W9-CRO-130

THE CARTOGRAPHY OF NORTH AMERICA

1500 - 1800

THE CARTOGRAPHY OF NORTH AMERICA

1500 - 1800

PIERLUIGI PORTINARO
and
FRANCO KNIRSCH

Crescent Books
A Division of Crown Publishers, Inc.

This edition published by
Crescent Books, distributed by
Crown Publishers, Inc.
225 Park Avenue South
New York, New York 10003

Produced by
Brompton Books Corp.
15 Sherwood Place
Greenwich, CT 06830
USA

Printed in Hong Kong

ISBN 0-517-03079-9

h g f e d c b a

Introduction

Development of ocean-going ships such as caravels and carracks in the fifteenth century made possible the Age of Discovery.

One day in 1832 the Dutch ambassador to France, Baron Walckenaer, happened upon an interesting-looking old map in a Paris antiques store. Painted on oxhide and signed by one Juan de la Cosa, it was a chart of the world that showed, among other things, some of the discoveries that had been made by Christopher Columbus and John Cabot in the Western Hemisphere during the eight years just prior to the date on the chart—1500. Thinking it might be important, the Baron purchased the chart for the equivalent of a few dollars. It was a good buy, for this immensely valuable 'Portolan World Chart' is now recognized as history's earliest authentic cartographic depiction of North America. It's creator had in fact been a member of Columbus's crew in 1492.

De la Cosa's chart marks the beginning of perhaps the most fascinating of all cartographic enterprises. For the next three centuries the mapping of America would record an unfolding story of daring exploration, tenacious settlement and fierce colonial rivalry. During this same period cartography itself—both as a science and as an art form—would come of age, and some of its most dazzling individual products would be dedicated to the subject of America.

The broad selection of maps and charts in this volume recapitulates this great enterprise, from its halting inception at the beginning of the sixteenth century to its final flowering in the early nineteenth century. Although the maps here presented are in generally chronological order, the reader will note numerous discontinuities in the degree of accurate geographic knowledge they reflect. New information reported by the early explorers—itself sometimes erroneous—was often jealously guarded and therefore was not disseminated at a uniform rate. Also, early cartographers did not always agree on such important technical matters as the exact size of the terrestrial globe or how best to project its curved surface onto a planar surface, with resulting discrepancies in the ways they represented both the position and scale of still-unfamiliar land masses. Finally, in matters of fine detail, the early mapmakers were still very much at the mercy of the developing printing techniques locally available to them.

Since this volume is concerned primarily with the cartographic history of the North American continent, perhaps a few words about the evolution of the term 'America' might be in order. The word was coined in 1507 by the famous German map-maker Martin Waldseemüller, who was convinced that the honor of discovering the New World belonged to Amerigo Vespucci. By the time Waldseemüller realized his mistake, so many copies of his influential map, the 'Universalis Cosmographia Descriptio in Plano', were in circulation that he was no longer able to erase the error from the minds of his contemporaries. When, in 1538, Gerard Mercator, perhaps the greatest cartographer since Ptolemy, produced a world map on which the New World was represented as being composed of 'North America' and 'South America,' the word became a permanent addition to the language of geography. In popular parlance, however, the unmodified term 'America' had, by the mid-eighteenth century, begun to take on a rather more specific connotation—that of English colonial North America, and particularly the portion of it that would eventually become the United States. That, of course, is how it is still used and how, unless otherwise specified, it will generally be used here.

In selecting the maps and charts to be reproduced on these pages the authors rated candidates against three separate criteria: historical significance, scientific merit and beauty. Surprisingly few of the final selections are deficient in even one of these categories.

A wood-block decoration from a 1493 edition of Columbus's Letters to Gabriel Sanchez. *It is based on an earlier (1486) illustration used in Braydenbach's* Pilgrimage.

Contents

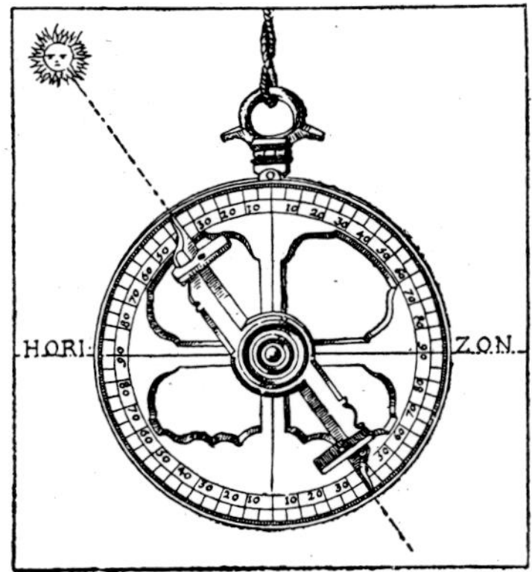

The nautical astrolabe was an instrument for determining latitude by measuring the angle of the sun at noon. It remained in use until the end of the sixteenth century.

A BRIEF HISTORY OF CARTOGRAPHY

Mapmaking, in the sense of making symbolic representations of configurations observed in the terrain or the heavens, must be a very ancient human activity, older than writing and at least as old as art. Doubtless the earliest terrestrial maps were comparatively narrow in focus and intention—guides to locating favored hunting grounds, delineations of territorial boundaries and the like. The oldest surviving town plan is Babylonian and dates from about 2200 BC, but in all probability it had far older predecessors.

Making world maps was obviously beyond the capacities of the most ancient cartographers, but it is nevertheless astonishing how early in history this task was undertaken. Precisely when it was first attempted we do not know, but in the British Museum there is a Babylonian clay tablet containing a crude map of the world that appears to date from the fifth century BC, and it is said that Anaximander of Miletus made a world map a century before.

By about 200 BC scholars in the Classical World had enough geographical, astronomical and mathematical knowledge at their disposal to begin constructing world maps with a certain degree of scientific rigor. Outstanding among the cartographers of this time was Eratosthenes of Cyrene, the librarian at Alexandria, who, by measuring shadows cast by the sun at the same time in Alexandria and Syene (which he assumed to be on the same meridian), was not only able to demonstrate that the earth was round but arrived at an estimate of its circumference that would have been almost exact if our planet were, as he believed, a perfect sphere. We have only descriptions of the map that Eratosthenes imposed on this sphere, but it must have been more symmetrical than accurate, showing the world as a central land mass composed of three continents—Europe, Asia and Libya (Africa)—surrounded by a vast and mysterious outer sea.

Although subsequent cartographers—notably Hipparchus, Strabo and Marinus of Tyre—added some changes and elaborations, this was essentially the world map that persisted for the remainder of the pre-Christian era and which was bequeathed in the second century of our era to the man destined to become the most influential cartographer of all time. Claudius Ptolemaeus, known to posterity as Ptolemy, was a Greek scholar who lived in Alexandria and had access to the greatest library in the ancient world. From that library and from personal contact with travelers, shipmasters, itinerant merchants and the like he assembled a formidable amount of geographical data which he organized into a cartographic system that would remain without serious challenge for the next 14 centuries.

The fruits of Ptolemy's labors were presented in his great *Geographia,* a work that consisted of a geographical index, a manual of cartography and 27 maps, including one world map. Again the 'habitable world' was represented by the three continents, Europe being separated from Libya (northern Africa) and Ethiopia (southern Africa) by the Pillars of Hercules and the Mediterranean and from Asia by the river Tanais (Don). Europe, Libya and the Near East and southern Russia were remarkably accurate in outline and contained a wealth of internal detail, but the peripheries of this ecumene were more fanciful. For example, Ptolemy freely admitted that the southern part of Ethiopia was *terra incognita,* but he nevertheless believed that it extended far to the east, eventually joining southern China and thus making the Indian Ocean land-locked. Though Ptolemy was the first to create a method for gridding his world map with lines of latitude and longitude, he both seriously underestimated the earth's total circumference and overestimated the east-west extent of the Eurasian land mass. The result, a radical reduction of the size of the ocean presumed to separate the western rim of Europe from the eastern shores of Asia, was to have a profound effect on the expectations with which Columbus undertook his epic voyage in 1492.

After the collapse of the Roman Empire, it was the East—Byzantium and the Moslem Empire—that became the principal heir to the Greek intellectual tradition. Here the Ptolemaic vision of the world was accepted without serious question or amendment, and manuscript copies of the *Geographia* were preserved for posterity. Some attenuated fragments of Greek ideas about geography penetrated the Western Europe of the Dark Ages, but the world maps prepared by medieval scholars owed little to historical or scientific thought and much to biblical tradition. Indeed, such maps rarely showed any lands not specifically mentioned in the Scriptures, and the distribution and outlines of these lands were entirely schematic.

The commonest type of medieval world map, now called the 'T and 0' type, was inscribed within a circle, the top of which represented east. Along the horizontal (or north-south) diameter lay a more-or-less continuous strip of water, the left half of which was the Don and the right, the Nile. Along the radius beneath and perpendicular to this diameter lay another strip of water, the Mediterranean. The circle of continents defined by this 'T' of waters were: Asia, the upper half, the land bequeathed by Noah to Shem; Europe, the lower left quadrant, the land of Japeth; and Africa, the lower right quadrant, the land of Ham. At the geographic center of the map lay Jerusalem, and at the top, or extreme east, either represented as contiguous with Asia or as an island, lay the Garden of Eden. Beyond, on all sides, was the outer ocean. Similarly arranged maps were also inscribed within squares and ovals, but all such world maps were essentialy diagramatic and not

A xylograph from Columbus's Letters to Sanchez. *Columbus watches Indians fleeing from his ship while the King of Spain observes the scene from the other side of the ocean.*

A print from a 1537 book by the geographer Giovanni de Sacrobosco. The ship in the background is a carrack.

really intended for utilitarian purposes.

By contrast, the charts prepared by medieval mariners were eminently practical and made substantial contributions to the science of geography. Sailors had apparently been making coastal charts—now usually called by historians *portolanos*—for their own use since antiquity, and it seems likely that some of the great geographers of Classical times may have had occasion to refer to such charts when constructing their own world maps. But all this must necessarily be speculative, since the first unmistakable written reference to the existence of portolan charts appears in a chronicle telling of a voyage made by Louis IX of France in 1270, and the earliest known example, the 'Carte Pisane' made by a Genoan named Pietro Vescante, dates from about 1311.

The supreme virtue of the portolanos was their strict adherence to observable fact, uninfluenced by any academic theory, religious tradition or popular myth. They were intended solely to help seamen to navigate from port to port, detailing as accurately as possible bearings and distances, prevailing winds, navigational hazards, salient landmarks and the general configuration of the coasts that lay along the route. Apart from such topographical features as mountain peaks or hilltop cities visible from the sea, the portolanos made no real effort to detail the interiors of the lands they dealt with, but in all other respects they were

In the frontispiece of another Sacrobosco book of 1519 the goddess of astrology reveals to a scholar the secrets of the armillary sphere while Ptolemy demonstrates the use of the astrolabe.

vastly superior to any other form of contemporary cartography. The earliest portolanos about which we know were concerned only with the Mediterranean and Black Sea, but by the mid-fourteenth century they were ranging as far afield as the Canary Islands and the Gulf of Guinea. Unfortunately, as a general rule, the portolanos were ignored by medieval scholars, though unmistakable portolan detail was added to at least one essentially Ptolemaic world map made for Charles V of France as early as 1375.

Ironically, the re-introduction of Ptolemy's geographical ideas into the mainstream of Western thought was to prove almost as inimical to the diffusion of the solid knowledge gained by the portolan chart-makers as was medieval unworldliness. Although Europeans had been vaguely aware of Ptolemy throughout the Middle Ages, the most accessible manuscript copies of the *Geographia* had been located in Byzantium and were written in Greek, a language few Western scholars understood. It was not until about 1406

An unknown author's 1483 world map based on the theories of the fifth-century philosopher Macrobius, in which Europe, Asia and Africa are treated as a single continent.

A typical medieval 'T and O' schematic map of the twelfth century. North is on the left. Asia fills the top half, and Europe and Asia the left and right quadrants below. The T's cross-bar is a chain of rivers, and its stem is the Mediterranean Sea.

that a Byzantine refugee, Emanuel Chrysolaras, and his Tuscan pupil, Jacobus Angelus, undertook to translate Ptolemy's work into Latin (for some reason changing its title from *Geographia* to *Cosmographia).* This translation was soon picked up by a German scholar, Nicolaus Donis, who, carefully following Ptolemy's prescriptions, prepared a set of maps to accompany the text. The stage was now set for technology to intervene, in the form of the newly-invented Gutenberg printing press. Between 1475 and 1500 no less than seven folio editions of the *Geographia* were published, with many more to follow, and for the next hundred years the Ptolemaic conception of the world so dominated scholarly Western thought that many geographers simply ignored contrary information based on recent discoveries.

The assumption on which Columbus undertook his first voyage of discovery—that by sailing west across the Atlantic he would inevitably reach Asia—was entirely Ptolemaic, as was his misidentification of his landfall. It was not until 1507, when Martin Waldseemüller published his famous world map, the 'Universalis Cosmographia,' that any cartographer was willing to commit himself to the proposition that the land discovered by Columbus might in fact be a continent separate from Asia, and even then, Waldseemüller's estimate of the breadth of the new continent was sufficiently low so as not to do too much violence to Ptolemy's mistaken figure for the

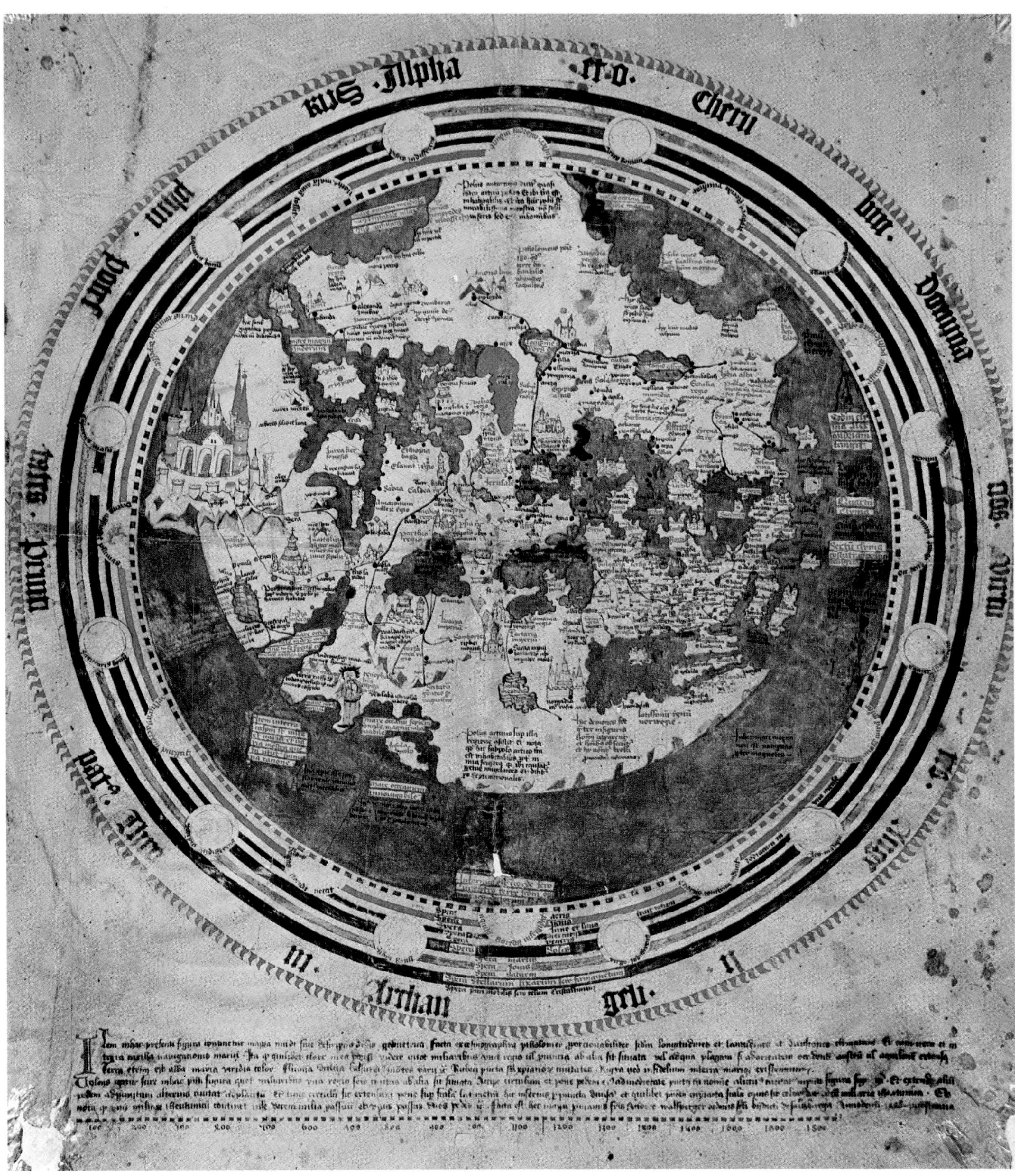

A 1448 world map painted on parchment by the Benedictine monk Andreus Walsperger. Here, north is at the bottom. As in 'T and O' maps, Jerusalem is at the center, and the continents are ringed by the mysterious outer ocean.

earth's circumference.

Yet as reports of the new discoveries made by Columbus's successors in the early sixteenth century began to multiply, it was impossible that Ptolemaic orthodoxy should remain completely unchallenged. Gradually a new school of mapmaking arose, one whose new-style maps, called *tabulae novae,* diverged increasingly from the tenets of the master. By mid-century the authority of these new maps was less a question of their scientific validity than of their public acceptance. The date on which that acceptance was finally won is conventionally said to have been 1570, the year in which Abraham Ortelius produced in Antwerp history's first new-style printed atlas, the *Theatrum Orbis Terrarum.*

The *Theatrum,* a collection of 53 maps by Ortelius and others, was an immediate success, running through four editions in its first year of publication. It was in its 16th edition when, in 1578,

C
A
B
The Deſcription of the Croſs-Staff.
This Inſtrument is of ſome antiquity in Navigation, and is commonly uſed at Sea, to take the Altitude of the Sun or Stars, which it performs with ſufficient exactneſs, eſpecially if it be leſs then 60 degrees, but if it exceed 60, it is not ſo certain, by reaſon of the length of the Croſs, and the ſmallneſs of the graduations on the Staff.

The most ancient instrument for determining latitude at sea was the cross-staff. Like the astrolabe it could measure the sun's angle, though less accurately. Sailors who could not afford the more expensive astrolabes used cross-staffs into the seventeenth century.

the next major new-style atlas was published by Ortelius's countryman, Gerard de Jode. And it was in its 21st edition in 1585 when by far the most important of the century's atlases (and the first to be so called) began its 10-year course of original publication. This was the enormously influential collection of 107 maps drawn by Gerard Mercator. By the middle of the seventeenth century nearly 50 editions of this monumental *Atlas*—progressively enlarged by Mercator's sons and successors—had been published in Latin, Dutch, French, German and English.

The Dutch continued to dominate mapmaking throughout the seventeenth century, with internationally famous atlases being produced by such great cartographers as Jodocus and Henry Hondius, Jan Jansson and Claes and Nikolaus Visscher. But in both the technical excellence of its printing and engraving and the lavish beauty of its decoration, the work of the Blaeu family—Willem Janszoon Blaeu and his sons Joan and Corneliss is outstanding. From their modestly titled *Theatri A Ortelii et Atlantis G Mercatoris,* published in 1631, to their mighty 12-volume *Atlas Maior* of 1662 (one of the most beautiful geographic works ever published) they produced a series of brilliantly executed and universally admired atlases, and at least one well-known modern authority has called Joan Blaeu's huge (20-sheet) world map, the 'Nova totius Terrarum Orbis Tabula' of 1648, the single 'highest expression of Dutch cartographical art.'

Pre-eminent though the Dutch were in the sixteenth and seventeenth centuries, notable cartographers flourished elsewhere in Europe. Sixteenth century Italy produced a large number of excellent map-makers, including Matteo Contarini, who in 1506 published the first printed map to show Columbus's New World discoveries, and Giacomo Gastaldi, perhaps the best Italian cartographer of the century. Sixteenth-century Italian publishers such as Lafreri, Bertelli and Duchetti were also notable for producing early map collections, quasi-atlases that slightly antedated the appearance of Ortelius's *Theatrum.* And throughout the seventeenth century Italy remained a major producer of maps, the technical quality of which ranged from mediocre to brilliant, two outstanding examples being the 1646 *Arcano del Mare* by the expatriate Englishman Sir Robert Dudley and the 1692 *Mercurio Geografico,* a collection of 155 maps edited by Giacomo Rossi.

Sixteenth-century Germany, too, maintained the high cartographic tradition initiated by Martin Waldseemüller in the subsequent work of Johann Schöner, Sebastian Münster, Peter and Philip Apian and others. There was, however, a marked slackening in German cartographic activity in the seventeenth century, due in part to the ascendency of the Dutch and in part to the appalling ravages inflicted on Germany in the Thirty Years War.

In both France and England, however,

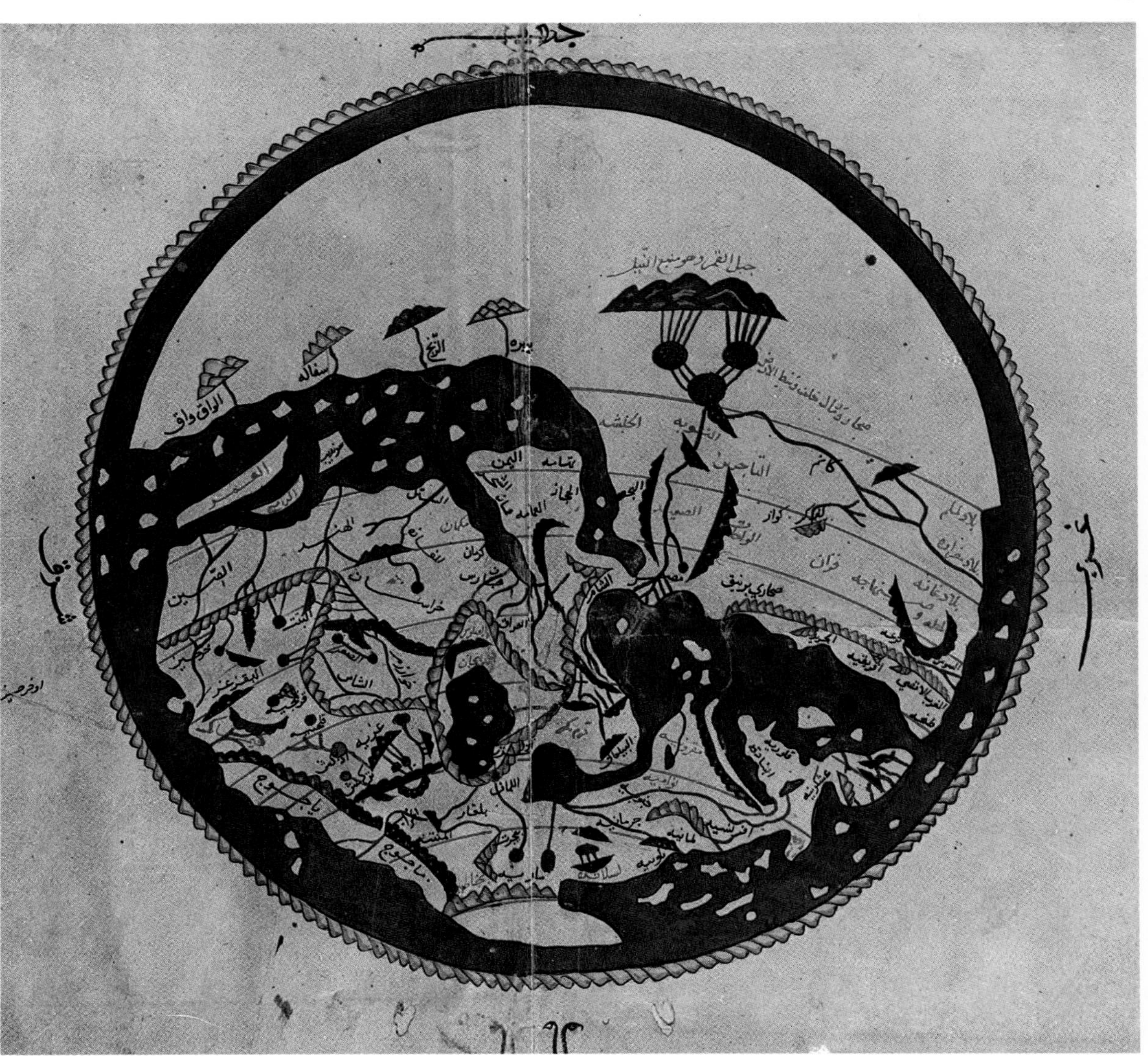

A twelfth-century world map by the Arabic cartographer Al Idrisi. North is at the bottom. At the center is the holy city of Mecca, and the outer ocean surrounds all the known world. The huge eastern extent of Africa accords with Ptolemy's hypothesis.

mapmaking flourished in the seventeenth century. The most prominent French map-maker of the sixteenth had been Oronce Fine, but the first French world atlas, that of Nicolas Sanson, was published only in 1654. It was soon followed by a spate of excellent atlases by Sanson, and his Sons Guillaume and Adrien, Alexis Jaillot, Pierre Duval and Nicolas de Fer. Well-known English atlas- and map-makers of the same period include Edward Wright, John Speed, John Seller, William Berry and Edmund Halley (he of the comet).

The 200-year cartographic supremacy of the Dutch finally ended in the eighteenth century. By this time the amount of accurate geographical information available to map-makers was relatively enormous. The size, position and outline of almost all the earth's major land masses were known, though a fair amount of interior detail, especially in America, Africa and Australia, had yet to be supplied. Also, because the general level of engraving and printing techniques was now very high, no one country could hope to maintain anything approaching a monopoly of map creation or production.

The Germans and the French both have good claim to be regarded as the greatest eighteenth century map-makers overall, but many fine individual products came from Italy, England and the Netherlands as well. The two foremost German cartographers of the century were undoubtedly Johann Baptist Homann (and family) and Matthias Seutter, both of whom produced a succession of atlases that were exceptional for their clarity and comprehensiveness, and, in the case of Seutter, for their richness of decoration. The same could be said of the atlases produced by the Germans' great French rivals, such as Guillaume de l'Isle, Philippe Bauche and Jean-Baptiste Bourguignon d'Anville. The maps contained in their works benefitted not only from the superiority of French survey techniques but also from the fact that their decorations were often supplied by such leading artists as Boucher, Cochin or Monnet. And as representative of the excellent work also being done in other countries, the fine Venetian craftsmanship displayed in Antonio Zatta's *Atlante Novissimo* (1779-85) and the incredibly minute detail that his countryman, Rizzi Zannoni, worked into his 1793 *Atlante Marittimo delle due Sicile* are especially worthy of mention.

But the eighteenth century was to mark the end of European cartography's 300-year Golden Age. Thereafter, thanks to the broad diffusion of geographic knowledge, it was no longer necessary to be an accomplished geographer in order to produce accurate and detailed maps. Nor was it necessary to be an accomplished artist, for, increasingly, high-speed presses would make possible the mass production of maps, with attendant emphasis not on their beauty but on their affordability. The result was undeniably progress, but, as usual, at a price.

This decorative frontispiece is from a geographical work called Sphaera Mundi *by Nauro Fiorentino, published in 1550 in Florence.*

The Production of Old Maps

The principal fascination of any old map of course lies in its content and what that implies about the state both of geographical knowledge and cartographic science at the time the map was made. This being so, we may be tempted to overlook another consideration that can bear strongly on a map's quality. The graphic techniques that were originally available for a map's production can influence its size, coloration, fineness of detail, rarity, state of preservation and much else. In the sequel we shall look briefly at how some of the maps included in this book were originally produced.

Until the Middle Ages all maps had either to be carved in clay or stone or hand-drawn on parchment. In either case, any copies had to be fresh works of draughtsmanship. The importation of paper-making technology from China in the twelfth century did more than alter the material on which medieval maps could be drawn, for at about the same time the Chinese technique of xylography, or wood block printing, was also introduced. ('Xylography' is simply a compound of the Greek words for *wood + writing).* Now, for the first time, maps and other drawings could be reproduced mechanically, and xylographic printing businesses soon sprang up in such cities as Venice, Rome, Strassburg, Antwerp and Amsterdam.

The earliest xylographic printing was done by the relief method—that is, only the raised protions of the carved printing surface of the wood block were inked, and it was they that transferred the design when the block was pressed down on a sheet of paper. But a second method, intaglio printing, was soon developed.

Intaglio is essentially the reverse of relief, in that the outline of a drawing is engraved on the surface of the block, and then the ink, instead of being applied to the raised surfaces, is used to fill the grooves made by the engraving tool. When the block is pressed down on paper the ink in the grooves is absorbed into the paper's surface. Obviously, in the intaglio method the engraving of the printing surface is much more simple and direct than is the more elaborate carving required by the relief method. And in fact, intaglio xylography could produce finer lines than could most relief xylography. It therefore soon became the preferred method for map printing.

Xylography was the most common method of printing maps until the end of the fifteenth century, but that was only because it was relatively cheap, for earlier in the century a much superior method had been discovered. This was calcography (from the Greek *copper + writing).* The lines that could be incised on a copper surface with a special engraving tool called a burin were finer than anything that could be achieved on wood, and hence vastly more detailed intaglio printing could be transferred to paper from an engraved copper plate. Later on the engraving process itself was simplified by the application of some elementary chemistry. The copper plate was first coated with a thin layer of wax, and the drawing was scratched lightly onto the surface through the wax. The whole plate was then dipped into a bath of nitric acid. The acid would leave all wax-covered areas unaffected but would, depending on how long the plate was immersed, etch all exposed metal to any depth desired. In addition to producing finer printed detail than wood blocks, copper plates had a significantly longer working life, thus allowing more copies of printed matter to be run off before the printing matrix was worn out.

Both xylography and calcography permitted a rudimentary kind of color printing, either through careful application of different-colored inks to a single matrix or through the use of more than one matrix. (The most important sixteenth century edition of Ptolemy—that produced by Johannes Schott in Strasbourg in 1513—made limited use of

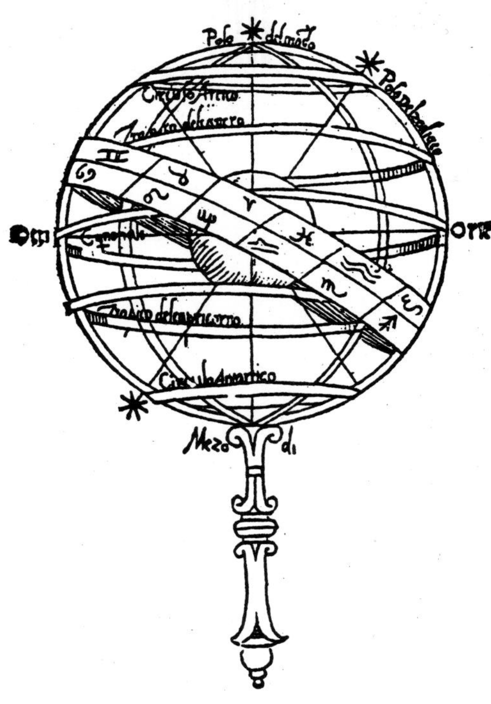

Another illustration from the Sphaera *of Fiorentino showing the armillary sphere of the heavens.*

a two-color xylographic printing process.) But throughout the period represented by the maps in this book most map-makers avoided color printing. Not only were the processes involved cumbersome and time-consuming, the results tended to be unsatisfactory because the colored inks were often too intense, tending to obscure rather than enhance small details.

Ortelius and some other map-makers painstakingly hand-tinted their maps after printing, but the majority left such embellishment to their customers. Thus many of the old maps that have come down to us bear colors and other decorations supplied by a succession of their owners. In fact, the coloring of printed maps became such a popular pastime that several instruction manuals were published for the benefit of, as one English author put it, 'those Gentry, and others, who delight in the Knowledge of Maps; which by being coloured...do give a better Idea of the Countries they describe, than they can possibly do uncoloured.' In addition to explaining to amateurs such arcana as sizing paper, preparing oil and water color pigments and laying gold leaf, these manuals helped to popularize certain conventions of map coloration and decoration—for example, how to represent political boundaries (dotted lines), or indicate principal cities (red dots or circles), or represent the figure of Boreas, the north wind (as an old man).

But color apart, the principal decorations on maps were usually the work of the map-makers themselves. The most universal decorative element was the cartouche, the enclosed area that contained the map's title, the name of the cartographer, the publication date, the dedication and other such written information. Very early the borders of the cartouches became vehicles for elaborate strap-work, swirls of cherubs and sirens, clusters of fruit and similar baroque embellishments. Very early, too, decorations began to be applied to the face of the map itself: puff-cheeked Zephyrs blew miniature sailing ships westward across the oceans, national and personal coats of arms appeared in more-or-less appropriate places and so on. Some maps, such as those produced by the Blaeus, went even farther, their margins being filled with perspective views of cities and towns, depictions of exotic plants and animals and scenes showing allegorical figures. Such decorative detail could on occasion be truly exquisite.

The question of who deserved the most credit for the production of a given map could be somewhat vexed. The cartographer who supplied most of the basic geographical information might not be the draughtsman who committed it to paper, and the draughtsman might not be the artist who supplied the decorations. The engraver who transferred the finished work to the matrix might be none of the foregoing. And of course the work of several different cartographers, draughtsmen, artists and engravers might be represented in a single atlas. Often, but by no means always, the name most prominently displayed on both maps and atlases was that of the editor, the person responsible for co-ordinating the work of all the other contributors.

How well the old maps that have come down to us have withstood the ravages of time varies enormously. The quality of the parchment or paper on which they were originally set down, as well as the chromatic stability of the various inks and paints used, obviously has much to do with their current state of preservation. So, too, do their individual histories of exposure to light, heat, dampness, oxygen and human handling. As a general rule, the best preserved maps are those that have been least consulted, those that have been kept in neglected private collections and out-of-the-way libraries. How many undiscovered cartographic treasures may yet be found in such places is the stuff that map-collectors' dreams are made on.

This handsome illumination from a fifteenth-century Greek parchment codex shows Ptolemy robed, crowned and holding the astrolabe that had become the conventional symbol of his geographer's calling.

An early sixteenth-century German printing press of the kind used in the production of the first modern maps.

The Exploration of North America

However attractive old maps may be in themselves, however well they may exemplify stages in the evolution of cartographic science and printing technology, they are above all else historical documents. In certain respects the maps in this book tell the story of America's discovery, exploration and settlement more vividly than any words. Yet of course they are best understood in conjunction with words, as illustrations, so to speak, meant to accompany an historical text. There is not space in these pages to recapitulate such a text—a whole library would hardly suffice to do the subject full justice—but perhaps a brief summary of some of the highlights in the growth of Europe's knowledge of North America might not be amiss, if only as an *aide-memoire.*

The Discovery of America

That the existence of North America should have remained unknown to all educated Europeans until the end of the fifteenth century is less an indictment of medieval enterprise than of medieval technology. The Polos, William of Rubruck and other daring medieval travelers had, after all, made some astonishing overland explorations of the Far East two centuries before Columbus's first voyage. But medieval Europe launched no significant maritime voyages of discovery, a fact due almost entirely to the undeveloped state of navigational science and marine architecture. The mariner's compass only came into general use in the fourteenth century, and a sea-going version of the astrolabe, an instrument capable of plotting latitude, was not widely available until the fifteenth century. Nor was it until the fifteenth century that a type of large ship able to undertake long ocean voyages, the caravel, was fully developed.

Once these and associated technologies were in place, the Age of Exploration not only dawned but fulminated. The Portuguese began their exploration of the west coast of Africa in earnest in the 1420s. By 1445 they had passed Cape Verde, and by 1488 they had doubled the Cape of Good Hope. In nine more years Vasco da Gama would extend this route of exploration all the way to India, thus finally laying to rest Ptolemy's theory of a land-locked Indian Ocean. But by then da Gama's accomplishment had already been overshadowed by that of a Genoese sailor who appeared to have found an even shorter route to Asia by sailing west across what was then called the Ocean Sea.

Columbus had followed the successive discoveries of the Portuguese navigators with mounting excitement, and in 1484 he presented to Portugal's exploration-minded king John II the radical proposal for his westward-directed 'Enterprise of the Indies.' Most educated people at that time accepted the essentially Ptolemaic idea that Asia lay on the far side of the great western ocean, but there were sharp differences of opinion as to how wide this Ocean Sea might be. The ever-optimistic Columbus had inevitably been attracted to the theories of geographers—notably the Frenchman Pierre d'Ailly and the Florentine Paolo dal Pozzo Toscanelli—who believed in both a modest terrestrial circumference and a Eurasian land mass of very great east-west extent, a combination that produced an Ocean Sea that was, in d'Ailly's words, 'of no great width.' On the basis of such theories Columbus was prepared to assert that the distance from Lisbon to Japan was only about 2400 miles, less than half the distance the Portuguese had already sailed down the west coast of Africa.

But neither the Portuguese monarch nor many other Europeans agreed with him, and it was not until 1492 that Isabella of Castile and Ferdinand of Aragon somewhat reluctantly agreed to finance Columbus's 'Enterprise.' In four successive voyages between 1492 and 1504 Columbus discovered and explored parts of Cuba, Hispanola, various smaller Caribbean islands, Venezuela, Panama and Honduras, all the while being convinced that he was on the eastern edge of Asia.

While Columbus was thus engaged, several other notable trans-Atlantic voyages of discovery were launched. In 1497 John Cabot, in the service of England's Henry VII, discovered Newfoundland, and in the following year he may (on the evidence of the de la Cosa chart) have explored the coast of North America as far south as Chesapeake Bay. In 1499 the Italian Amerigo Vespucci explored the coast of South America as far south as Brazil, and in 1501, as far south as Argentina. It was on the basis of these latter explorations, and on Vespucci's speculations that the lands being investigated might be part of a continent independent of Asia, that the cartographer Martin Waldseemüller coined the name 'America' for the New World.

The Sixteenth Century

Immediately upon learning the results of Columbus's first voyage, the Spanish rulers had persuaded Pope Alexander VI to set a north-south line of demarcation 100 leagues west of the Azores, beyond which all newly discovered lands not held by a Christian prince as of 25 December 1492 would belong to Spain. As the result of Portuguese protests this arrangement had been modified in the 1494 Treaty of Tordesillas, whereby the line, 'la Raya,' was moved 370 leagues west of the Cape Verde Islands, all new lands to the west belonging to Spain, and all those to the east to Portugal. However advantageous this division might have been to Spain in terms of the Hispano-Portuguese rivalry, it had virtually no effect on the activities of other European nations, which had never taken 'la Raya' seriously in the first place.

A northern shipyard in the late fifteenth century. Naval architecture in the north was at this time less developed than in the Mediterranean, a fact that favored the Spanish and Portuguese in mounting voyages of discovery.

England, which had staked an early claim in the New World with John Cabot's voyages, issued royal patents to a number of merchant adventurers who explored portions of the North American seaboard during the first decade of the sixteenth century. Of these perhaps the most famous was Cabot's son, Sebastian, who claimed to have discovered Hudson Bay in 1509. France, though a late starter, soon strongly entered the race for discovery as well. In 1524 Giovanni da Verrazano, serving France's Francis I, explored a large section of the American coast from Florida to Nova Scotia, along the way discovering, among many other things, New York harbor. Later, in three voyages between 1534 and 1542, the great Malouin captain Jacques Cartier explored Newfoundland, Nova Scotia and the St Lawrence River as far inland as Montréal.

Meantime, both Spain and Portugal had been too busy with their own explorations and conquests to make more than token protests against these Anglo-French 'incursions.' In 1513 the Spanish explorer Vasco Nuñez de Balboa had crossed the Isthmus of Panama to discover the Pacific Ocean, only a few months after his compatriot, Juan Ponce de León, had discovered Florida. Between 1519 and 1522 a Spanish expedition led by the Portuguese Fernando Magellan had circumnavigated the entire globe, during which time Hernando Cortes had brought all of Mexico under Spanish dominion. The great wealth that was soon flowing into Spanish coffers from Mexico and the Indies permitted Spain's Charles V to continue to finance exploration at a rate beyond the means of other sovereigns, and in North America the years between 1539 and 1543 were to produce an especially rich harvest of Spanish discoveries. It was during this period that Hernando de Soto, in his vain search for the mythical El Dorado, both discovered the Mississippi River and penetrated as far inland as present-day Arkansas. Simultaneously, Francisco Vasquez de Coronado was exploring parts of Texas, Colorado and New Mexico, and in the Far West a series of Spanish navigators—notably Hernando de Alarcon, Juan Rodriguez Cabrillo and Bartolome Ferrelo-cruised the Pacific coast from Baja California to perhaps as far north as Oregon.

Following the accession of Elizabeth I of England in 1558 there was a new wave of English exploration of the New World. Between 1576 and 1606 Martin Frobisher, John Davis, George Weymouth and John Knight all vainly sought a northwest passage around America to Asia, in the course of which they discovered Baffin Land, Frobisher Bay and Hudson Strait and significantly enlarged Europe's knowledge of Labrador and Newfoundland. Between 1577 and 1580 Sir Francis Drake duplicated Magellan's feat of global circumnavigation, along the way discovering and claiming for the English crown San Francisco Bay.

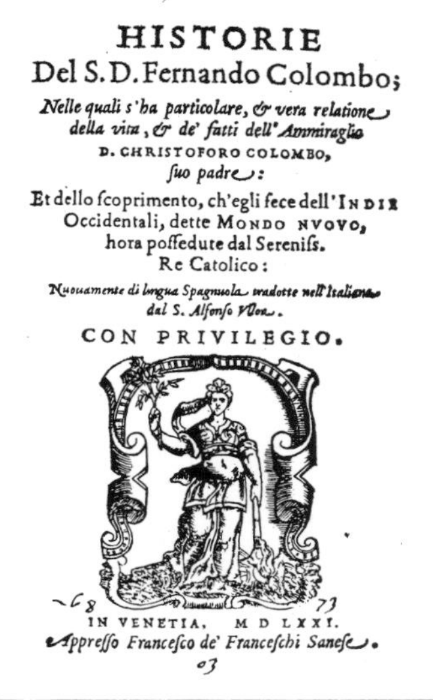

HISTORIE
Del S. D. Fernando Colombo;
Nelle quali s'ha particolare, & vera relatione della vita, & de' fatti dell'Ammiraglio
D. CHRISTOFORO COLOMBO,
ſuo padre:
Et dello ſcoprimento, ch'egli fece dell'INDIE Occidentali, dette MONDO NUOVO, hora poſſedute dal Sereniſs. Re Catolico:
Nuouamente di lingua Spagnuola tradotte nell'Italiana dal S. Alfonſo Vlloa.
CON PRIVILEGIO.
IN VENETIA, M D LXXI.
Appreſſo Franceſco de' Franceſchi Saneſe.

Frontispiece of the Venetian first edition (1571) of the Historie *by Columbus's son, Don Fernando Columbus.*

And in 1583 Sir Humphrey Gilbert made the first abortive attempt to establish a permanent English colony in the New World (in Newfoundland). Two years later, in 1585, Sir Walter Raleigh, Gilbert's half brother, organized a second attempt at colonization, this time off the coast of North Carolina on Roanoke Island; but though settlers were actually established on shore, by 1590 they had all mysteriously vanished, presumably the victims of Indian attack.

By the end of the sixteenth century several European nations had established ephemeral commercial outposts in North America, but only the Spanish in Florida could claim even limited success in setting down colonial roots. Yet colonization was now clearly the order of the day for any power that wished to make good its claims to North American territory, and in the seventeenth century such colonization would proceed apace.

The Seventeenth Century

In 1606 Elizabeth's successor, James I of England, granted patents to two private companies to establish permanent settlements in America. One of these, the London Company, in the following year dispatched three ships to Virginia, and on 24 May 1607 they landed a party of 105 would-be colonists at Jamestown. At first it seemed that this frail enclave might go the way of its luckless predecessors, but thanks to timely resupply by sea and the forceful local leadership of John Smith the Jamestown Colony endured and by 1609 was both self-sustaining and growing. In 1624 the Company went into receivership and Virginia thus became the first New World Royal Colony.

The French had settled in North America even earlier, though in a somewhat different way. Unlike the English, the French were less interested in founding stable agricultural communities in the New World than in establishing a permanent network of commercial centers for traders, hunters, trappers, fishermen, miners and the like. This approach, at least at first, permitted the French to extend their influence rapidly over much wider areas than those inhabited by the English, but the degree of control the French exercised over the lands they colonized so thinly was less firm.

The French had begun to fish the waters off Newfoundland intensively around 1505 and in the remainder of the century had set up numerous fishing stations along the coast. After Cartier's expedition in 1534 French fur trading posts also began to appear, and these rapidly expanded into the interior. How permanent these small and intermittently-manned posts may be said to have been is moot, and many historians prefer to cite the Acadia colony on Nova Scotia, founded by Samuel de Champlain in 1604, as the first permanent French settlement. In all, between 1603 and 1635, the tireless de Champlain made 11 voyages to the New World. He founded Québec in 1608, gave his name to Lake Champlain in 1609 and eventually, as Royal Governor of New France (after 1633), oversaw various explorations that

Prima Columbi in Indiam nauigatio. Anno 1492. VIII.

A sixteenth-century engraving by De Bry showing Columbus saying goodbye to his Spanish patrons, Queen Isabella and King Ferdinand.

A fresco in the Castello de Albertia in Genoa shows two of Columbus's ships on the day of their departure from Palos in 1492. The lefthand ship is the nao Santa Maria. *The caravel, right, probably should have lateen sails on the fore and main masts, as Columbus did not re-rig his two caravels until he reached the Canary Islands.*

The most famous portrait of Columbus was painted nearly 40 years after his death by Ridolfo Bigordi, the son of the great Ghirlandaio.

certainly extended as far west as eastern Wisconsin and may even have reached the Mississippi.

Meantime, in 1620, the English had established a second major New World colony at Plymouth, Massachusetts, and a few years later the Dutch began to exploit the territory about the lower reaches of the Hudson River. They called this area New Holland and established its principal settlement, New Amsterdam, in 1626.

As settlements along America's eastern seaboard proliferated the first serious symptoms of colonial rivalry began to appear. Taking advantage of a war between England and France in the late 1620s, English colonists seized the French settlements around the Bay of Fundy and in 1629 captured Qúebec. In 1632, under the Treaty of St-Germain-en-Laye, the English were obliged to restore most of these captures, but the stage for future conflict had clearly been set. More immediately decisive was England's bloodless seizure of New Holland in 1664, for this effectively ended the history of Dutch presence in North America and began the history of English-dominated New York and New Jersey.

By the latter part of the century the European spheres of influence in North America were fairly well defined. Between the Appalachian plateau and the coast the English firmly controlled the eastern seaboard from the northern border of Florida through Maine, as well as eastern Newfoundland and the southern coast of Hudson Bay. The French more loosely controlled a broad swath of territory that ran southwest from the Gulf of St Lawrence, surrounded the Great Lakes and extended (thanks largely to the explorations of the Sieur de la Salle and others) south through the Mississippi basin all the way to the Gulf of Mexico. The Spanish controlled Florida, Mexico and much of Texas, New Mexico and Arizona, as well as parts of the California littoral. The distribution of these territories virtually guaranteed that further colonial expansion—and especially English expansion—in North America could not be accomplished without war.

This miniature from Enea de Azuraza's Cronica de Guiné *is the best portrait of Henry the Navigator, the fifteenth-century prince who founded Portugal's great tradition of maritime discovery.*

King Ferdinand of Aragon and Queen Isabella of Castile: details from a painting now in the Prado, La Vergine dei Re Cattolici, *artist unknown.*

Above and right: These four sketches, in the de Albertis collection in Genoa, show the routes of Columbus's voyages of 1492, 1493, 1498 and 1502. On the third voyage (above) he made his first landfall on the mainland. On the fourth voyage (right below) he got as far as Panama but turned away, unaware that less than 50 miles distant lay another great ocean, the Pacific.

The Eighteenth Century

Although geography alone would doubtless have made armed conflict between the English and French colonists inevitable, that conflict was both hastened and intensified by the nearly incessant series of wars fought by the two mother countries in Europe between 1689 and 1763. As the result of the first three of these wars—the War of the League of Augsburg (called in America King William's War), the War of the Spanish Succession (Queen Anne's War) and the War of the Austrian Succession (King George's War)—the British had, by 1748, extended their control over all of Newfoundland and Nova Scotia, Hudson Bay and part of New Brunswick. But it was the fourth war, the Seven Years War (French and Indian War), that was to prove decisive, for by the Treaty of Paris, concluded in 1763, France ceded to Britain Canada and all areas (except for New Orleans) formerly claimed by France east of the Mississippi. Yet the British were to enjoy undisputed control over this vast territory for only a little more than a decade, for in 1775 the thirteen original Anglo-American colonies rebelled and by 1783 had compelled Britain to recognize the sovereign status of the United States of America.

By the time of the American Revolution the general dimensions and configuration of the North American continent were fairly well understood, and most of the important internal detail was known about areas that lay to the east of the Mississippi. But this was less true of the West. To be sure, throughout the century maritime explorations of America's western seaboard were made: In 1728 and again in 1741 the Dane Vitus Bering discovered and navigated the northern strait that separates America from Asia, and both the British captain James Cook and the American captain Robert Gray made important reconnaissances of the western coast between 1778 and 1792. As for the interior, various bands of largely forgotten hunters and trappers had been probing westward for many years, but it was not until 1793 that the man usually credited as being the first to cross the continent, the Canadian Alexander Mackenzie, reached the Pacific.

The United States only began to mount major government-sponsored explorations of the West after its purchase of Louisiana (the name given the immense tract of land lying between the Mississippi and the Rocky Mountains) from France

The coat of arms granted to Columbus by the monarchs of Spain when they created him Admiral of the Ocean Sea.

in 1803. The first of these was the famous expedition led by Meriwether Lewis and William Clark that, between 1803 and 1806, ascended the Missouri River, crossed the Rockies and came within sight of the Pacific (in 1805). Between 1805 and 1807 Zebulon Pike explored the sources of the Mississippi, Colorado and New Mexico. And much more exploration followed. By the mid-1850s not only had all the essential remaining exploration of the West been completed but the boundaries of the contiguous United States had assumed their present form.

In terms of general cartographic interest, the maps of America made after the first few years of the nineteenth century yield diminishing returns. Though the maps continue to tell the story of America's political growth, most of the mysteries of America's geography had been solved, and the maps themselves assume an ever more utilitarian, ever less artistic aspect. The great age of New World discovery that began with Columbus was now over, and so too was that dazzling period in the history of mapmaking that began when Juan de la Cosa first sat down to paint a crude portolano on a piece of oxhide.

Above: A 1590 engraving from a drawing by De Bry showing Columbus's initial landing on San Salvador.

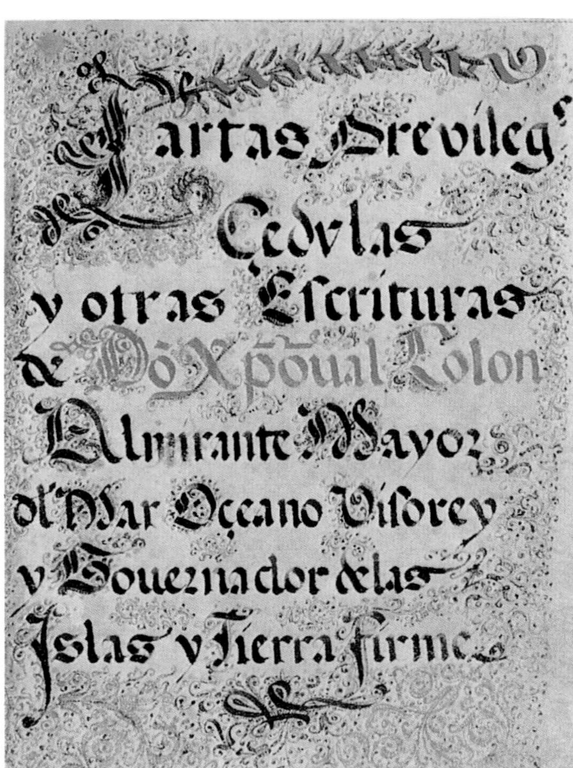

Cartas Previleg[s]
Cedvlas
y otras Escrituras
de Dõ Xpoual Colon
Almirante Mayor
dl Mar Oçeano Visorey
y Gouernador de las
Islas y Tierra firme

Right: The frontispiece of The Book of Privileges Granted by the Catholic King of Spain to Columbus and his Sons.

Opposite: More engravings by De Bry showing scenes of the discovery of the New World. The ships are represented as galleons, appropriate to the time of De Bry (1590) but not to that of Columbus.

F. Maij

2

F. Delfinum

Henricus Martellus made this portolan world chart in 1489, just before the discovery of the New World. His elaborate rendering of the West African coast suggests his excitement about the recent voyages made by the Portuguese.

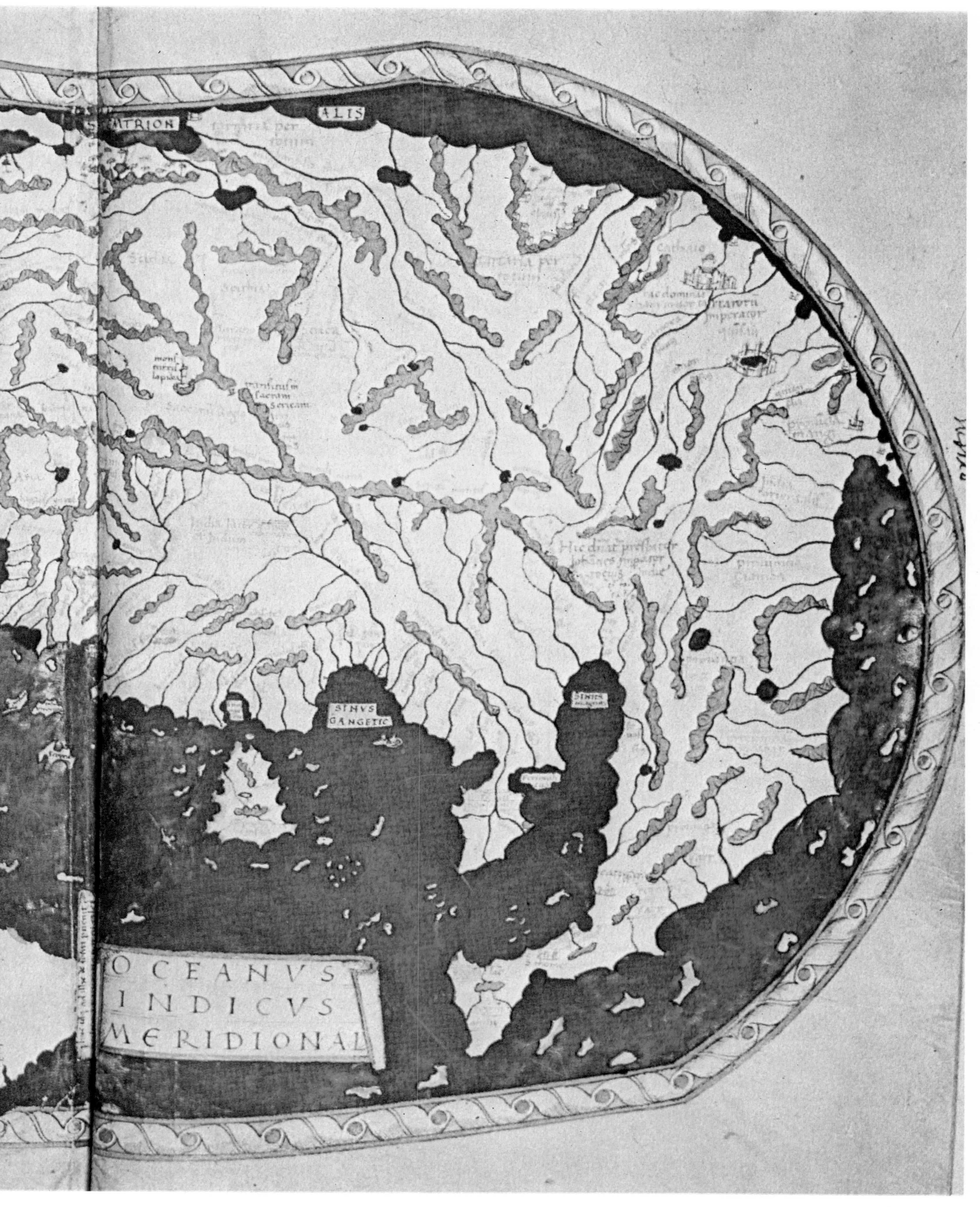
ALIS
SINVS GANGETIC
OCEANVS
INDICVS
MERIDIONAL

A carrack, probably Flemish of about 1470.

INDEX OF THE PLATES

A stern view of a fifteenth-century carrack.

North American Maps 1500-1600

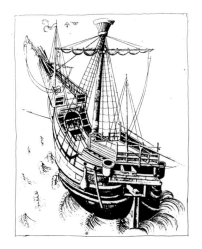

The North American maps of the sixteenth century are in some ways the most fascinating, for in their many eccentricities and inaccuracies we can trace the unfolding story of how geographers rooted in Ptolemaic concepts tried to come to grips with the astonishing information the New World explorers were bringing back to Europe.

At first the two foci of 'hard' knowledge were confined to the areas first explored by Columbus and the Cabots—*ie,* Central America and the Antilles and the area around Newfoundland—and only gradually did details of other sections of the eastern coasts of North and South America emerge. But for geographers there remained the overriding question of whether these new lands were part of Asia, as both Columbus and the Cabots maintained and Ptolemaic orthodoxy strongly suggested. It is remarkable how early some cartographers began to speculate to the contrary, Waldseemüller's 'Universalis Cosmographia' of 1507 being the earliest known and certainly most famous example. But as the maps in this section clearly show, the matter remained unsettled for most of the rest of the century. Even despite the knowledge of the America's western coasts that accumulated in the years during and after Magellan's circumnavigation, there still remained a widely-held conviction that somewhere, well to the north, there must nevertheless be a land bridge that clearly linked North America to Asia.

Of the geographers who opposed this view, many were North Europeans who very much wanted to believe in the discovery of a far-north sea passage around America to India—*ie,* a new route not already under Spanish or Portuguese control. Optimistic explorers' reports, such as those returned by Martin Frobisher after his deep penetrations of the Hudson Strait during 1576-8, continued to fuel hopes into the following century that the fabled Northwest Passage might yet be found.

Cartographers dealt with the dispute about the Asian connection in one of three ways. The more prudent did not commit themselves, leaving the northwestern part of North America blank or conveniently letting it run off the edge of the map—a form of cartographic reticence that persisted in many maps well into the eighteenth century. Other mapmakers confidently drew in the land bridge, though in many different forms. The majority of the dissenters showed America separated from Asia by a considerable northern ocean, often called the Eastern or Japanese Ocean. Only a small minority guessed that the separation might be no wider than a strait. Possibly the first of these was Giacomo Galstaldi, who first posited what we now call the Bering Strait (and he called the Straits of Anian) in 1562. The first known cartographic application of this theory appeared on a 1566 map by Zaltieri of Bologna, a later copy

These fanciful illustrations are from the 1493 edition of Columbus's Letters to Sanchez. *Both show scenes of the island of Hispaniola—a European-looking town and, almost as absurd, a shallow-water oared Spanish galley cruising off the island's coast.*

DANTHES
Aligerius
Florentinus
Poëta, Anno
Sal. M.CCC.
descripsit
IIII. ſtellas
Antarcticas
cap. pr. purg.
DANTHES ALIGERIUS
His verbis
ab Americo
Vespuccio
. in ſuis
Epis tolis
adductis.
Io mi volſi a man deſtra, e poſimente
A l'altro polo, e vidi quattro ſtelle
Non viſte mai fuer ch'a la prima gente,
Goder pareua il ciel di lor fiammelle;
O Settentrional vedruo ſito,
Poi che priuato ſei di mirar quelle.
Ego inde versus intuebar æthera,
Poli Nothi adnotaui ibi astra quattuor,
Nisi à priore gente, visa nemini.
Nitet, micatq; flamma quadrupla æthere,
Mihi plaga orbis orba noſſe cerneris
Nequit, videre quando tanta lumina.

A sixteenth-century engraving showing an allegorical scene in which Amerigo Vespucci studies the earth's sphericity by observing the constellation of the southern cross. In the cartouche appears an apposite quotation from Dante.

of which appears in Plate LI.

Some other points of debate about America were settled fairly quickly via exploration, though it is surprising how long disproven ideas persisted on many maps. Such notions as that North and South America were separated by a strait or even a fairly wide sea, or that Florida was an island, did not survive past mid-century. But smaller points, such as whether Yucatan was a peninsula or an island, took longer to resolve.

And numerous other points were not resolved at all. The idea that North America must be connected to Greenland somewhere above the Arctic Circle gathered force throughout the century and continued to be accepted by most cartographers for the next 200 years. The speculation that California was an island was also put forward in the sixteenth century, though it was not so widely held as in the seventeenth and early eighteenth centuries. And there was no real consensus about the breadth of North America—certainly none about the northern latitudes where the continent might or might not join Asia, but little, as well, about the mid-continent (say, from modern Vancouver to Québec or from San Francisco to Washington, DC). Nor was this question satisfactorily resolved until the eighteenth century.

One of the more curious errors that persisted on many maps until late in the sixteenth century had to do with the so-called 'Sea of Verrazano.' In 1524, while cruising off the North Carolina coast, Giovanni da Verrazano came upon the long barrier of sandbars and low islands that separates the Pamlico and Albermarle sound from the open ocean. He mistook this for an isthmus that separated the Atlantic from another large body of water, which he named the Western Sea and which he rather daringly guessed must be connected to the Pacific. This mythical Mare Indicum began appearing on some maps as early as 1526, and belief in its existence does not seem to have been finally abandoned until about 1590. Plates XVI, XXIII and XXIV show how Münster and Agnese imagined Verrazano's sea in the 1540s.

This woodcut from a 1537 book printed in Lubeck portrays Columbus and friend standing on a ship whose design would have been considered primitive by the real Columbus.

Dyt ys dat högeste vnde
öldeste water recht / dat de gemene
Kopman vnd Schippers geordinert vnde
gemaket hebben tho Wißby / dat sick eynn
yder (de thor Sewert vorkeret)
hyr na richten mach.

Gedrückt in der Keyserliken
Stadt Lübeck dorch Jurgen Richolff
Wanhafftich in der Mölenstraten.
Int jar M. CCCCC. XXXvij.

Plate I

'Portolan World Chart,' Juan de la Cosa, 1500. The first known representation of the New World, it was painted on oxhide by a Basque pilot who sailed with Columbus on his voyages of 1492 and 1493. It not only depicts the discoveries of Columbus but those made by the Cabots in 1497-8. The many wind roses and the (inaccurate) latitude scale are typical portolano features. The St Christopher figure on the left is meant to stand for Columbus
955 x 1770 mm. Museo Naval, Madrid.

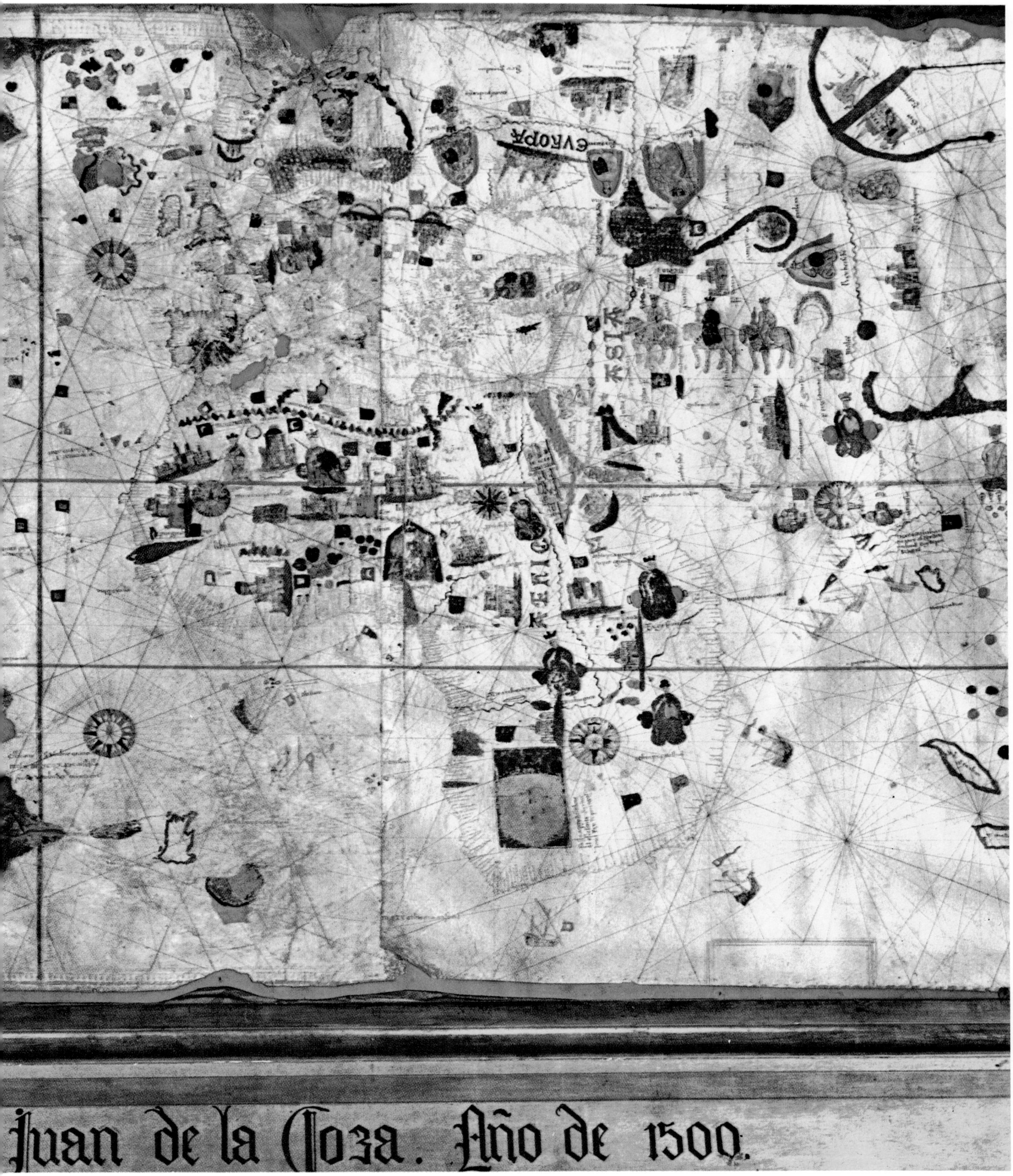
EVROPA
ASIA
AFRICA
Juan de la Coza. Año de 1500.

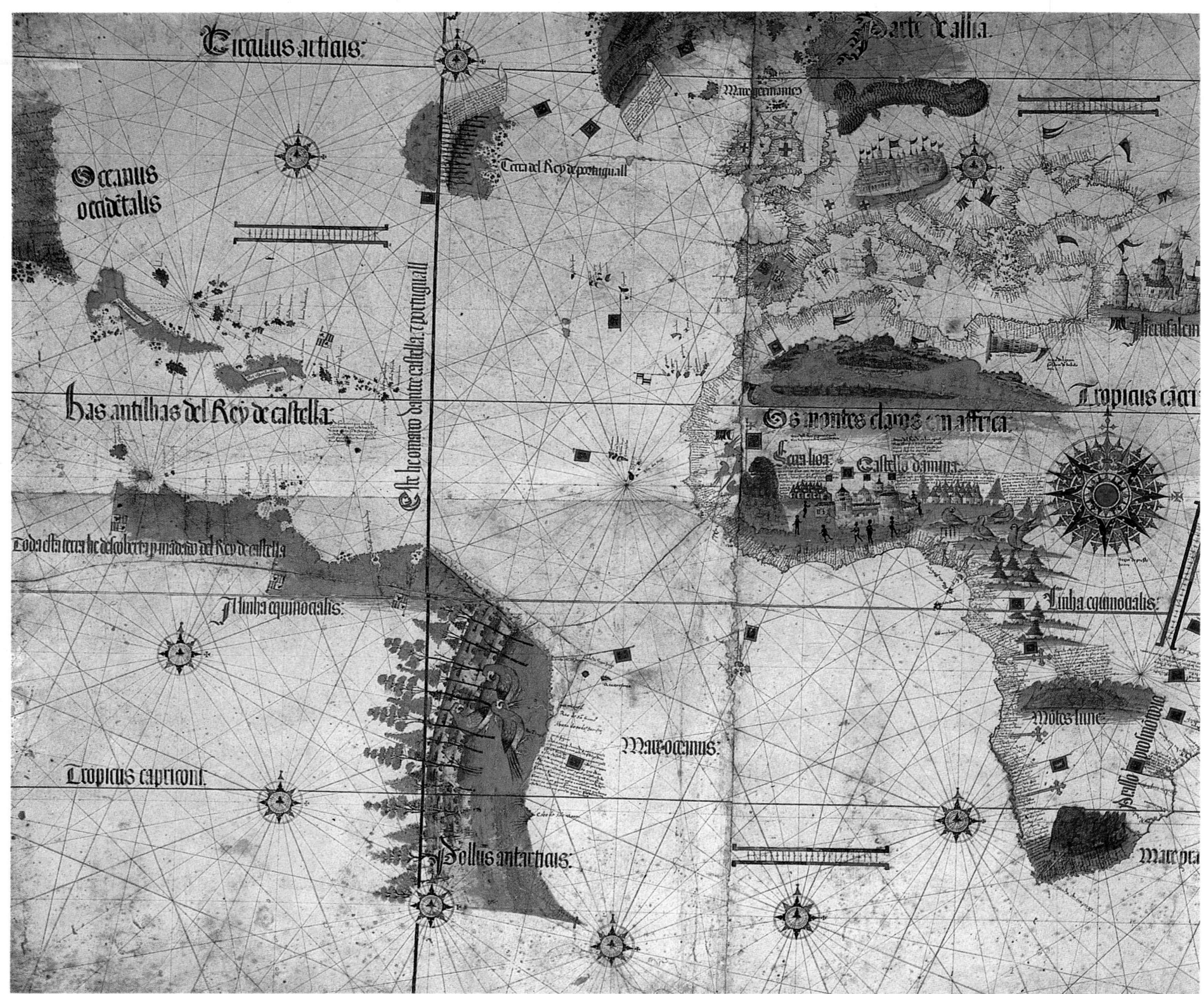

Plate II

'Cantino Planisphere,' anon, 1502. This hand-colored parchment map is a copy of one that was locked in the royal archives of Portugal. It was smuggled out of the country by the envoy of the duke of Ferrara, Alberto Cantino. It shows the line set up in 1494 by the Treaty of Tordesillas to distinguish new lands claimable by Spain and Portugal. Eastern Brazil is correctly shown on the Portuguese side of the line, but Newfoundland, recently discovered by Corte Real, is also set partly east of the line, a 15-degree displacement.
1050 x 2200 mm. Biblioteca Estensa, Modena.

Plate III

'Planisphere,' Nicola Caverio, *c* 1505. This 10-section world map drawn on parchment by the Genoan cartographer Caverio clearly shows the influence of the Cantino map: The depiction of the New World is almost identical, even to the disingenuous eastward displacement of Newfoundland.
1150 x 2250 mm. Bibliothèque Nationale, Paris.

Plate IV

'Universalis Cosmographia,' Martin Waldseemüller, 1507. A copy of the famous wood-block map made by the German cartographer who first both showed the new lands as separate continents and gave them the name by which we know them. (The legend 'America' is visible at the latitude of the Tropic of Capricorn.) The continents are made narrow so as to conform to an underestimated global circumference and an exaggeration of the extent of Asia. At the top of the map are the figures of Ptolemy and Amerigo Vespucci, after whom the New World had been named.
The original, 1370 x 2440 mm, is in Schloss Wolfegg, Würtemberg.

universal de 1507

(Primero con el nombre América)

scrito por Carlos Sanz en su obra

OMBRE DE AMERICA"

Mapas y Libros que lo impusieron

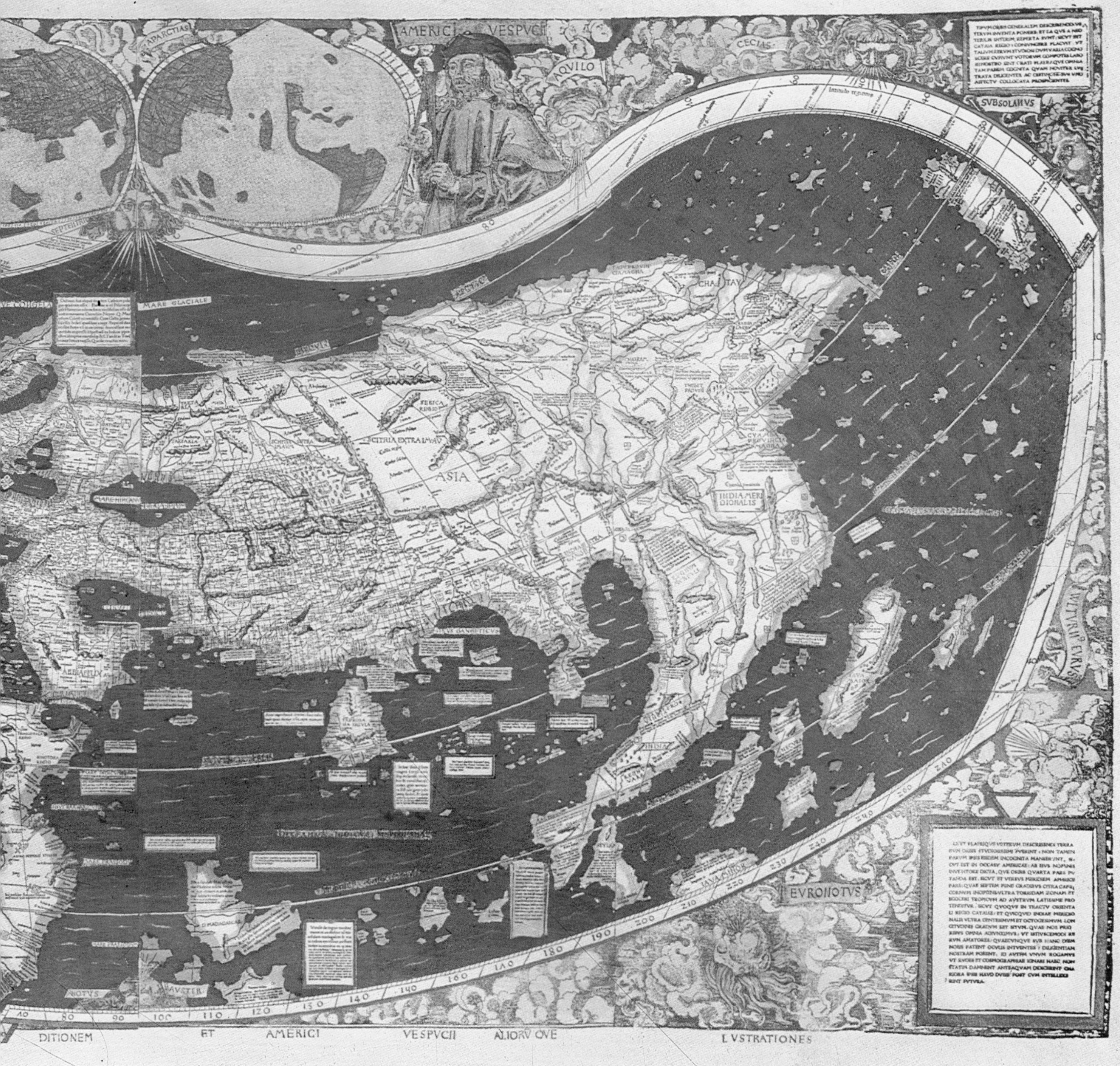

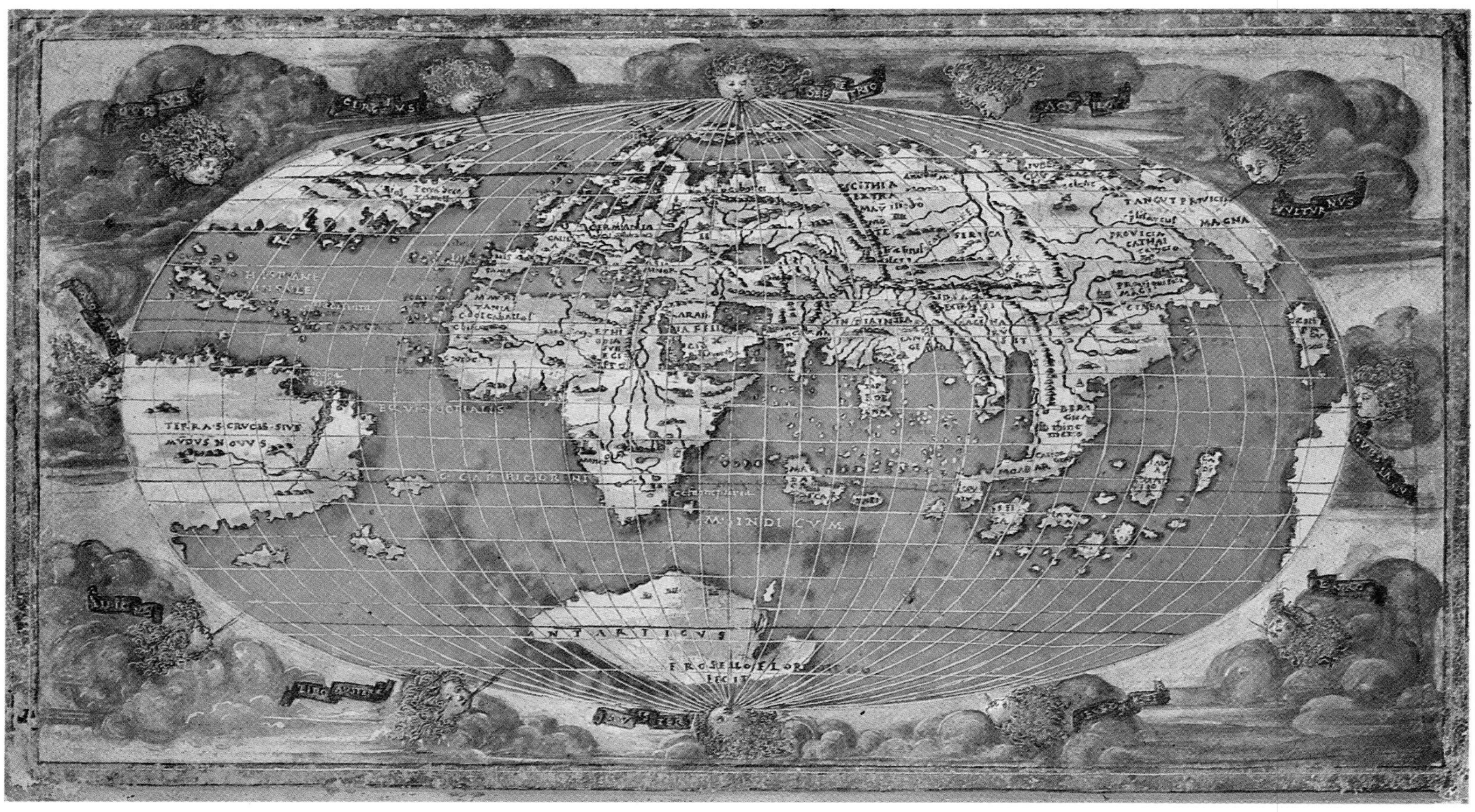

Plate V

'World Map,' Francesco Roselli, 1508. This copperplate map, the first to use an oval projection, shows well the early discoveries of Columbus, the Cabots and Vespucci but divides North from South America by a wide sea and links North America to the Asian mainland. Roselli engraved the first printed map of America, one drawn by Contarini, in 1506.
1800 x 3350 mm. National Library, Florence.

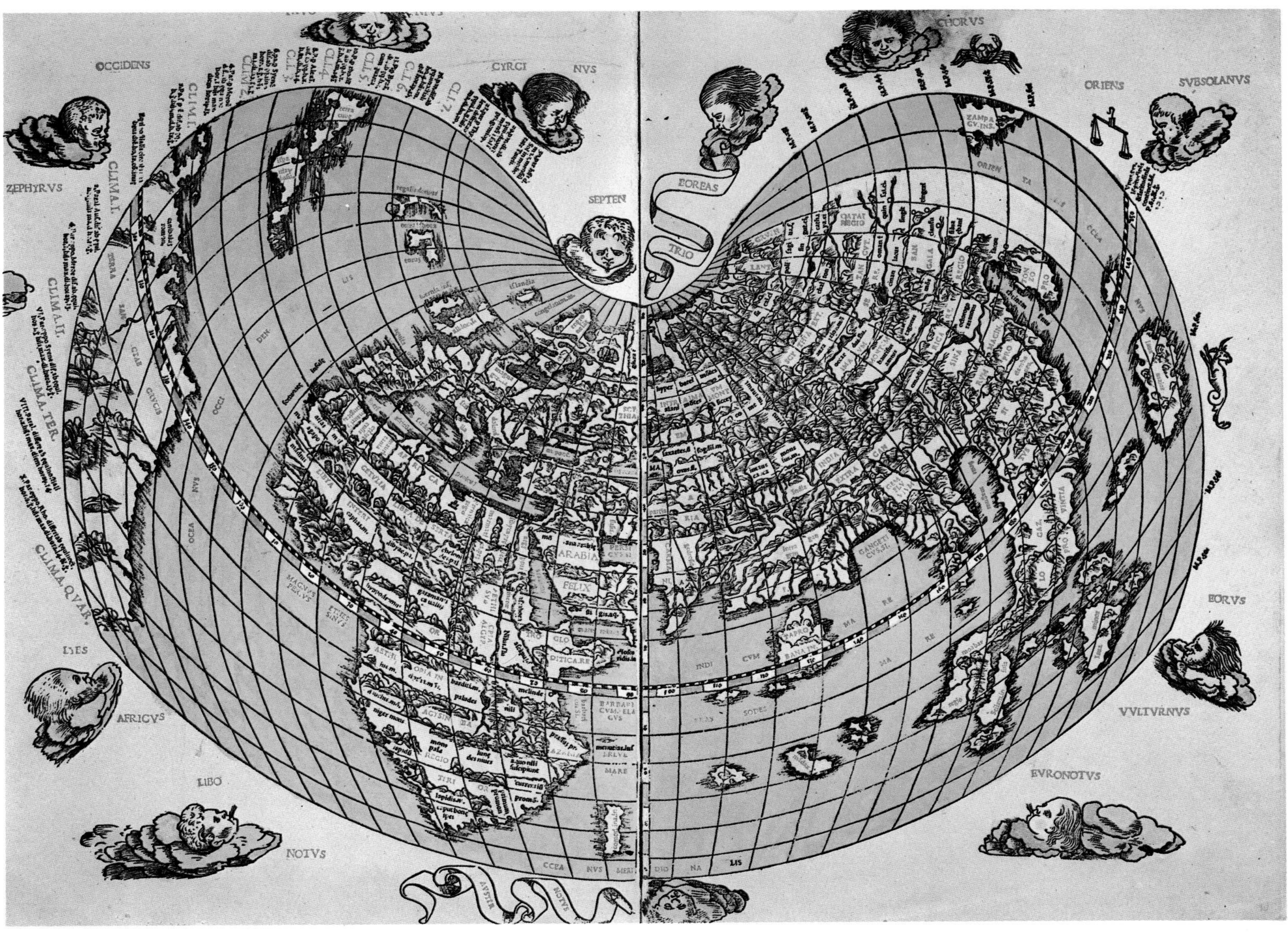

Plate VI

'World Map', Bernardo Silvano da Eboli, 1511. This color-printed xylographic map was included in an edition of Ptolemy published in Venice. It shows North America as a collection of islands—Hispaniola, Cuba and Newfoundland—considerably apart from South America, here called 'Terra di Santa Croce.' But clearly the cartographer was uneasy about the western extent of the new lands. He lets South America run off the map and is vague about a possible linkage between North America and the Asian mainland. 415 x 565 mm.

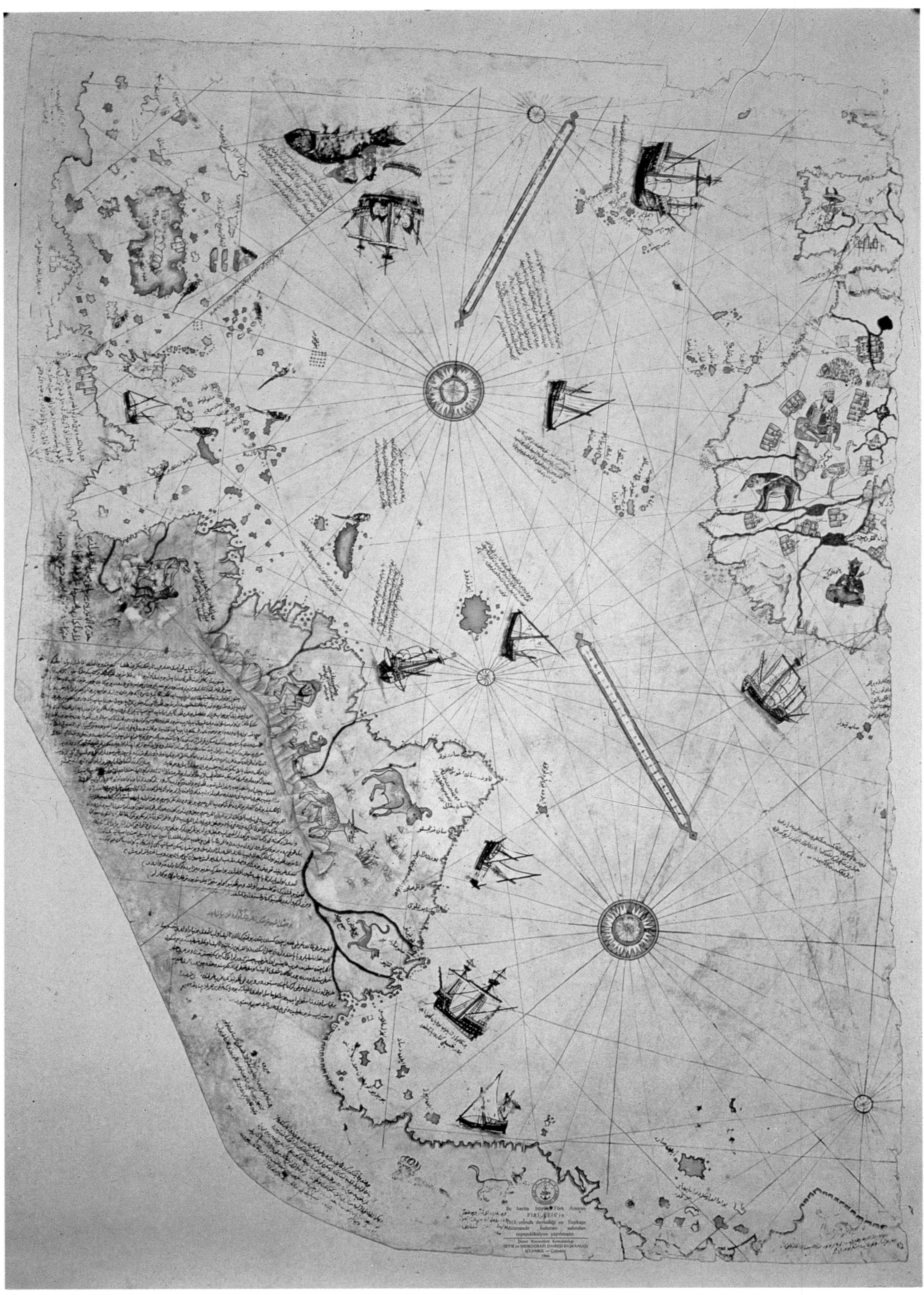
Bu harita büyük Türk Amirali
PIRI REIS'in
1513 yılında derlediği ve Topkapı
Müzesinde bulunan aslından
reprodüksiyon yapılmıştır.
SEYIR ve HIDROGRAFI DAIRESI BAŞKANLIĞI
ISTANBUL — Çubuklu

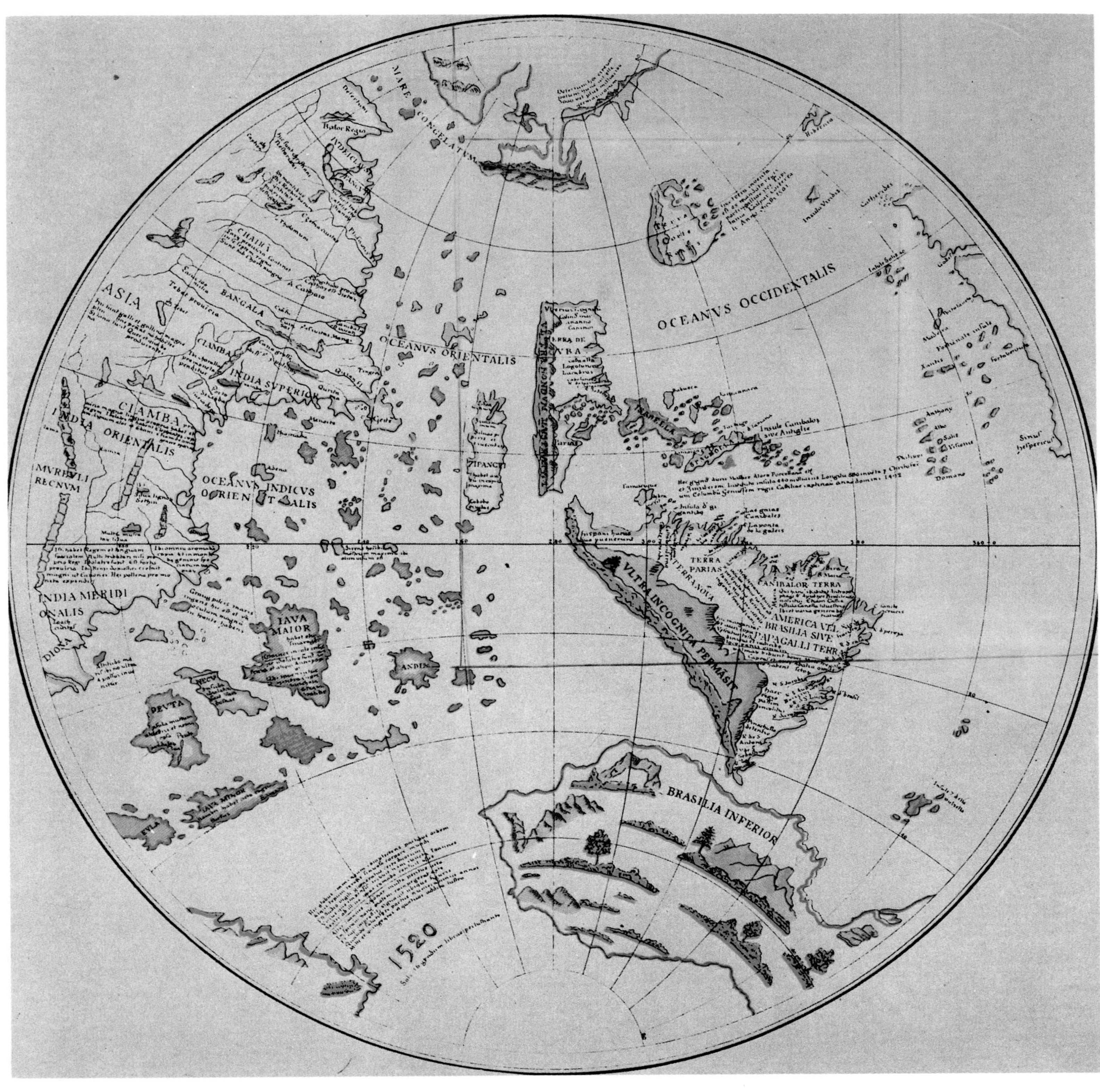

Plate VII (left)

Planisphere,' Piri Reis, 1513. There is some mystery about this fragment of a lost planisphere by an Ottoman cartographer. Legend has it that it is based on a map drawn by Columbus himself. Turkish pirates are said to have captured the original from a Spanish ship, and Reis later drew this hand-colored copy on a sheet of parchment. 900 x 650 mm. Topkapi Museum, Istanbul.

Plate VIII (above)

'Globe,' Johann Schöner, 1520. This modern copperplate is a facsimile of part of a globe in the Nuremberg Museum. North and South America are separated, but North America, here called 'Cuba,' is otherwise close to Waldseemüller's model. Note that Schöner correctly speculated on the existence of the Strait of Magellan, the discovery of which was not reported in Europe until two years later.

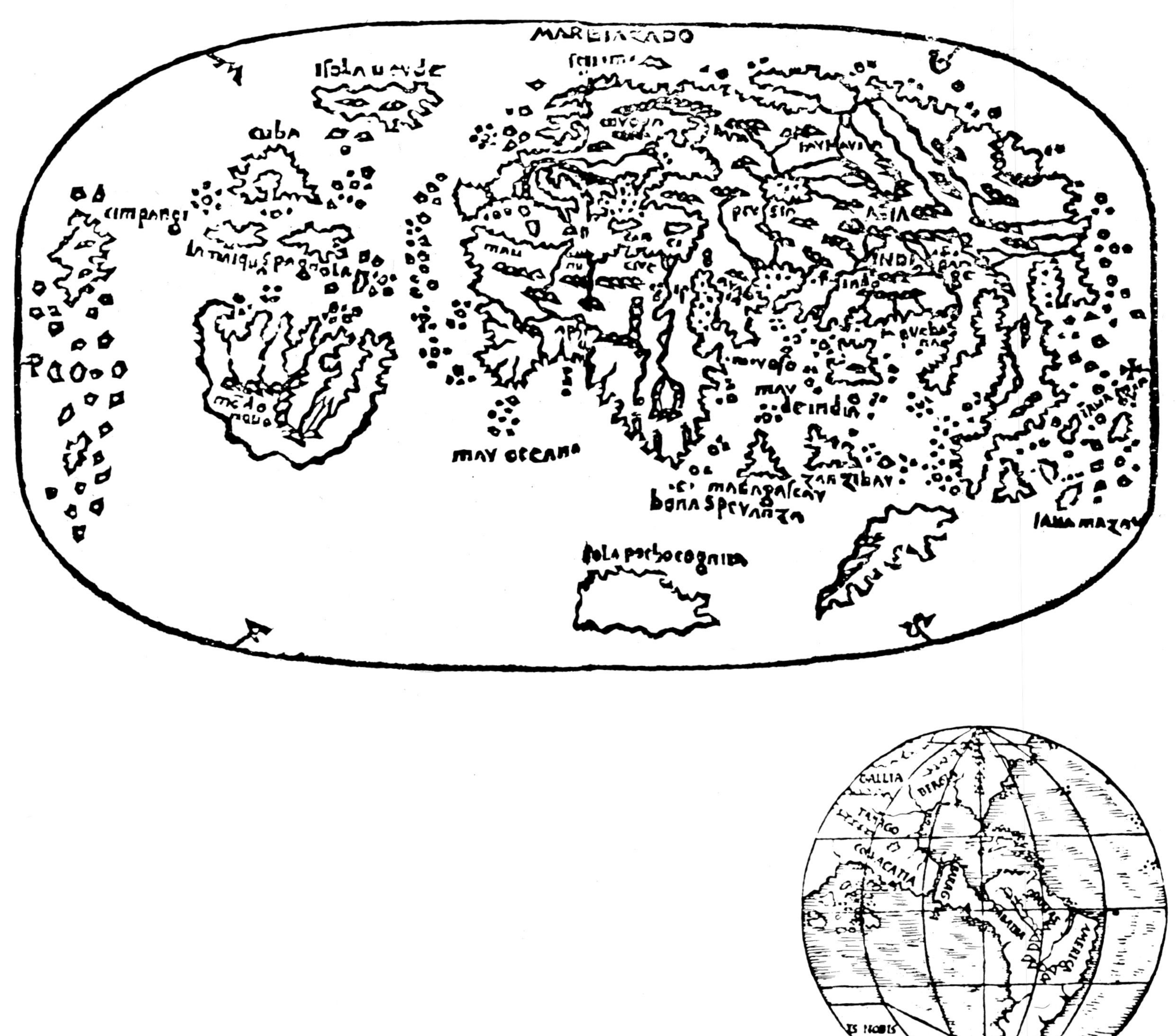

Plate IX (top)

'Portolan World Chart,' Pietro Coppo, 1528. This crude wood-block map, published in Venice, makes Central and North America an archipelago of many islands, large and small. A curious feature of the map is the dense chain of islands that runs down the mid-Atlantic.
80 x 135 mm. City Museum, Pirano

Plate X (above)

'De Orbis Situ,' Franciscus Monachus, 1527. This woodcut, included in a book by a Franciscan friar that was published in Antwerp, is one of the first to show a continuous coast from Florida to Labrador, though the coast belonged to Asia. Note the canal-like strait in the isthmus.
65 mm diameter. PNB

The portrait of Sebastian Cabot by Manescardi in the Doge's Palace in Venice. Although Sebastian claimed to have accompanied his father on the voyages of 1497-8, it is not certain he did so. He did, however, make some important explorations of his own and may be the discoverer of Hudson Bay (c 1508).

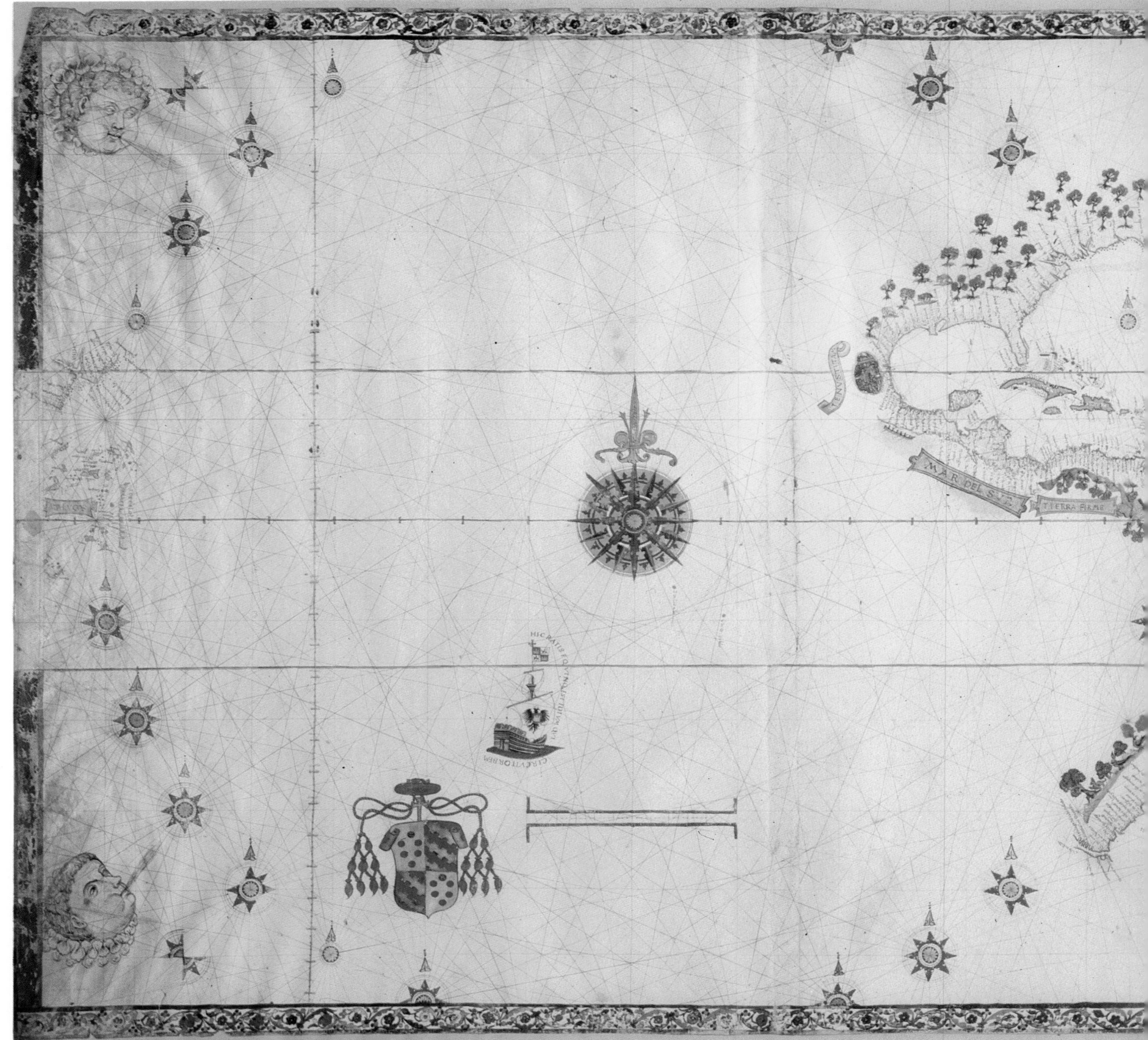

Plate XI

'Salviati World Map,' anon, *c* 1526. This exceptional map may have been a gift from Charles V of Spain to Cardinal Giovanni Salviati, the papal nunzio, whose crest appears on the lower right and left. Its delineation of the eastern coast of the Americas is excellent and includes details of explorations of Florida and Chesapeake Bay reported by Ponce de León and Vasquez de Ayllón, respectively. The realistic extent of the Pacific shows clearly how Magellan's circumnavigation affected cartographic thinking. The map is of parchment, hand-colored.
930 x 2100 mm. Medicea-Laurenziana Library, Florence.

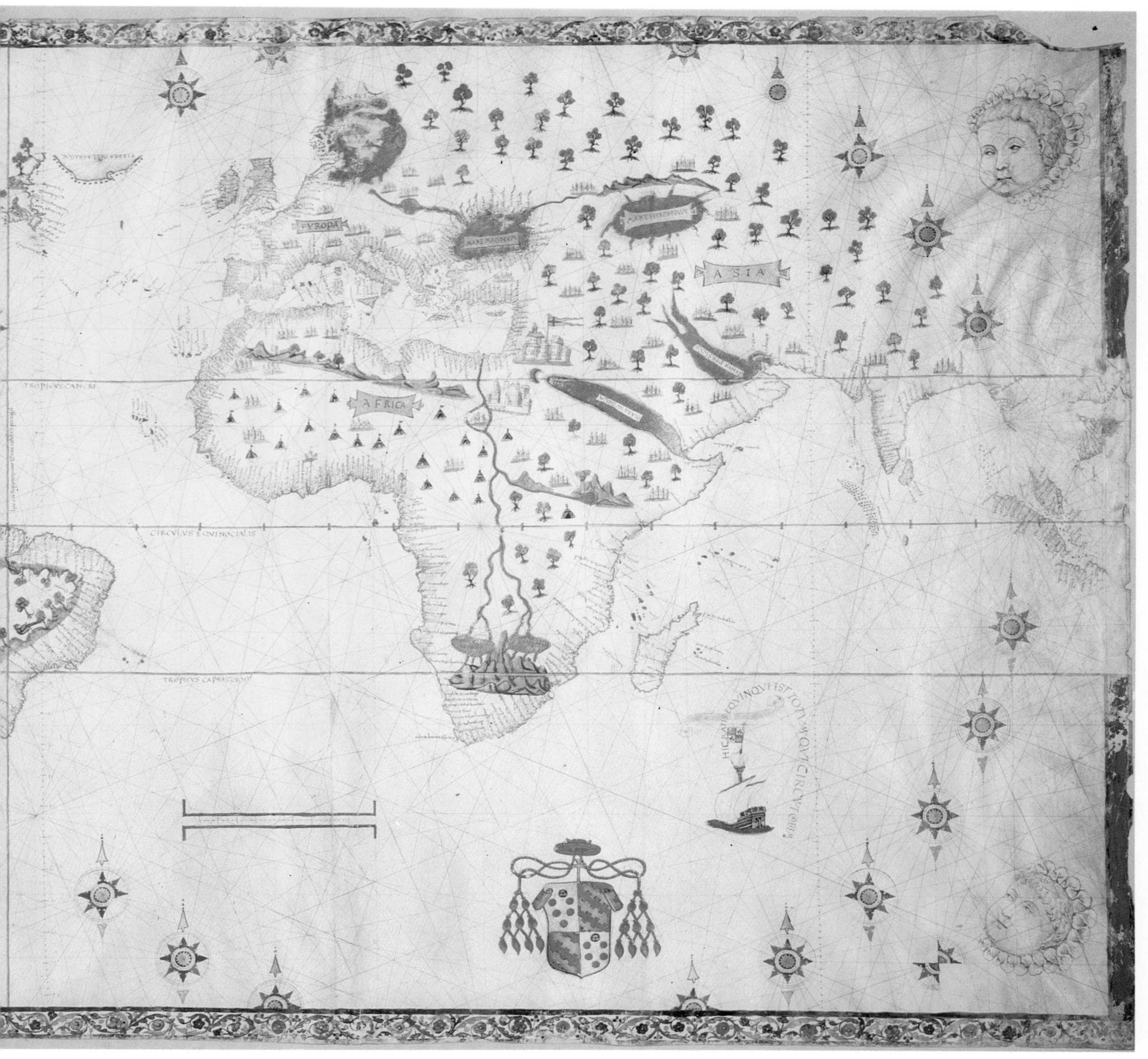
EVROPA
MARE MAGNVM
ASIA
AFRICA
TROPICVS CANCRI
CIRCVLVS EQVINOCIALIS
TROPICVS CAPRICORNI

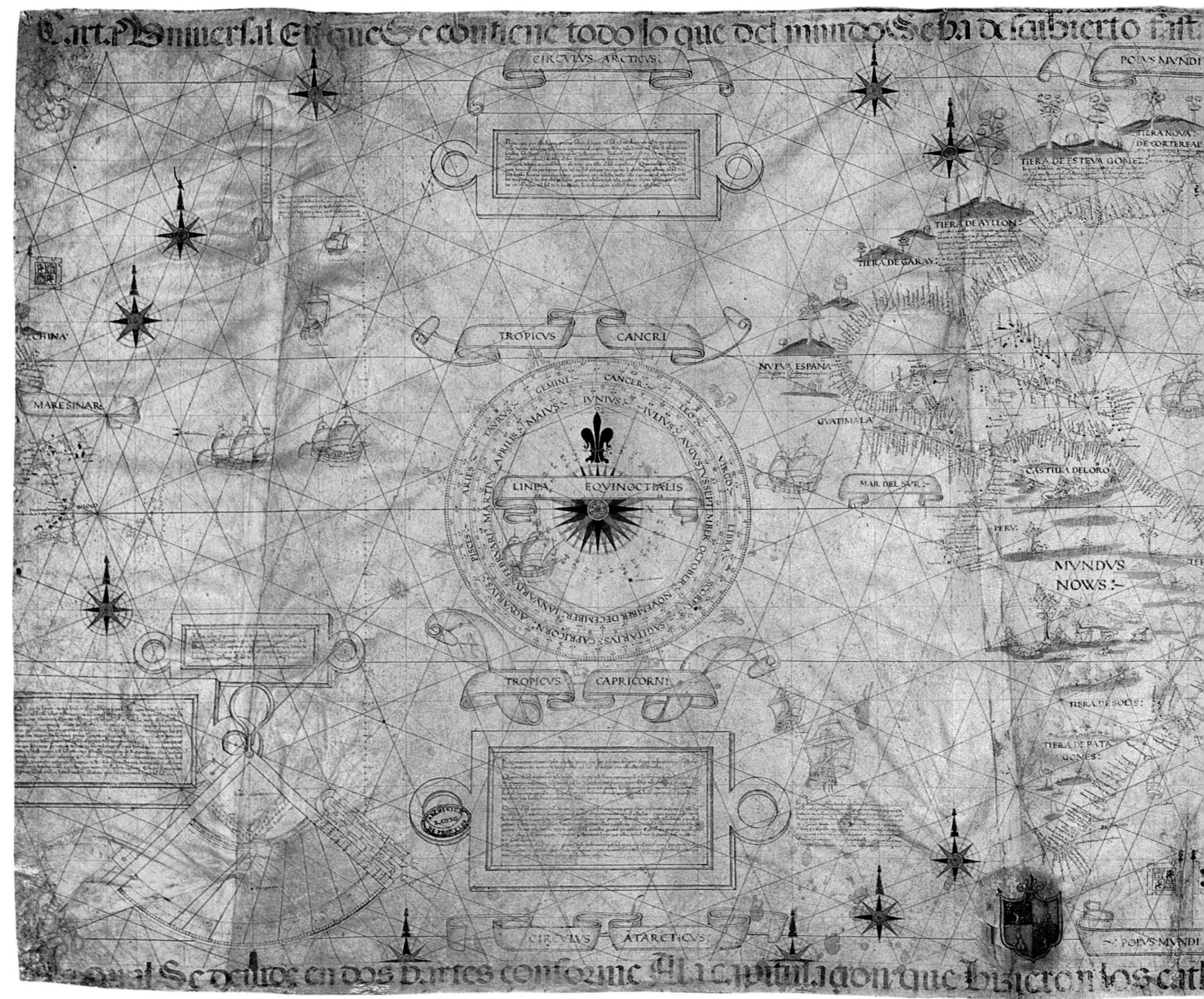

Plate XII

'World Map,' Diego Ribiero, 1529 Whoever drew the Salviati map (Plate XI) may have been influenced by Ribiero, Cosmographer Major after 1523 in the Casa de Contratación, the great Spanish hydrographic center in Seville. This parchment manuscript map is widely considered to be his masterpiece and one of the most handsome maps produced in the sixteenth century. The legends along the American coastline form a kind of capsule history of New World exploration up to that time, and the longitude scaling is remarkably advanced. At the bottom the arms of the Roveres and Chigis flank those of the late Pope Julius II.
850 x 2045 mm. Vatican Library

OCCEANVS SEPTETRIONA LIS
MARE HYPERBOREV
HYPERBOREI MONTES
SARMATIA EVROPE
SARMATIA ASIATICA
GERMANIA
FRANCIA
GRETIA
PONTVS EVXINVS
ASIA MINOR
ARMENIA
MEDIA
HIRCANIA
SCITHIA ITRA IMAV MOTE
SCITHIA EXTRA IMAV MOTE
ARACHOSIA
PAROPANISVS
GEDROSIA
INDIA ITRA GAGE
INDIA EXTRA GAGE
MAVRITANIA
NVMIDIA
MARE MEDITERANEV
IVDEA
ARABIA DESERTA
ARABIA PETREA
ARABIA FELIX
GETVLIA
GVINEA
DESERTA LIBIE
ETHIOPIA
ETHIOPIA SVB EGIPTO
REGIO ETHIOPV
PALVDES NILI
SINVS GAGETICVS
SINVS BARBARICVS
MAREETHIOPICVM
MARE INDICVM
INSVLA DIVI LAVRETII
PROMOTORIV BONÆ SPEI
OCCEANVS MERIDIONALIS

This shield, now in the Royal Armory in Madrid, belonged to Charles V. The gold and silver relief design is an allegory of the discovery of the New World and of the riches that flowed from it.

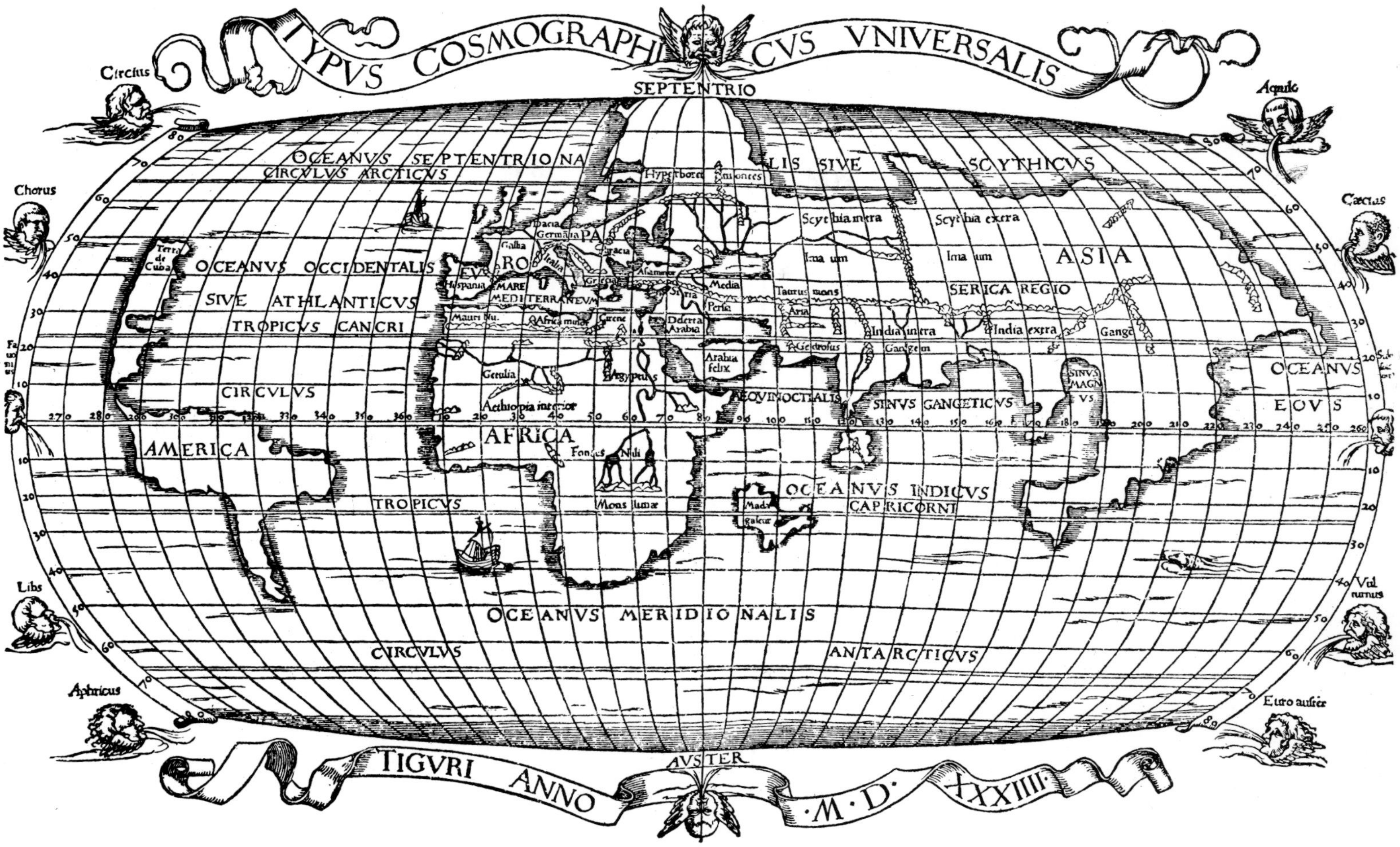

This woodcut from Columbus's Letters to Sanchez *has the admiral sailing through an incoherent jumble of the islands he has just discovered.*

Plate XIII

'Typus Cosmographicus Universalis,' J Watte, 1534. This wood-block map published in Zürich illustrates the uneven way in which geographic knowledge spread. Far from including the sophisticated information on the Salviati and Ribiero maps (Plates XI and XII), it does not even come up to the level of Waldseemüller's 1507 map (Plate IV).

Plate XIV

'The North Atlantic,' Pedro Reinel, 1535. This parchment portolano by a Portuguese chart-maker outlines the American coastline with the same accuracy as Ribiero (Plate XII). The 'Raya' of the Treaty of Tordesillas, shown by a dotted line, continues to give most of Newfoundland, and perhaps some of Labrador as well, to Portugal.
702 x 1020 mm. National Maritime Museum, Greenwich.

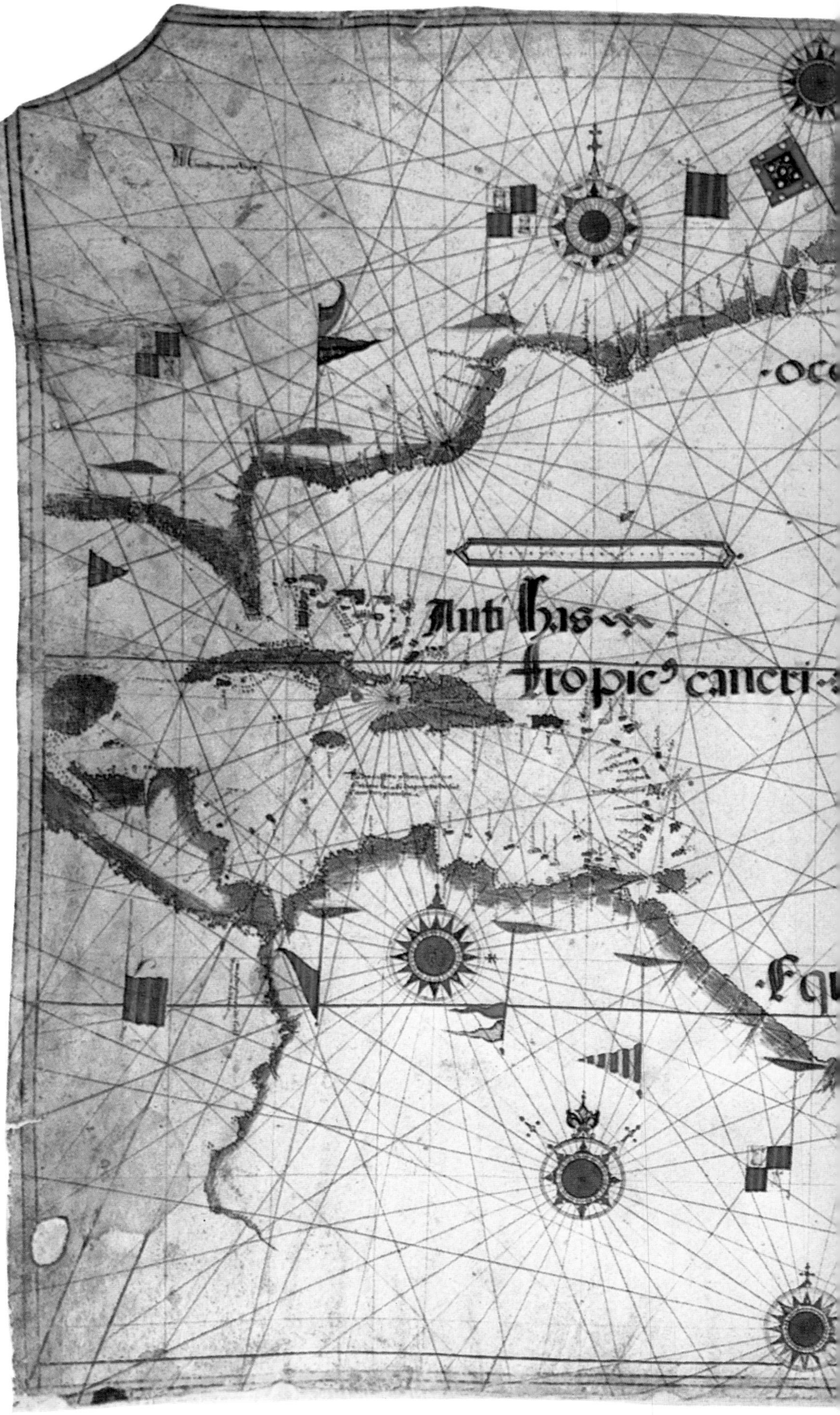

Europa
Partes da frica
terra do brasil
tropic' capricorni

Plate XV

'Orbis Descriptio,' Oronce Finé, 1534. Finé, the most prominent sixteenth-Century French cartographer, drew this map in 1534. It was engraved on wood and printed in 1536 and became a great success. In showing North America as an extension of Asia it may be somewhat retrograde, but the workmanship, decoration and heart-shaped projection (something of a Finé specialty) are impressive.
501 x 570 mm. Biblioteque Nationale, Paris.

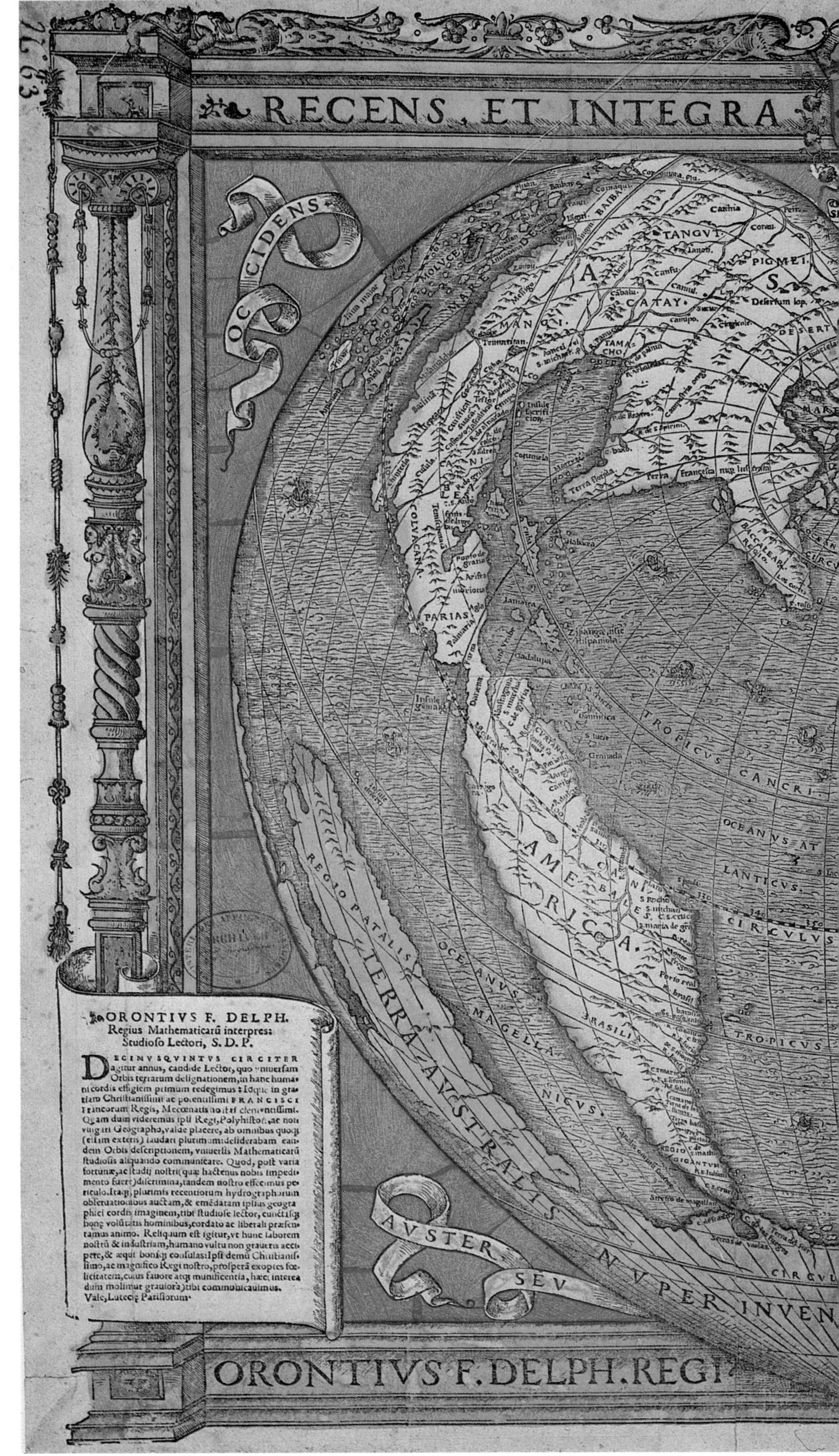

ORBIS DESCRIPTIO
ORIENS
AEQVINOCTIALIS
OCEANVS INDICVS
SED NONDVM PLENE EXAMINATA
MERIDIES
ANNOTATIO.
EX HAC PLANA TERRARVM ORBIS descriptione, duorum quorūcunq; locorum, datarum longitudinum atq; latitudinum, directū itineris interuallum (modò illud nonaginta non superet gradus) prope verum supputare licebit. Numeratis itaq; eorundem locorum lōgitudinibus atq; latitudinibus, eisdēve locis in Charta coassumptis: imposito vnū circini pedē super altero locorū, aliū vero extendito in reliquū. Dein traducito circinū inuariatū in eā rectā, quæ figurā bifariā diuidit, & in suos gradus distributa est: & animaduertito, quot gradus capiat ipse circinus. Hos enim si per 62 miliaria, aut gallicas leucas 31, seu 20 cōmunes, quidecimve maiores multiplicaueris: viatoriā eorundē locorū distātiā obtinebis.
REGALI PORRO CAVTVM est sanctione, ne quispiā hāc geographici cordis effigiem, hinc ad decennium, absq; manifesto opificis consensu imprimat, seu venditet, aut quouis modo distrahat, sub graui mulcta, concesso apud Lugdunū diplomate luculenter expressa.
Parisiis,
MATHEMATIC9 FACIEBAT.

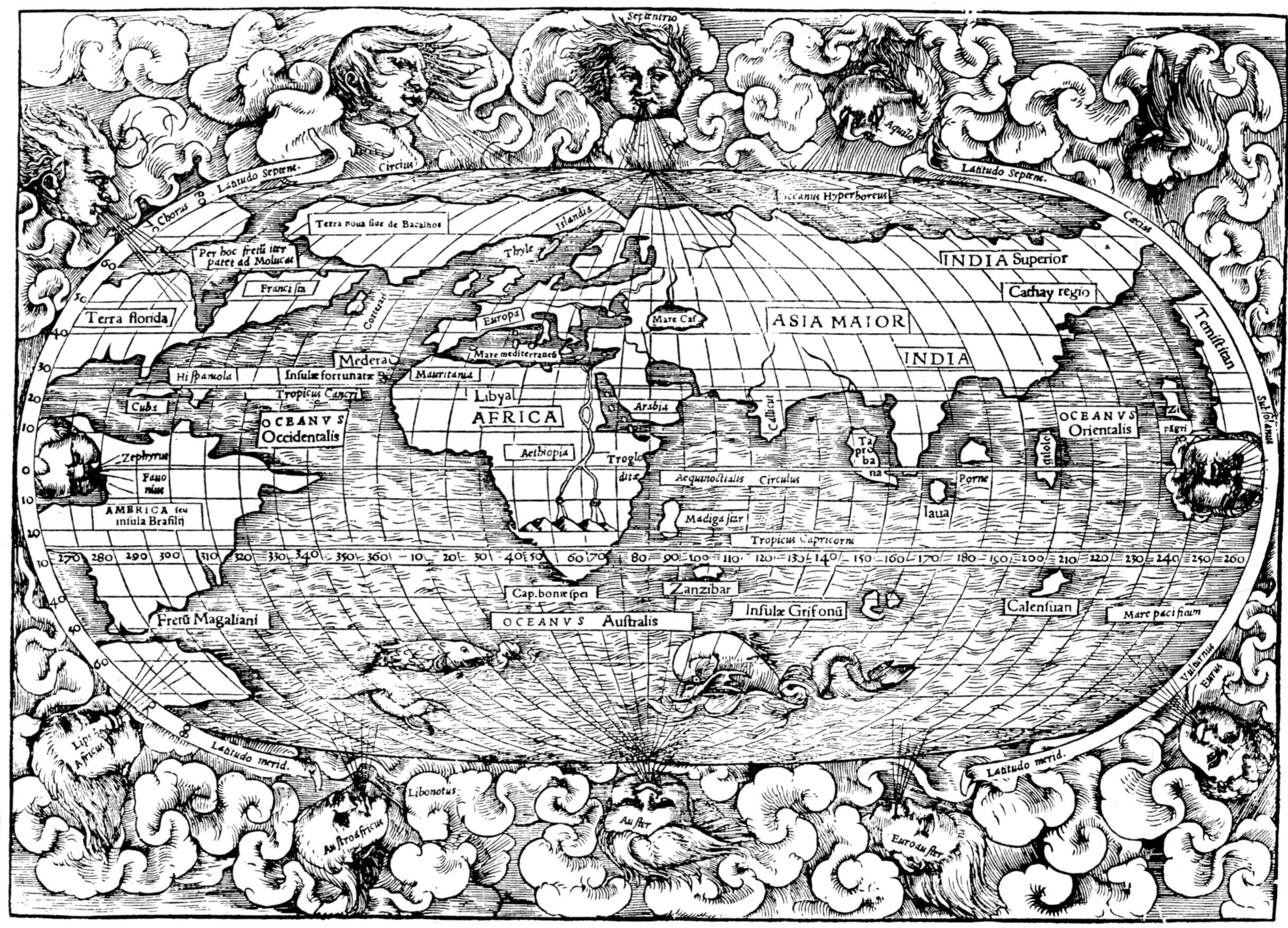

Plate XVI

'Typus Orbis Universalis,' Sebastian Münster, 1540. Münster was one of the more eccentric cartographers of the mid-sixteenth century. This woodcut from his book *Geographia Universalis,* published in Basle, shows North America as being nearly bisected by the imaginary 'Sea of Verrazano' and Newfoundland arcing across the North Atlantic to join with Scandinavia. The name he gave to northern North America, 'Terra Francisca,' may be a reference to Cartier's explorations of 1534-5.
245 x 360 mm.

Two details from maps by the French portolan chartmaker Pierre Descelier. They both chart and illustrate the discoveries of Cartier along the St Lawrence River. The earlier (1544) map, top, clearly displays the name 'Canada,' a word that Cartier first heard from the Indians. On both maps north is at the bottom.

Plate XVII

'Tabula Orbis,' Gaspar Treschel, ed, 1541. This wood-block map is one of 50 included in a 1541 edition of Ptolemy's *Geographia* published in Vienne, France, by Treschel. It appears to have been drawn in 1522 by an unknown hand, but it is not, except for the crude representation of America, in any sense a modern map. It thus stands as a reminder of the extraordinary persistence of Ptolemy's ideas even in the midst of the Age of Discovery
468 x 415 mm. Civic Library, Ivrea

tione ventorum.
Hypertias
Boreas
Aquilo
RADITIONEM.EXACTISSIME.DEPICTA.1522.L.F.
Vulturnus
Cecias
Subsolanus
Leuans
Eurus
Euro auster
Nothus
Auster
Euronothus
ASIA
halor regio
Tangul
Cathaia
India superior
India intra gangem
India extra gangem
Quinsai
Cathaio
mangi
Sinus magnus
Sinus gangeti cus
Java maior
Java minor
Seia
Sera
Seria regio
Sogdiana
Bactrianа
Alexandria
Drangiana
Taprobana
Sabana
Tine
Moabar
mare indicū
130
140
150
160
170
180
190
200
210
220
230
240
250
260
270
280
290

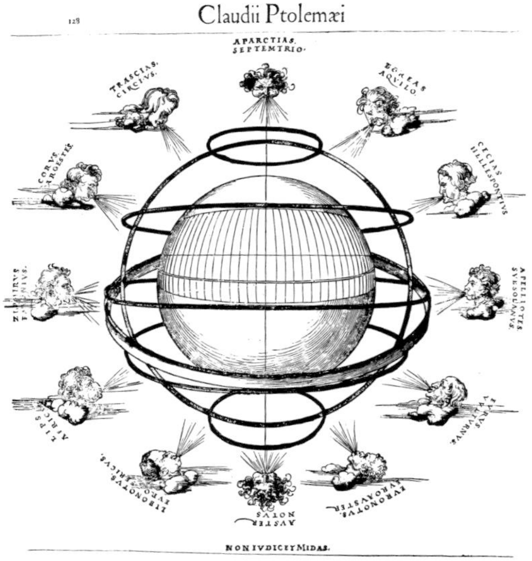

A decorative 12-point wind rose, one of the illustrations in Treschel's 1541 edition of Ptolemy. Wind roses were ancient navigational aids that indicated the directions from which certain winds usually blew (eg Boreas and Aquilo from northeast). The 32-point rose was the basis for the modern compass card.

Plate XVIII

'Oceanus Occidentalis,' Gaspar Treschel, ed, 1541. Another map in Treschel's 1541 edition of Ptolemy shows more New World detail than the one reproduced in Plate XVII. That is doubtless because it is a copy of a map, 'Tabula Terre Nove,' inserted in a 1513 edition of Ptolemy by the 'modern' cartographer Martin Waldseemüller.
268 x 415 mm. Civic Library, Ivrea

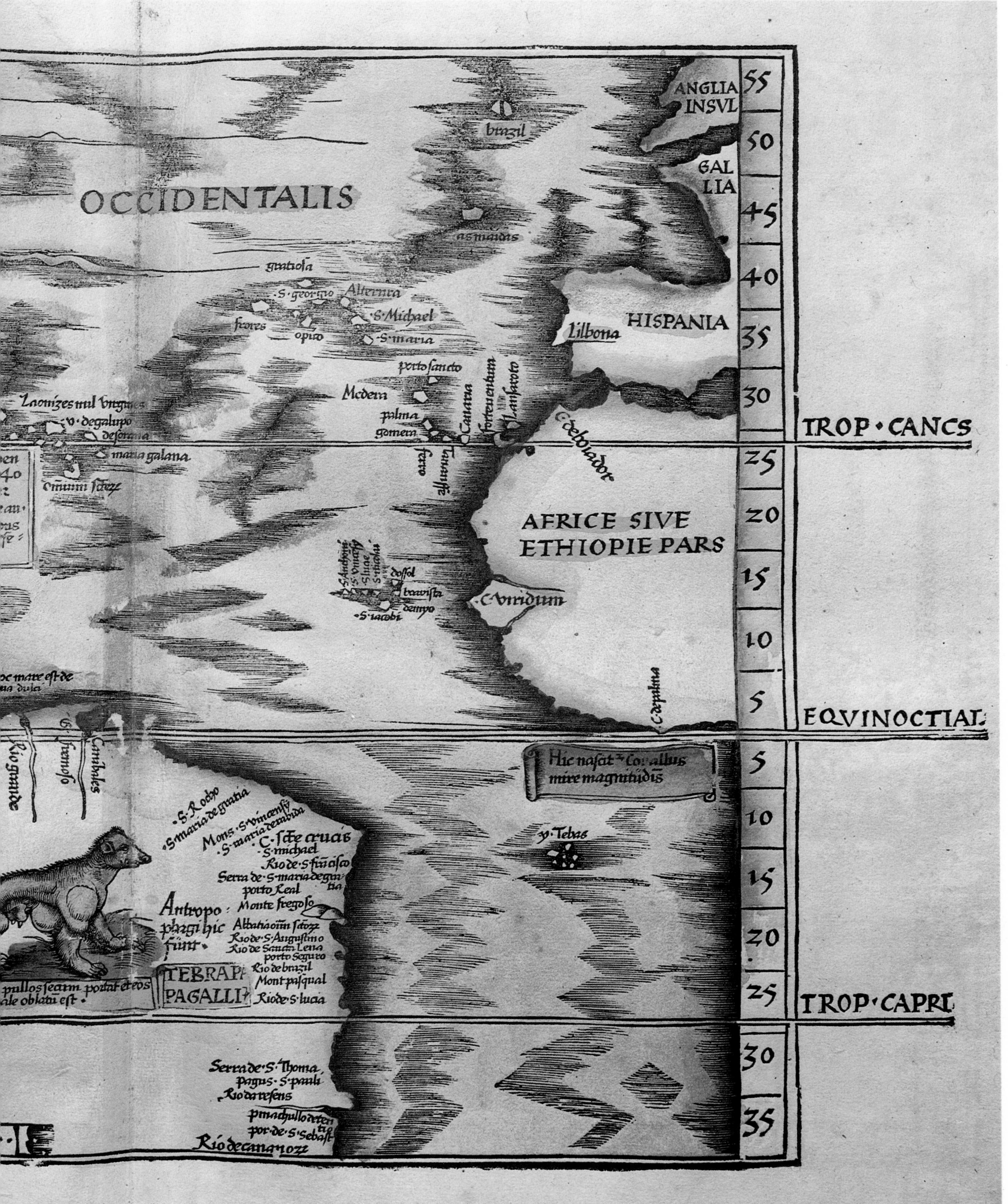
ANGLIA INSUL
GALLIA
OCCIDENTALIS
HISPANIA
Lilbona
TROP · CANCS
AFRICE SIVE ETHIOPIE PARS
EQUINOCTIAL
Hic nascit^r Corallus mire magnitudis
TROP · CAPRI
Antropo plagi hic sunt
TEBRAP PAGALLI
55
50
45
40
35
30
25
20
15
10
5
5
10
15
20
25
30
35

Plate XIX

'Atlantic Ocean,' Jean Rotz, 1542. Rotz, a French portolan chartmaker of the Dieppe school, included this parchment map in a collection he prepared for England's Henry VIII. Oriented with north at the bottom, it shows Newfoundland as a conjuries of islands and Labrador extending far out into the Atlantic, almost to Iceland.
595 x 770 mm. British Library, London

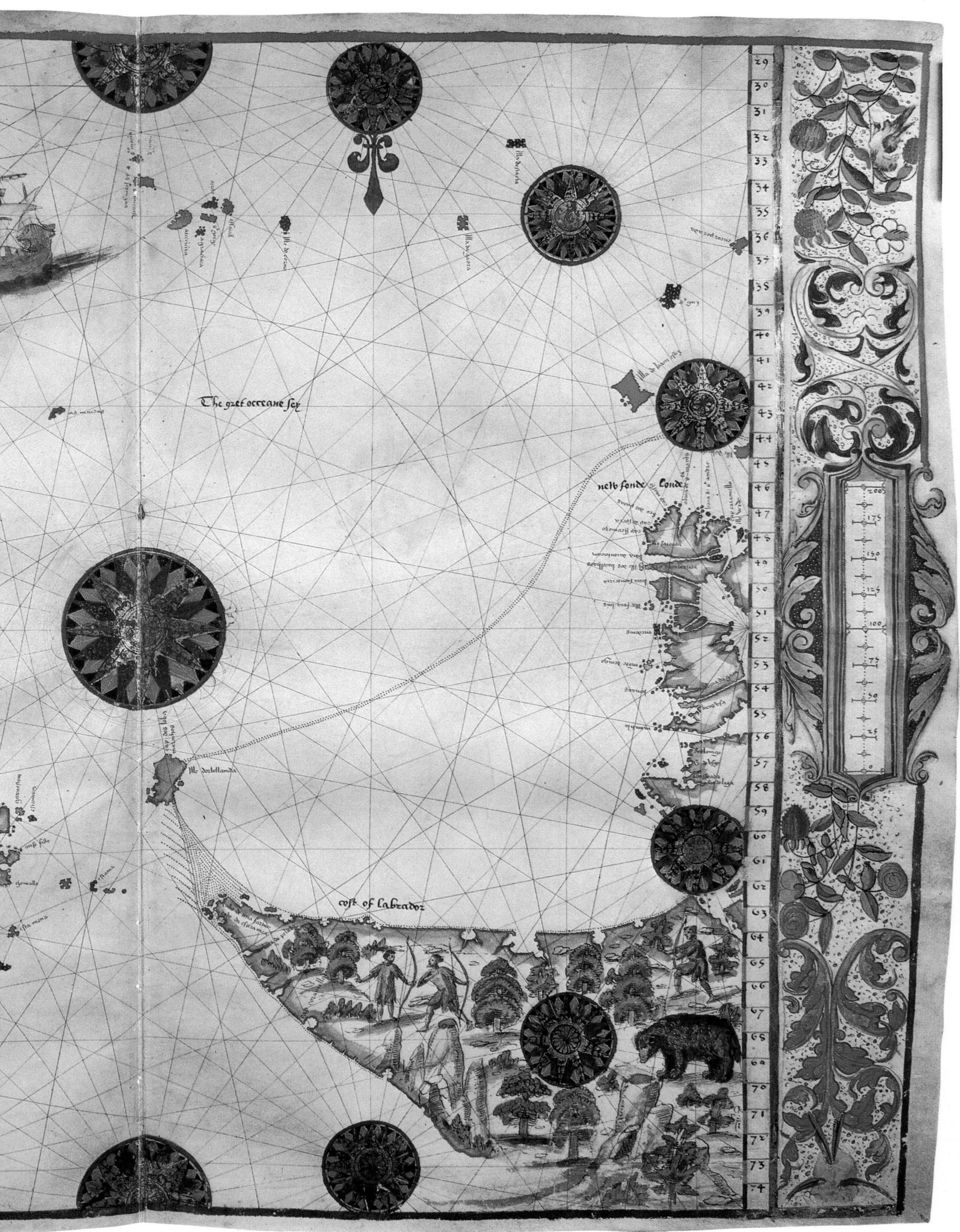
The gret occeane sey
new fonde londe
cost of Labrador

Plate XX

'North America and West Indies,' Jean Rotz 1542. Another map in the collection Rotz presented to Henry VIII (see Plate XIX), this is also oriented with north at the bottom. Because it shows the Gulf of St Lawrence but does not show the St Lawrence River it must be based solely on the information that Cartier reported from his first voyage, for he discovered the river only on his second voyage. Note the Indian wigwams, the first ever to appear on a map. 595 x 770 mm. British Library, London

the cost of peron
The Indis of occident quhar the spaniartis
doith occupy
espagnolla
Couba
Lucaia
Land of florida

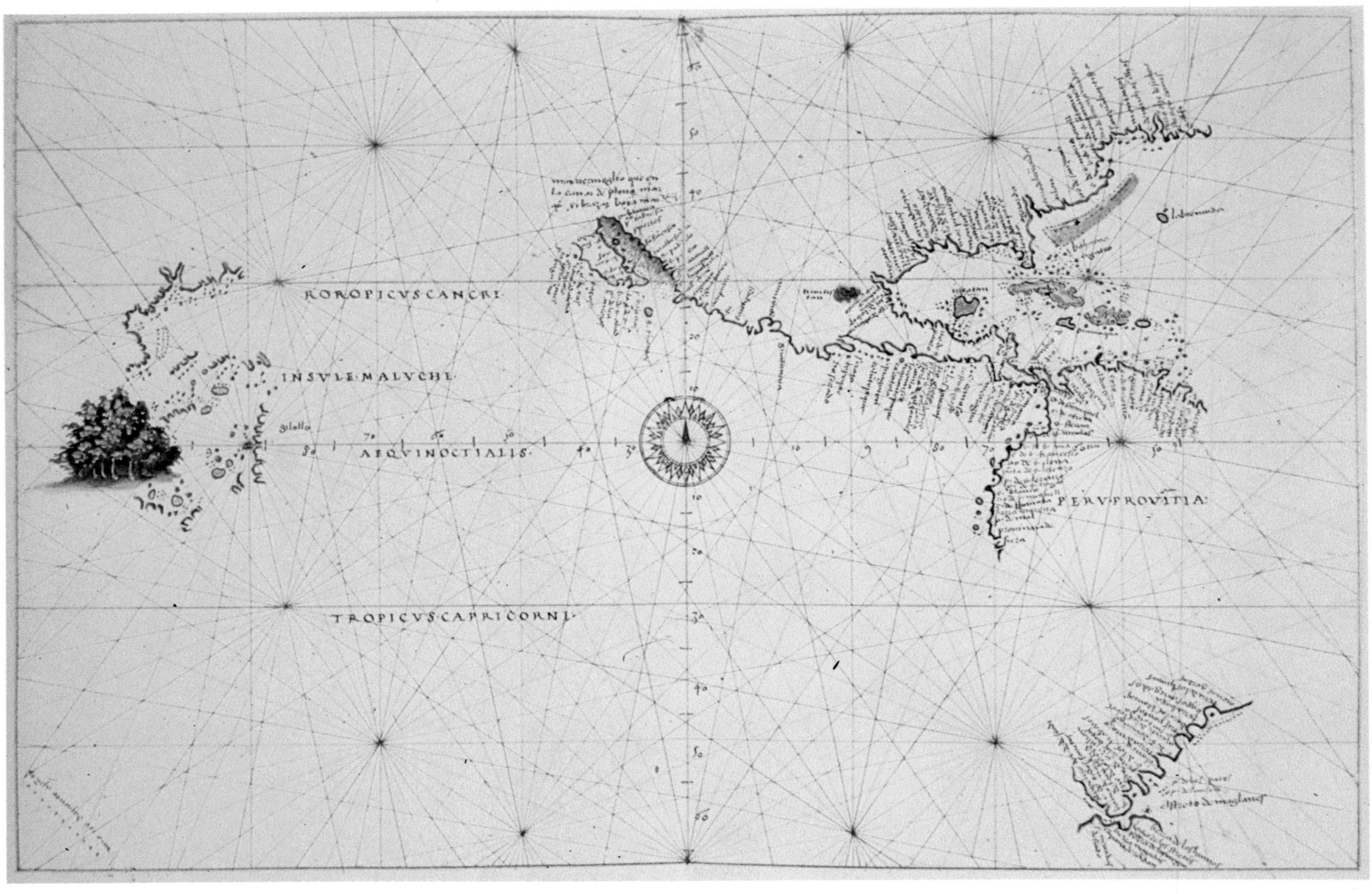

Plate XXI

'Pacific Ocean,' Battista Agnese, *c* 1543. Agnese was a prolific Genoan cartographer who did most of his work in Venice. This parchment map was included in a collection once owned by Charles V. In addition to showing such refinements as Cape Cod and the Gulf of Maine, it also presents details of the Gulf of California based on explorations made by Ulloa in 1539. Some of the east coast of South America is left blank only because it would not fit conveniently on the map.
245 x 340 mm. Medicea-Laurenziana Library, Florence

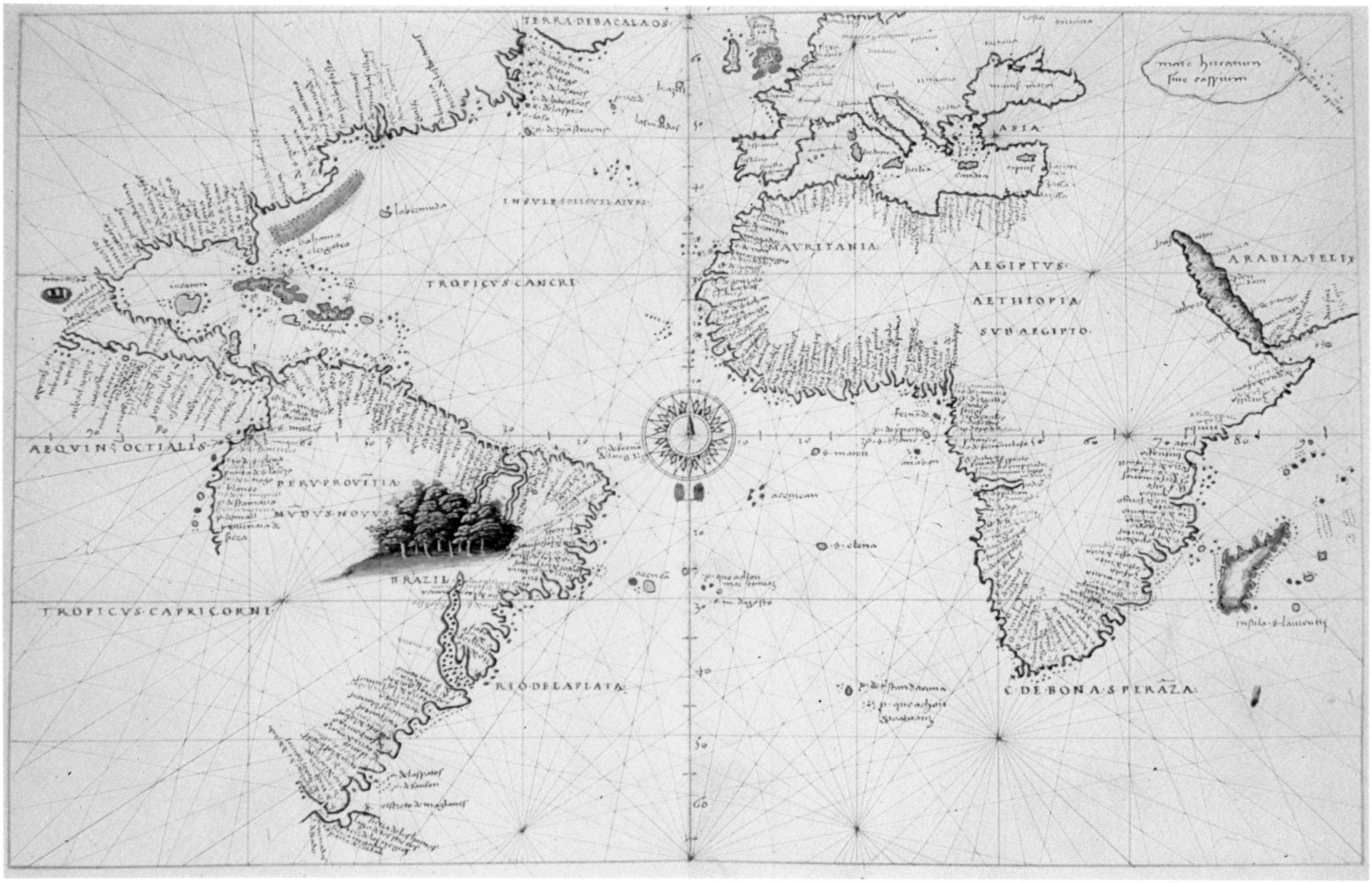

Plate XXII

'Atlantic Ocean,' Battista Agnese, *c* 1543. This parchment map, also in the Charles V collection, fills in details of the American east coast missing in Plate XXI. Its general accuracy and the profusion of place names are impressive.
245 x 340 mm. Medicea-Laurenziana Library, Florence

This portrait of Magellan by an unknown artist now hangs in Vienna's Kunsthistorisches Museum.

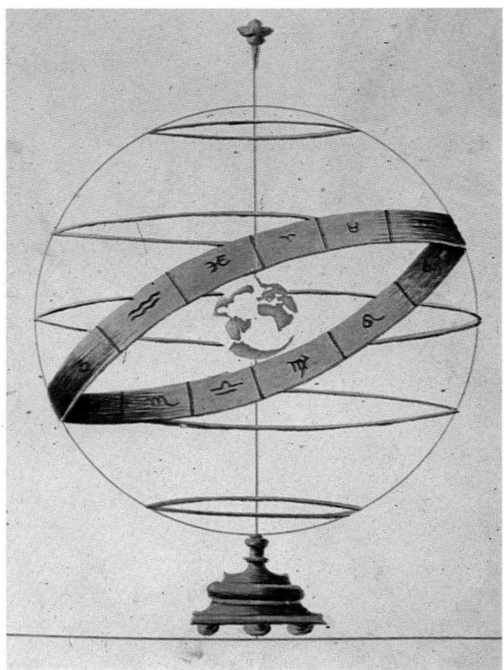

This painting of an armillary sphere is a detail from one of Agnese's portolanos.

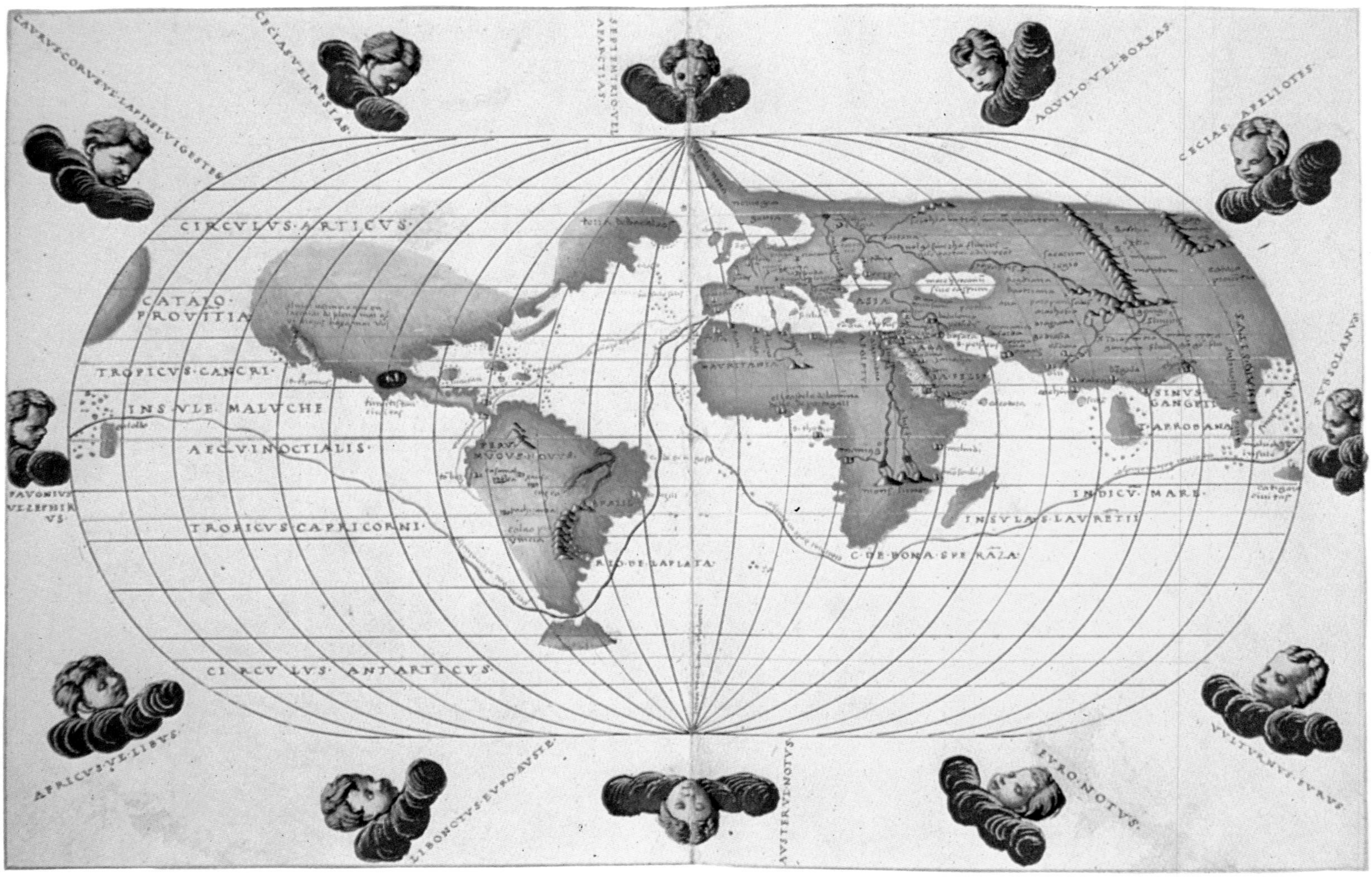

Plate XXIII

'Magellan's Voyage,' Battista Agnese, *c* 1543. This planisphere, painted on parchment, traces the route taken by Magellan on his voyage of 1519-1522. Of interest is the indication of the false 'Sea of Verrazano' in North America.
245 x 340 mm. Medicea-Laurenziana Library, Florence

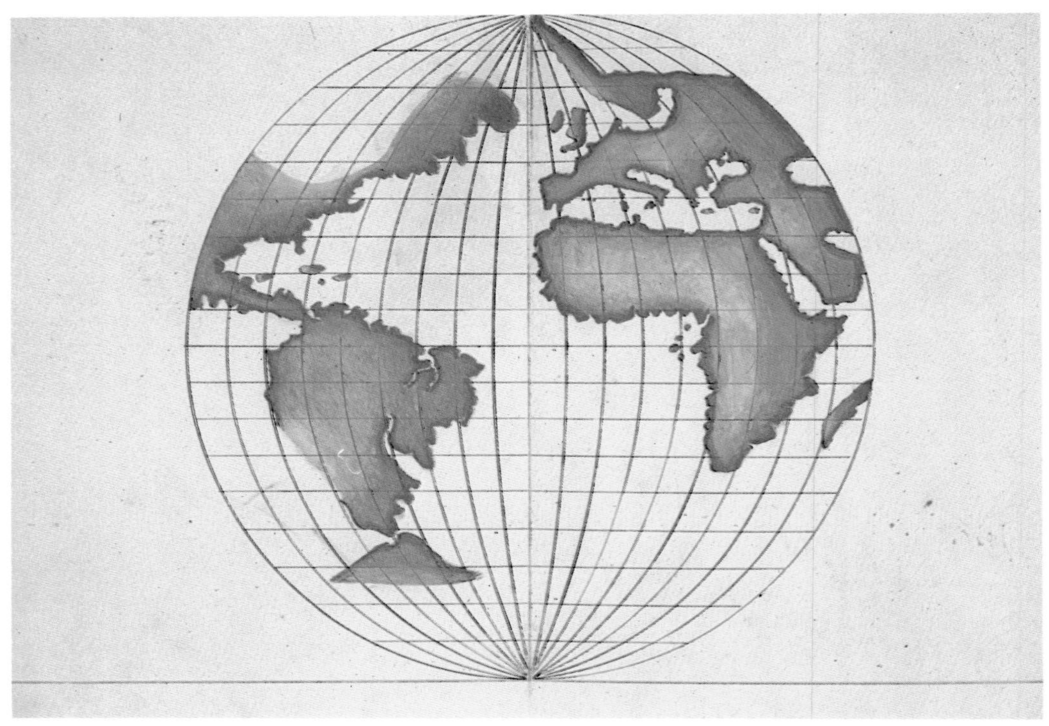

Plate XXIV

'Planisphere,' Battista Agnese, *c* 1543. Also a planisphere drawn on parchment, but this time made with a circular projection.
245 x 340 mm. Medicea-Laurenziana Library, Florence

Plate XXV

'Planisphere,' (detail) Guillaume G Brouscon, 1543. Of little geographic import but very handsome is this French parchment portolano.
450 x 650 mm. Huntington Library, San Marino, CA

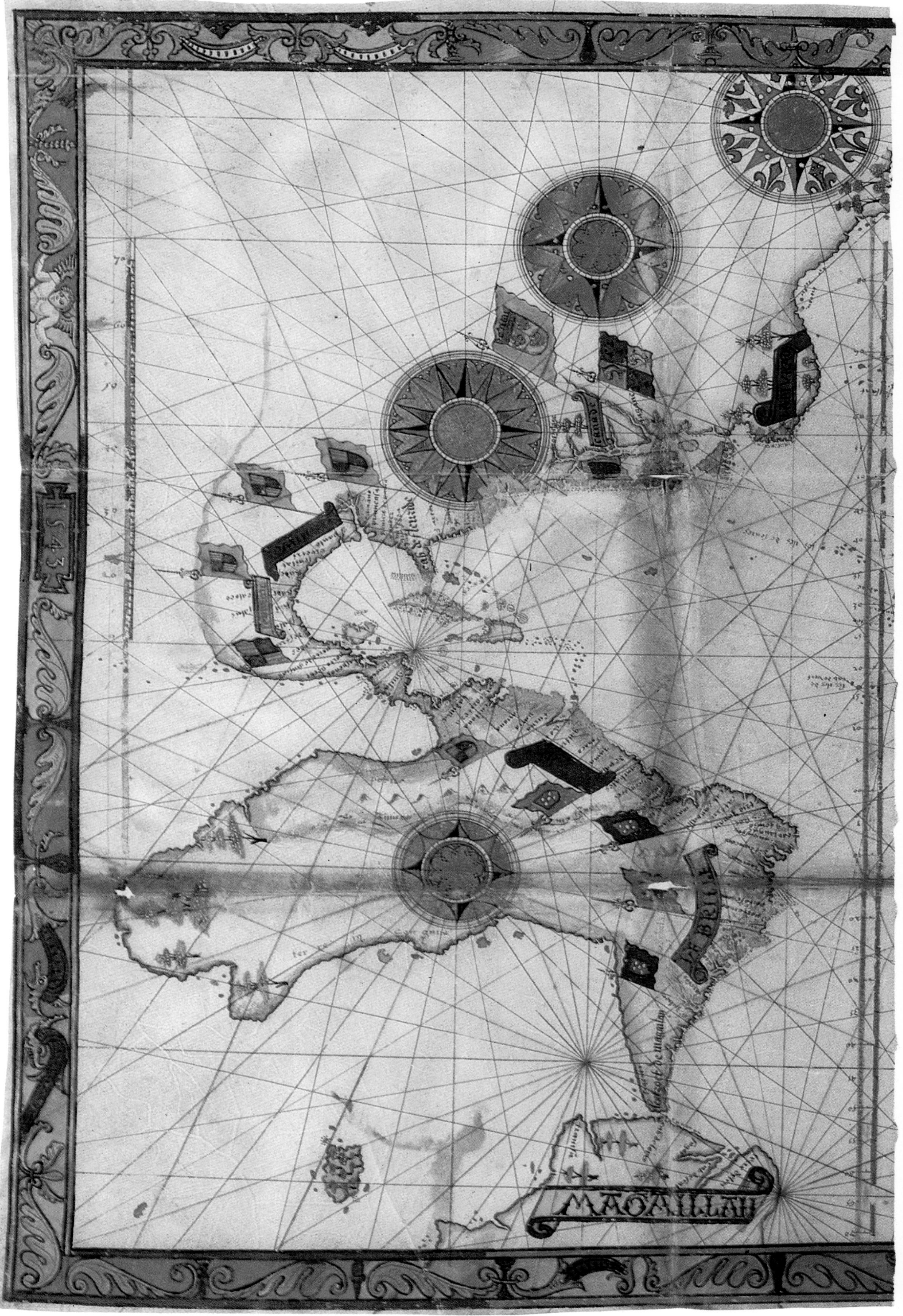
1543
MAGAILLAN

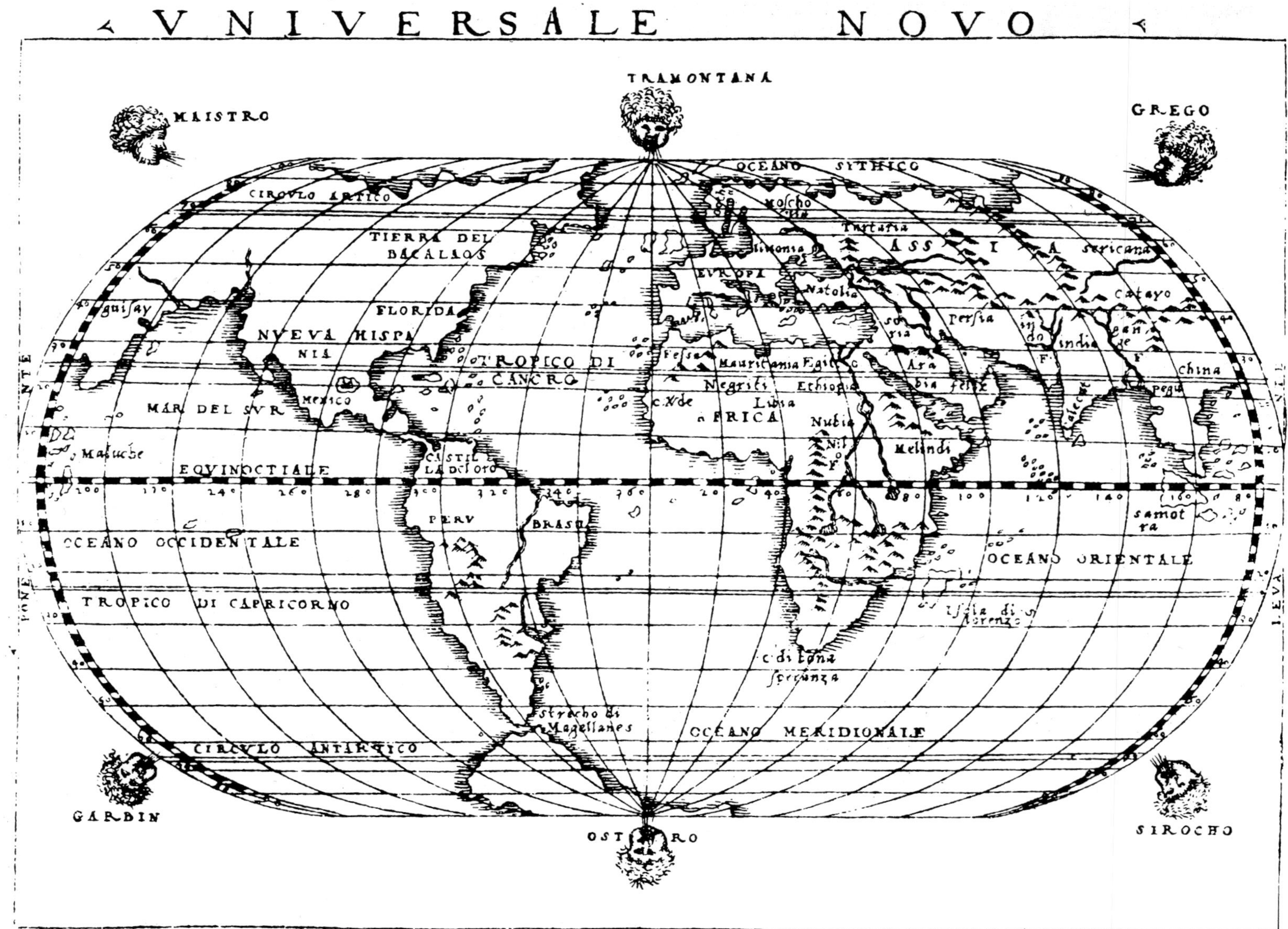

Plate XXVI

'Universale Novo,' Giacomo Gastaldi, 1548. This little copperplate map from a pocket atlas is a simplified version of a larger map Gastaldi made in 1546. It still shows the Asian land bridge, although 14 years later Gastaldi would be the first to speculate that a strait separated North America from Asia. On the other hand, the depiction of the Lower California peninsula shows that the map is based on up-to-date information. Note also that the winds surrounding the map now bear modern names.
135 x 175 mm. (Printed by Nicolo Bascarini, Venice)

Plate XXVII

'Planisphere' (detail), Pierre Desceliers, 1550. Two of the four parchment sheets forming a portolan world map. The geographic detail is copious and up-to-date (*eg,* note the elaboration of the St Lawrence River and western South America), and the decoration is splendid.
1350 x 2150 mm. British Library, London

REGION FROIDE:
CANADA
MER DE FRAN CE:
MER DESPAIGNE:
MER OCCEANE:
DE CANCER:
MER DES ENTILLES:
AFRIQVE
LA LIGNE:
LA ZONA TORRIDA:
LE PERV:
MER DV SV:
AMERIQVE
TROPIQVE
DE:
MER AVSTRALLE:
MER DE MAGELLAN:
LA TERRE:

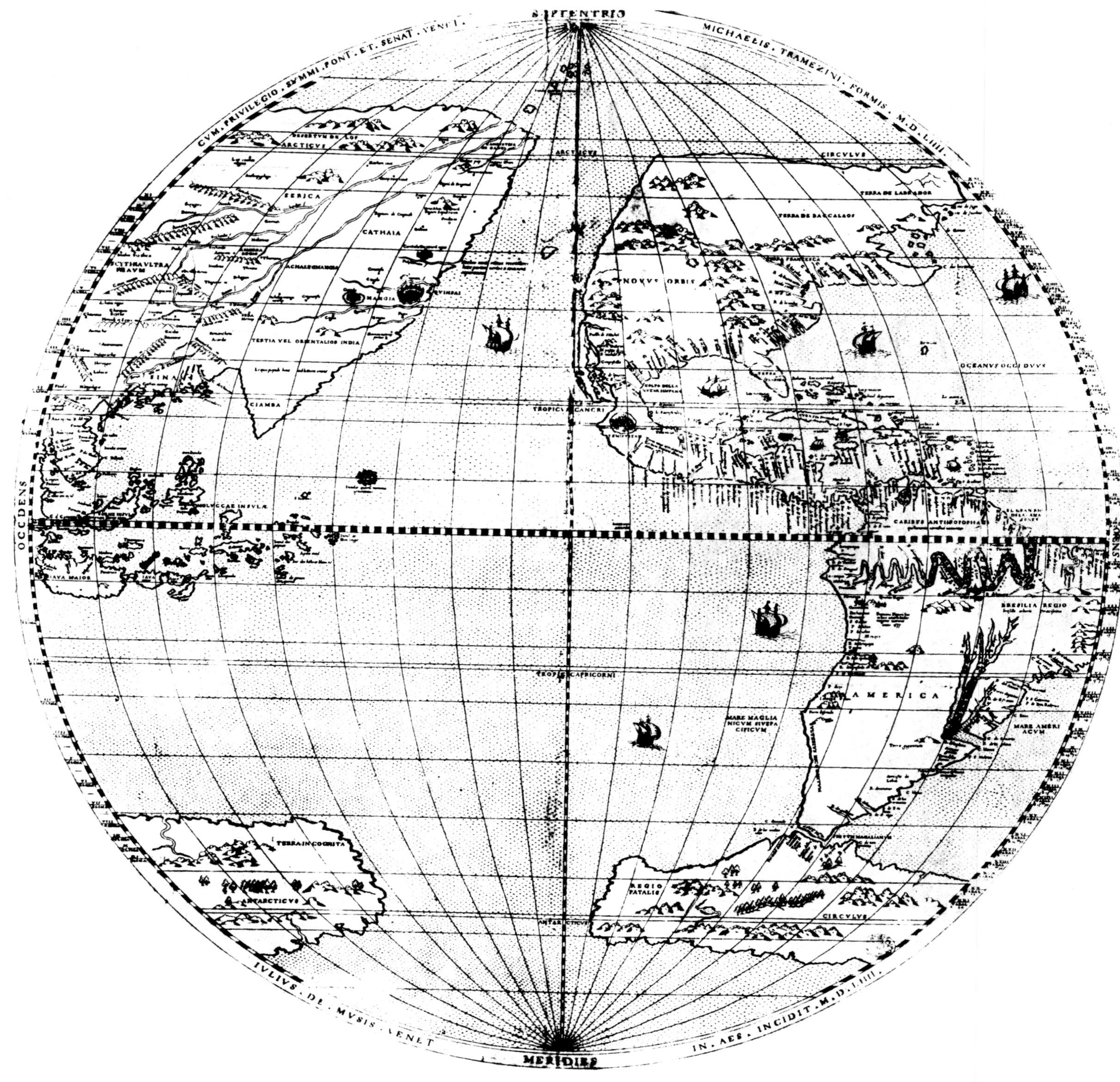

Plate XXVIII

'Western Hemisphere,' Michaelis Tramezini, ed, 1554. Interestingly, this is one of the few mid-century Italian maps not much influenced by the ideas of Gastaldi. Engraved on copper, it firmly asserts the separation of North America and Asia, in this case by a broad sea. It also hints at a theory that would be adopted by many mapmakers in the seventeenth century: that all of California was an island.
750 x 1500 mm. Bibliothèque Nationale, Paris

Plates XXIX and XXX

'Mondo Novo,' Pedro de Medina, 1555. A wood-block map included in the Venetian edition of Medina's *L'Arte de Navigar.* (Plate XXX is a detail of Plate XXIX.) New World discoveries are shown in crude but reasonably accurate detail. Yucatan is depicted as an island, a point about which there was no consensus among cartographers at this time. The Amazon is shown as slanting northwest-southeast, a less popular speculation.
220 x 340 mm

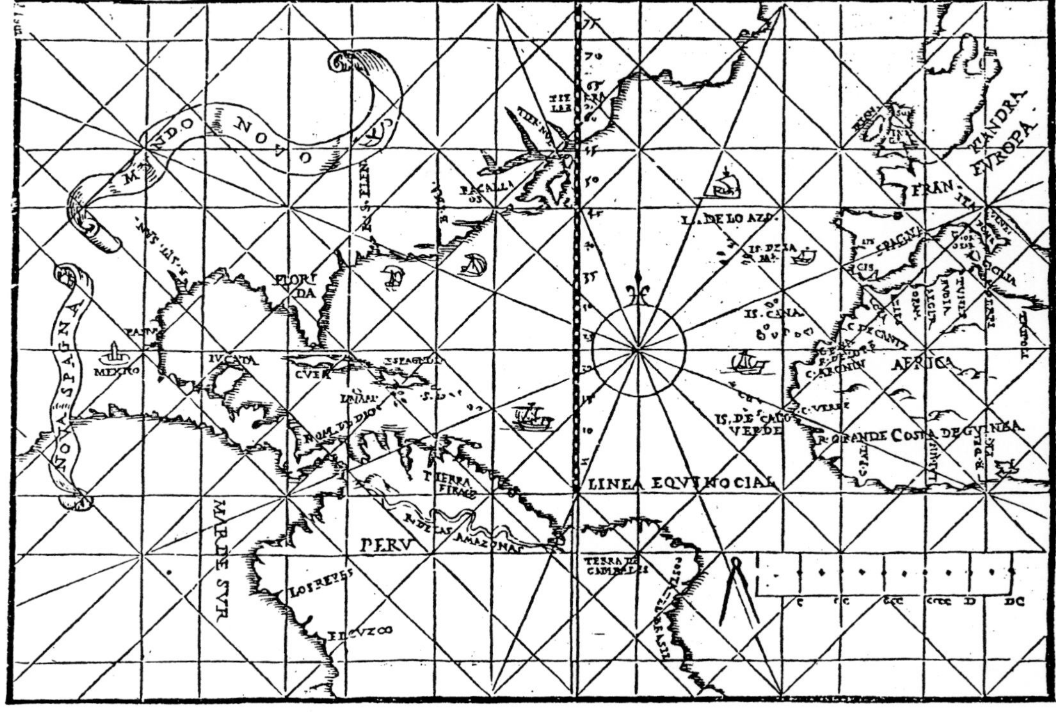

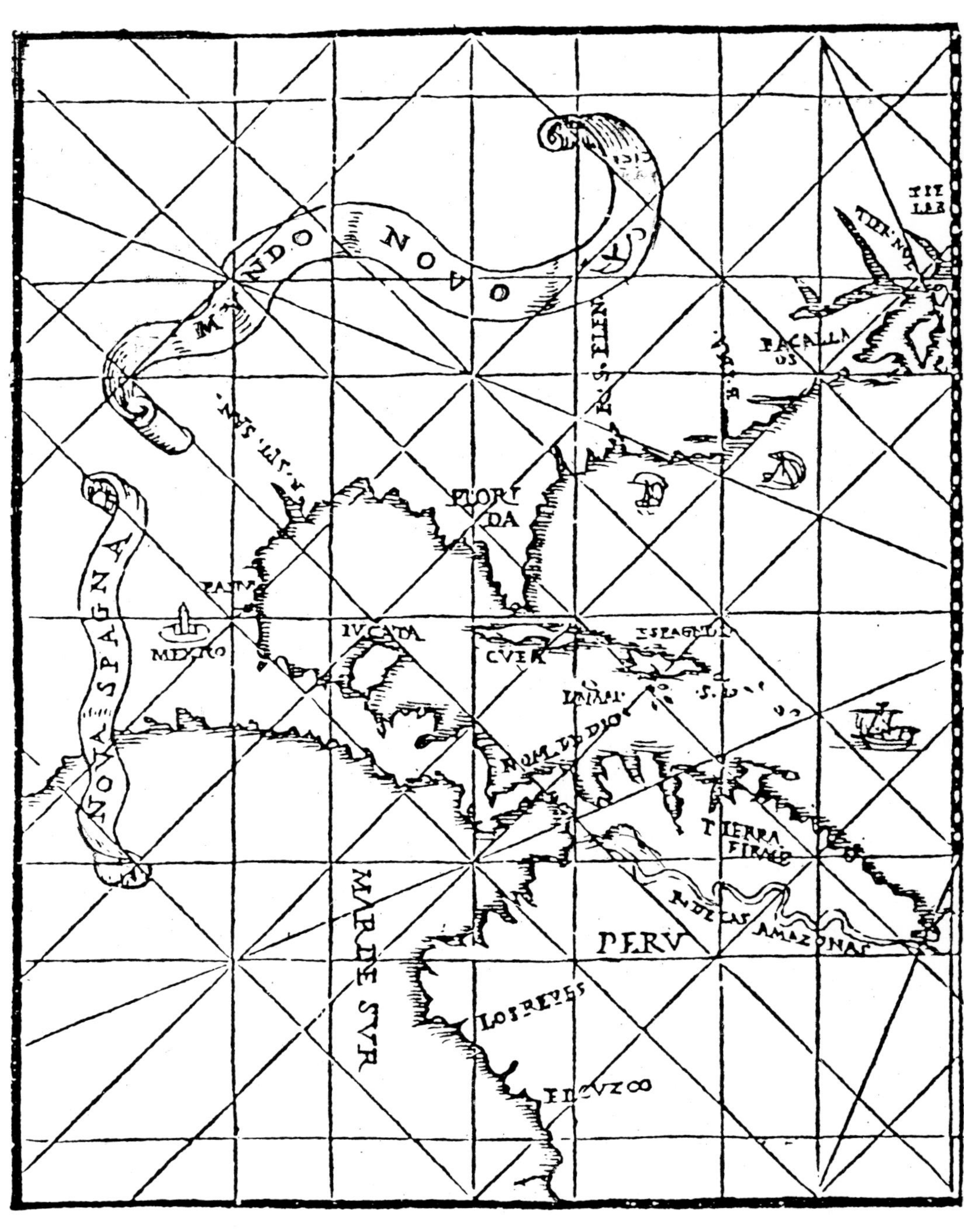

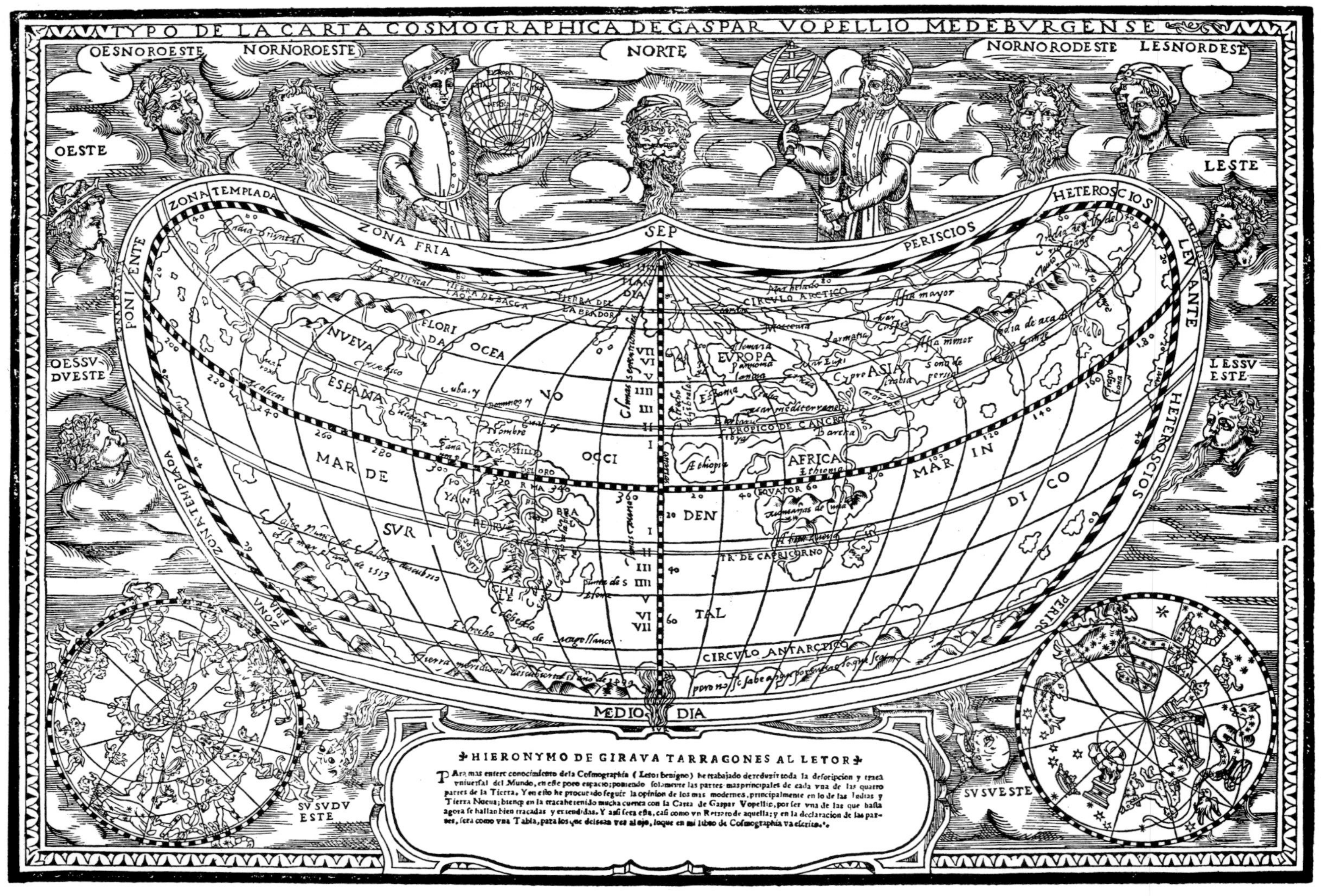

Plate XXXI

'Carta Cosmographica,' Juan de la Girava, 1556. Girava, Cartographer to Charles V, made this wood-block map as a simplified copy of an earlier work, now lost, by a German named Vopel. Astonishingly crude for a royal cartographer in 1556, it nevertheless is nicely decorated and carries an interesting note (lower left) about Balboa's 1513 discovery of the Pacific. 285 x 405 mm.

Plate XXXII (right)

'Terre de Floride,' Guillaume le Testu, 1556. This handsome map is from a MS atlas, *Cosmographie Universelle,* compiled by a French portolan chartmaker. By far the most detailed map of the region to date, it gave many place names, of which only Cape Canaveral remains today. It was one of the maps used by the Huguenots who came to settle in the New World in 1644. 350 x 480 mm. Bibliothèque de l'Armée de Terre, Ch de Vincennes

TERRE·DE
LA·FLORIDE
PARTIE·DE·LA·MER·OCEANNE
LA·COVBE
ESPAIGNOL
PARTIE·DE·LA·MER·DES·LENTILLE

Plate XXXIII

'La Nouvelle France,' Guillaume le Testu, 1556. Another manuscript map from le Testu's *Cosmographie* (see Plate XXXII), laden with place names and decoration. Information based on Cartier's exploration of the St Lawrence River is lavishly displayed. Newfoundland is still shown as being composed of three separate large islands.
370 x 530 mm. Bibliothèque de l'Armée de Terre. Ch de Vincennes

Plate XXXIV

'Neuve Espagne,' Guillaume le Testu, 1556. Also from *Cosmographie,* this map contrasts oddly with the one shown in Plate XXXV in that it shows us not fanciful monsters, but only ordinary Europeans and Blacks at work under the benign protection afforded by the coat of arms of the Spanish royal house. On this map north is on the right.
370 x 530 mm. Bibliothèque de l'Armée de Terre. Ch de Vincennes

Plate XXXV

'Terre Neuve,' Guillaume le Testu, 1556. In several respects this map, also from the *Cosmographie,* seems more primitive than the other le Testu maps reproduced in this book (Plates XXXII-XXXIV). Not only are the monstrous decorations slightly medieval, much of the exact detail that appears on his other maps of the St Lawrence area is absent or distorted. But other details of the New England coast are interestingly and well presented. Again, the map is oriented with north on the right.
370 x 530 mm. Bibliothèque de l'Armée de Terre, Ch de Vincennes

Terre de labrador
TERRE NEVFVE
MER OCEANNE

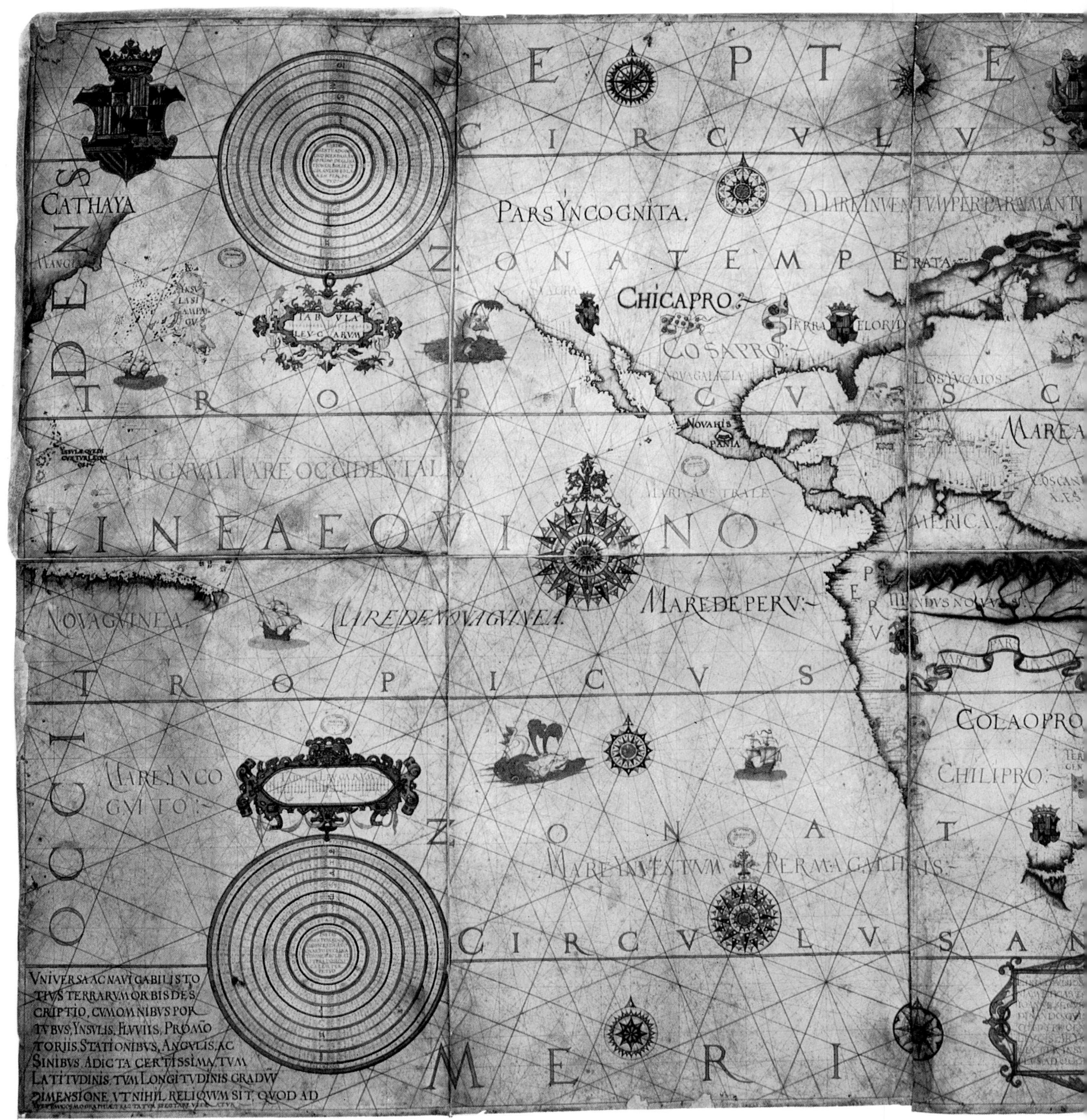

Plate XXXVI

'Portolan World Map,' Andreas Homen, 1559. This enormous planisphere is made up of 10 parchment sheets and is Homen's only extant work. In its details and proportions it is for the most part excellent, though it does show the Sea of Verrazano.

The arms in the upper left and right corners are those of Spain and Portugal, symbolic of the division of the world by the line set up in the Treaty of Tordesillas.
1500 x 2940 mm. Bibliothèque Nationale, Paris

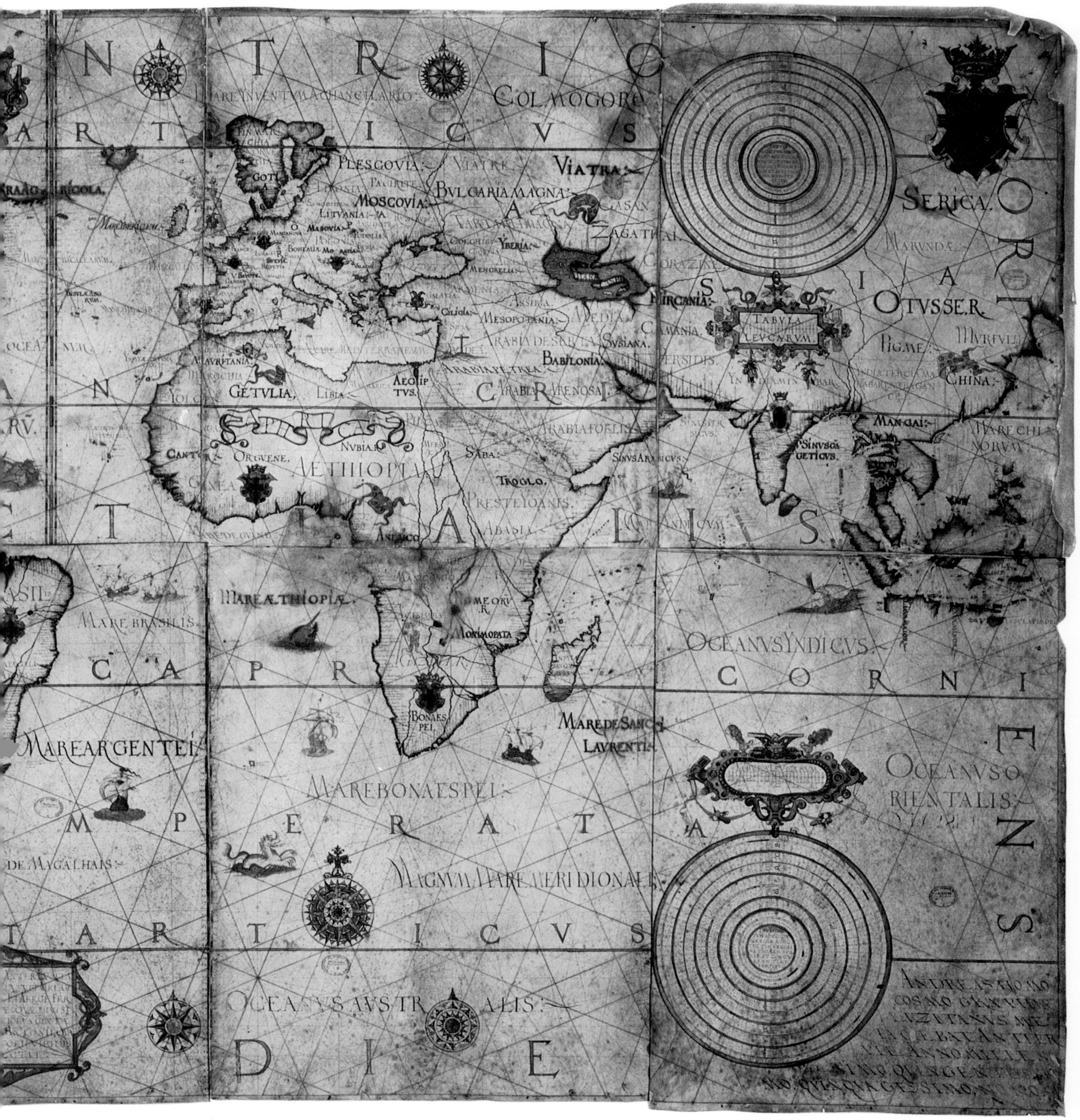
COLMOGORO
PLESCOVIA
VIATRA
BVLGARIA MAGNA
MOSCOVIA
LITVANIA
SERICA
TABVLA LEVCARVM
HIRCANIA
BABILONIA
PIGME
CHINA
MANGAI
GETVLIA
LIBIA
NVBIA
AETHIOPIA
SABA
TROGLO
PRESTEYOANIS
MAREAETHIOPIAE
MARE BRASILIS
MAREARGENTEI
OCEANVS YNDICVS
MAREBONAESPEI
OCEANVS ORIENTALIS
MAGNVM MARE MERIDIONALE
OCEANVS AVSTRALIS

Plate XXXVII

'Mediterranean Portolano,' Jacobus Maiolo, 1561. An unusual map of the world appears as a kind of bonus on this highly decorated parchment map of the Mediterranean by a Genoese cartographer, for it is sketched in on a largely blank space devoted to the Sahara Desert. The New World part of the map is remarkably well outlined.
880 x 1200 mm. Pegli Naval Museum, Genoa

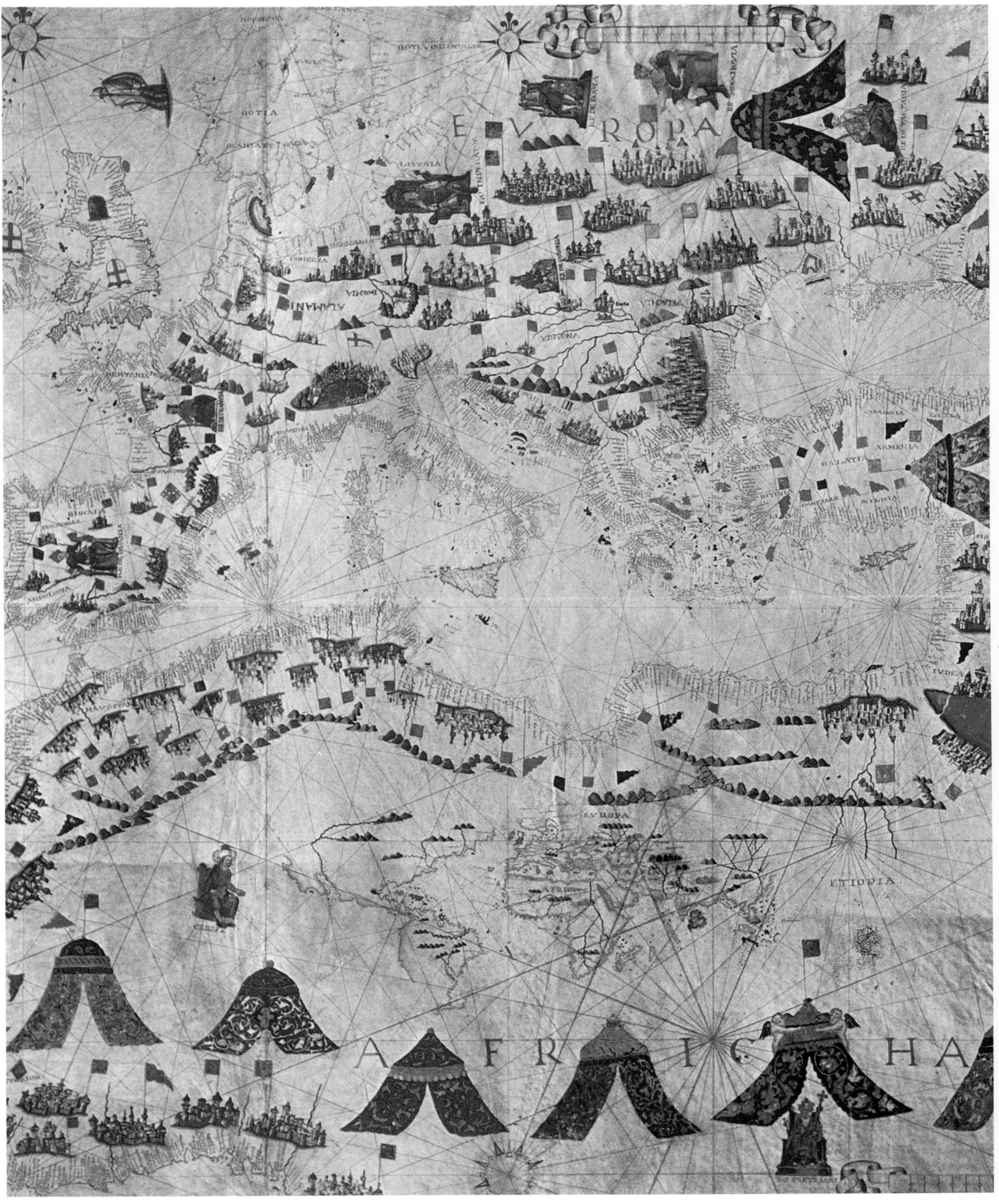
E V R O P A
ARMENIA
ETIOPIA
A F R I C H A

Plate XXXVIII

'North Atlantic,' anon, mid-sixteenth century. This parchment map is one of 27 in a manuscript atlas by an unknown member of the French Dieppe school of portolan chartmakers. The St Lawrence River is shown in some detail as far as Quebec, and Newfoundland at last appears as a single island (though, to be sure, Nova Scotia is shown as an island also). The locations of various French fishing stations are noted, as well.)
385 x 290 mm. Bibliothèque Municipale, Lyon

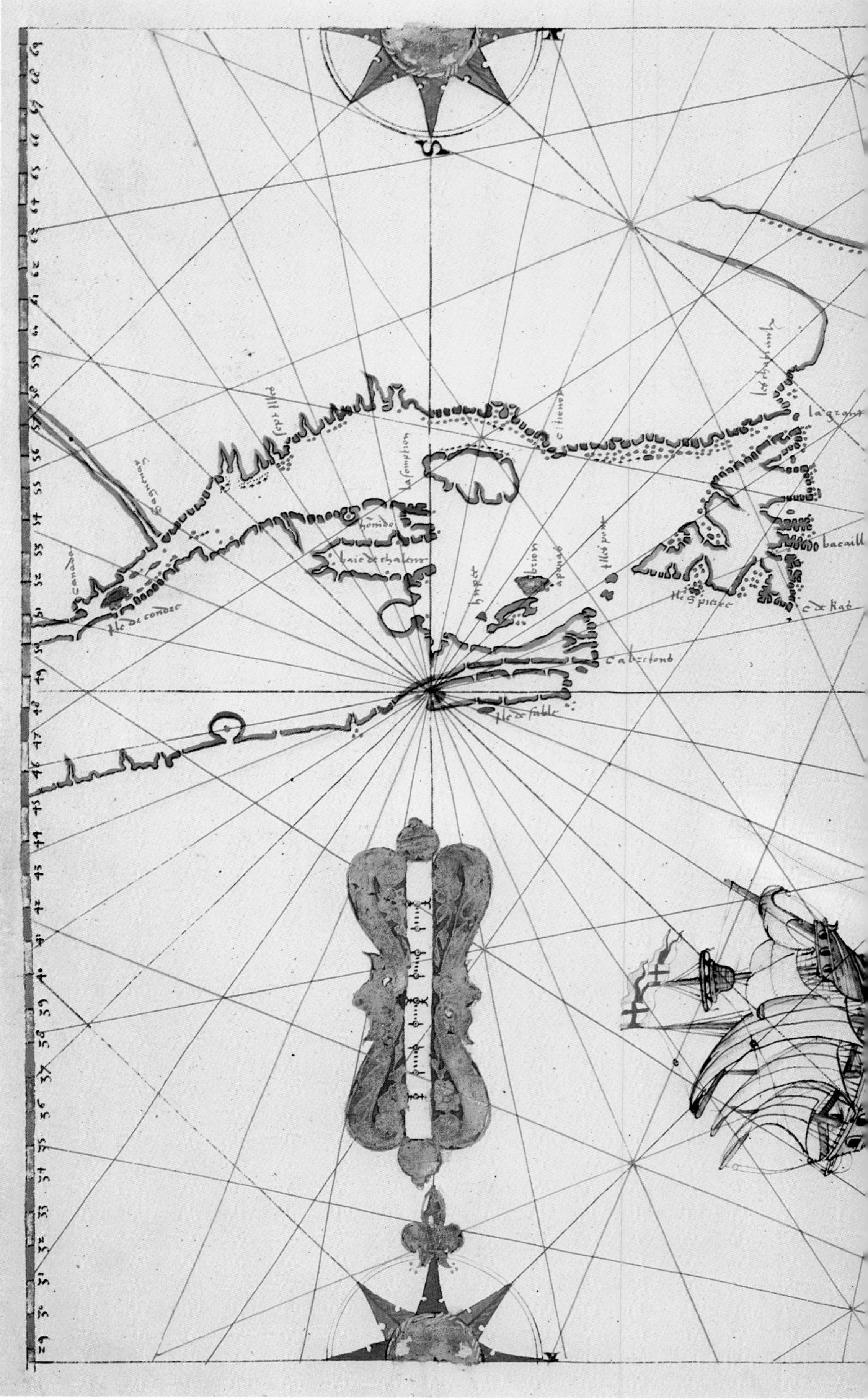

Yslam
la terre de labonrador
brasil
S. michel
S. marie
madere
finisterre
baione
lisbonne
S. vincent
S. marie
cadis
bordeau
Rochelle
fontarabia
londe

Plate XXXIX

'North American East Coast,' anon, mid-sixteenth century. Also from the same MS atlas illustrated in Plate XXXCIII, the map shows on a larger scale the whole coast of North America from Labrador to Florida, with north now facing the bottom. As before, the map is much concerned with locating fishing grounds and fishing stations, a major aspect of France's interest in the New World at this time (though why the emphasis on Labrador above Hamilton Inlet is unclear).
290 x 385 mm. Bibliotèque Municipale, Lyon

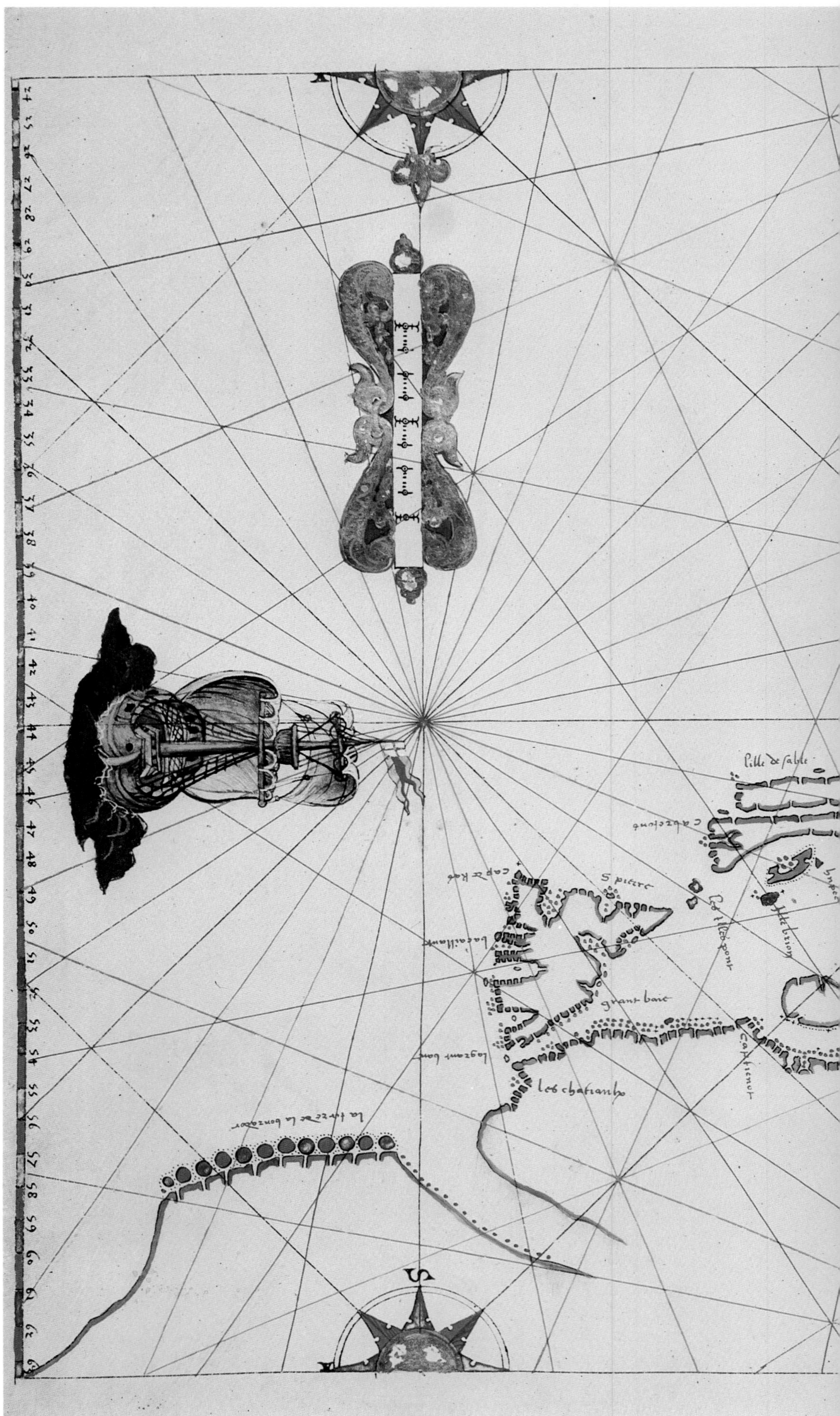

Plate XL

'Orbis Terrarum,' Ortelius, 1564. This copperplate map is now famous because it was one of 70 included in Ortelius's monumental *Theatrum Orbis Terrarum* of 1570, history's first 'modern' printed atlas. The regular edition of the atlas went through 42 editions between 1570 and 1612, and 31 editions of the reduced-format edition had been published by 1697. For this reason the map was hugely influential, even though it added little new detail to that shown on earlier maps. One comparative novelty is the narrow sea separating Asia and North America. The fabled Northwest Passage is also clearly shown.
380 x 468 mm

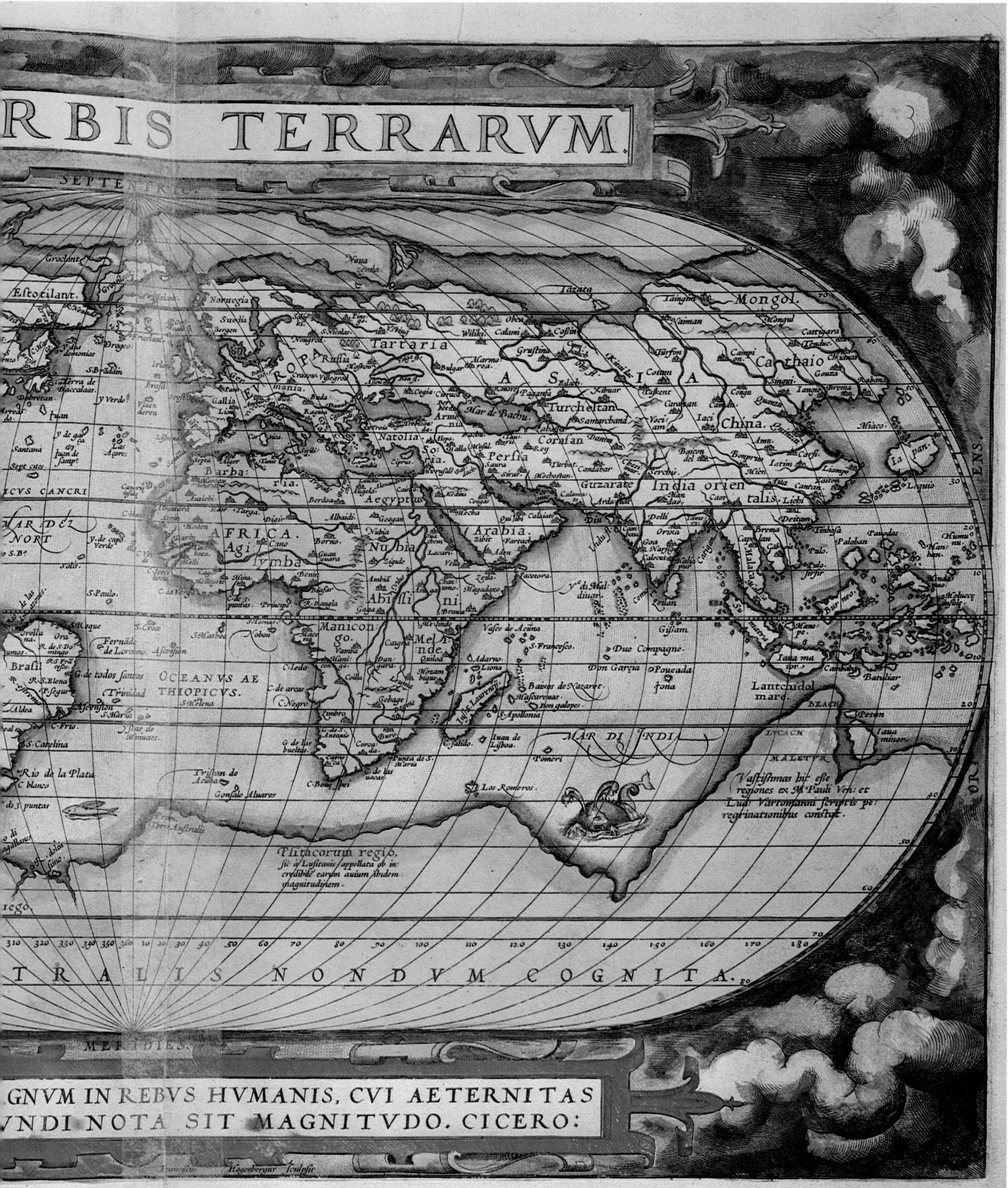
RBIS TERRARVM
SEPTENTRIO
ASIA
EVROPA
Tartaria
Mongol.
Carthaio
China.
Turcheſtan
Perſia
India orientalis
Arabia
AFRICA.
Aegyptus
Abiſſini
Manicongo.
OCEANVS AETHIOPICVS.
MAR DI INDIA
MAR DEL NORT
TROPICVS CANCRI
Brasil
Lantchidol mare.
Pſitacorum regio, ſic à Luſitanis appellata ob incredibilē earum auium ibidem magnitudinem.
Vaſtiſſimas hic eſſe regiones ex M. Pauli Ven: et Lud. Vartomanni ſcriptis peregrinationibus conſtat.
TRALIS NONDVM COGNITA.
MERIDIES.
ORIENS
GNVM IN REBVS HVMANIS, CVI AETERNITAS
VNDI NOTA SIT MAGNITVDO. CICERO:
Hagenbergus ſculpſit

By the late sixteenth century the caravels and carracks of earlier times had given way to the galleon, a fast and seaworthy new design that featured a low fo'c's'le and a sweeping sheer to a high poop.

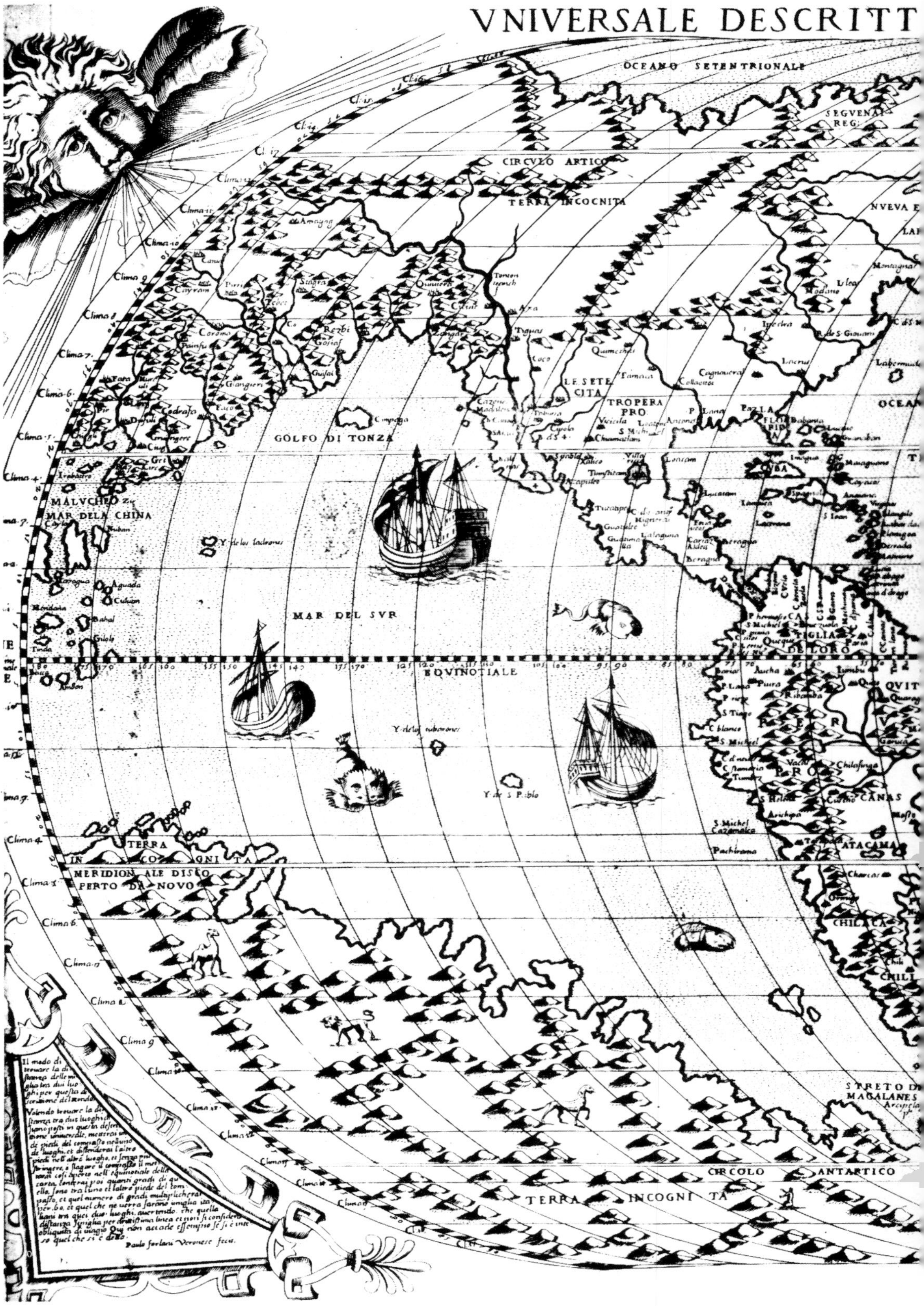

Plate XLI

'Mappamondo,' Paulo Forlani, 1565. The influence of Gastaldi's 1546 world map (of which Plate XXVI is a simplified version) is evident on this Italian copperplate made at a time when Gastaldi had already ceased to believe in an Asian land bridge. Forlani differs from the Gastaldi of 1546 only in his details and his decorations.
370 x 450mm

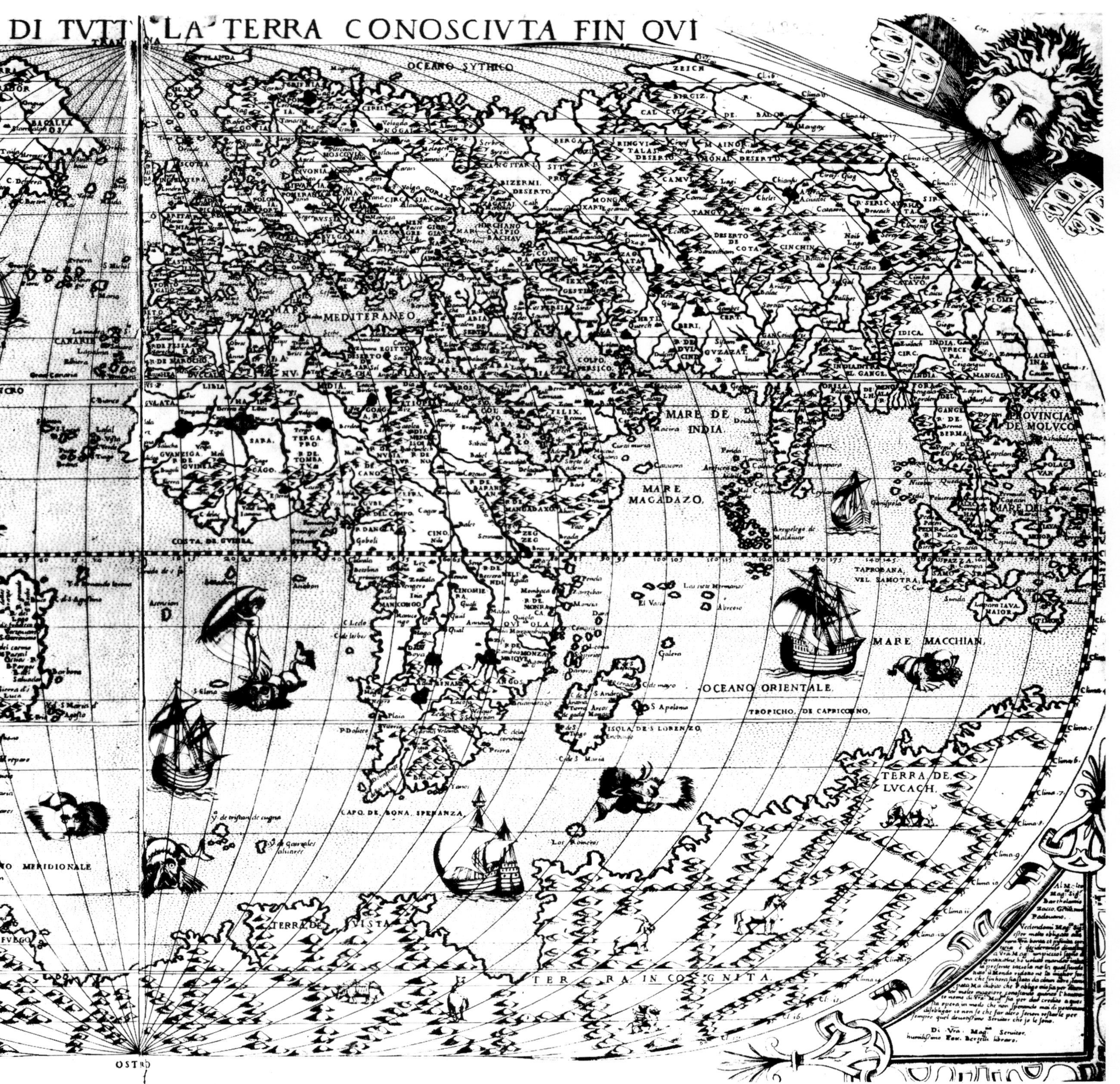
DI TVTT LA TERRA CONOSCIVTA FIN QVI
OCEANO SYTHICO
MARE MEDITERANEO
MARE DE INDIA
MARE MAGADAZO
PROVINCIA DE MOLVCO
MARE MACCHIAN
OCEANO ORIENTALE
TROPICHO DE CAPRICORNO
ISOLA DE S LORENZO
CAPO DE BONA SPERANZA
TERRA DE LVCACH
TERRA DE VISTA
TERRA INCOGNITA
OSTRO

Plate XLII

'Planisphere,' Nicolas Desliens, *c* 1566. On this very handsome but somewhat schematic parchment map Desliens, a French chartmaker of the Dieppe school, takes pains to stress France's political claims in the New World. Not only is all of North America included in Nouvelle France, but even the North Atlantic is called Mer de France. North is, of course, at the bottom. 270 x 450 mm. Bibliothèque Nationale, Paris

Plate XLIII (right)

'Planisphere' (detail), Nicolas Dealiens, 1566. Although at first glance this might appear to be a detail of Plate XLII, in fact it is a detail from another planisphere by Desliens, a copy meant for a different customer. The geographic differences are small but enough to show the drawbacks of hand copying.
270 x 448 mm. British Museum, London

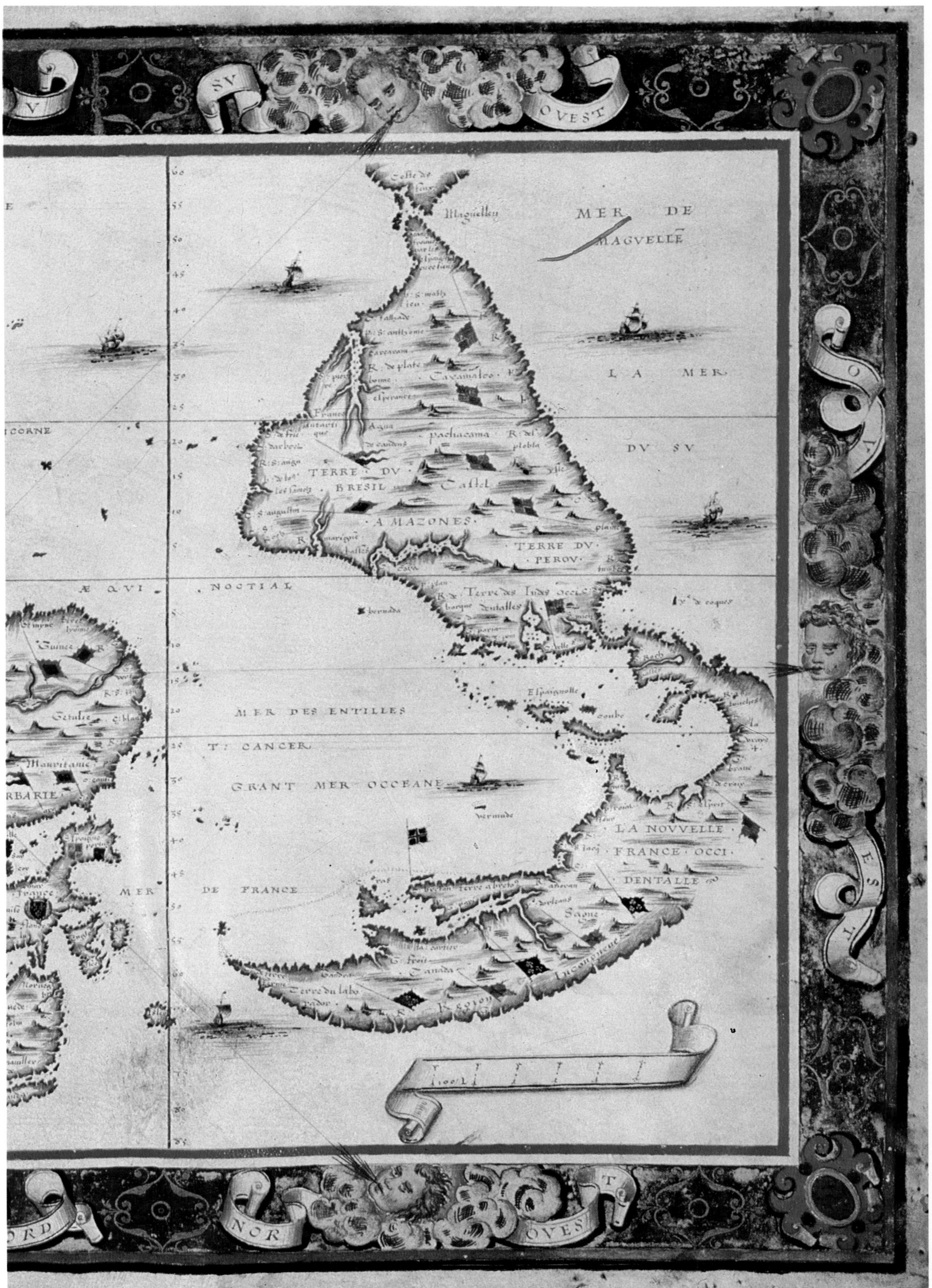
SV OVEST
MER DE MAGVELLE
LA MER
DV SV
TERRE DV BRESIL
AMAZONES
TERRE DV PEROV
Cavamalco
pachacama
Castel
Terre des Indes occidentalles
Æ QVI NOCTIAL
MER DES ENTILLES
T: CANCER
GRANT MER OCCEANE
LA NOUVELLE FRANCE OCCIDENTALLE
MER DE FRANCE
Canada
Terre du labo rador
Saghe
Guinee
Getulie
Mauritanie
BARBARIE
France
NORD
NOR OVEST

Plate XLIV

'Americae Sive Nove Orbis,' Ortelius, 1570-87. One of the great works of the sixteenth century is this New World map from Ortelius's *Theatrum.* It is not the New World map of the first edition, for it shows a corrected profile of the west coast of South America (*cf* Plate XL) that was introduced later. North America, however, appears essentially as it did in the first edition, with place names such as Canavaral, Apalchen and Sierra Nevada clearly visible. California is a peninsula and a sea separates the continent from Asia. Had the map been extended 10 degrees north the Northwest Passage would likely have been shown.
380 x 470 mm (copperplate)

SEPTENTRIO.
ESTOTILANT
SAGVENAI
TERRA CORTEREALIS.
CANADA.
NOVA
CHILAGA.
FRANCIA
NORVMBEGA.
MOCOSA
AVACAL
APALCHEN.
CALICVAS.
CAPASCHI.
TERLICHICHI MECHI.
TAGIL
LA FLORIDA.
La emperadada
La bermuda
Santana
Las Açores
SPANIA NOVA
TOVA
TOPIRA
MEXICO
CVBA
HISPANIOLA
Antillas
Insulæ de C. Verde.
S.Paulo
ORIENS.
SVR, quod
Caribana.
Tisnada.
PE
RV.
Paguana.
Amazones
Picora
BRESILIA
à Lusitanis A°. 1504. inuenta.
PARANA.
CVTA
CHARCAS
CHILI.
PATAGONES,
REGIO GIGANTVM
Rio de la Plata
Golfo de S. Sebastiano
Archipelago del C. desseado.
MERIDIES.
TERRA DEL FVEGO.
FRETVM MAGELLANICVM
Cum Priuilegio decennali Ab. Ortelius delineab. et excudeb. 1587.

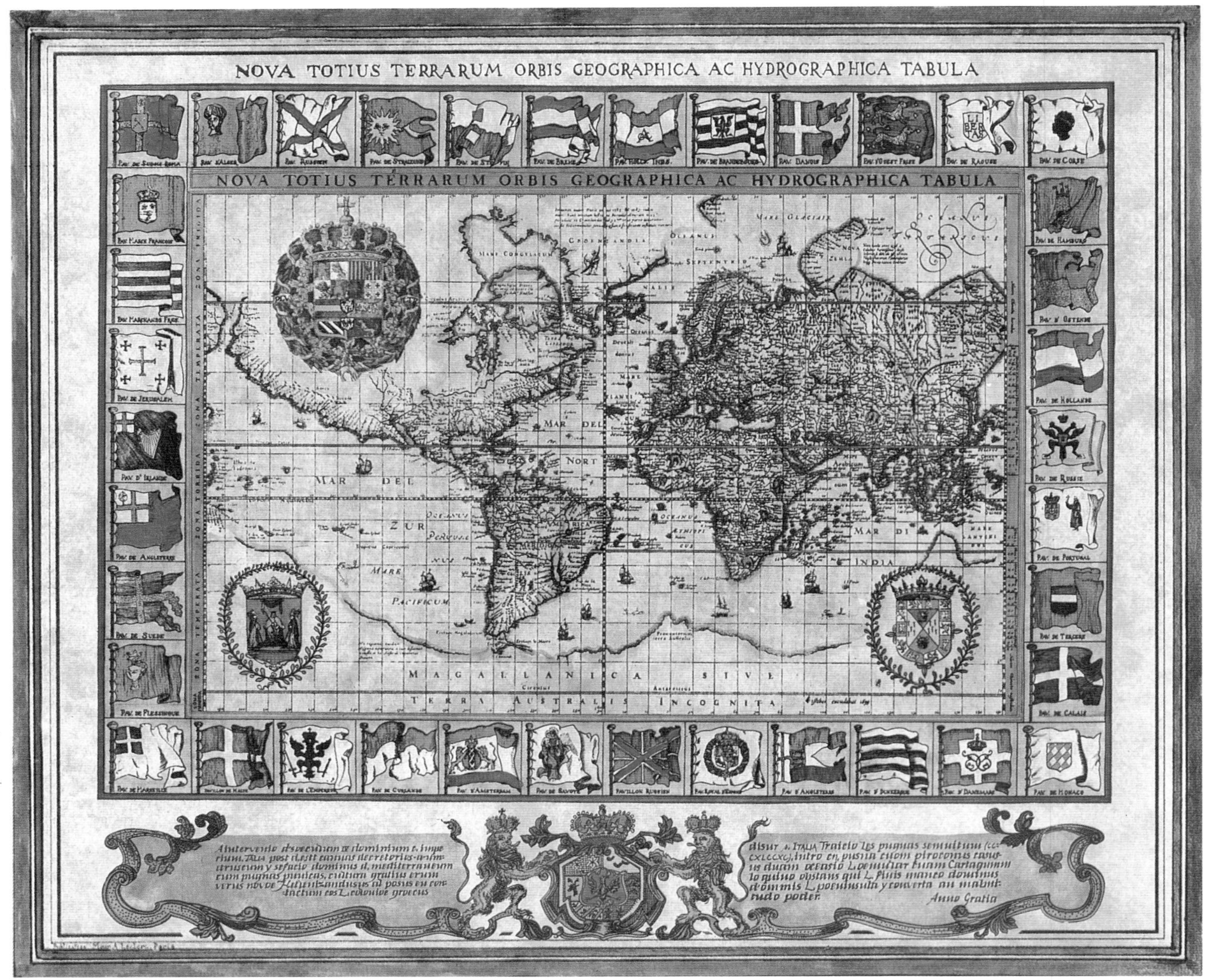

Plate XLV

'Typus Orbis Terrarum,' Ortelius, 1570. Along with 'Americae Sive Nove Orbis' (Plate XLIV) this great copperplate world map from Ortelius's *Theatrum* is considered one of the 'mother maps' of western cartography because of its profound influence on subsequent mapmaking. With the advent of the *Theatrum* the center of European cartography shifted decisively to Holland.
335 x 495 mm

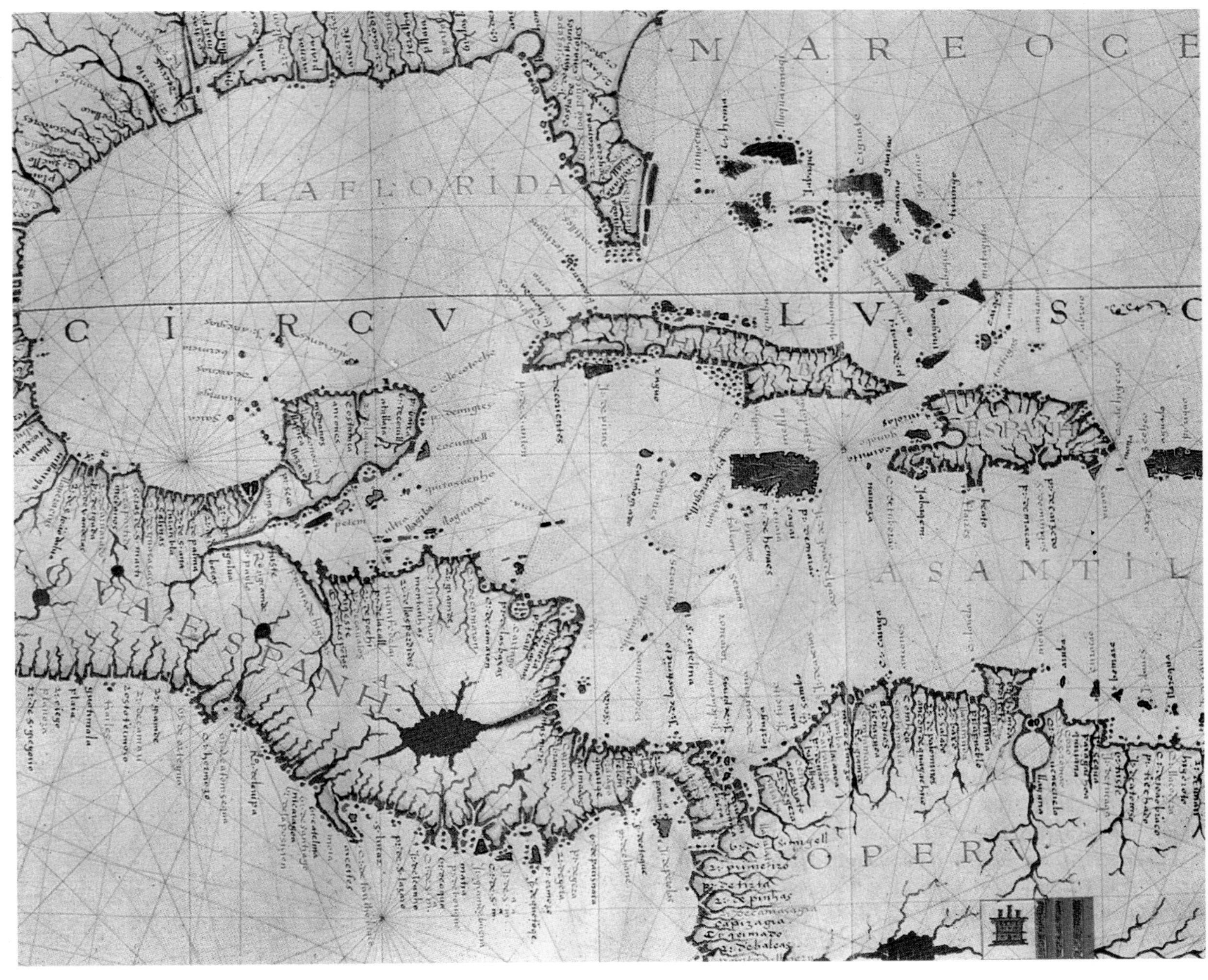

Plate XLVI

'Central America' (detail), Fernam Vaz Durado, 1571. This parchment portolano shows Central America and the Caribbean with considerable accuracy and in great detail and is probably the best representation to date of the North American coast from the Rio Grande to about Savannah. The map is from the Portuguese MS *Atlas Hydrografico,* now in the Torre de Tombo Archive in Lisbon.

Plate XLVII

'Portolan Planisphere,' anon, *c* 1585. This Portuguese parchment chart of the world is primarily interesting for the detail it lavishes on the Northwest Passage, and especially on its western entrance. The first man to claim to have found this entrance was a Greek sailor named Apostolos Valerianos, better known as Juan de Fuca, who said that he discovered it in 1592 in the vicinity of what is now called Vancouver Island. This map does not entirely agree with de Fuca's description, but it is close enough to cast some doubt on its provisional dating of 1585. 1145 x 2130 mm. Bibliothèque Nationale, Paris.

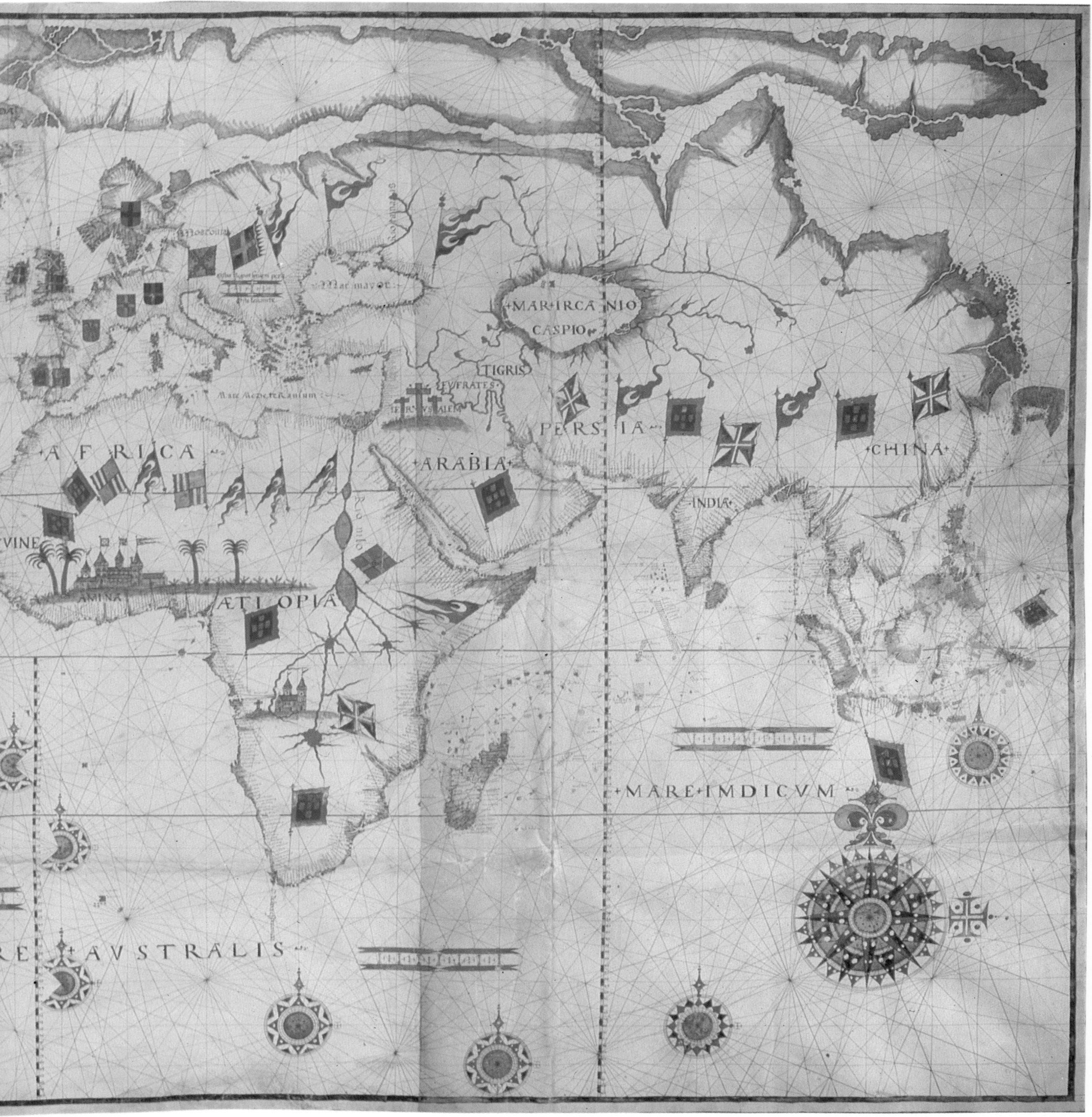
MAR IRCANIO
CASPIO
TIGRIS
EVFRATES
PERSIA
ARABIA
CHINA
INDIA
AFRICA
GVINE
AMINA
ÆTIOPIA
MARE IMDICVM
RE AVSTRALIS

Plate XLVIII

'Mappamonde,' Gerard Mercator, 1587. Waldseemüller first applied the name 'America' to the southern continent of the New World, but when Mercator, the greatest cartographer of the age, used it for both continents, they could never again be called anything else. This Mercator copperplate is a later, more conventional version of a 1569 world map in which he used his radical isogonic cylindrical projection for large-scale maps. In his rendering of North America there is a fairly clear indication of the Hudson River, and the Appalachians are shown as a continuous chain of mountains, something Mercator was the first to do. Note that, as on most sixteenth-century maps, there is no suggestion that Greenland and Canada are joined. This was an idea that would only really take root in the next century, but it would then persist for nearly 200 years. 385 x 450 mm.

AFRI
ASIA
Aequator
Tropicus Cancri
Tropicus Capricorni
TERRA AVS TRALIA
Circulus Antarcticus

Sir Walter Raleigh, navigator, adventurer, courtier and sponsor of the colonization of Virginia.

Plate XLIX

'Maris Pacifici,' Ortelius, 1589. This copperplate of the Pacific Ocean appeared in the 24th edition of the *Theatrum.* The delineation of the west coasts of North and South America and of the islands of the Pacific have evolved greatly since Ortelius's 'Orbis' of 1564 (Plate XL). Some familiar names can be seen on the California coast. 378 x 472 mm

MARIS PACIFICI,
(quod vulgò Mar del Zur)
cum regionibus circumiacentibus, insulisque in eodem
passim sparsis, novissima descriptio.
MARIS ATLANTICI,
SIVE MAR DEL NORT
PARS.
Noua Hispania.
Florida.
Bermuda
Cuba
Spagnola
Iamaica
S. Ioan
La Trinidad
Cartagena
Caribana.
Quito.
Peru.
Charcas.
Chili.
Patagones.
AMERICAE
MERIDIONA-
LIOR PARS.
Circulus Aequinoctialis.
QVOD VVLGO
NOMINANT
MAR DEL ZVR.
Archipelagus insularum.
Fretum Magellanicum.
Tierra del Fuego.
Mar del Nort.
SEPTEMTRIO
MERIDIES.
Prima ego velivolis ambivi cursibus Orbem,
Magellane novo te duce ducta freto.
Ambivi, meritoq; vocor VICTORIA: sunt mi
Vela, alæ; precium, gloria; pugna, mare.
Cum privilegijs Imp. & Reg. Maiestatum,
nec non Cancellariæ Brabantiæ, ad decennium.

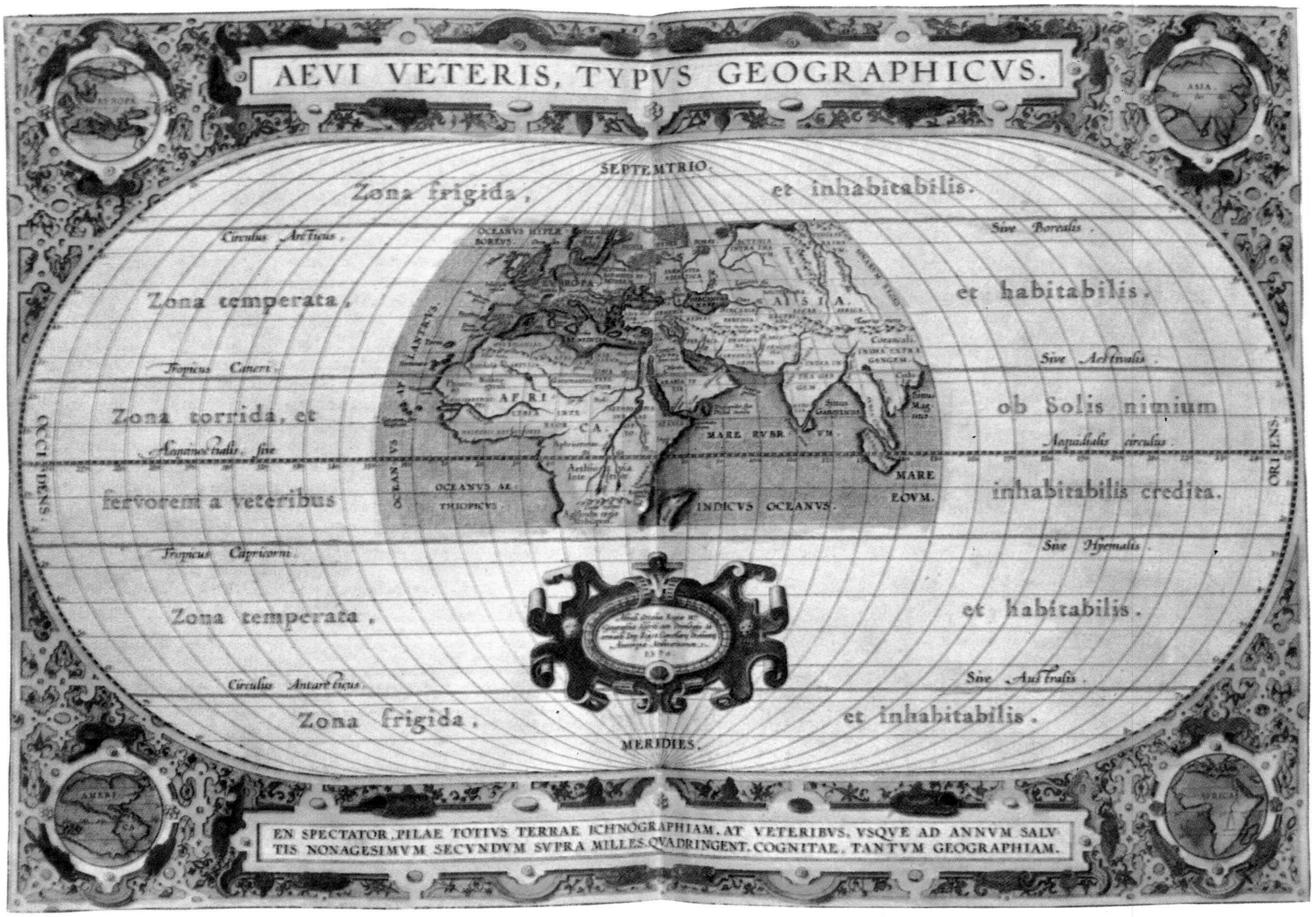

Plate L

'Aevi Veteris, Typus Geographicus,' Ortelius, 1579. Here Ortelius makes an interesting comparison of ancient and modern geography. On an old schematic projection of the globe he has superimposed a modern map of Eurasia and Africa. Inset in each of the four corners of this copperplate are maps of each of the four continents.
378 x 472 mm

Cornelius Ketel's portrait of Sir Martin Frobisher, the Elizabethan explorer-adventurer who believed that during his explorations of northeast Canada in 1576-8 he had found the Northwest Passage's entrance.

ER
La beaute, la Vertu, l'Ornement, et les graces,

A charming miniature of England's Elizabeth I, under whose long reign (1558-1603) the English colonization of America began and for whom the colony of Virginia was named.

L'Isole piu Famose del Mondo, *an atlas of the world's islands, was published in Venice in 1572 by Thomaso Porcacchi and was highly popular. This is the frontispiece of the 1590 edition*

Theodore de Bry, a French author of several copiously illustrated books on geography, included this fanciful depiction of the island of Roanoke. The island had been described in 1584 in a report made by Raleigh to Queen Elizabeth.

Pasquenoke
WEAPEMEOC
samonguepeuc
Roanoac
Trinety harbor
T B
2

Plate LI

'Mondo Nuovo,' G Porro, 1590. One of the maps in Thomaso Porcacchi's *L'Isole piu Famose del Mondo,* was a loose copy, made by an engraver named Porro, of a 1566 map that was originally drawn by Zaltieri of Bologna. It is crude cartography for 1590, but at least Zaltieri's was the first map to show the strait Gastaldi had predicted between Asia and North America.
70 x 140 mm

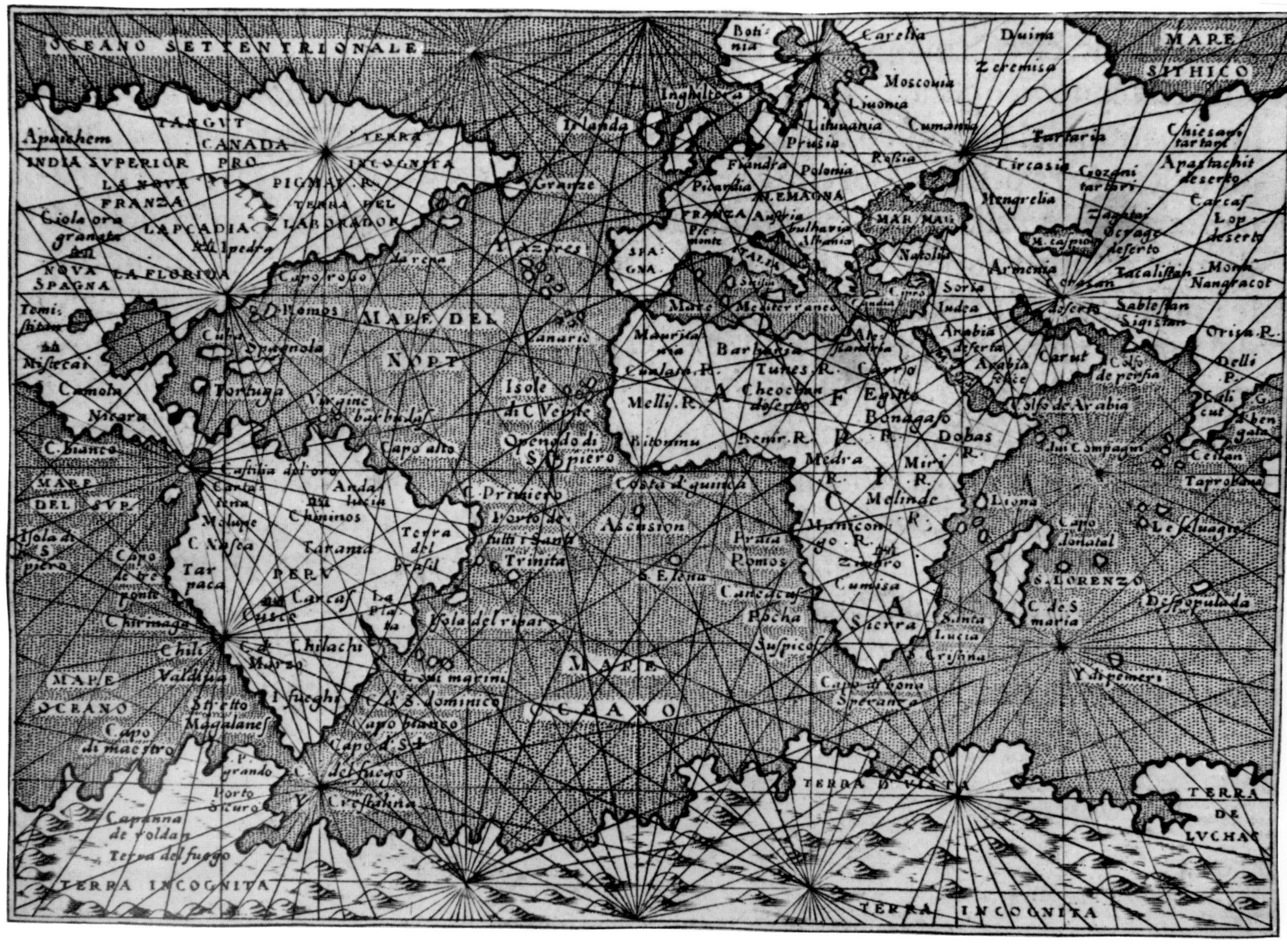

Plate LII

'Navigational Chart,' G Porro, 1590. Another map included in Porcacchi's *L'Isole piu Famose del Mondo* and engraved by Porro. The spiderweb of lines on such charts was merely an extension of compass bearings. They had some utility on large maps of small areas, but virtually none on small maps of large areas such as this one. 105 x 140 mm

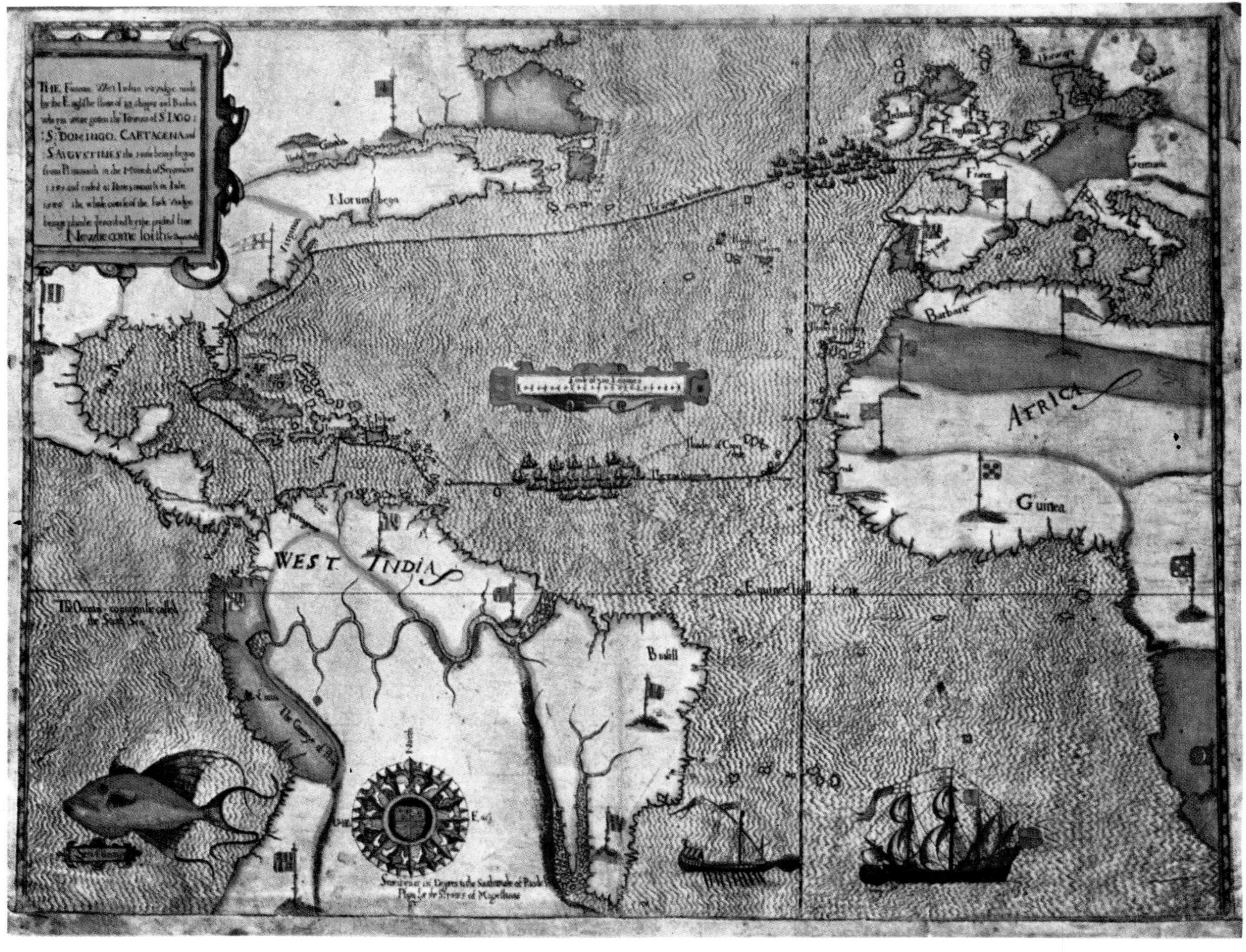

Plate LIII

'Drake's Itinerary,' anon, 1590(?). This handsome copperplate traces the route followed by Sir Francis Drake on his expedition of 1585-6. He sailed with 25 ships against the Spanish Indies, harrying Hispaniola, Cartagena and Florida before going on to Virginia to remove some 190 dispirited would-be colonists.

Plate LIV

'Nova Totius Terrarum Orbis,' Nikolaus Visscher, 1652. This is a relatively recent reproduction of a mid-seventeenth-century map. (The more decorative original is shown in Plate LXXXIV.) It is included here to suggest some of the changes that would occur in geographic knowledge in the next half century. Compared to, say, Mercator's 1587 world map (Plate XLVII) or its 1595 up-date (Plate LX), the map gives many more North American place names, notably on the west coast, and has filled in the whole area between the western shores of Hudson Bay to southern Labrador. The Great Lakes do not appear, but all five had already been shown on French maps by 1650. Note that the Greenland-Canada land bridge is also now asserted.

Sir Francis Drake

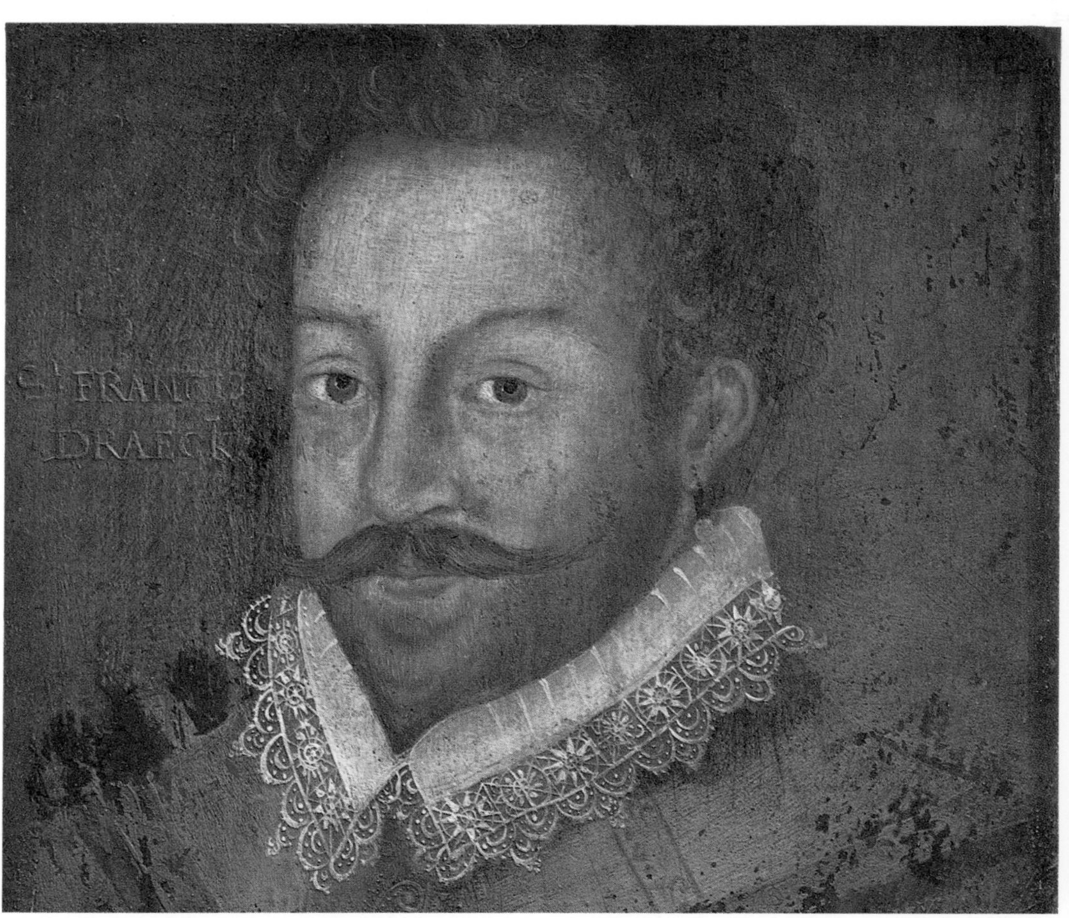

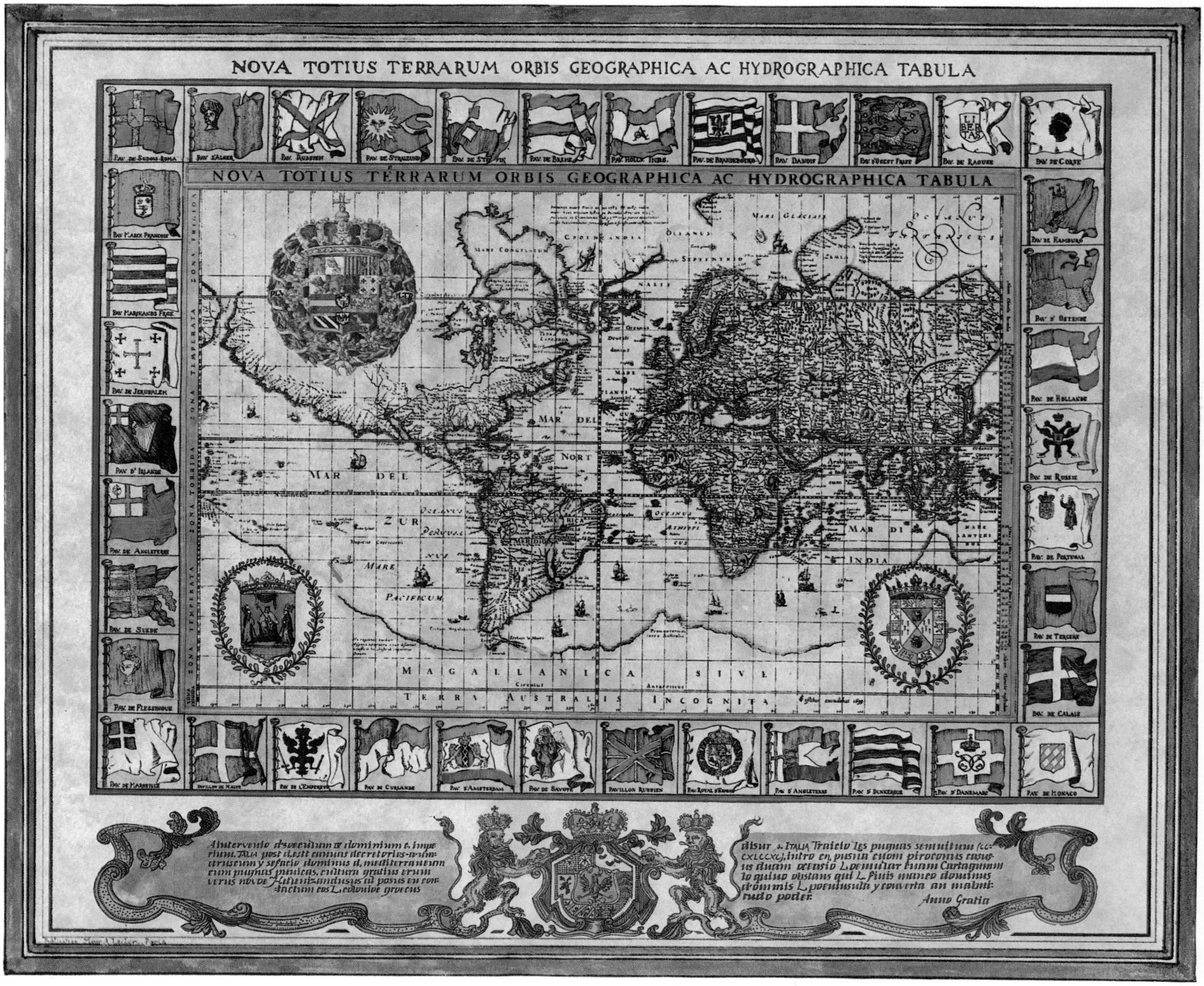

NOVA TOTIUS TERRARUM ORBIS GEOGRAPHICA AC HYDROGRAPHICA TABULA
NOVA TOTIUS TERRARUM ORBIS GEOGRAPHICA AC HYDROGRAPHICA TABULA
MAR DEL NORT
MAR DEL ZUR
MARE PACIFICUM
MAGALLANICA SIVE
TERRA AUSTRALIS INCOGNITA
Anno Gratia

Plate LV

'The Hemispheres,' Cornelis de Jode, 1593. Gerard de Jode published, in 1578, what is generally regarded as history's second 'modern' atlas, *Speculum Orbis Terrarum,* but it was overshadowed by the earlier *Theatrum* of Ortelius and the later *Atlas* of Mercator. In 1593 his son, Corneliss, issued a new and much enlarged edition of *Speculum,* and in it was this fine copperplate of the hemispheres drawn on polar projections.
320 x 520 mm

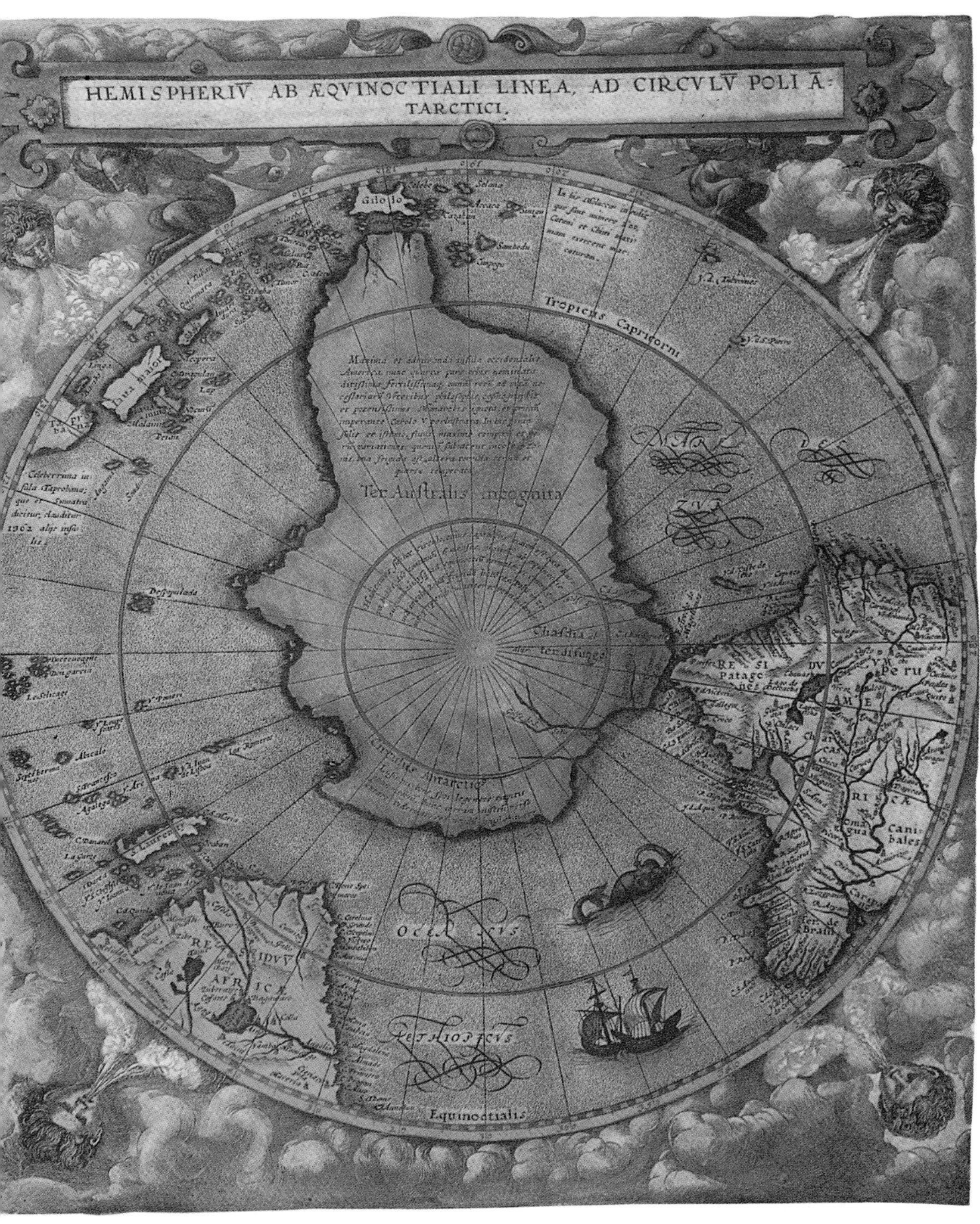
HEMISPHERIV AB ÆQVINOCTIALI LINEA, AD CIRCVLV POLI ATARCTICI.
Tropicus Capricorni
Ter Australis incognita
Equinoctialis

GERARDUS MERCATOR NATUS
RUPELMUNDÆ III NON. MARTII ANNO
CIƆIƆXII: VIXIT ANN. LXXXII. M. VIII. D.
XXVI: DENATUS IV NON. DECEMBRIS
ANNO CIƆIƆXCIV.
IUDOCUS HONDIUS NATUS IN
PAGO FLANDRIÆ DICTO WACKENE XVI
KALEND. NOVEMBRIS ANNO CIƆIƆLXIII:
VIXIT ANN. XLVII. M. VII. D. XXIX: DENAT
US XIV KAL. MARTII ANNO CIƆIƆCXII.

The two great Flemish cartographers Gerard Mercator and Jodocus Hondius are shown on this copperplate from a mid-seventeenth-century atlas.

Plate LVI

'Quivirae Regnum, cum aliius versus Boream,' Cornelis de Jode, 1593. This copperplate map from the 1593 edition of *Speculum Orbis Terrarum* is one of the first regional maps of the American west coast, covering an area from the Tropic of Cancer to the Pole. The Northwest Passage and the Strait of Anian (Bering Strait) are prominently displayed, but the Gulf of California is oddly absent.
350 x 240 mm.

QVIVIRÆ REGNV, cum alijs versus Borea.
Septentrio.
Oceanus 19 ostijs inter has insulas irrũpens, 4 euri-pos facit, quibus indesinenter in Septentrionem fertur, atq ibidem, mire vehementerq absorbetur.
Polus Magnetis respectu insularũ capitis Viridis.
El Streto de Anian.
Circulus
Anian Reg.
Hic hominũ societates cernuntur ruri, in ten-torijs habitantes, more Hordarũ, quas apud Tar-taros videmus.
Bergi.
Regio hæc plana est et sil-vestris, in qua boves, vac-cæq reperiuntur, gibbũ ca-melorũ habentes, cauda ve-ro, et pedibus leones referũt.
Ories.
Tuchano
Cabo de Corri-entes
Cabo Mendocino
Quiuira Regnũ.
C. Blanco
Las dos Hermanas
OCEANVS
Los Mongos
La Vezina
La desgraciada
Meridies.

Plate LVII

'Orbis Terrae,' Peter Plancius, 1596. Less well known than his fellow countrymen Mercator, Ortelius, de Jode or Hondius, Plancius was nevertheless an influential cartographer in his time. The lavish decoration on this handsome copperplate world map is a sort of foretaste of the Flemish style of the next century. In North America, Florida, Virginia and Norombega (New England) are named, and a peninsular California, the Northwest Passage and the Strait of Anian are shown. 395 x 575 mm.

peritissimorum totius orbis Gæographorum operibus desumta. Antverpiæ, apud Joannem Baptistam Vrient.
ASIA
Polus Arcticus
Oceanus Tartaricus
AFRICA
OCEANUS INDICUS
Aequator
Mare Lantchidol
Golfo Bengala
Iapan
Archipelagus
S. Lazari
Timor
Noua Guinea
Los Romeros
Tristan d'Acunna
De Iaua minori
TERRA AUSTRALIS MAGALLANICA
Circulus Antarcticus
Polus Antarcticus
AFRICA

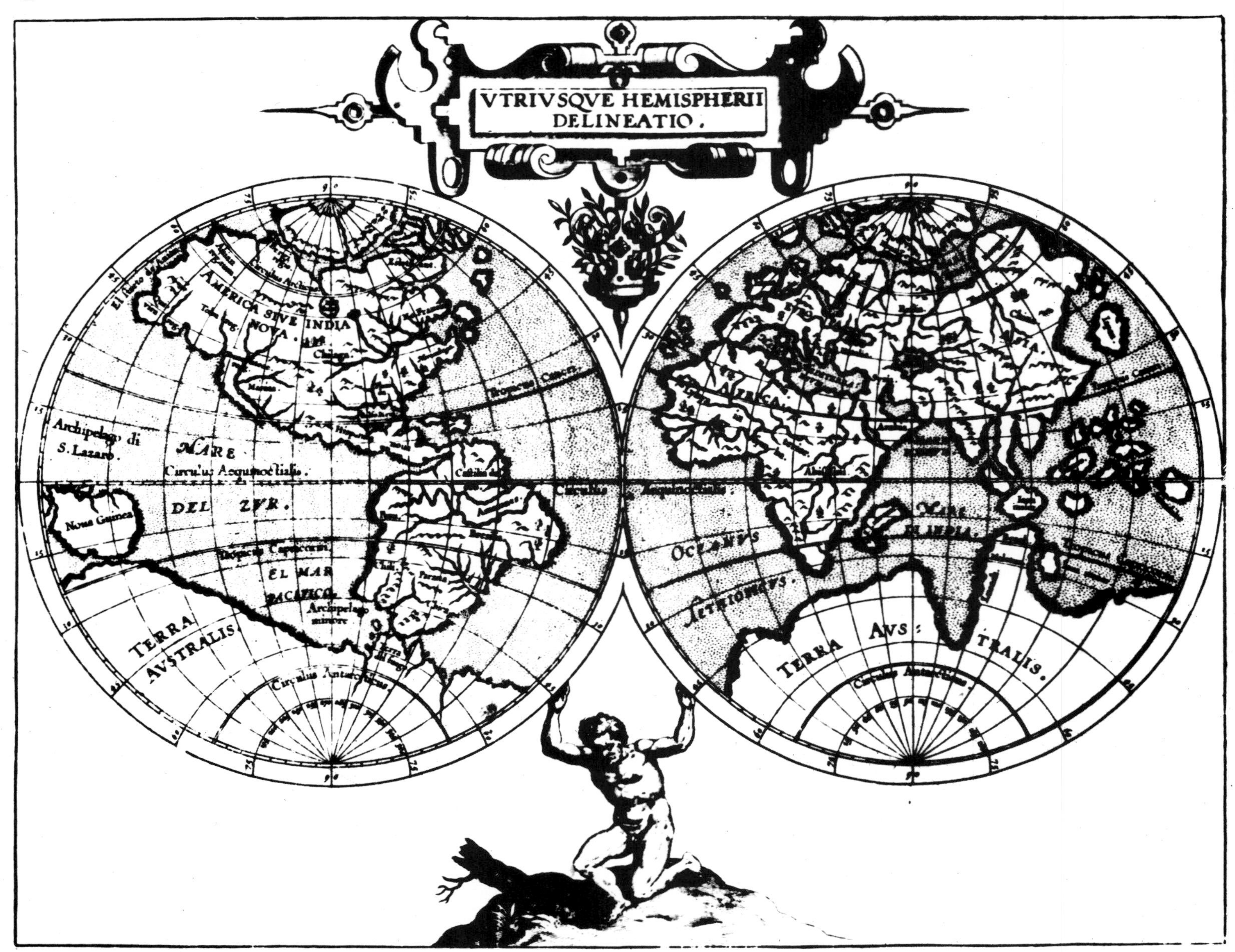

Plate LVIII

'Utriusque Hemispheri Delineato,' Cornelis van Wyfliet, 1597. This map is of interest primarily because it was included in the first atlas that was devoted exclusively to America, *Descriptionis Ptolemaicae Augmentum*, a collection of 19 copperplate maps published in Louvain in 1597 as a supplement to Ptolemy's *Geographia.* 230 x 290 mm.

The decorative frontispiece of a 1595 Dutch book on the navigation of the Far East, based on recent Portuguese and Spanish discoveries.

REYS-GHESCHRIFT

Vande Navigatien der Portugaloysers in Orienten / inhoudende de Zeevaert / soo van Portugael naer Oost Indien/als van Oost Indien weder naer Portugael; Insgelijcx van Portugaels Indien/nae Malacca, China, Iapan, d'Eylanden van Iava ende Sunda, soo in't heen varen/ als in't weder keeren; Item van China nae Spaenschs Indien/ ende wederom van daer nae China; Als oock van de gantsche Custen van Brasilien/ende alle die Havens van dien; Item van't vaste landt/ende die voor Eylanden (Las Antillas ghenaemt) van Spaenschs Indien/met noch de Navigatie vande Cabo de Lopo Gonsalues, naer Angola toe/aen de Custe van Æthiopien; Mitsgaders alle die Coursen/Havens/Eylanden/diepten ende ondiepten/sanden/drooghten/Riffen ende Clippen/met die gheleghentheydt ende streckinghe van dien. Desghelijcks die tyden vanden jare dat de winden waeyen / met die waerachtighe teeckenen ende kennisse van de tyden / ende het weer/wateren/ ende stroomen/ op alle die Orientaelsche Custen ende Havens/ghelijck sulcks alles gheobserveert ende aen gheteyckent is/van de Piloten ende s'Coninghs Stuer-luyden / door de ghestadighe Navigatie/ende experientie vyde selfde ghedaen ende bevonden.

Alles seer ghetrouvvelijcken met grooter neersticheyt ende correctie by een vergadert, ende uyt die Portugaloysche ende Spaensche in onse ghemeene Nederlandtsche Tale ghetranslateert ende overgheset,

Door IAN HUYGHEN van LINSCHOTEN.

t'AMSTELREDAM.

By Cornelis Claesz. op't VVater, in't Schrijf-boeck, by de oude Brugghe.

Anno M. D. XCV.

A late sixteenth-century galleon as depicted in Crescienzo's 1602 Nautica Mediterranea. *The twin mizzen masts were typical of many galleons of the period.*

Jacques Cartier, the great Malouin explorer (he was born in St Malo the year before Columbus's first voyage) whose discoveries between 1534 and 1542 did much to spur the French to begin colonizing Canada.

Plate LIX

'Septentrionalum Terrarum,' Gerard Mercator, 1595. A copperplate map of the North Pole inserted in the 1595 (third) edition of Mercator's *Atlas.* America is shown from the Davis Strait to the Strait of Anian, and the Shetlands, Faroes and the peculiar 'Friesland' are in the insets. 380 x 460 mm.

Plate LX

'America sive India Nova,' Gerard Mercator, 1595. A copperplate from the first complete edition of the *Atlas,* published in 1595 by Michael, Mercator's son, a year after his father's death. The representation of America is fairly conventional for large-scale maps of this period, and the marginal insets add a touch of welcome detail. Note that New Guinea is on the same meridian as Alaska. 385 x 480 mm.

AMERICA
siue
INDIA NOVA,
ad magnæ Gerardi Merca:
toris aui Vniversalis imi:
tationem in compendi:
um redacta.
Per Michaelem Mercatorem
Duysburgensem.
Polus 90 Arcticus
Polus 90 Antarcticus
Circulus Arcticus
Circulus Antarcticus
Tropicus Cancri
Tropicus Capricorni
Circulus Aequinoctialis
OCEANVS ATLANTICVS
MAR DEL NORT
EL MAR PACIFICO
CVBA
Matanca
Santiago
La Trinidad
Iamaica
NOVA
Canada
Chilaga
Hochelaga
Golfo Mexi
Cuba
Hispaniola
La Bermuda
Gorgades
S. Paulo
Quitaaieno
Ascension
La Trinidad
Circulus Antarcticus

North American Maps 1600-1700

The frontispiece of Peter Goos's 41-map marine atlas De Zee Atlas ofte Water-weereld *of 1666.*

By the beginning of the seventeenth century it was well established that the Americas were continents separate from Asia—or that if North America *were* connected with Asia by a land bridge, it lay so far to the north as to make little practical difference. It had also become clear from circumnavigations and from revised estimates of America's breadth both that the distances involved in any westerly trade routes from Europe to China and India were impractically vast and that they were in any case beset by formidable obstacles. The rigors of the southern route via the now-infamous Strait of Magellan were well known, and though explorers continued to search for a Northwest Passage, it was obvious that if such a thing existed it would necessarily be long, intricate and probably ice-bound for most of the year.

The result was a re-focusing of attention on the possibilities of America itself. The Spanish had already grown rich by exploiting the mineral wealth of Central and South America, and while North America seemed to offer less obvious prospects for the mining of precious metals, it was clearly rich in more mundane ways, in bounties potentially to be harvested from hunting, fishing, trapping, logging and, perhaps above all, agriculture. Thus the three great Northwest European maritime powers—England, France and the Netherlands—now began to make serious efforts to set up permanent colonies in North America.

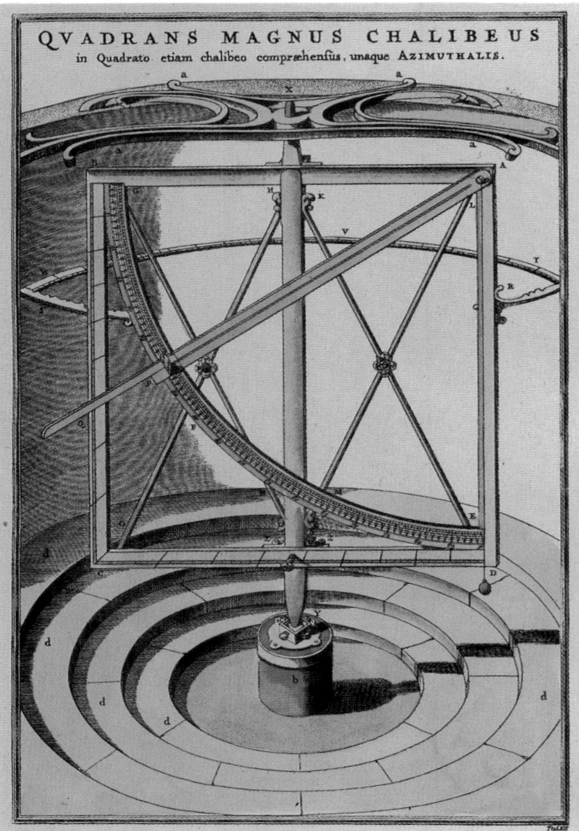

An explanatory drawing of a quadrant from one of the Blaeu's atlases.

This readjustment in thinking can be inferred from many of the maps produced in the seventeenth century. There is a steady increase in the production of maps that would be of maximum use to prospective settlers, maps that depict relatively restricted areas in great detail, with much emphasis on the configuration of coastlines, the course of rivers and other inland topographical features and the assignment of place names. Two of the most famous such maps, de Champlain's map of New England and southeastern Canada and John Smith's map of Virginia, are reproduced here as Plates LXIII and LXIV. Among the other seventeenth-century cartographers who produced similar regional maps were Wright, Wood, Tatton, Lescarbot, Duval, de Laert and Block.

Although for the average seventeenth-century reader detailed area maps might have been expected to have somewhat less appeal than decorative general maps, area maps were nevertheless widely disseminated through the still relatively new medium of the atlas. The great successes of the Ortelius, de Jode and Mercator atlases at the end of the sixteenth century had inspired a host of seventeenth-century immitators, and sheer comprehensiveness now became one of the criteria of competition. Each new atlas, and each new edition of older atlases, seemed to strive to include more maps than its predecessors, something like a culmination being achieved with the publication of the Blaeus' enormous 12-volume *Atlas Maior* in 1662.

The effect of regional mapping on general maps of North America was, of course, healthy, but it produced certain inconsistencies. The overall accuracy with which the eastern coast of North America was depicted increased rapidly throughout the century, but the greatest emphasis still fell on three areas: the Gulf of St Lawrence-St Lawrence Valley region, the Chesapeake Bay region and, to a lesser extent, the Hudson Valley region. Once away from the American east coast, however, the maps became far more speculative. For example, a delusion shared by many of the century's cartographers (though not, interestingly, by many in the preceeding century) was that all of California was a gigantic island; and it was not until 1701 that this idea was at last conclusively disproven.

More illustrations from a Blaeu atlas: two types of armillary spheres, a Ptolemaic sphere and a sextant.

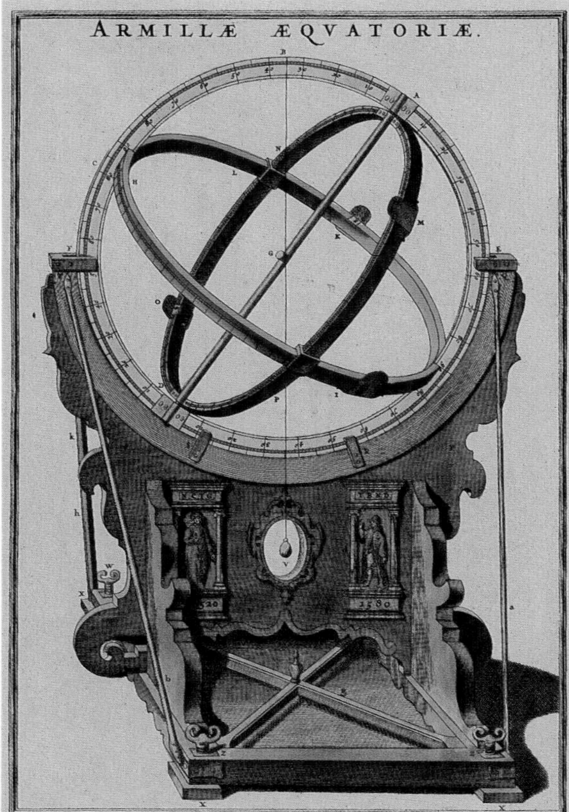

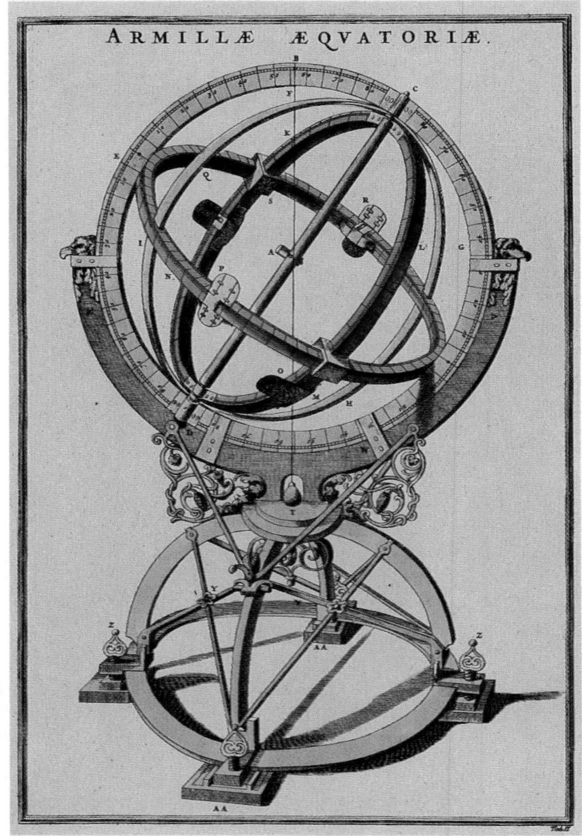

Numerous maps in this section show the California island, beginning with Plate LXX and going all the way through Plate CII.

But to try to judge seventeenth-century mapmaking solely on the grounds of geographic accuracy is probably to miss the main point. Simply in terms of color, decoration, calligraphy and overall exquisitness of execution the best of these maps have never been equalled. If the Blaeus stand, by general consensus, at the top of the list, the Visschers and Jansson are surely not far behind. Nor, for that matter are the leading exemplars of the French school, such as the Sansons and Jaillot. And several Italian and English cartographers are not very far behind them. Thus the plates in this section of our book reproduce works that are as much monuments to art as they are to geography, works that have earned the seventeenth century the undisputed title of 'Golden Age' of modern mapmaking.

The study of the Danish astronomer Tycho Brahe, as depicted in the great 12-volume Atlas Maior *published by the Blaeus in 1662.*

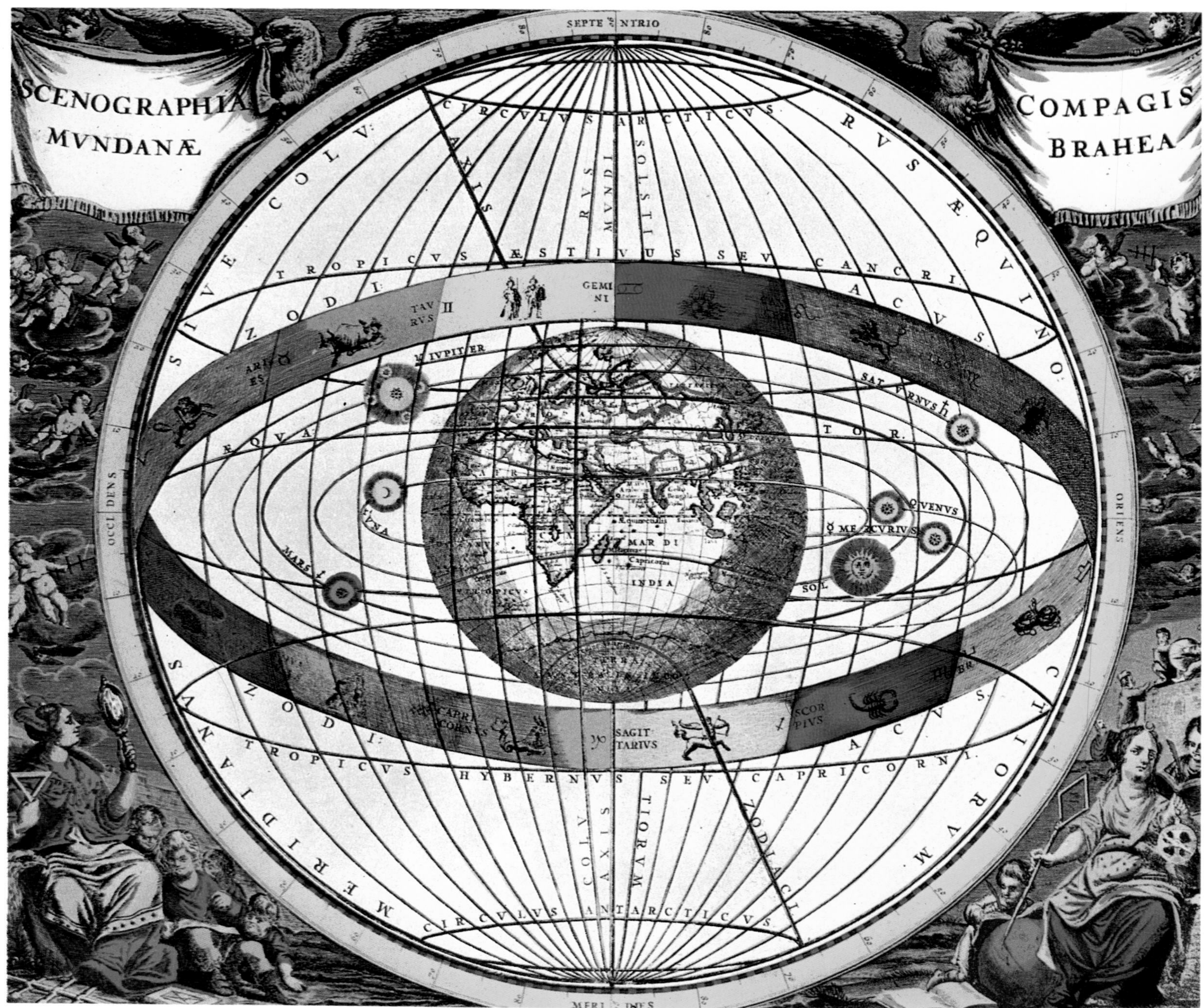

A plate illustrating Tycho Brahe's astronomical system taken from the Atlas Universalis *published by the German mapmaker Cellarius in 1660.*

Another plate from the Atlas Universalis, *this time illustrating the Copernican astronomical system.*

From Jacques de Vault's Cosmographia *of 1583 a plate showing an astronomer using a crude instrument to plot the direction and angle of celestial bodies.*

IL SAGGIATORE
Nel quale
Con bilancia esquisita e giusta
si ponderano le cose contenute
nella
LIBRA ASTRONOMICA E FILOSOFICA
DI LOTARIO SARSI SIGENSANO
Scritto in forma di lettera
All'Ill.mo et Reuer.mo Mons.r D.
VIRGINIO CESARINI
Acc.o Linceo M.o di Camera di N.S.
Dal Sig.r
GALILEO GALILEI
Acc.o Linceo Nobile Fiorentino
Filosofo e Matematico Primario
del
Ser.mo Gran Duca di Toscana.

MATEMATICA

IN ROMA MDCXXIII
Appresso Giacomo Mascardi

The frontispiece of the 1523 book Il Saggiatore *by Galileo, the brilliant Italian physicist and astronomer who risked his life defending Copernican astronomical theories in the face of official Church disapproval.*

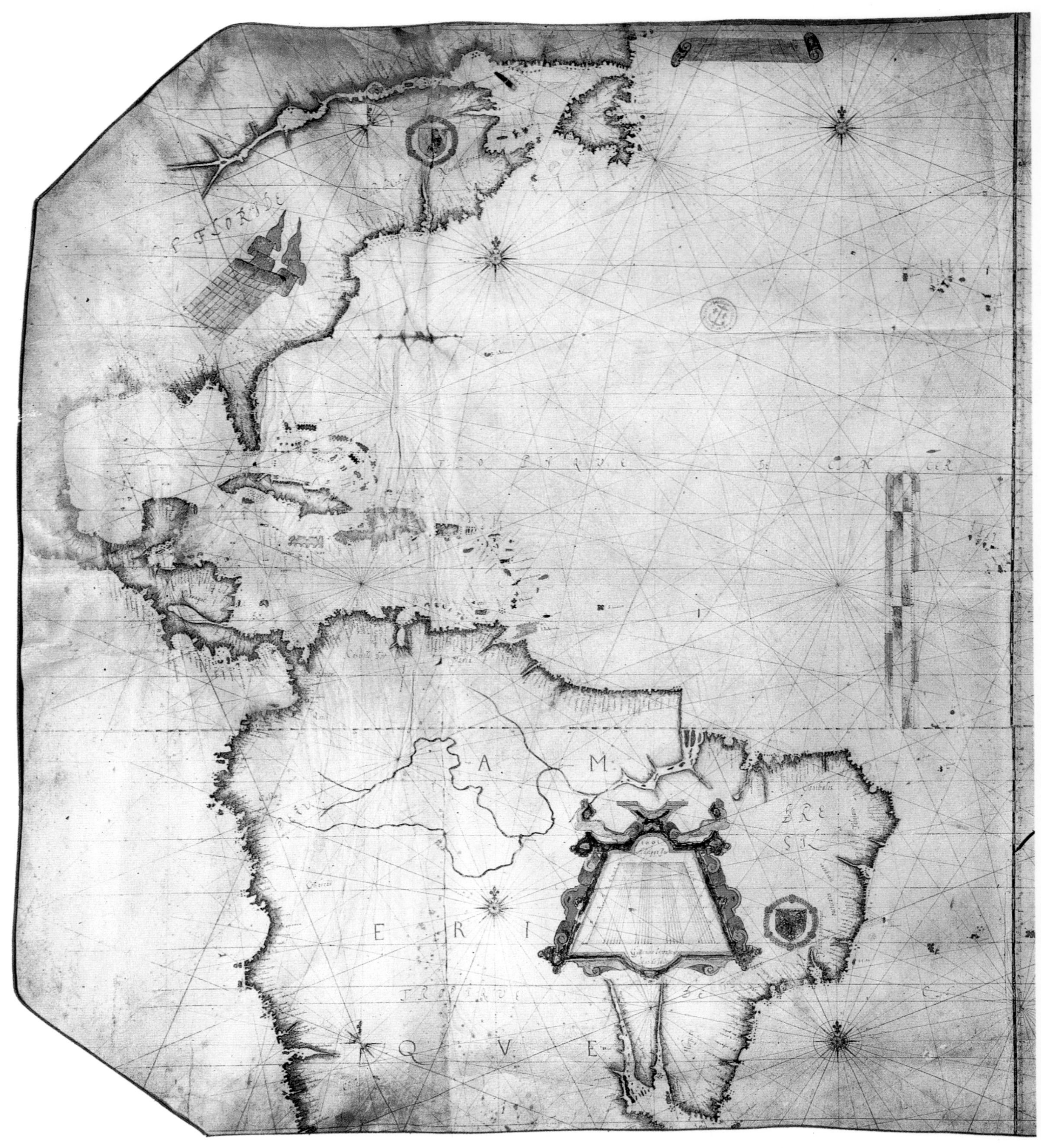

Plate LXI

'Océan Atlantique' (detail), Pierre Levasseur, 1601. A parchment chart of the Dieppe school illustrating the high degree of accuracy with which the portolano-makers continued to render coastal outlines.
744 x 990 mm. Bibliothèque Nationale, Paris.

The lavishly decorated frontispiece of Pierre Mortier's 1693 sea atlas.

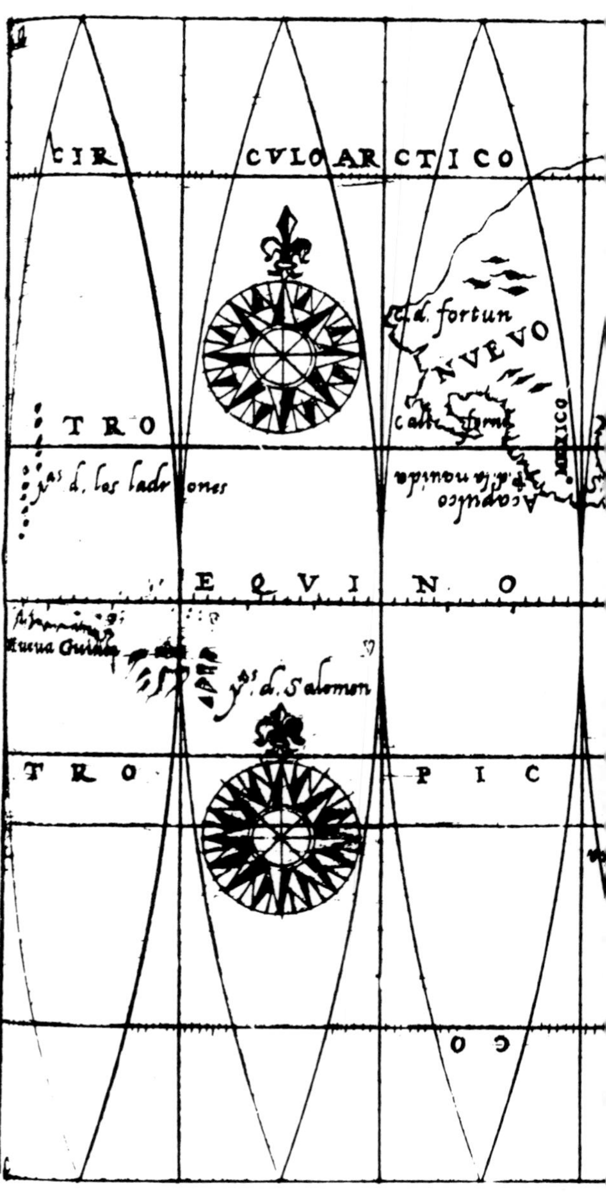

Plate LXII

'World map,' G de Cespedes, 1606. This copperplate from the Spanish book *Regimiento de Navigación* is curious in that it resembles a gore map but is in reality nothing more that 12 segments drawn over a conventional projection. If it were a true gore many parts of the world, including Labrador, western Alaska, Greenland and Iceland would simply vanish.
140 x 280 mm. British Library, London.

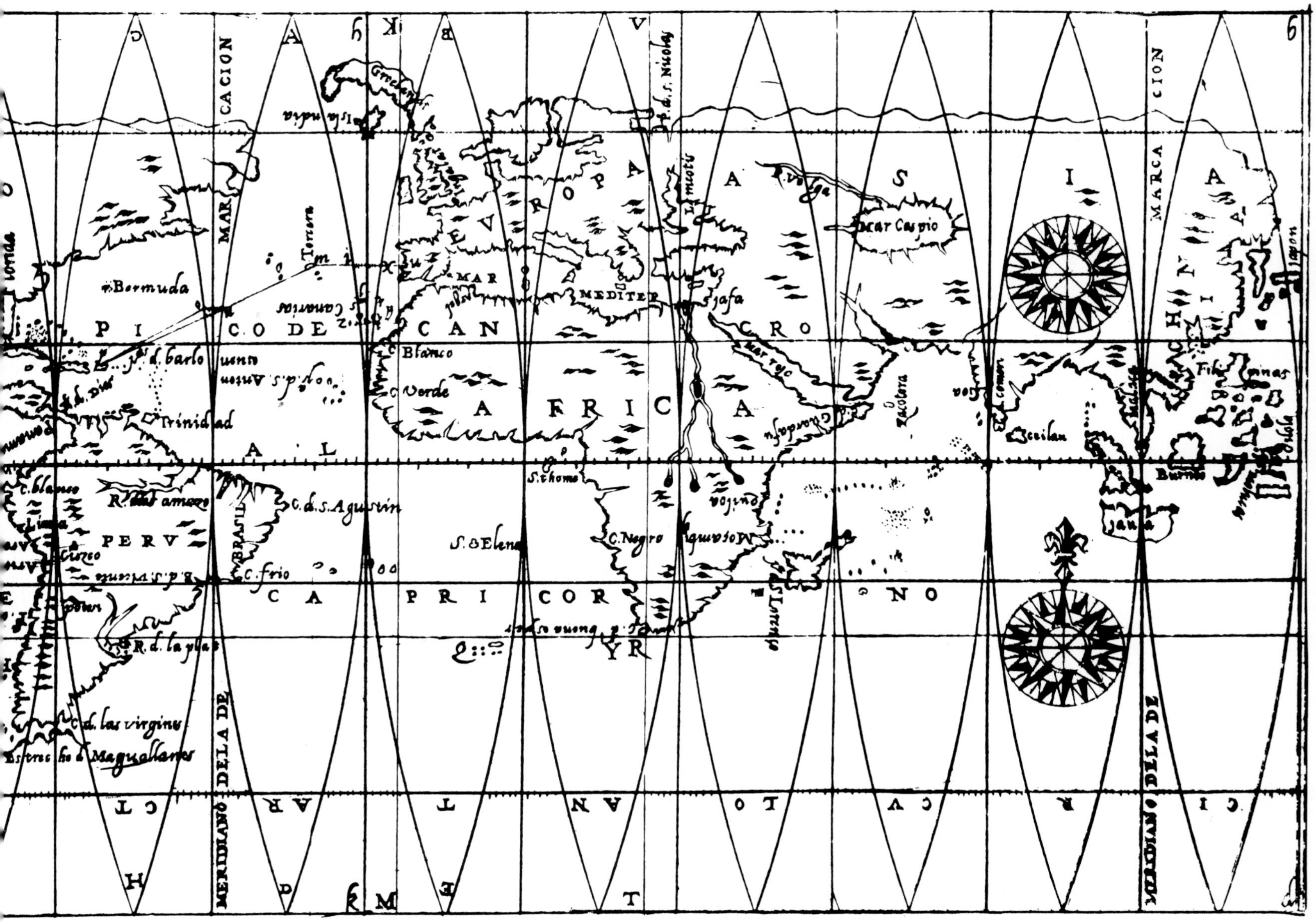

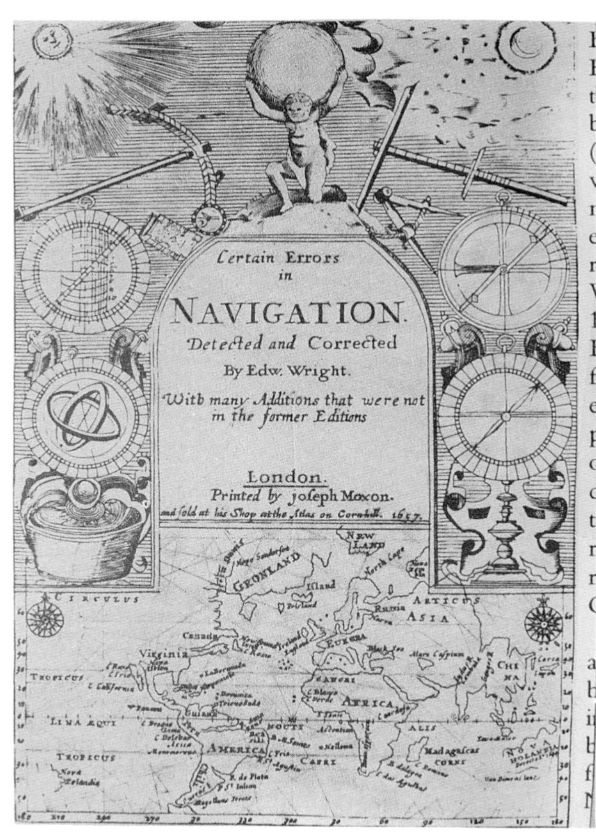

The frontispiece of a 1545 French history of the exploration of Canada.

A detail from the frontispiece of Théodore de Bry's Grands Voyages *(1601) showing van Nort, the first Dutch circumnavigator.*

1619

LES
VOYAGES
du Sr de Cha-
mplain Capita-
ine ordinaire
pour le ROY
en la nouvelle
France es an-
nees. 1615.
et 1618.
dedies au
ROY.
chez C. Collet au
Pallais a Paris.

Grands Voyages

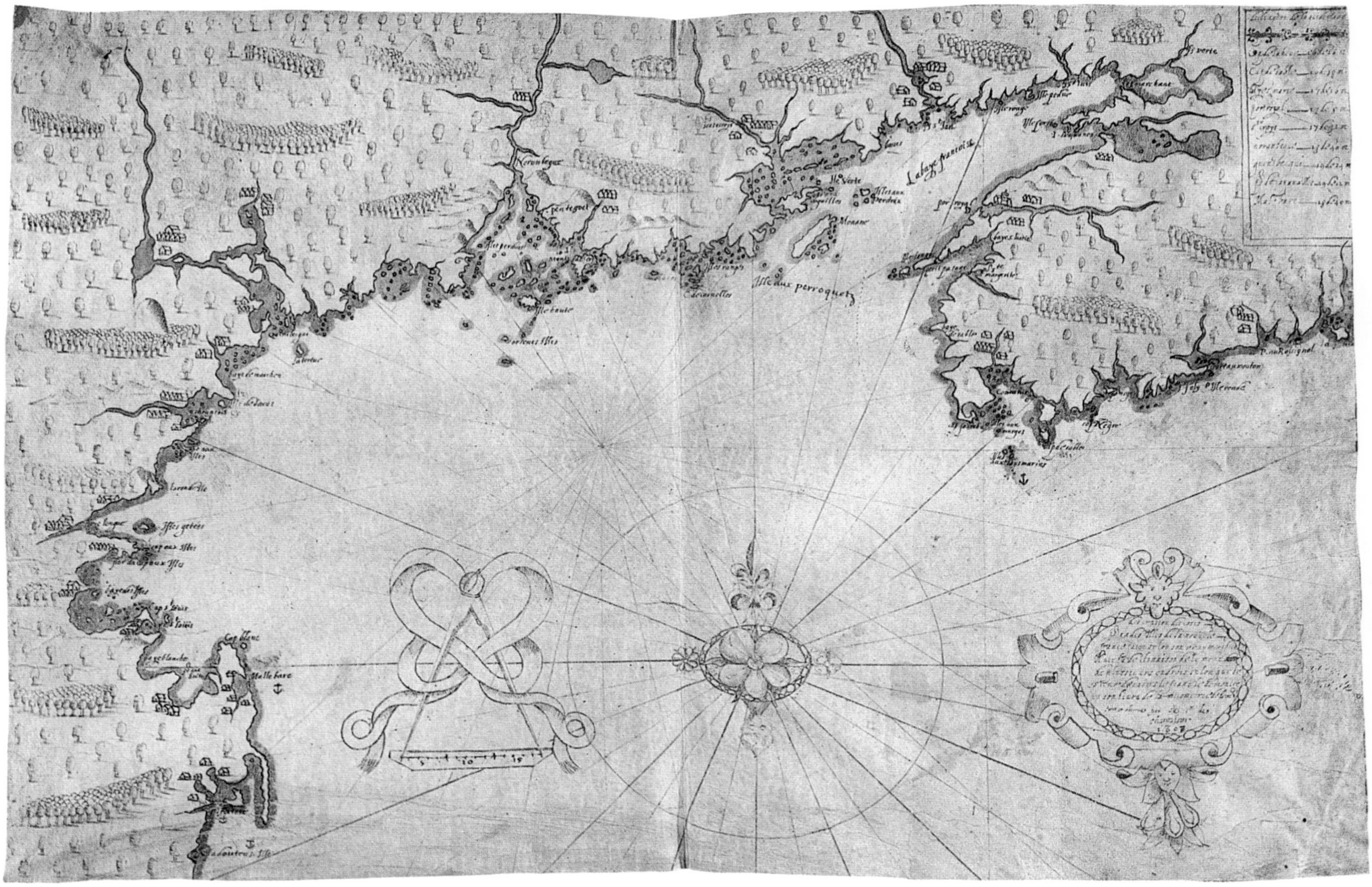

Samuel de Champlain, cartographer, explorer, colonizer and, eventually, governor of New France.

Plate LXIII

'La Nouvelle France,' Samuel de Champlain, 1607. This parchment map was the result of two voyages that de Champlain made to America between 1603 and 1606. Among the place names noted are La Baye Françoise Bay of Fundy, Norombegue (Penobscot River), Cap aux Iles (Cape St Ann) and Cap Blanc (Cape Cod)—the last named for its gleaming white beaches.
370 x 545 mm. Library of Congress, Washington.

Plate LXIV

'Virginia,' John Smith, 1612. Based on a description given by Smith and engraved in England by William Hole, this immensely influential regional map, oriented north to the right, is full of fascinating detail. Among the surviving place names are Jamestowne, Appamatuck, Capes Henry and Charles, and Poynte Comfort. The different types of trees indicate the nature of various forests. Note the inset of Chief Powhatan's council chamber.
322 x 406 mm.

VIRGINIA
To the crosses hath bin discouered what beyond is by relation
Kings howses
Ordinary howses
HONI SOIT QUI MAL Y PENSE
NN AHOACKS
The Sasquesahanougs are a Gyant like people & thus atyred
SASQVESAHANOUGH
PEACK BAY
TOCKWOGHS
SKARAWAOKS
ATQVANACHUKES
and halfe
Seale of Leagues
Leagues
Chickahokin
Discouered and Discribed by Captayn John Smith

Plate LXV

'Theatrum Mundi,' Juan Lavanha and Luis Teixeira, 1612. This parchment map is from an elaborate MS atlas ordered by an Austrian duchess but not completed until after her death. Each of its 32 pages was separated by a layer of red satin. It offers few cartographic innovations but stands as a good summary of the geographic knowledge of the day.
385 x 524 mm. Royal Library, Turin.

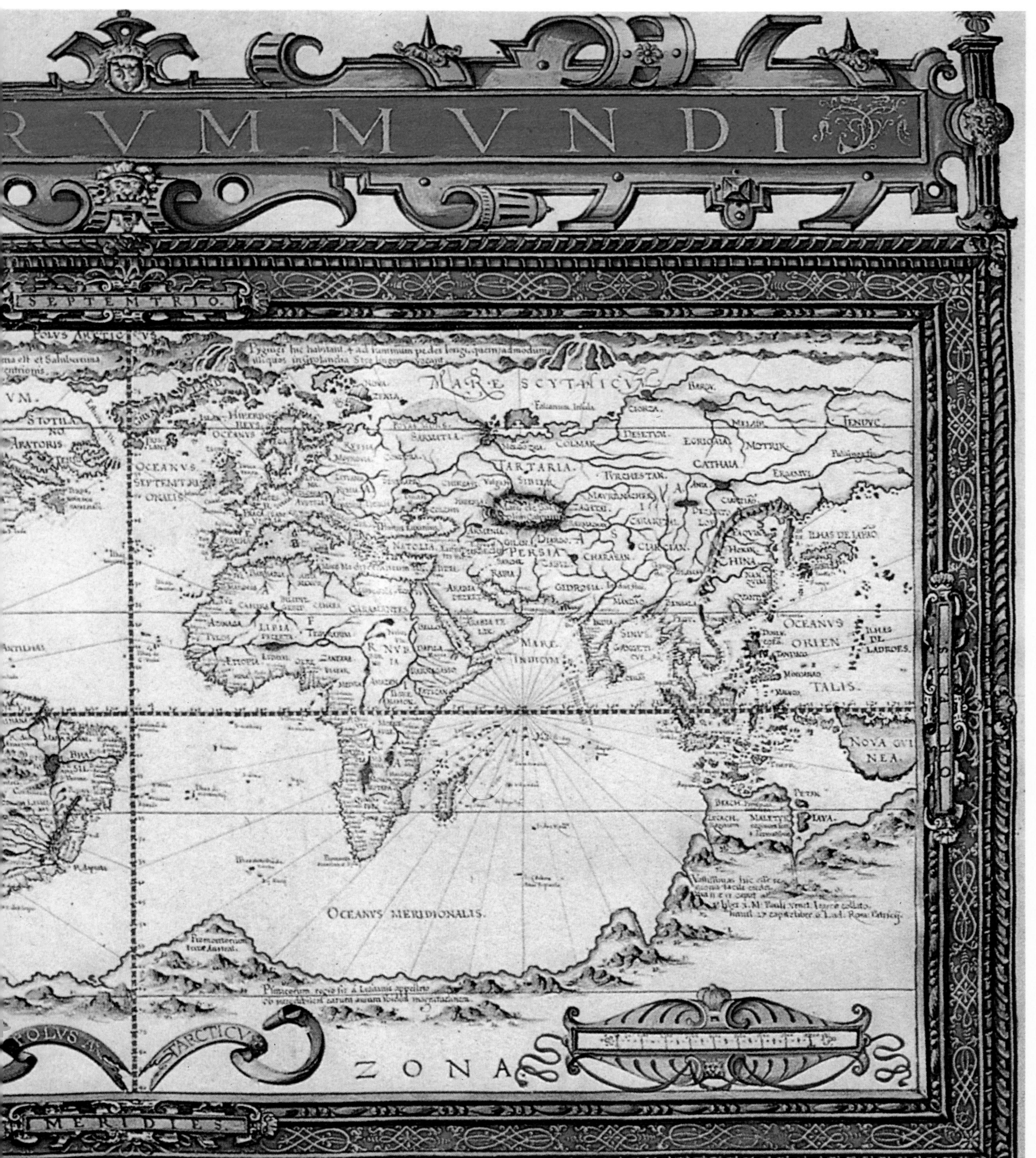
RVM MVNDI
SEPTEMTRIO
MARE SCYTICVM
TARTARIA
PERSIA
CHINA
OCEANVS ORIENTALIS
NOVA GVINEA
MARE INDICVM
OCEANVS MERIDIONALIS
ZONA
MERIDIES

Plate LXVI

'Océan Atlantique,' Pierre de Vaulx, 1613. A handsome parchment chart in the portolan style, its restrained, elegant decoration suggests that it was meant for an important client. If it adds little new geographically, it is nevertheless admirably detailed and free from speculation. 681 x 958 mm. Bibliothèque Nationale, Paris.

Flandres
DE·FRANCE
Gasconne
Prouece
Navarre
Isles-des-Esores
B·de·Argez
BAR BARIE
Toutone
B·de·Sanaga
PARTIE·DAFRICQVE
Isles du cap de vert
La·serleone
Chasteau de·Minne
le·benin
ÆTHIOPIE
LA·LIGNE
ÆQVINOCTIALLE
les cambales
La france Antartique
LE·BRESIL
Ceste·carte·A·Este·faicte
Au·haure·de·Grace·Par
Pierre·deuaulx·Pilote
Geographe·Pour·le·Roy
l'an·1613

Plate LXVII

'Carta Maritima,' Oliva da Messina, 1616. Like de Vaulx's chart (Plate LXVI) this fine Italian parchment portolano, in its scrupulous detail and tasteful decoration, is a worthy representative of the ancient—but by this time waning—tradition of portolan cartography.
720 x 930 mm. Museo di Storia della Scienza, Florence.

TROPICVS · CANCRI
LANOVA ANDALVCIA
TISNADA
AMASONES
BRASIL
DOVRADO
PICORA

NINUS
IANUARIUS
ASI
A
MARTIUS
MAIUS
IULIUS
SEPTEMBER
NOVEMBER
ALEXAN DER MAGNUS
VER
TERRA
IGNIS
AUTUMNUS
AMERICA SEPTENTRIONALIS Sive MEXICANA
OCEANUS OCCIDENTALIS
MAR DEL ZUR
MAR DEL NO
Tropicus Cancri
Circulus Æquinoctialis
Tropicus Capricorni
MARE PACIFICUM
ARCHIPELLAGO DE SANT LASARO
NOVA GUINEA
AMERICA MERIDIONALIS sive PERUANA
MERIDIES
Columbus anno Domini 1492 Americam nomine Regis Castellæ detexit Americus Vespucius 1499 nomen suum illi dedit.
En tibi Ferdinandum Magallanu qui Fretum hoc primus detexit et totum terræ ambitum circumnavigavit: cum effigie Heroum qui maxima cum gloria idem prestiterunt.
Hæc sunt opera charitatis
In carcere eram et venistis ad me
Aegrotus eram et invisistis me
Peregrinus

CYRUS MAIOR
PERU VIANA
MAGALLANICA
FEBRUARIUS
APRILIS
IUNIUS
AUGUSTUS
OCTOBER
DECEMBER
C. IULIUS CÆSAR
AQUA
AESTAS
SEPTENTRIO
OCEANUS TARTARICUS
MARE
ATLANTI
OCEANUS
ÆTHIOPI
CUS
Tropicus Cancri
Tropicus Capricorni
OCEANUS CHINENSIS
Philippinæ Insulæ
MAR DI INDIA
MARE LANTCHIDOL
BEACH
TERRA AUSTRALIS INCOGNITA
MERIDIES
AER
HYEMS
collegistis me
Nudus eram et amicivistis me
Sitivi et dedistis mihi potem
Esurivi et dedistis mihi quod ederem

The frontispiece of Planitarum Effectus, *engraved by John Sadler.*

Plate LXVIII (previous two pages)

'World Map,' Claes Visscher, 1617. This spectacular Dutch copperplate map is almost a caricature of the lavish decorative style that made Flemish cartography preeminent in the seventeenth century. Among other elements: in the corners, Alexander the Great, Ninus, founder of Ninevah, Cyrus the Great and Julius Caesar; across the bottom, acts of charity; along the sides, the months; across the top, the other three continents pay homage to Europe; in the New World map, Magellan, Cavendish, Nort and Drake stand beside the busts of Columbus and Vespucci.
545 x 825 mm. Austrian National Library, Vienna.

Plate LXIX

'Mar Oceano,' Domingo Sanches, 1618. Another fine parchment portolano, this time Portuguese, replete with patron saints, blazons, galleons and scenes of native life. In terms of North American geography it is slightly inferior to the de Vaulx and de Messina charts (Plates LXVI and LXVII).
840 x 950 mm. Bibliothèque Nationale, Paris.

OVA FRANCA
CORTES REAS
EV RO PA
TVRQVIA
MAROCEANO
T^o DECANCER
COSTA DE BER
BE RIA
AFRICA
MAR MEDITERANO
LIBIA
GUINE
MINA
CALABAR
ABIXIM
BRA
T^o DECAPRICORNIO
Mar Etio Pico
MARINDICO
RIO DA PRATA
S. IO SEP
DOMINGO SANCHES
A FES EM LISBOA ANNO 1618

Plate LXX

'The North Part of America,' Henry Briggs, 1625. This copperplate map by a prominent English mathematician was to have considerable influence on other mapmakers. It was published in *Purchas his Pilgrimes,* a work that included Briggs's 'Treatise of the North-West Passage.' It is the first large map to show California as an island and the first to name Hudson Bay (though here apparently applied to James Bay). Among others it names Cape Codd, Plymouth (but not Boston), the Hudson River and Santa Catalina Island, and with the notation 'Po. Sr. Francisco Draco' it roughly locates modern San Francisco.
285 x 355 mm.

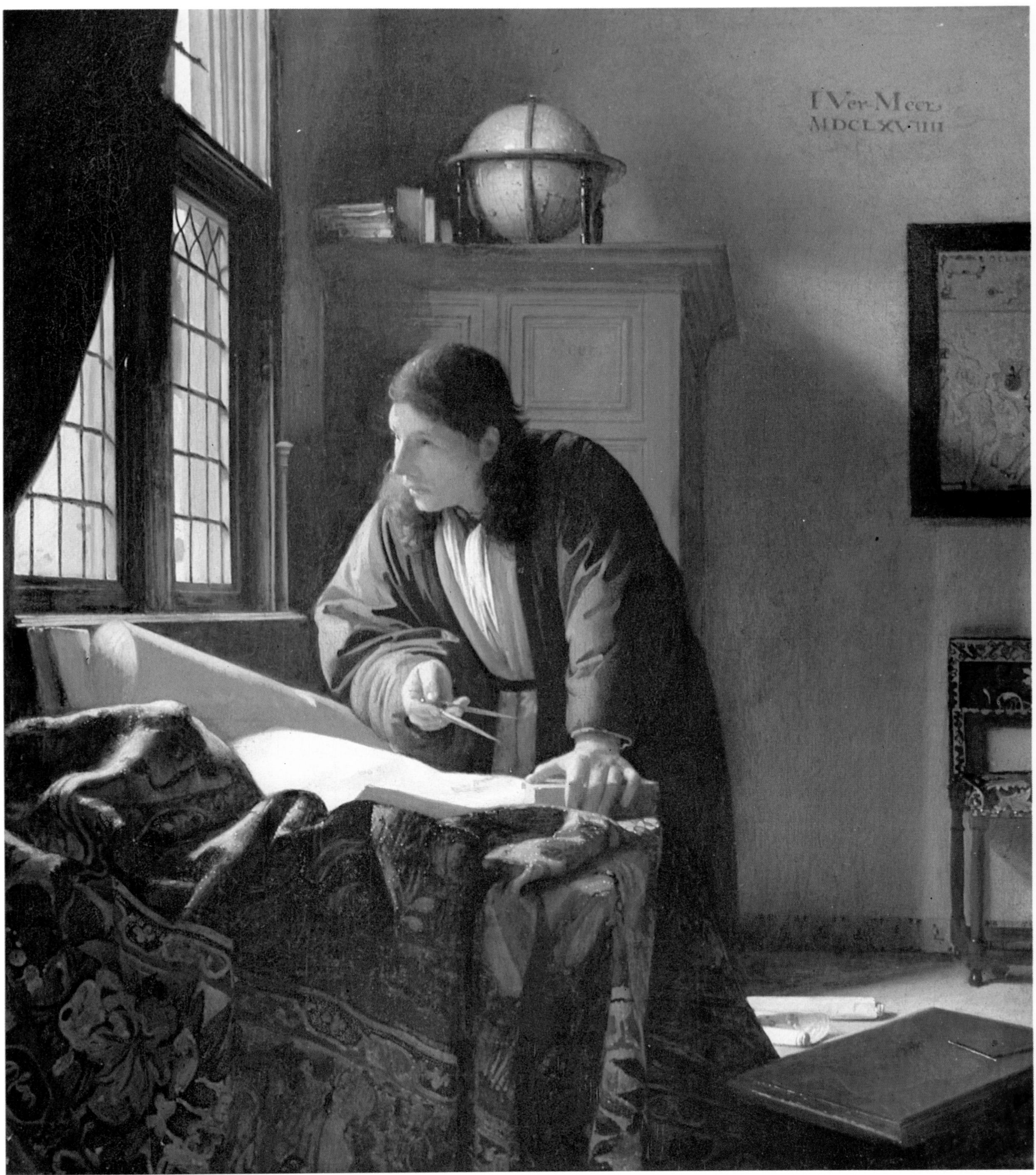

Jan Vermeer's famous The Geographer *suggests the importance the artist's contemporaries—and especially his Dutch contemporaries—attached to geography and the art of mapmaking.*

Plate LXXI

'Typus Orbis Terrarum,' Juan Teixeira Albernas, 1628. A parchment world map from an atlas belonging to the duchess du Berry. Its general configuration, the exaggerated east-west extent of North America and the depiction of the Northwest Passage suggest that this chartmaker owed a good deal to Ortelius. 270 x 340 mm. Bibliothèque Nationale, Paris.

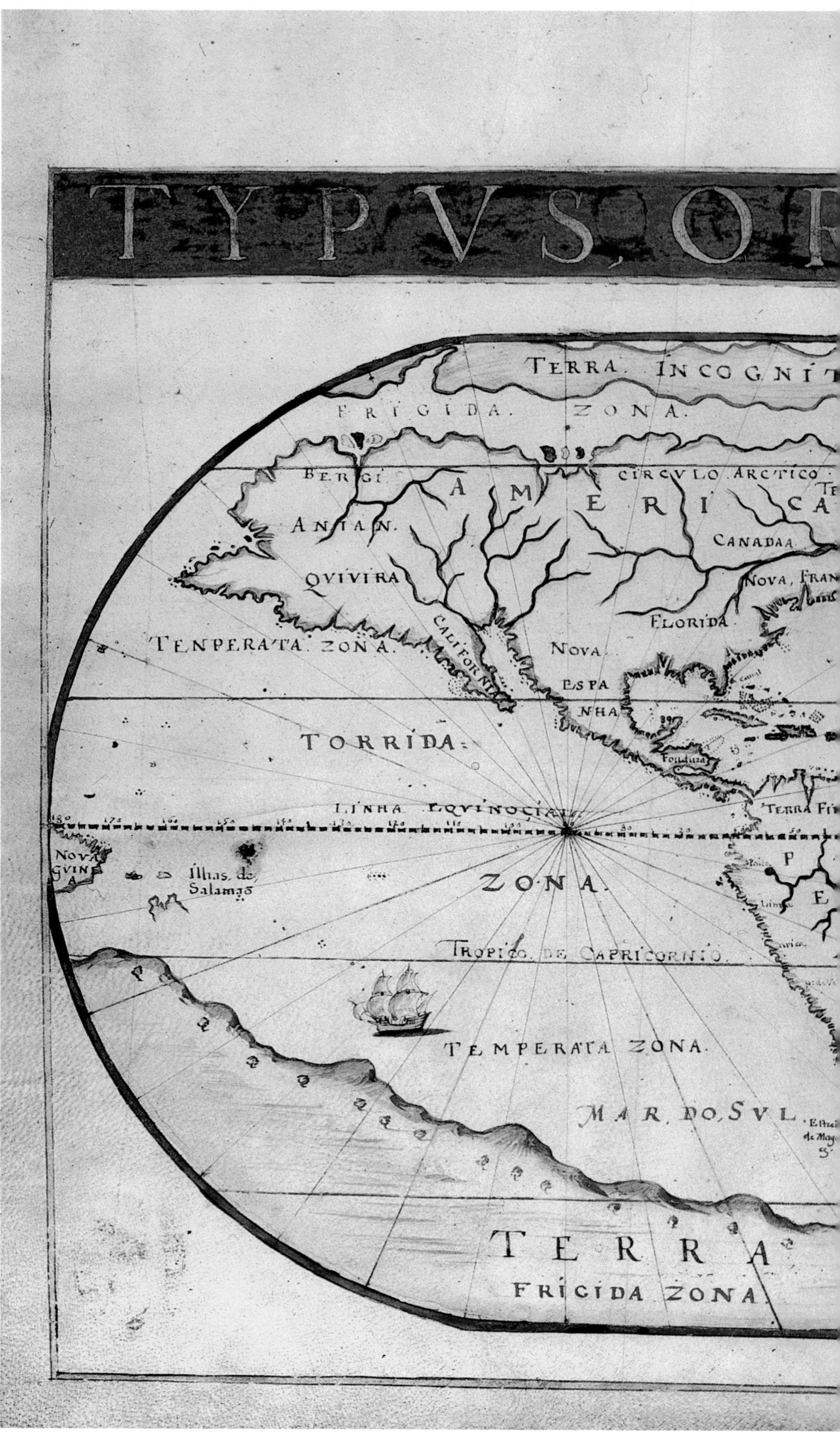

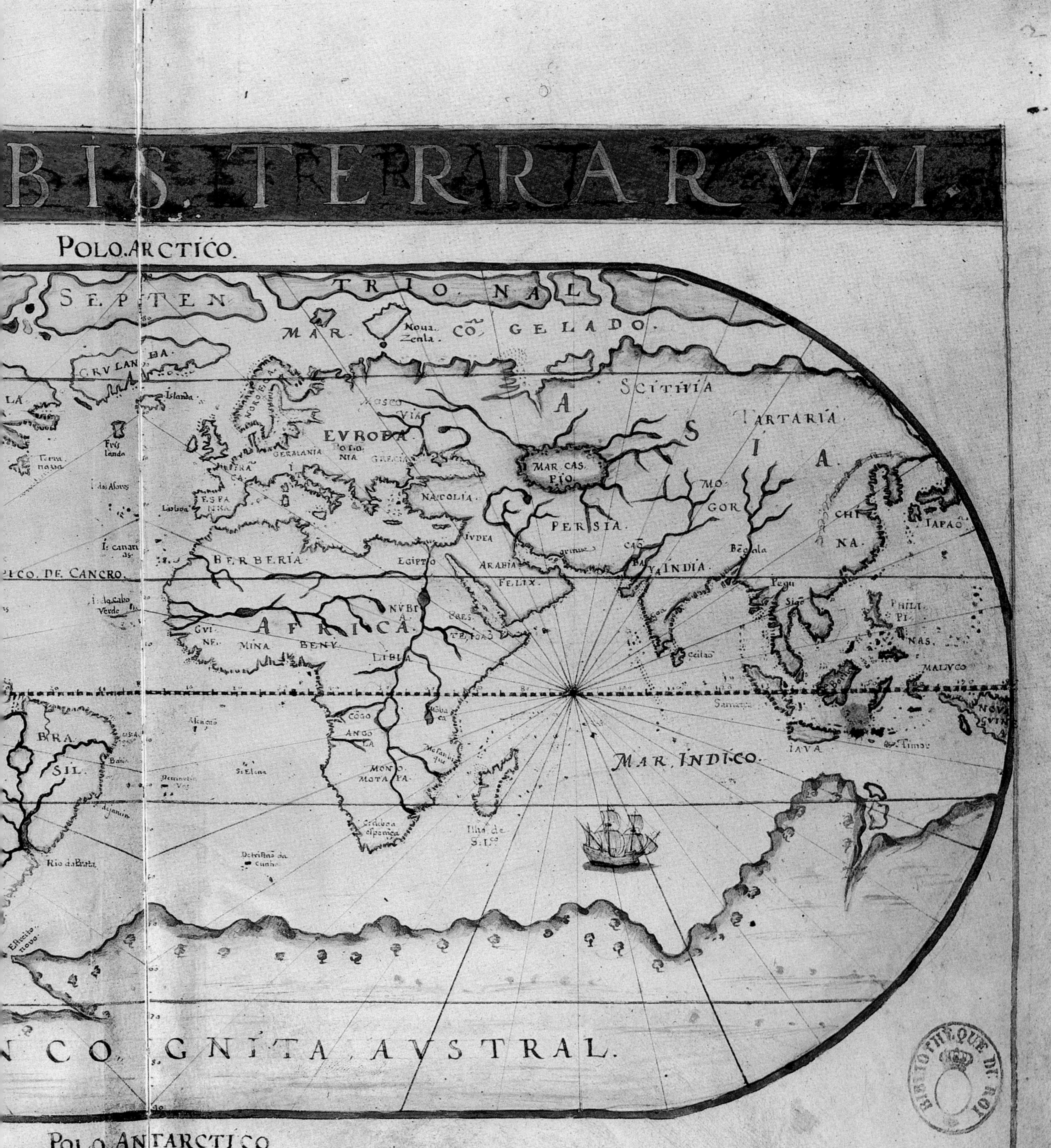
BIS. TERRARVM.
POLO.ARCTICO.
SEPTENTRIONAL
MAR CO GELADO
Noua Zenla
SCITHIA
TARTARIA
ASIA
EVROPA
MAR CASPIO
NATOLIA
PERSIA
MOGOR
CHINA
IAPAO
ESPANHA
Lisboa
BERBERIA
EGIPTO
IVDEA
ARABIA FELIX
INDIA
Begala
Pegu
PHILIPINAS
MALVCO
AFRICA
NVBIA
GVINE
MINA
BENY
LIBIA
CONGO
ANGOLA
MONOMOTAPA
BRASIL
Bahia
Rio da Prata
MAR INDICO
IAVA
Timor
Ilha de S. Lo
Estreito nouo
TERRA INCOGNITA AVSTRAL.
POLO ANTARCTICO.

Plate LXXII

'Hemispheres,' Melchior Tavernier, 1630. This French copperplate world map is certainly decorative, but adds little to the arts of cartography or geography. Four years later Tavernier would produce *Théatre Géographique du Royaume de France,* one of the earlier French national atlases.
200 x 130 mm. Service Historique de la Marine, Paris.

Plate LXXIII

'America,' Jodocus Hondius, 1630. This copperplate map by the younger Hondius presents a good summary of the knowledge of the geography of the Americas in 1630, with a profusion of place names and fairly accurate contours, but still with about a 35-degree overestimate of the breadth of North America. One result of this exaggeration is that it places the continent too close to Greenland (still shown with 'Friesland' to its southeast). The decorations, which include various types of ships and boats and a panel showing scenes of Indian life, are full of typically Flemish interest and charm.
460 x 560 mm.

Plate LXXIV

'Nova Virginia Tabula,' Willem Blaeu, 1630. A representative example of how cartographers appropriated the work of others, this Blaeu copperplate is, of course, a nearly direct copy of John Smith's 1612 'Virginia' (Plate LXIV), even to the major decorations.
460 x 560 mm.

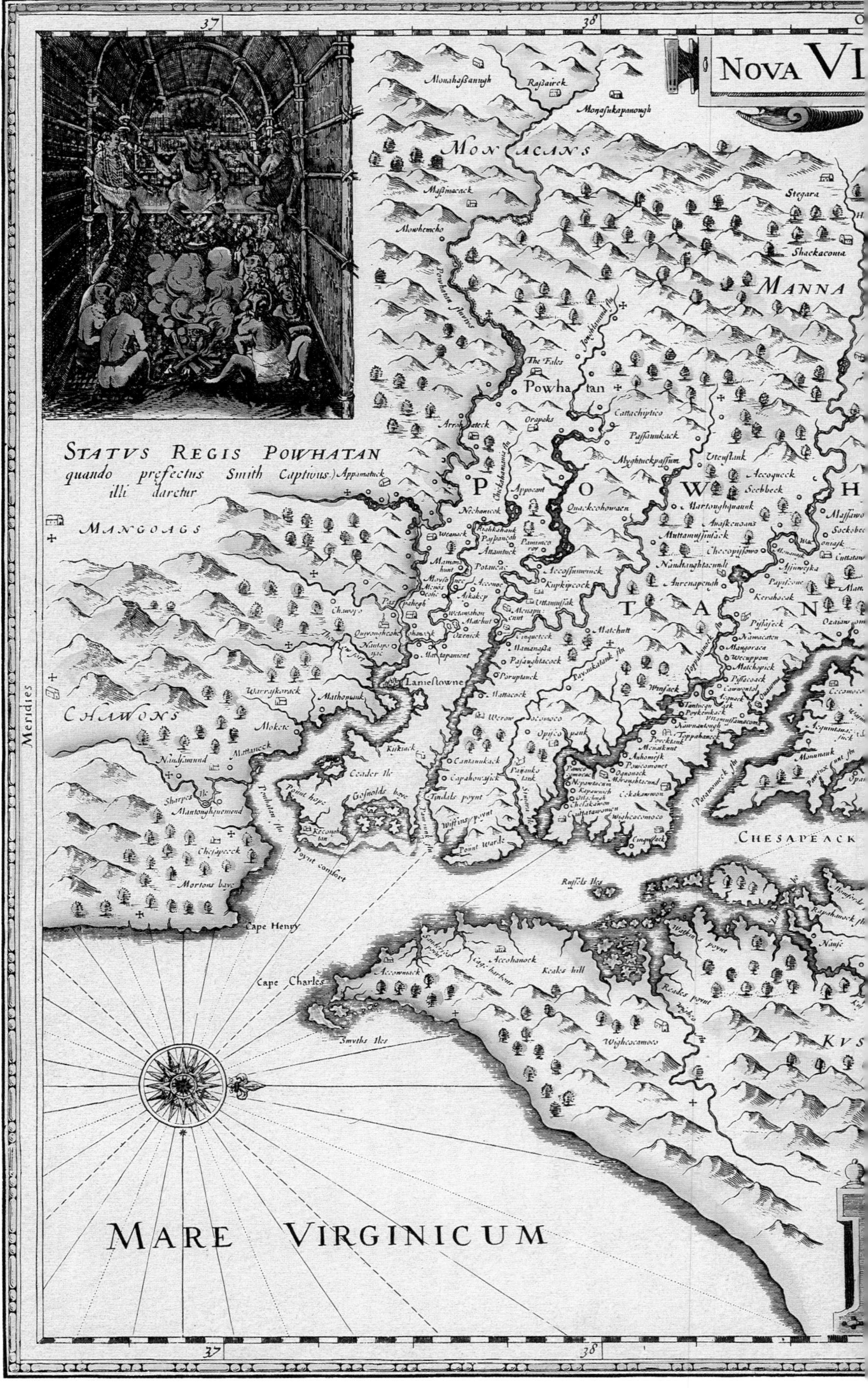

INIÆ TABVLA
Maſſawomeck
Maſſawomecks
Notarum explicatio
Domus Regum
Ordinariæ Domus
Lucubrationes Anglorum
Habitus foeminarum in Provincia Sasquesahanougs
Septentrio
Pamacocack
Tauxenent
Cepowig
Uchowig
Attaock
Tesinigh
Quadroque
Powels Iles
SASQVESAHANOVGH FINITIMA
Sasquesahanough
Ozinies
Tockwogh flu
TOCKWOGHS
Peregrys mount
Atquanachuke
ATQVANACHVKES
Chickahokin
Macocks
Germanica communia 15 pro Uno gradu
cina Guiljelmi Blaeuw.
Sculpt
39
40
41

Plate LXXV

'Carte Universelle Hydrographique,' Jean Guérard, 1634. This elaborate French parchment world map, bearing the arms of Cardinal Richelieu, has, in its depiction of North America, some noteworthy features. There is a hint that the St Lawrence River rises from a body of water looking a little like Lake Ontario. California is shown as an island, and above it a legend implies the possibility of the Northwest Passage opening west from Hudson Bay. On the east coast, next to the legend 'Virgines,' is a notation 'Habitation des Hollandais,' presumably a reference to the Dutch settlement at New Amsterdam.
369 x 469 mm. Bibliothèque Nationale, Paris.

RAPHIQVE; Faitte par Iean Guerard, l'an, 1634
TERRE VERTE,
OCEAN TARTARIQVE
MER GLACIALE
NOVA ZEMLA,
GROEN LAN DE
L'ocean Caledonique,
EVROPE
ASIE
AFRIQVE
TARTARIE
PERSE,
CHINE
L'OCEAN DE CHINE.
JAPAN
L'OCEAN D'ETHIOPIE
MER DES INDES
DE CAPRICORNE
TERRE AVSTRALLE INCOGNVE
ORIENT
NOMBRE DES CLIMATS BOREAVLX
SEPTENTRION
MIDI

Plate LXXVI

'America.' Henry Hondius, 1641. This fine copperplate was included in one of the Mercator-style atlases that H Hondius and Jan Jansson produced between 1635 and 1657. Although it shows little that is geographically new, it nevertheless summarizes well the knowledge of the time. 480 x 640 mm.

AMERICA
noviter delineata
Auct: Henrico Hondio.
1641
Amstelodami, Excudit Ioannes Ianssonius.
OCEANUS
AT
LAN
TICUS
MAR
DEL
NORT
OCEANUS
PERUVIANUS
PACIFI
EUROPÆ
HISPANIA
PARS
AFRICÆ PARS
NOVA
FRAN
CIA
Canadẽses
Acores Insulæ
Flandricæ
I.Canariæ ol.
Fortunatæ
I. de C. Verde
BRASI
LIA
GUIANA
Caribana
PERU
Patagones
CHICA
Fretum Magellanicum
Frislant
Circul. Arcticus
TENTRIONALIS
LA FLORI
SINUS MEXICA NUS
Spanniola
Amazo nes
A
M
E
R
I
C
A
MERI
DION
A
LIS
Oma gua
R. de la Plata id est Argenti fluvius
La Bermuda
Tabaiar
GUAIRA
Toupinam bauli

Plate LXXVII

'Nova Totius Terrarum Orbis,' Henry Hondius, 1641. Though published in the same year as Hondius's 'America' (Plate LXXVI) this copperplate world map shows some differences in how North America is depicted (*eg,* the breadth of Hudson Bay is about twice as great, and California has become an island). In the corners of the map, Ptolemy, Mercator and Henry's father, Jodocus, share places of honor with Julius Caesar.
510 x 715 mm.

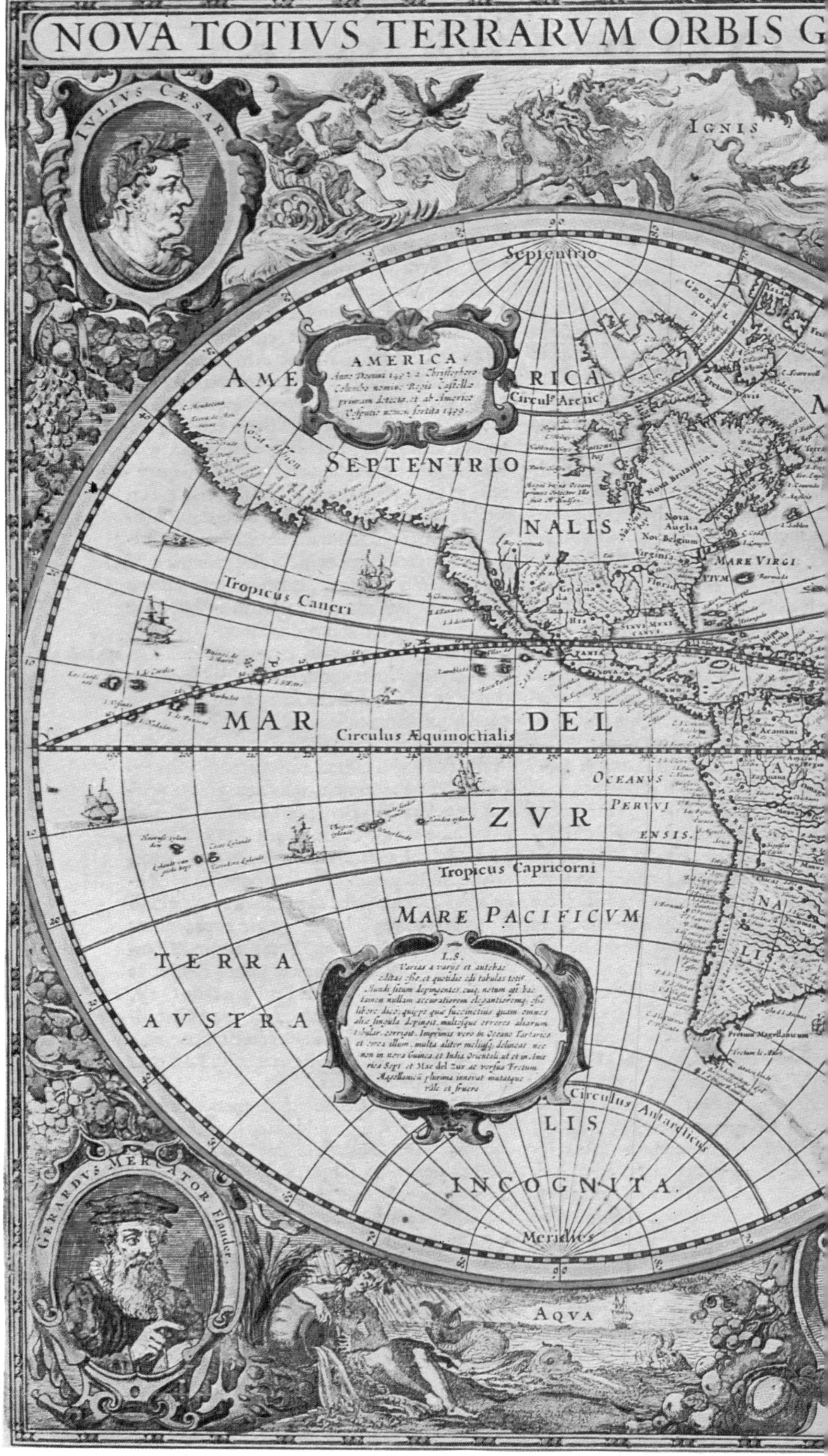

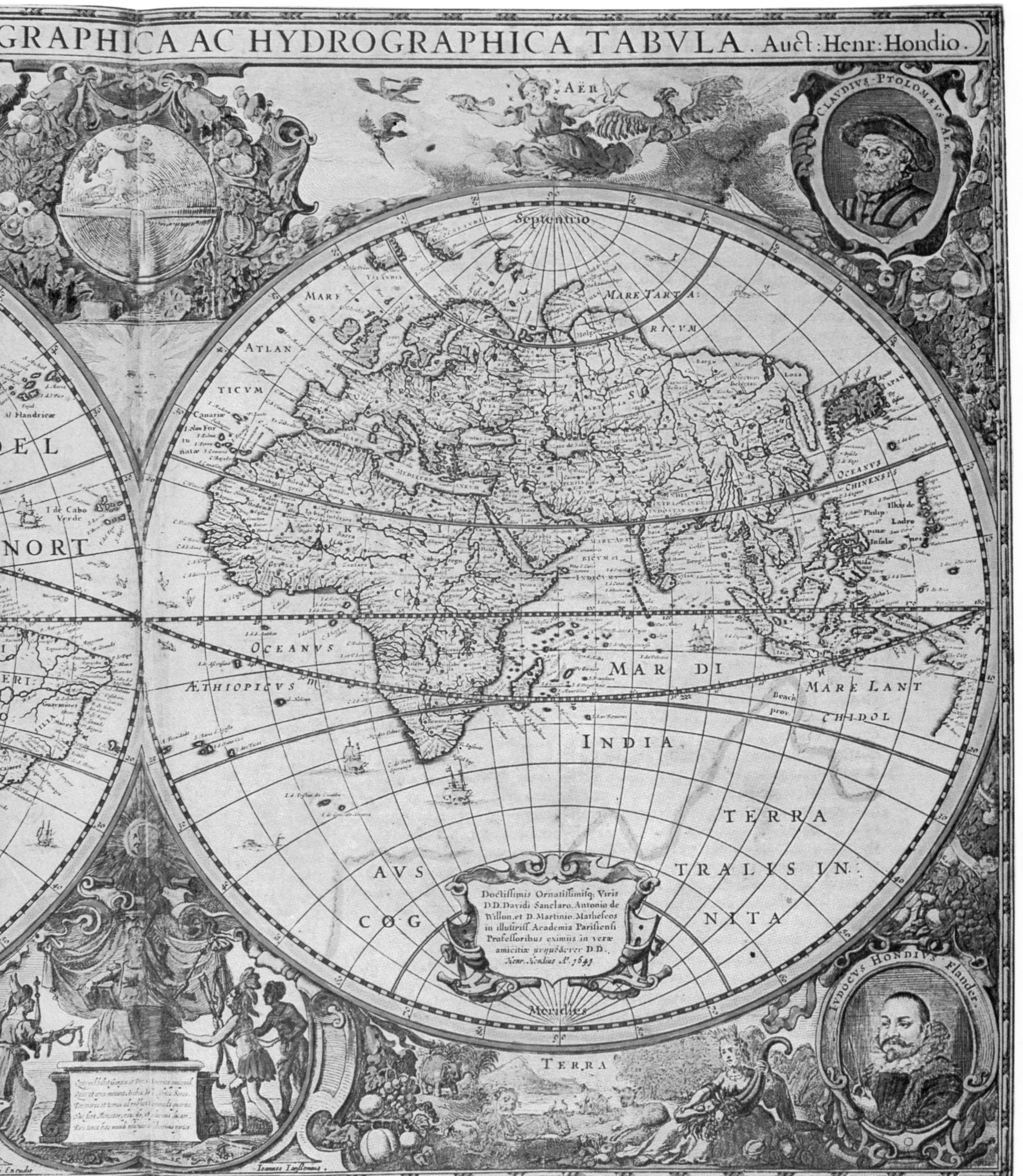
GRAPHICA AC HYDROGRAPHICA TABVLA. Auct: Henr: Hondio.
AËR
CLAVDIVS PTOLOMÆVS ALE.
Septentrio
MARE TARTA RICVM
MARE ATLAN TICVM
I de Cabo Verde
NORT
OCEANVS ÆTHIOPICVS
MAR DI INDIA
MARE LANT CHIDOL
OCEANVS CHINENSIS
TERRA AVSTRALIS INCOGNITA
Doctissimis Ornatissimisq; Viris
D.D. Davidi Sanclaro. Antonio de
Willon. et D. Martinio. Matheseos
in illustriss. Academia Parisiensi
Professoribus eximiis in veræ
amicitiæ
Henr. Hondius
Meridies
TERRA
IVDOCVS HONDIVS Flander.
Ioannes Iansonius

Plate LXXVIII

'Totius Terrarum Orbis...,' Melchior Tavernier, 1643. The North America that appears on this copperplate map of the world appears to be basically the same as the one that appears on Tavernier's 1630 map (Plate LXXII), with California an island and Canada joined to Greenland above the Arctic Circle. The decorations illustrate very well the hulls and rigging of early seventeenth-century ships.
520 x 715 mm.

RAPHICA AC HYDROGRAPHICA TABVLA
SEPTENTRION
ISLE D'ISLANDE
MER
ATLAN
TIQUE
OCEAN
TARTARIE
OCEAN DE LA CHINE
ISLES DES PHILIPPINES
Le Tropique de Cancer
MER ARABIQUE
INDIQUE
Equinoctialle
OCEAN
ÆTHIOPIQUE
MER DES
Tropicus Capricorni
LANTCHIDOL
INDES
Le Tropique de Capricorne
TERRE
AVSTRALLE
INCOGNVE
AVSTRALIS
COGNITA
TERRA
IN
CARTE DE L'EUROPE ET D'ASIE aussi L'AFRIQUE
MIDI
sculp. del.

Plate LXXIX

'Nova Totius Terrarum Orbis...,' Willem Blaeu, 1645. This splendid copperplate from the Blaeus' four-volume third edition of the *Theatrum Orbis sive Atlas Novus* is typical of their style: sound geography mixed with lush baroque decoration. On the left border are the four elements; on the right, the four seasons. Along the top are the seven planets and along the bottom, the seven wonders of the ancient world.
412 x 520 mm.

SOL
MARS
IUPITER
SATURNUS
QUATUOR ANNI TEM PESTATES
VER
ÆS TAS
AUTUM NUS
HYEMS
OGRAPHICA AC HYDROGRAPHICA TABULA auct: Guilielmo Blaeuw
MARE GLACIALE
NOVA ZEMLA
Mare Pitzorke
MARE ATLAN TICUM
MAR DEL NORT
MEDITERRANEUM
OCEANUS ÆTHIOPI CUS
MAR DI INDIA
Mare Arabicum
MAGALLANICA
TERRA AUSTRALIS INCOGNITA
GALL ANI CA
Psittacorum regio
Amplis.s Prudentis.s viro D. Cornelio Petri F. Hooft inclytæ Reipub. Amsterodamensis Consuli dignis.s mihi multis nominibus Colendo. Hanc universalem geographicam terreni orbis tabulā L.M. Q. D.D.D. Guilh. Blaeuw.
J.s vanden Ende sculpsit.
MAUSO LEUM
DIANÆ TEMPLUM
IUPITER OLYMPICUS
PHAROS

Plate LXXX

'Americae Nova Tabula,' Willem Blaeu, 1645. Also from the third edition of *Theatrum Orbis sive Atlas Novus* is this more detailed depiction of the Americas. It varies in several ways from the Americas shown on the world map in the same atlas (Plate LXXIX), and in fact seems very similar to the 1641 Hondius map shown on Plate LXXVI. Yet if Willem Blaeu was truly the author, the map may have predated the Hondius version, since Willem died in 1638. The perspective views of Latin American cities on the upper border and the drawings of Indian costumes along the sides are of special interest.
415 x 525 mm.

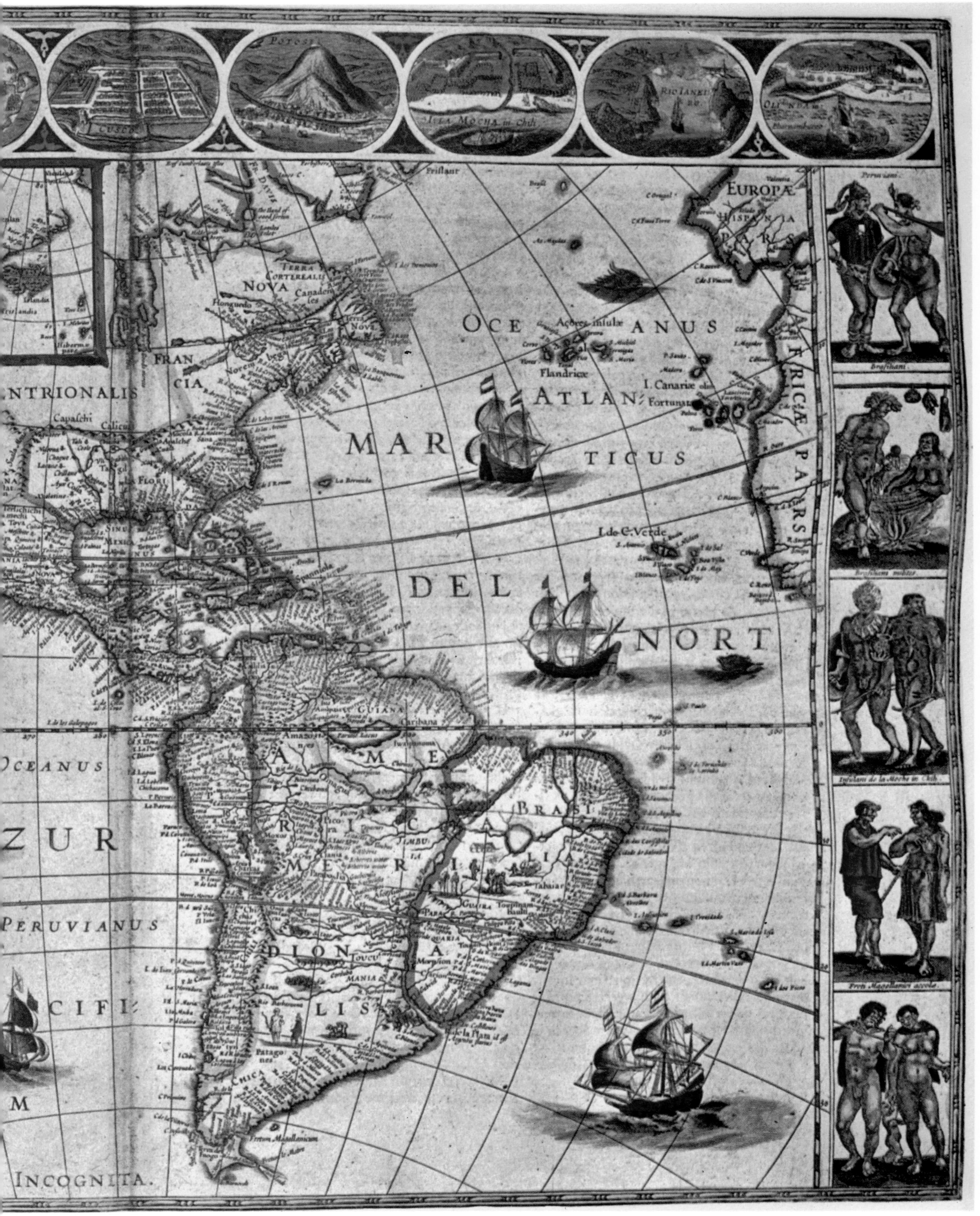
CUSCO
POTOSI
ISLA MOCHA in Chili
RIO IANEIRO
OLINDA
EUROPÆ
HISPANIA PARS
TERRA CORTEREALIS
NOVA
FRAN CIA
NTRIONALIS
OCE ANUS
Açores insulæ
Flandriæ
I. Canariæ
Fortunatæ
ATLAN TICUS
MAR
AFRICÆ PARS
I. de C. Verde
DEL NORT
GUIANA
OCEANUS
AMERICA
MERIDIONALIS
BRASILIA
ZUR
PERUVIANUS
CIFI
Patagones
CHICA
Fretum Magellanicum
M
INCOGNITA.
Peruviani
Brasiliani
Insulani de la Mocha in Chili
Freti Magellanici accolæ

Plate LXXXI

'Extrema Americae,' Joan Blaeu, 1648. This copperplate of New France comes from the fourth edition of *Theatrum Orbis sive Atlas Novus.* It seems to be derived from a famous map made by de Champlain, the last and best of the four great maps he drew of the region between 1607 and 1632. But there are subtle differences. Blaeu, for example, has rendered the northeast coast of Labrador in much finer detail and has affixed many more (Dutch) place names, yet it is still de Champlain's map that is the more accurate in general outline.
398 x 496 mm.

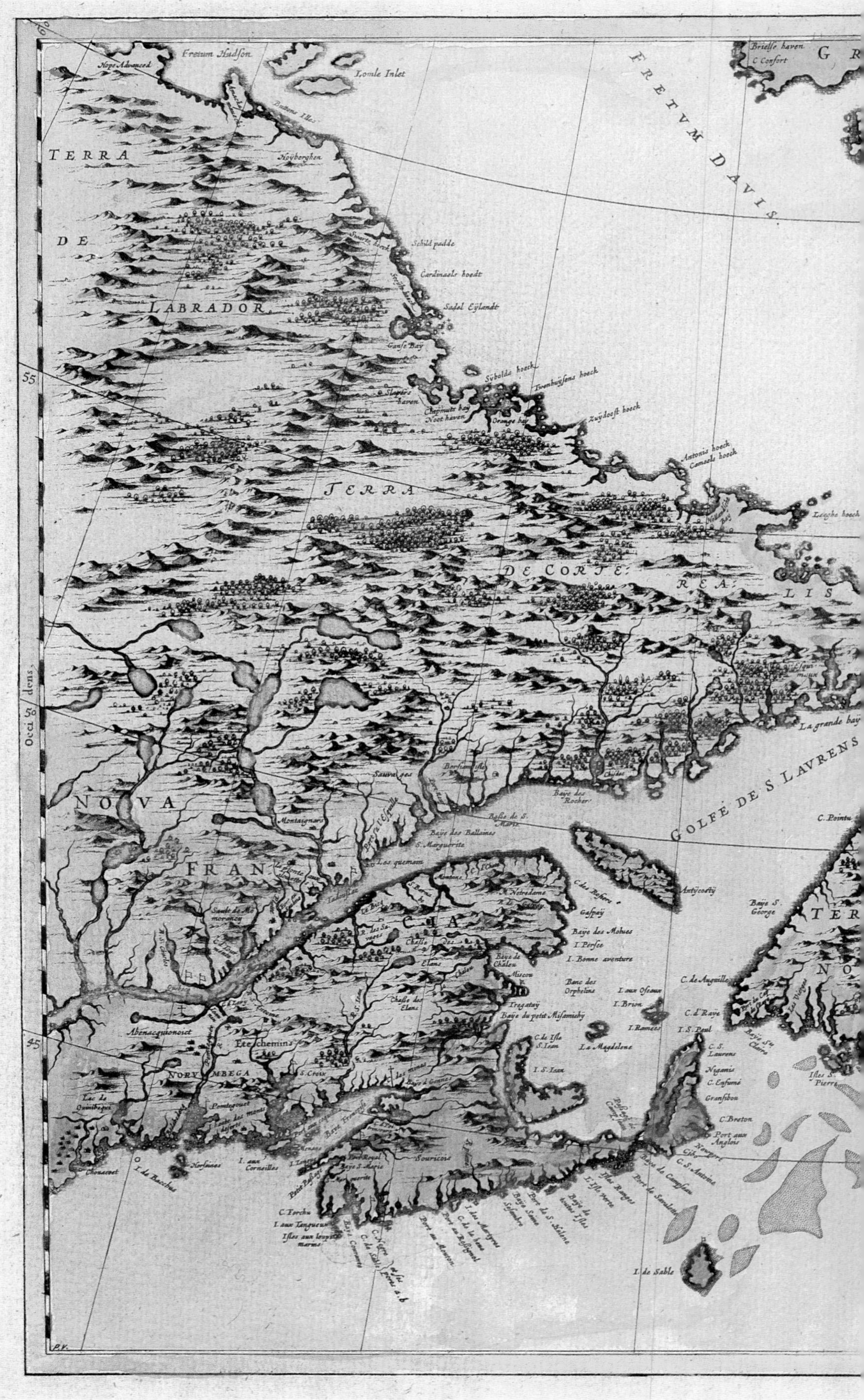

EXTREMA AMERICÆ
Versus Boream, ubi
TERRA NOVA
NOVA FRANCIA, Adjacentiaq.
Amstelędami Io: Blaeu Exc.
C. Goede hoepe
Withe Cape
C. Discord
Croix Blanche
Belle Isle
I. Fichot
C. de Grat
Belle Isle
Isle aux Aposres
I. das Aves
C. S. Iean
I. des Fogues
C. de Bona vista
I. de Bacalaos
Baya de Conception
C. S. Francisco
C. de Raso
55
45
50

Plate LXXXII

'Insulae Americanae,' Nikolaus Visscher, 1650. In terms both of accuracy and detail this copperplate map of the Caribbean region by Claes Visscher's son is exceptional. The outline of Florida, for example, is far better than on many later maps. But Visscher was also capable of making much poorer maps. As with many other mapmakers, from whom he copied could make a big difference. In this case, it was from the Blaeus.
720 x 980 mm.

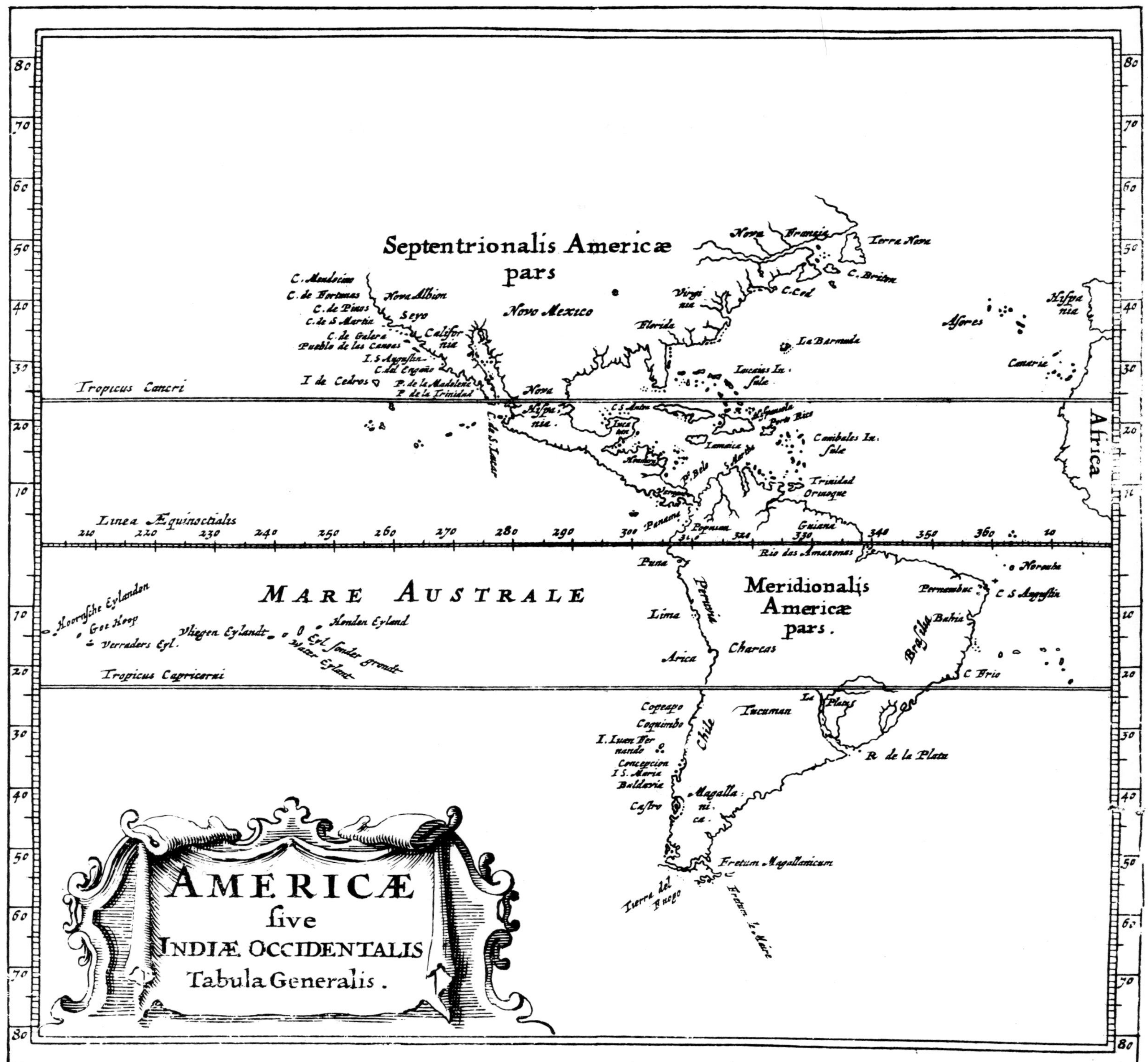

Plate LXXXIII

'Americae,' anon, 1650. This sketchy copperplate from a small Venetian atlas neither contains much that is geographically new nor is it very decorative. But by the standards of the day it is nevertheless quite up-to-date and sound, a testimonial to the growing diffusion of geographic knowledge by the mid-century.
120 x 125 mm.

Plate LXXXIV

'Nova Totius Terrarum Orbis,' Nikolaus Visscher, 1652. Compared with his Caribbean map (Plate LXXXII) this elaborate Visscher world map is geographically backward, but it is sumptuous in its decoration. In the corners are the four continents. The top and bottom borders depict 12 Roman emperors, and along the sides are views of cities and scenes of life in Europe, Asia, Africa and America.
415 x 525 mm.

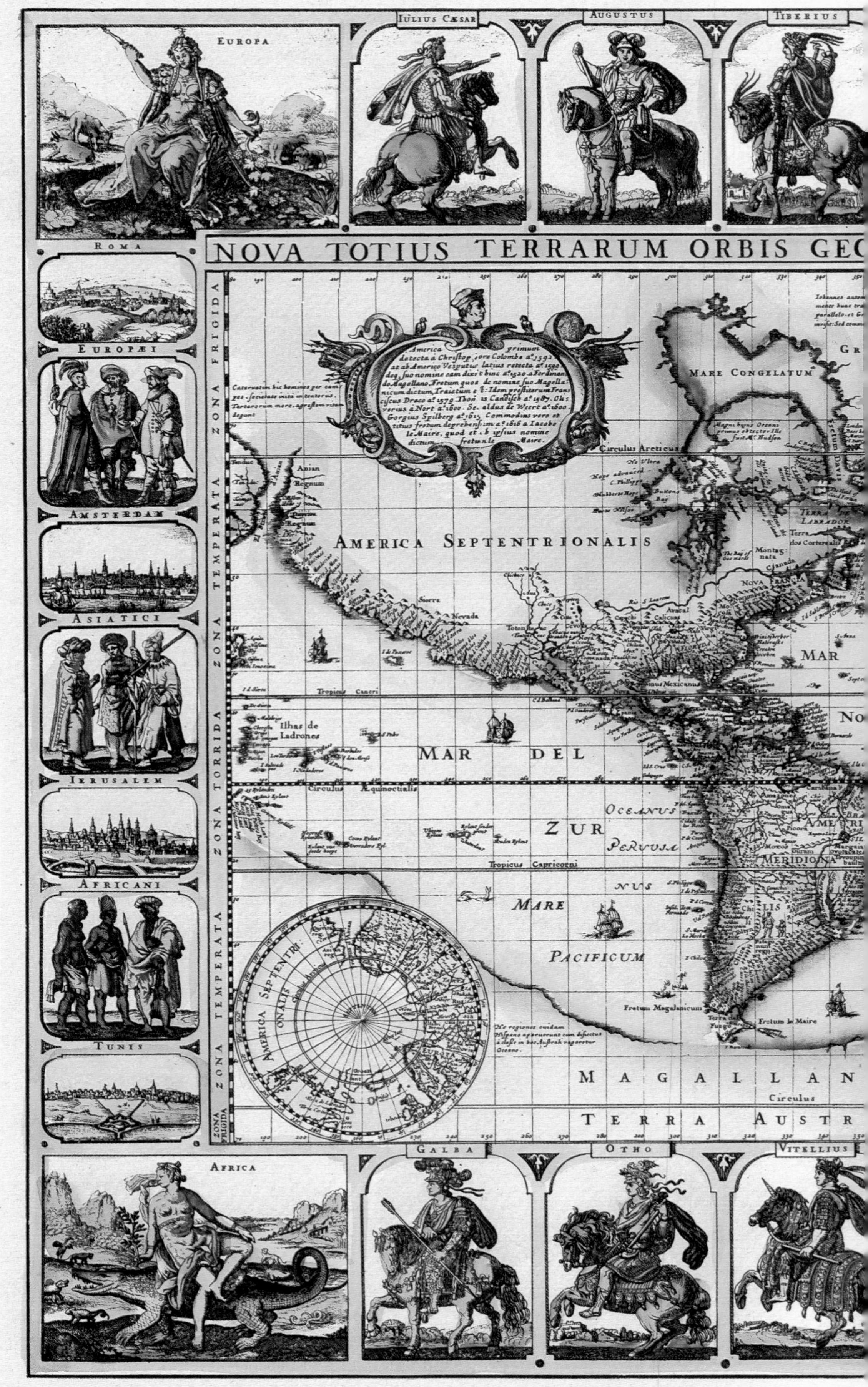

CALIGULA
CLAUDIUS
NERO
ASIA
PHICA AC HYDROGRAPHICA TABULA
Autore N. I. Piscator
MEXICO
AMERICANI SEPT.
HAVANA
AMERICANI MERID
PARNAMBUCO
MAGELLANICI
B. DE TODOS SANTOS
S. Salvador
MARE GLACIALE
OCEANUS TARTARICUS
NOVA ZEMLA
SEPTENTRIO
Mare Arabicum
MAR DI
INDIA
MAGALLANICA
TERRA AUSTRALIS INCOGNITA
Promontorium terræ Australis
A S I V E
I N C O G N I T A
excudebat 1652
VESPASIANUS
TITUS
DOMITIANUS
AMERICA

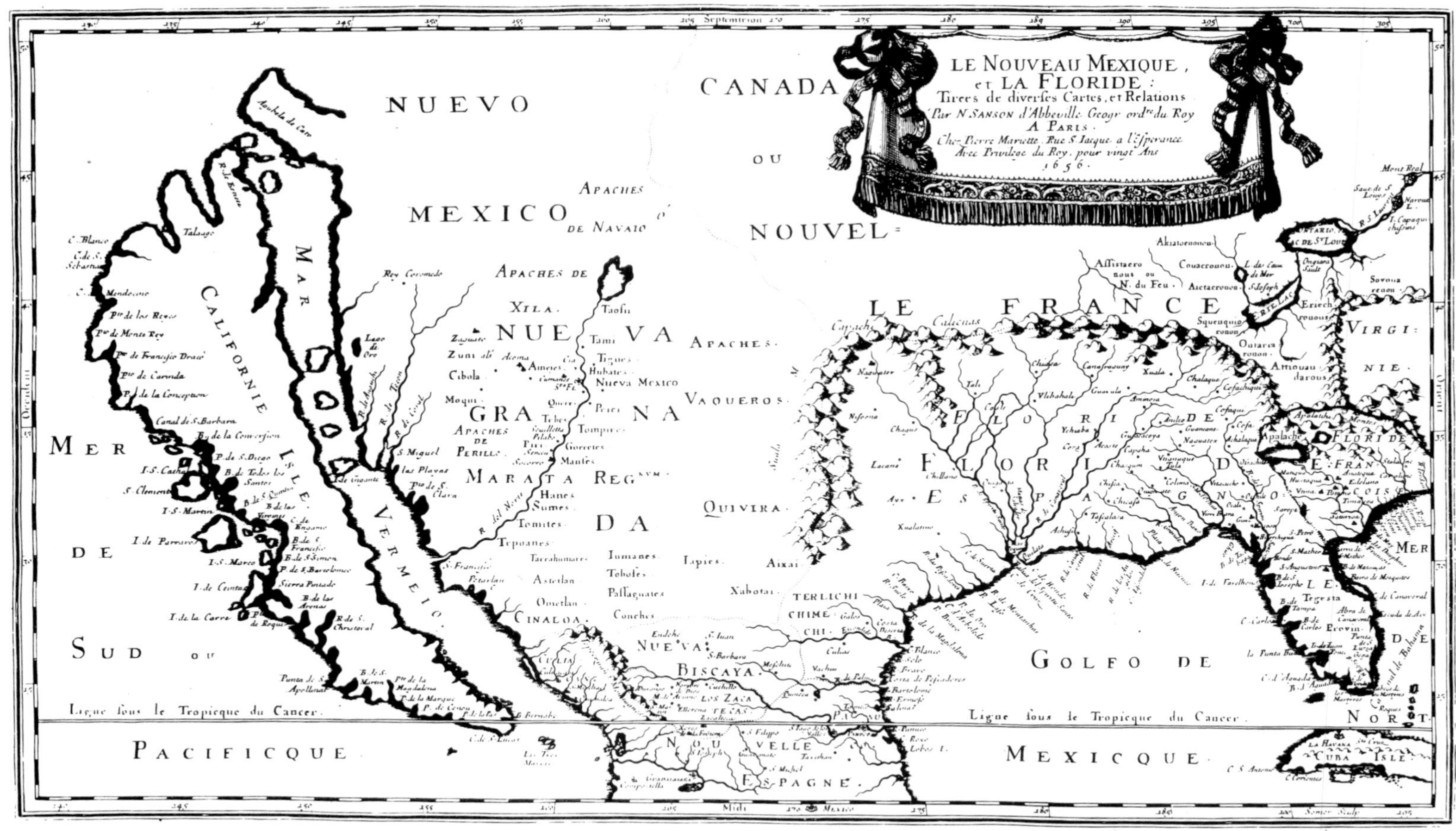

Plate LXXXV

'Le Nouveau Mexique et la Floride,' Nicolas Sanson, 1656. Sanson, the first great French atlas-maker, in 1656 published *L'Amérique*, an atlas devoted solely to the New World. No doubt the most arresting feature of this map of North America is the way Sanson details insular California, showing—and even naming—lesser islands in the sea between it and the mainland. But of equal interest is the fact that Lakes Ontario and Erie are also both shown and named.
310 x 540 mm.

A detail from Plate LXXXVI is this dedication by Blaeu to his patron.

Plate LXXXVI

'Insulae Americanae,' Willem Blaeu, 1660. This copperplate chart of the Caribbean is only nominally dated 1660, for it must have been drawn by Blaeu at least 22 years before that. It is in fact, the basis for the Visscher copy shown in Plate LXXXII. 365 x 430 mm.

Plate LXXXVII

'Virginia and Florida,' Joan and Cornelis Blaeu, 1660. By the second half of the seventeenth century the number of detailed regional maps of North America was rising rapidly, and atlas publishers were expected to include them in their collections. Thus the younger Blaeus, using then-current information, made this fine copperplate of the coast of Georgia, the Carolinas and Virginia and added it to their 1662 *Atlas Maior.*
400 x 520 mm.

Powhatan
Chesapeack Bay
Sanawa noock
Weape catching meoc
VIR GINIA
SECOTAN
MONGOAC
Medano, Hispanis
PTENTRIO NALIS.
MAR DEL NORT
Chicola
Stalane
Sandhoeck
Porto Royal
Hoc loco Galli Fortalitium exstruxerunt duce Laudonerio. A° 1562
Milliaria Germanica communia

Plate LXXXVIII

'Planispherium Terrestre,' Nikolaus Visscher, 1660. The North America that appears on this ornate world map is a considerable improvement over the one Visscher put on his map of 1652 (Plate LXXXIV). He confines the known part of the continent to an arc of about 100 degrees and is less dogmatic in speculating about the presumed remaining 50-60 degrees. The contours of the eastern seaboard are much better, though he continues to insist on a link between Canada and Greenland. Note too that he has now shown and named all five of the Great Lakes. The decorations mostly have to do with various aspects of astronomy and cartography, but under the two main hemispheres are a series of drawings illustrating selected natural phenomena such as the tides, a rainbow and a Norwegian whirlpool.
365 x 430 mm.

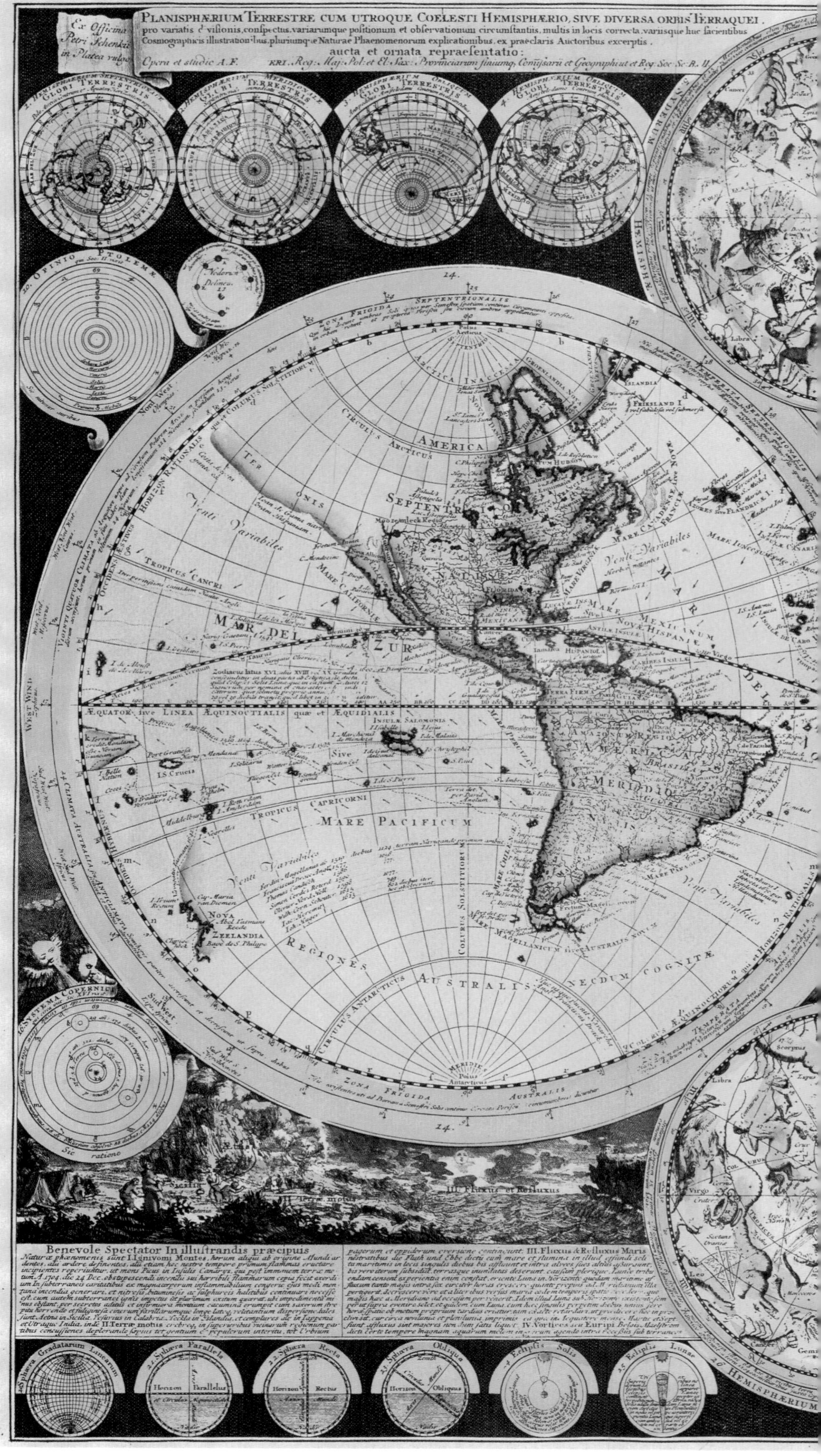

Plate LXXXIX

'New England,' John Smith, 1660 (1614). The date 1660 is notional for this map, referring only to the date when this particular edition of it was printed. In fact the map was first drawn by Simon Passe in 1614, based on descriptions given by John Smith, and was published in various engraved versions throughout the rest of the century. The Pilgrims knew of it and accepted its name, Plimouth, for the place where they settled. Other familiar place names are Cape Anna, the River Charles and Boston, the last mislocated at the site of present-day York, Maine.
360 x 420 mm.

Plate XC

'Planisphere,' anon, mid-seventeenth century. A distinct oddity is this parchment map drawn by a Chinese artist under the direction of Matteo Ricci, a Jesuit missionary. It is at least as accurate in general outline as many maps produced by famous European cartographers of the time.
1050 x 2110 mm. Biblioteca Ambrosiana, Milan

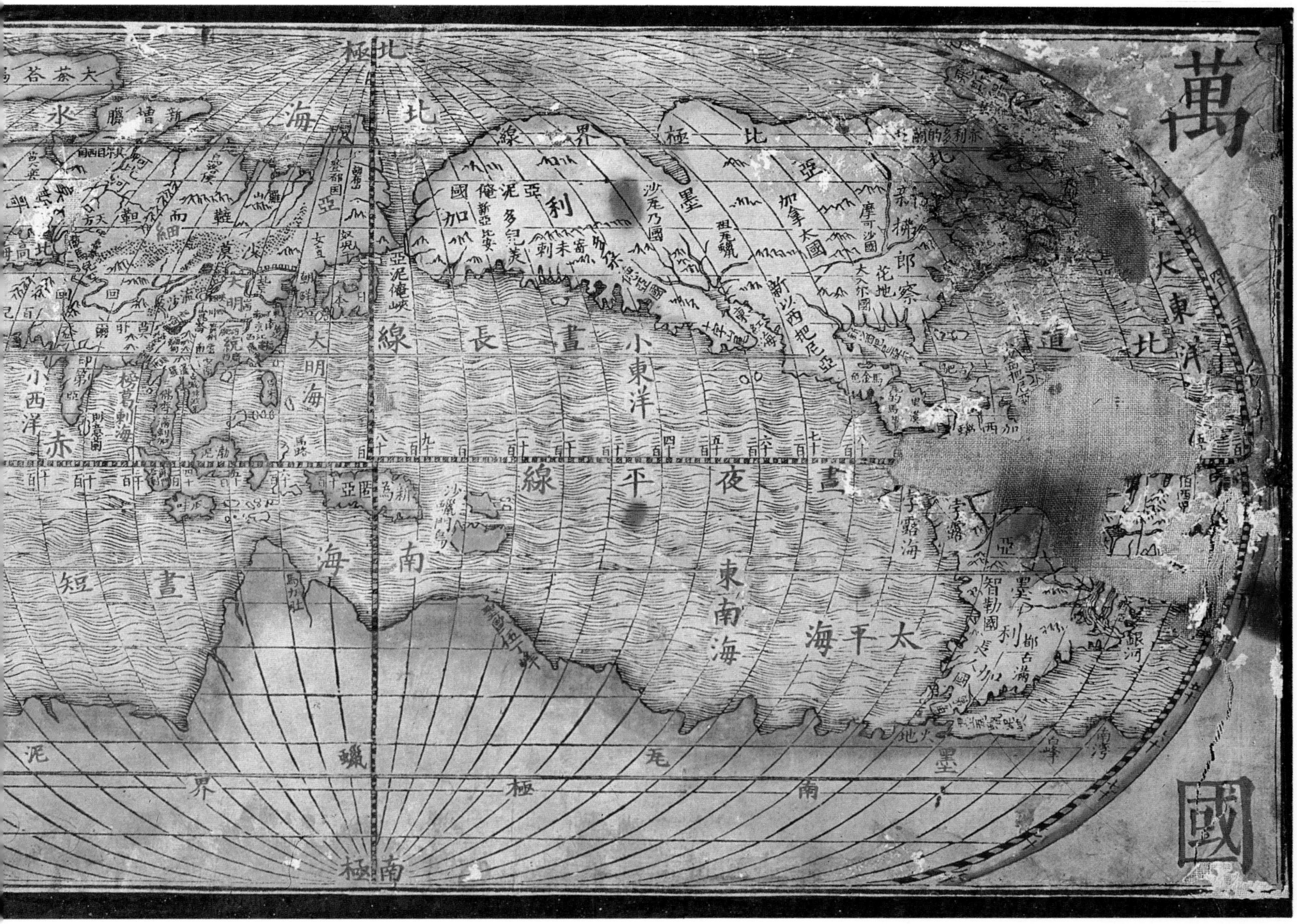

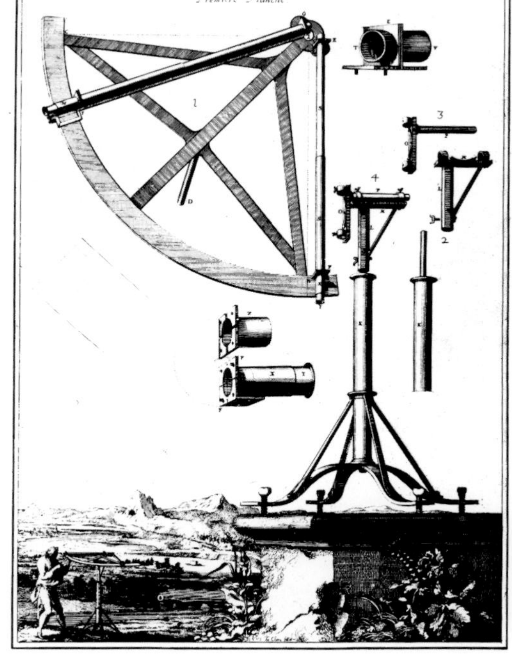

French engravings of some tools of the surveyor's trade. The French at this time excelled in the art of scientific survey. One of their greatest astronomer-surveyors, Jean Picard, designed these quadrants and the zenith selector (left drawing, top).

Plate XCI

'Novissima Totius Terrarum Orbis Tabula,' John Seller, *c* 1673. Seller, Hydrographer to Charles II and James II, produced numerous terrestrial and marine atlases. This engraved map of the world, included in his 1675 *Atlas Maritimus,* is basically Dutch in spirit, for Seller much admired Flemish cartography and often put Dutch maps into his atlases.
445 x 550 mm.

Plate XCII

'New France' (detail), G F Pesca, late seventeenth century. Part of a copperplate map commissioned by the church for missionaries in the North American interior. The term Huron in the inset appears to refer more to the Ontario shoreline than to the lake, which is called Mare Dulce. The territory of the Algonquins is accurately located, and the drawings of Indians, animals and birch bark lodges and canoes are convincing. Note the converted Indian family in the upper left corner.
515 x 400 mm. (overall).

HVRONVM EXPLICATA TABVLA
OÑENDITIAQVI
OENTARONK LACVS
TIONONTATE pop:
Seu Natio Vulgo del tabaco
Scala leucarum francicarum horariarum
Scala Milliar. Italicorum Mediocrium
lacus Ontario
Scala leucarum francicarum horariarum
Scala Milliar. Italicarum Comunium vel Mediocrium
LACVS SVPERIOR
LACVS OZOLARVM
MARE DVLCE
ALGOM
CHINI
TIONNONTATE
GÄSISTAGVE
ONTARIO lacus seu SANCTI LVDOVICI
HIRO
NOVVM BELGIVM
NOVA SVECIA
VIR GI NIA
Concilium
Erie populi

Plate XCIII

'Nova Totius Terrarum Orbis Tabula,' Frederick de Wit, 1665. This lushly decorated Dutch copperplate world map is notable for the political bias it betrays in its depiction of North America. Despite the fact the Dutch and English were then fighting a naval war, de Wit seems to have considered Louis XIV's expansionist France the greater menace, for the name Nouvelle France appears nowhere on the continent and eastern Canada is now called New Brittannia.
430 x 580 mm.

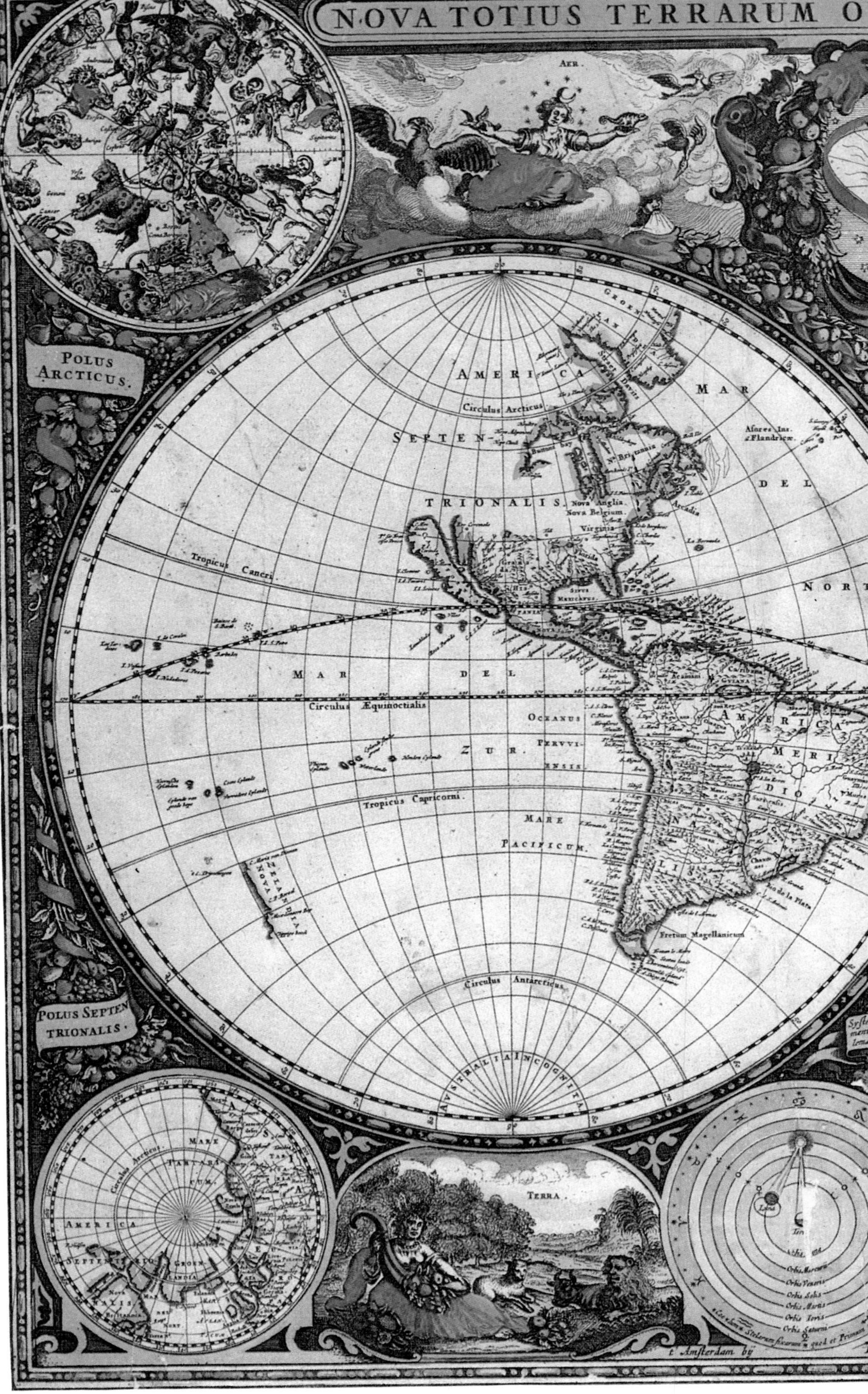

TABULA AUCTORE F. DE WIT.
IGNIS.
POLUS ANTARCTICUS.
MARE TARTARICUM.
OCEANUS CHINENSIS.
Ilas de las Vealas.
Archipelagus S.Lazari.
OCEANUS ÆTHIOPICUS
MAR DI INDIA.
HOLLANDIA NOVA.
POLUS MERIDIONALIS.
AUSTRALIA INCOGNITA
AQUA.
Fretum Magellanicū
Fretum le Maire
T.ª del Fuego
Circulus Antarcticus.
Orbis Lunæ et Terræ
Orbis Martis
Orbis Iovis
Orbis Saturni
Stellarum fixarum
Sphæra mundi
inde Witte Paskaert, 1660

Plate XCIV

'Totius Americae Descriptio,' Frederick de Wit, 1690. The biases de Wit showed on his earlier map (Plate XCIII) are both more explicit and quite different on this copper-engraved New World map. France is now awarded all the area between southern Labrador and Florida, and, with the exception of Newfoundland, English claims along the east coast are ignored. 420 x 490 mm.

GROENLANDIA
VETUS
TERRA LABRADOR
NOVA BRITANNIA
OCEANVS
Açores Insulæ
alias Flandricæ
ATLANTICVS
MAR
DEL
NORT
MARE
VIRGINIÆ
Isles Bermudes
Porto Sancto
Canariæ Insf.
Fortunatæ
Inf. de Cabo Verde
AFRICÆ PARS
AMERICA
BRASILIA
MERIDIO
OCEANVS
ÆTHIOPICVS
P. de Wit excudit.

Plate XCV

'Totius Terrarum Orbis Tabula,' Joan Blaeu, 1662. A world map from the Blaeu's great 12-volume *Atlas Maior.* The North American geography is perfunctory, with the Greenland-Canada link shown, the Great Lakes omitted and the issue of Californian insularity somewhat fudged. In its decoration the map is painterly, but the intricate detail that made some earlier Blaeu maps so fascinating is missing. 460 x 590 mm.

ARVM ORBIS TABVLA. Auctore IOANNE BLAEV.

Plate XCVI

'L' America Settentrionale,' Giovanni de Rossi, 1687. De Rossi's map is a slightly edited version of a map drawn earlier by the French mapmaker Guillaume Sanson. Here the political divisions are distinctly pro-French, with Nova Francia embracing most of the eastern half of North America. England is given only upper Labrador and Hudson Bay, New England and Virginia, while Connecticut, New York, New Jersey and Delaware are implicitly given to the Dutch and Swedes, though neither now seriously claimed the area. In addition, France gets 'French Florida' (part of South Carolina and Georgia). Note how carefully the island of California is detailed and that Alaska and western Canada are given to Denmark.
380 x 535 mm.

Settentrione
OCEANO SETTENTRIONALE
GRONELANDA
VIEIL GRONELANDA
Baffins Bay
Stretto di Davis
TERRE ARTICHE
Cumberland Isles
Hoye Sanderson
Horn Sound
Wemeas Isle
London Coste
Bare Barbier
C. Chidley
Warwick Forland
Gilberts Sound
Lancaster
Briolsheuen
I. de Resolution
Buttons I.
C. Conforte
C. Chrystian
C. Farwel
C. Discord
Elisabeth Forland
Goede hope
Forbisher
Hudson
MAR CHRISTIANO
ESTOTILANDA ò TERRA DE LABORADOR ò
NADA ouero
NUOVA BRETAGNA INGLESE
ESTOTILANDA DANESE
Schild Paads
Gemsse Bay
Orange Bay
Hollandsche Bay
Lageboeck
Bare Sauvage
Port de Quadier
Brest
Bell Isle
de Grace
C. Fichet
GOLFO DI S. LORENZO
NUOVA I.
TERRA
dela Conceptio
C. de S. Francesco
la Grand Banc
la Piccola Banc
Islandа I.
Horn
Langa ness
Skalholt
Reka ness
Cerchio del Polo Articho
I. de Schetland
Isole del Ferro
ISOLE BRITANNICHE
I. Orcades
SCOTIA
IRLANDA
Edinbou
Dublin
Westernes I.
Primo Meridiano
MAR DI NUOVA FRANCIA
MAR DI CANADA ò NUOVA FRANCIA ouero
MAR DEL NORT
OCEANO ATLANTICO
Oriente
I. de Cuervo
I. Gratiosa
I. Terzere
I. Fayal
I. de Pico
I. S. Miguel
S. Maria
ISOLE ASSORE
Isles Bermudes
LESAGUENAY
QUEBEC
CANADA
I. S. Ioan
I. de Sable
Aux loups Marins
Port Rossignol
Bristou
Londen
Plymouth
Amsterdam
L. Dockvois
L. di S. Louis
Lago de Frontenac
Lago de Ilinois
Nation Auteu
Forte Maimis
Maimis Nat.
Rio Ouabache
NUOVA FRANCIA
Bella Riviera
Lago Palaxi
C. Charles
Chesapeac
Pomejoc
Iourdain
Carolina
S. Agostino
Barra de Malancas
Barra de Mosquitos
Spiritu Santo
FLORIDA
TEGESTA PROV.
MAR DEL MESSICO ouero
MAR DI MESSICO
ISOLE LUCAYE
Lucayoneque
Ciguatao
Cuarao
Guanahanio
S. Saluador
Triangulo
Somana
Yumeta
Maiagnana
Caicos
M. Christo
Anguilla
Cotomere
Cerchio del Tropico di Cancro
los Alcaxanes
C. S. Antonio
de Cotoche
Cozumel
YUCATAN
ISOLE ANTILLE
Caiman grande
Caimanes
Sevilla dell Oro
Jamaica I.
Bueras
Serranilha
Serrana
Roncador
Golfo de Honduras
HONDURAS
Trugillo
NICARAGUA
S. Catelina
S. Andero
Cartagena
Porto Rico
S. Domingo
Vaca
ISOLE BARLOVENTO
Anguilla
Barbada
Antigoa
Guadalupe
Margalante
la Dominique
la Martinique
S. Lucia
S. Vincent
la Barbonde
Granadilla
Granada
Tabago
la Trinidad
NUOVA SPAGNA
ISOLE CARIBE
ISOLE SOTTO VENTO
Bon Ayre
Curacao
la Margarita
S. Martha
Rio de la Hacha
Coro
Panama
Nata
Darien
de Paria ò Orenoque
AMERICA MERIDIONALE
Giorgio Widman Sculp.
Mezzo 29° di
285 295 300 305 310 315 320 325 330 335 340
80 75 70 65 60 55 50 45 40 35 30 25 20 15 10

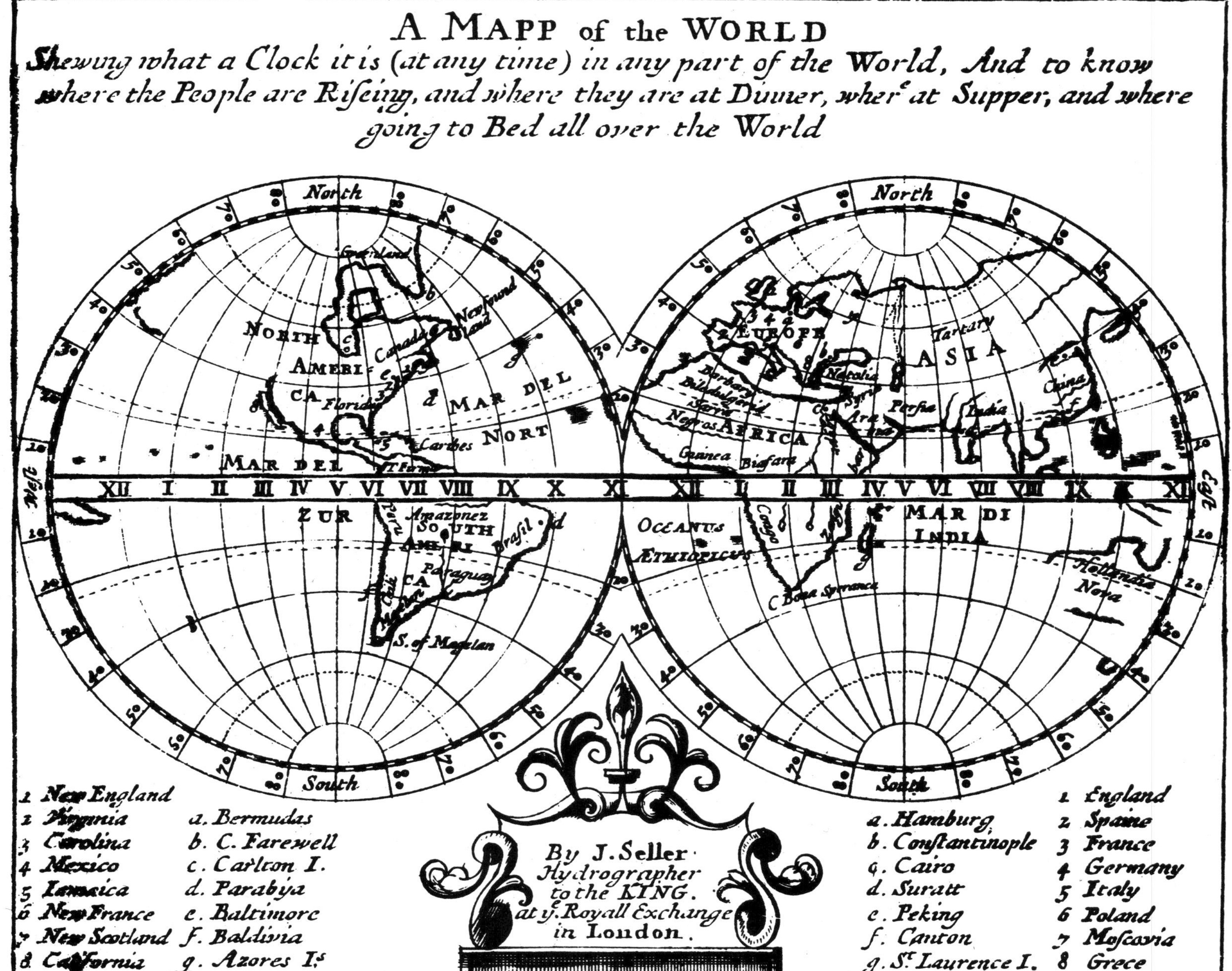

Plate XCVII

'A Mapp of the World,' John Seller, 1685. This little copperplate comes from Seller's 1685 book *New System of Geography*. It divides the world into time zones calculated from the prime meridian and international date line.
125 x 150 mm.

Plate XCVIII

'Canada Orientale,' P Coronelli, 1690. A Jesuit priest, Coronelli was the Cartographer of the Republic of Venice in 1690. This copperplate map of the St Lawrence Gulf, Terra Nova (Newfoundland) and Acadia (Nova Scotia), with its careful depiction of the location of the major fishing grounds, is doubtless derived from French sources. 390 x 540 mm.

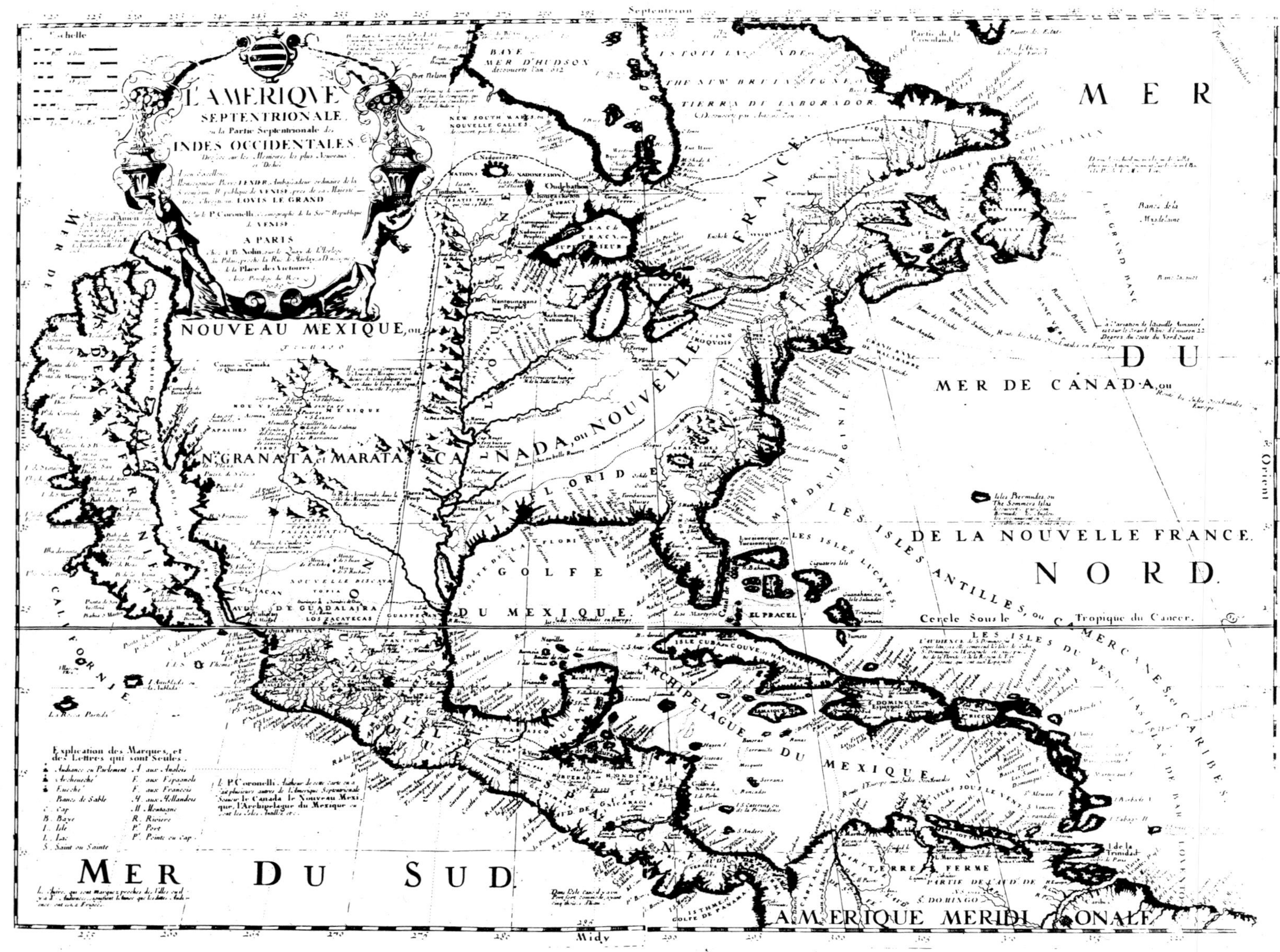

Plate XCVIX

'L' Amérique Septentrionale,' P Coronelli, 1689. This Coronelli map of North America was engraved and published in France. Like the Rossi map shown on Plate XCVI it appears to be based on a Sanson model.
430 x 590 mm.

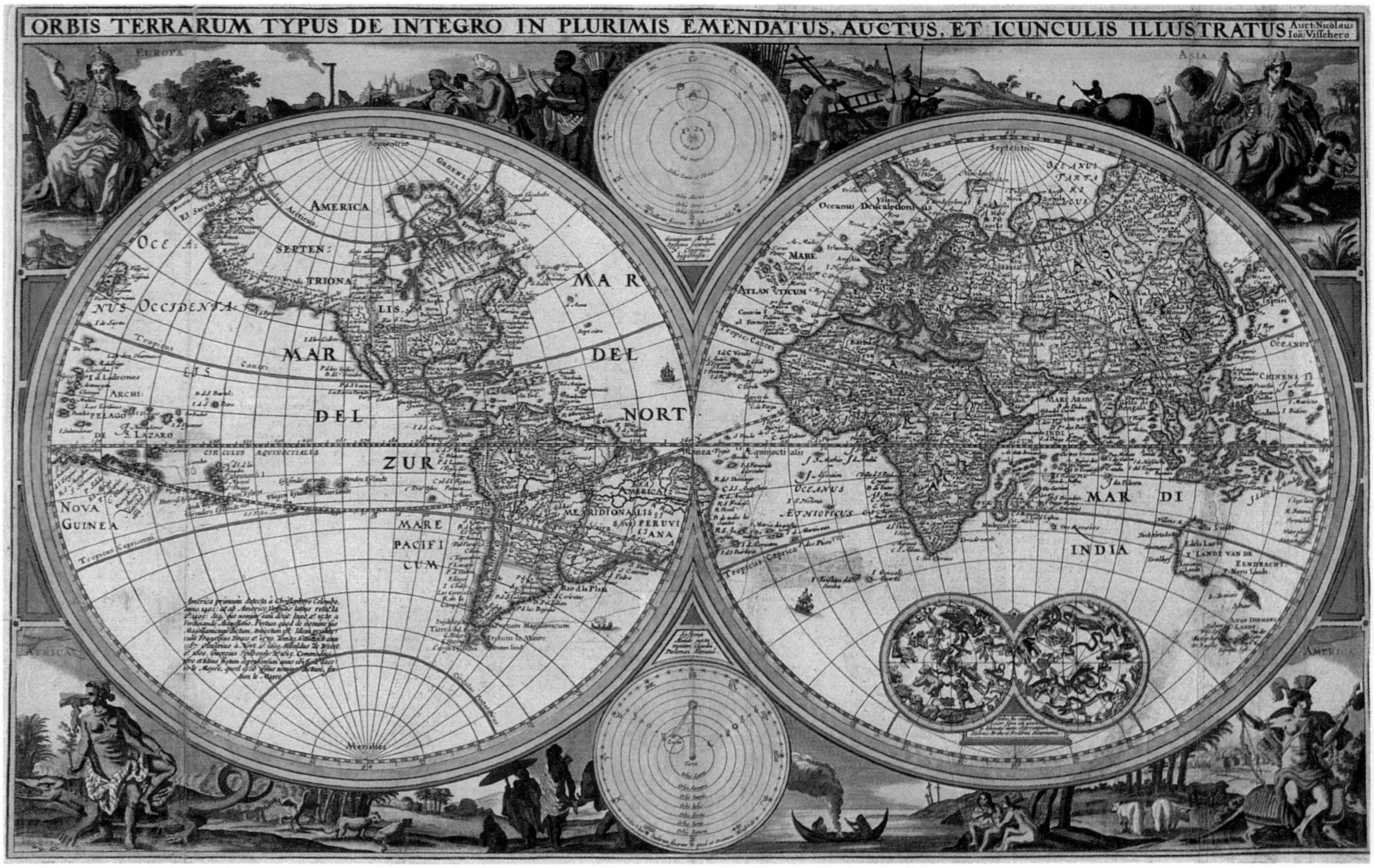

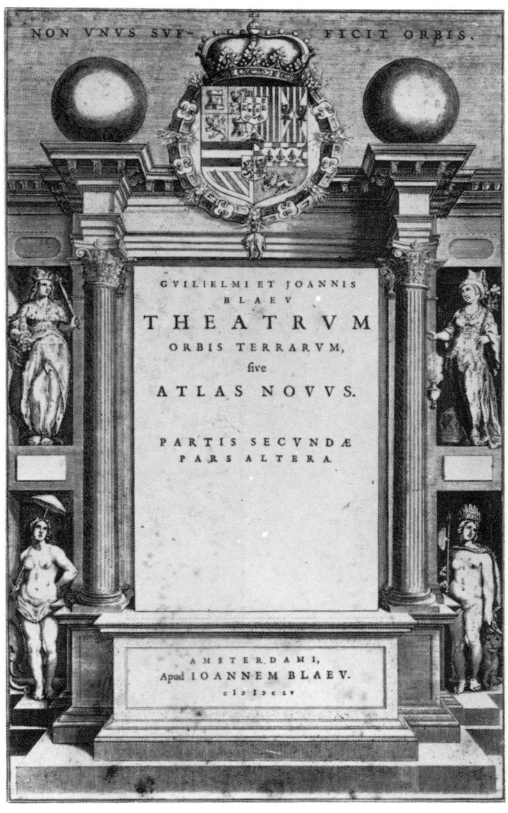

Plate C

'Orbis Terrarum,' Nikolaus Visscher, 1690. This ornate Visscher world map adds little to geographic knowledge of North America (it does not even show the Great Lakes), but it does indicate political divisions. Like most maps of the period, it shows much too much continental breadth. Estimates tended to vary between about 150 and 170 degrees, whereas the reality is closer to 115 degrees.
430 x 580 mm.

The frontispiece and an illustration from different editions of the Blaeu's Theatrum. *There were five major editions of the work, or if one counts foreign language versions separately, 20.*

Plate CI

'North Atlantic,' anon, late sixteenth century. This parchment portolano of an earlier age is placed here as a reminder of the enormous increase in geographic knowledge that occurred during the seventeenth century. The depiction of Labrador, Greenland and Iceland (with a non-existent island lying between the latter) seems almost whimsical by late seventeenth century standards. But the drawings of the two English galleons are exquisite and valuable to naval historians. 380 x 410 mm. Greenwich Naval Museum, London.

Plate CII

'America Settentrionale,' P Coronelli, 1696. Another Coronelli copy of a map by the Sansons, this copperplate, which purports to show western North America as understood in 1688, was published in Venice in 1696. Its most notable feature is the large amount of trans-Mississippian detail it supplies, most of it nonsense. 450 x 610 mm.

Settentrione
AMERICA SETTENTRIONALE
Colle Nuoue Scoperte sin all'Anno 1688
Diuisa nelle sue parti secondo lo stato presente,
e Descritta
dal P. Mrô Coronelli M.C.
Cosmografo della Sereniss.ma Repub.ca di Venezia.
Dedicata
All'Ill.mo et Reu.mo Monsig. Fehe Antonio Marsily,
Archidiacono della Catedrale di Bologna
MARE D'HUDSON, ò CHRISTIANO
Scoperto dagl' Danesi
NUOUO MEXICO, ò
NUOUO MEXICO
N. GRANATA, e MARATA
Scoperta da Spagnuoli l'anno 1598
LA NUOUA BISCAIA
IL MARE DI CALIFORNIA
GOLFO DEL
Occidente
Oriente
MARE DEL SUD
Mezzo Giorno

A high-sterned Dutch ship of the late seventeenth century.

North American Maps 1700-1800

The number of maps devoted to North America increased dramatically in the eighteenth century. The greatest increase was in regional maps—hardly surprising, since the level of colonization was now such that it had produced a fierce armed rivalry between England and France, and the value of both military and boundary maps was at a premium.

As before, many of these detailed regional maps found their way into the atlases of the day, and the information they provided helped to improve the overall quality of general mapping as well. But not uniformly. It is astonishing, given the amount of geographic knowledge available by mid-century, how inaccurate some continental maps could be even in the 1790s. To be sure, this was partly a matter of poor communication. The supposed insularity of California, for example, had been disproven in 1701, but maps continued to show California as an island well into the 1750s, even, indeed, after Ferdinand VII of Spain had gone to the trouble of issuing a royal decree in 1747 to the effect that California was definitely part of the mainland.

In general, eighteenth-century maps of North America were quite accurate about most of the eastern littoral (with the possible exception of Florida, which seems always to have been a problem) and displayed a steadily increasing knowledge of the interior up to about the longitude of the Mississippi. The Pacific coast, too, was fairly well mapped up to about the latitude of the Juan de Fuca Strait, though proper mapping of the Northwest coast had to await the explorations of Cook in 1778 and of Vancouver in 1792-4. But the trans-Mississippi interior still was largely unknown, and would remain so until the following century.

As usual, where knowledge was wanting fantasy flourished. An interesting example of this is Jefferys' 1768 map (Plate CLIX), reproduced in Diderot's *Encyclopédie* in 1780, which speculates that the Queen Charlotte and Juan de Fuca Straits in all probability represent the western end of that 200-year-old fata morgana, the Northwest Passage.

Jeffery's supposition was based on a story about a Spanish admiral named de Fonte who, in 1640 was said to have discovered a network of rivers and bays emptying into the Pacific at about 53^{0} north latitude. Pursuing this waterway inland, de Fonte encountered an American ship coming west. The owner of the ship, a Major Gibbons of Boston, said that he had sailed it all the way across America from the Atlantic. Not only Jefferys, but also J N de l'Isle and Buache were so taken with this tale that they incorporated it on their maps, as did several lesser lights over a period of nearly 50 years. But the whole story was pure nonsense, concocted by an English journalist named Petiner in 1708. The fact that cartographers of the stripe of Jefferys could do such wonderfully precise work about eastern America makes their credulity about the unknown West all the more striking.

Yet however tempting it may be to dwell on the eighteenth century's cartographic eccentricities, the larger truth is that opportunities for conjecture were disappearing rapidly, and by the century's end there were few left. The time was nearly at hand when mapmaking would become wholly subservient to the authority of comprehensive geographic knowledge. As if in recognition of this, the amount of decoration lavished on eighteenth-century maps declined steadily. From being objects of art they were now well on their way to becoming simply objects of utility.

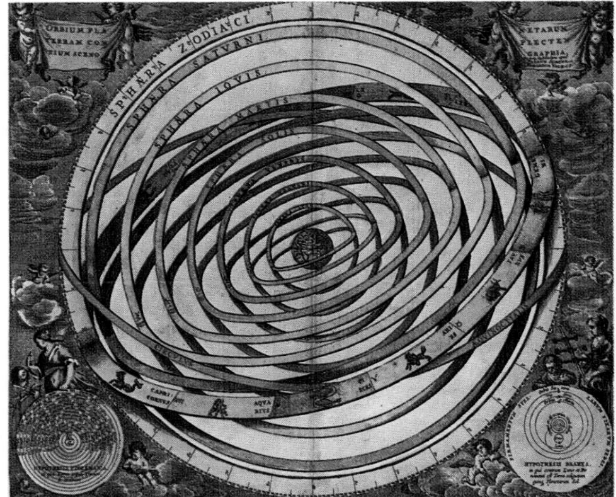

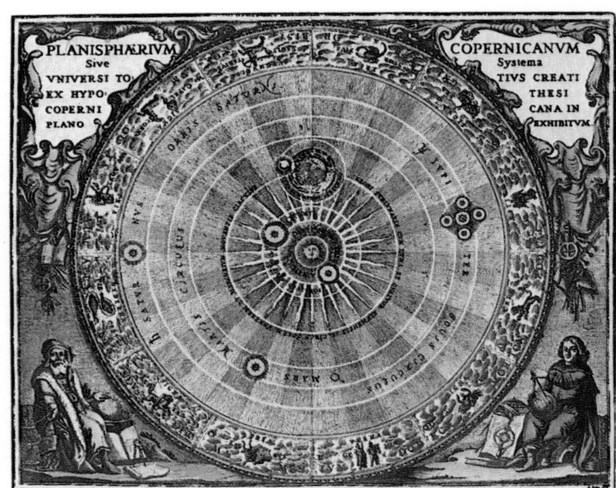

The solar system according to, left, Ptolemy and, right, Copernicus.

The royal arms of France.

The Sun King, Louis XIV of France. The first two Anglo-French wars in North America were fought during his reign (1643-1715).

The royal arms of England.

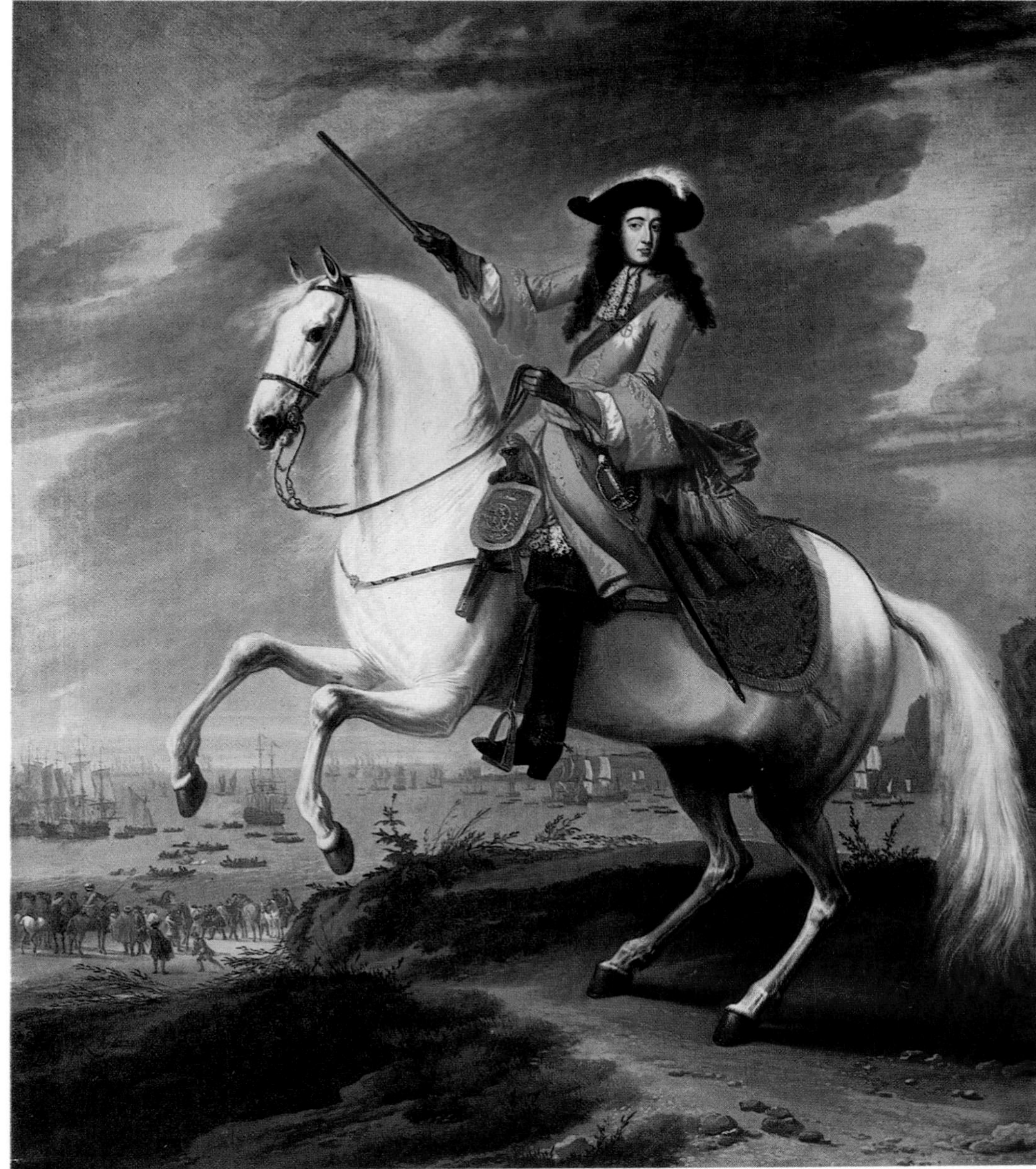

England's William III, the dedicated enemy of Louis XIV, reigned during the first Anglo-French colonial war.

In North America the second Anglo-French colonial war was named 'Queen Anne's War,' since it was fought—1702-13—during all but the final year of the English monarch's reign.

George Washington at the age of 23. (The portrait was painted later, in 1772.) He fought in the fourth and decisive Anglo-French colonial war in North America.

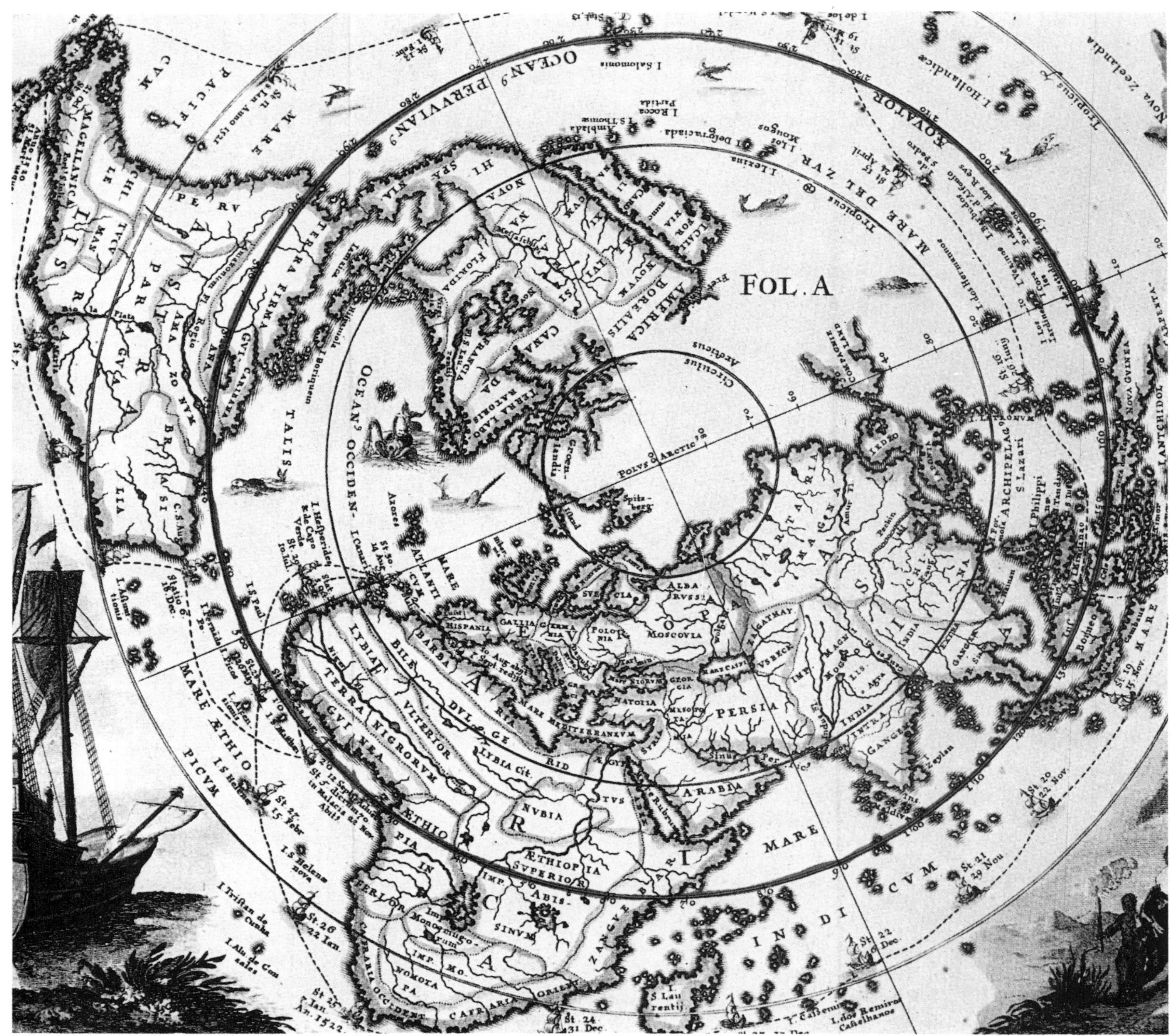

Plate CIII

'Northern Hemisphere,' H Scherer, 1700. This copperplate is from the seven-volume *Atlas Novus dei Sphere,* a 1700 German work largely concerned with showing the diffusion of the Jesuit missions throughout the world. On a polar projection it traces the route taken by Magellan and depicts his ship, *Victoria.*

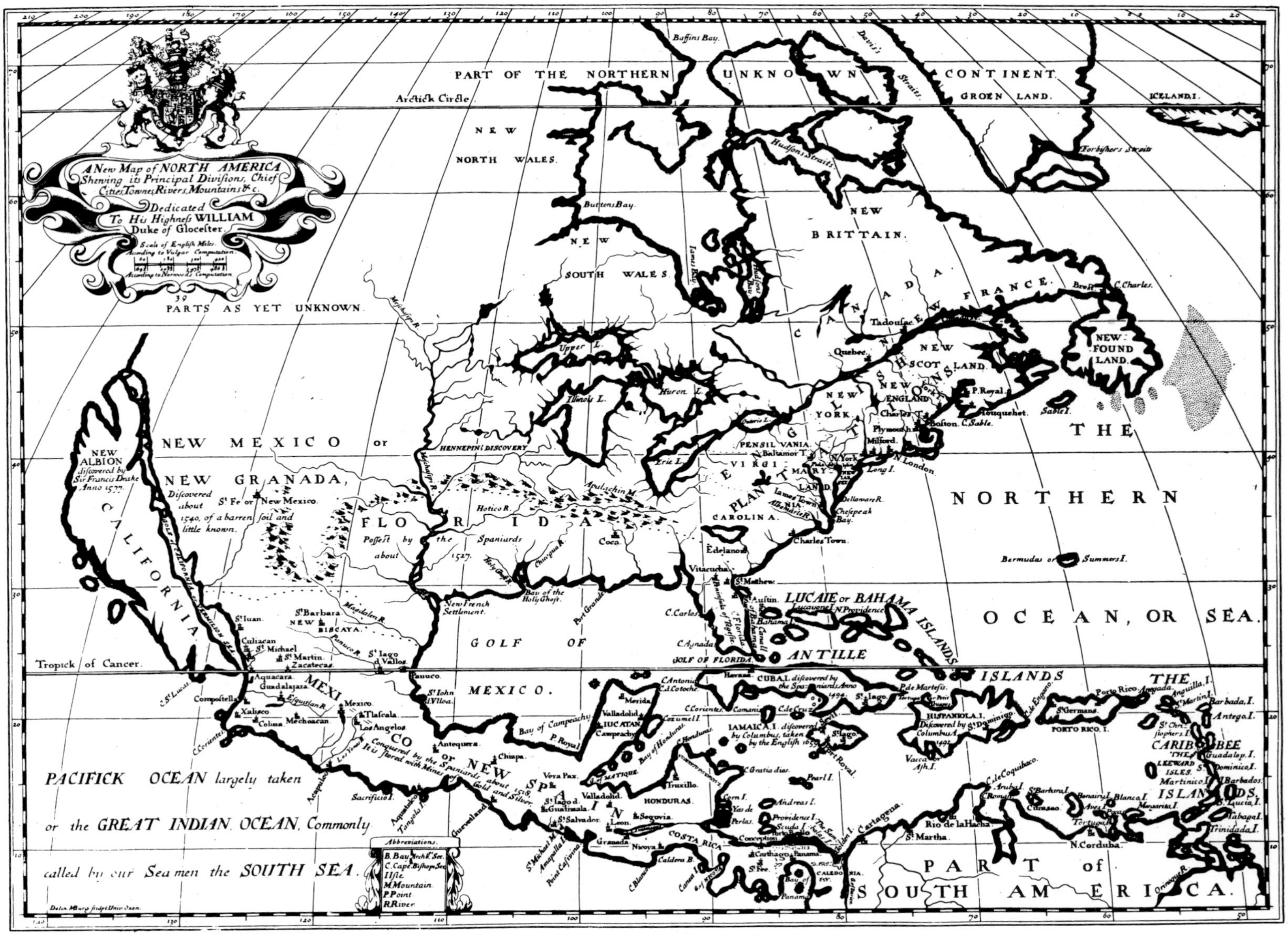

THE
GENERALL HISTORIE
OF
Virginia, New-England, and the Summer
Isles: with the names of the Adventurers,
Planters, and Governours from their
first beginning. Ano: 1584. to this
present 1624.
With the Procedings of those Severall Colonies
and the Accidents that befell them in all their
Journyes and Discoveries.
Also the Maps and Descriptions of all those
Countryes, their Commodities, people,
Government, Customes, and Religion
yet knowne.
Divided into sixe Bookes.
By Captaine John Smith sometymes Governour
in those Countryes & Admirall
of New England.
London
Printed by I.D. and
I.H. for Michael
Sparkes.
1624.

The decorative frontispiece of John Smith's Generall Historie of Virginia, New England and the Summer Isles *of 1624.*

Plate CIV

'A New Map of North America,' Edgar Wells, 1700. This copperplate comes from Wells's *A Set of Ancient Maps and Present Geography.* Although its detail is scant, it does take pains to list the English settlements and claims in America. New Scotland, New England, New York and New Jersey are plainly visible, as are Pennsylvania, Maryland, Virginia and Carolina. On the California island Nova Albion, the site of Drake's landing, is also duly noted.
360 x 490 mm.

Plate CV

'Indiarum Occidentalium,' Louis Renard, 1703. Renard, a French marine cartographer and atlas-maker, worked in the Dutch style and sometimes, as on this Amsterdam-printed map, used Dutch as well as Latin titles. The detail here is very fine, and the mapping of Manhattan, Long Island and the Connecticut shoreline are of special interest.
480 x 560 mm.

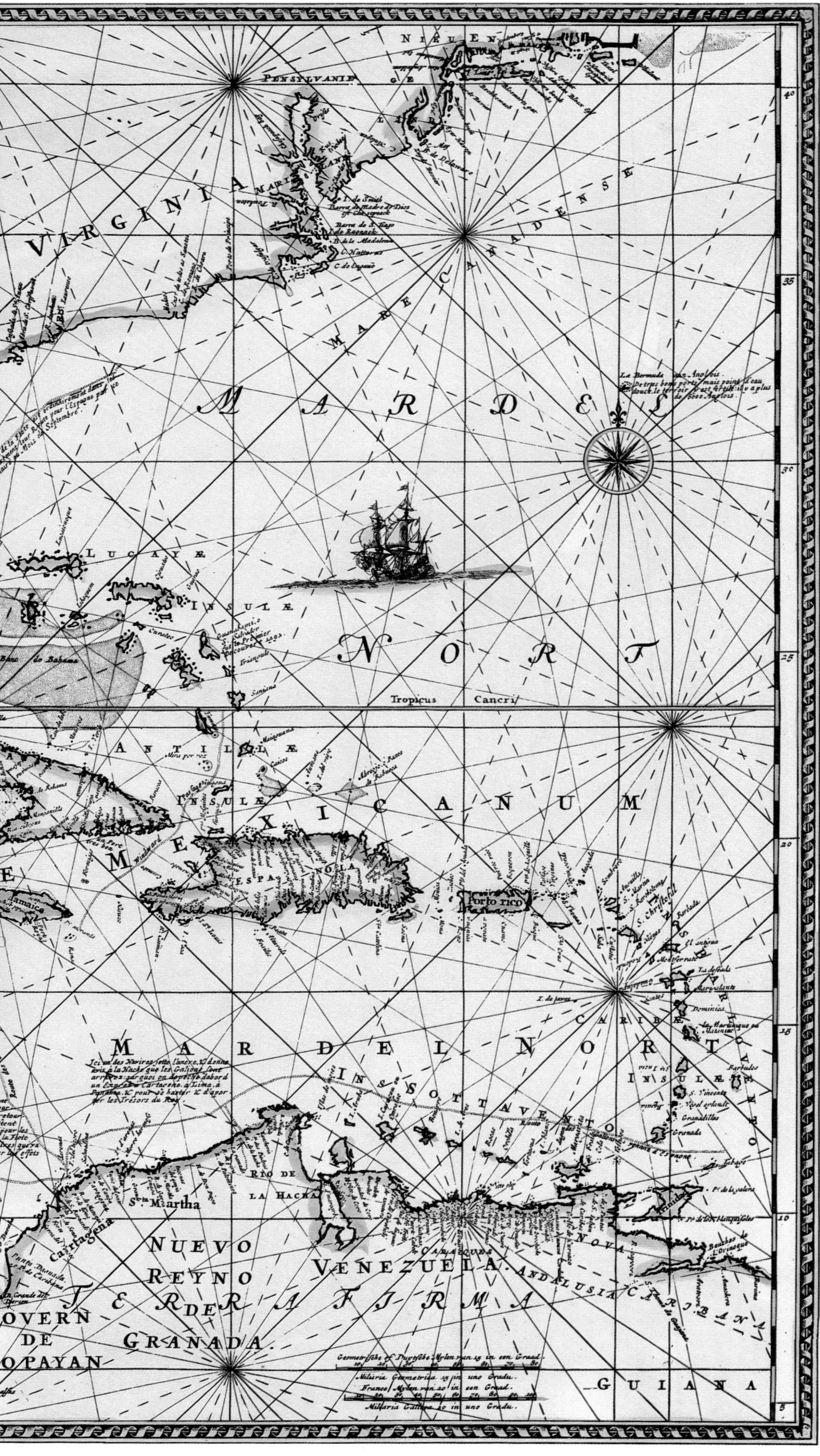

PENSYLVANIE
VIRGINIA
MARE CANADENSE
La Bermude aux Anglois
MAR DE L NORT
LUCAYÆ
INSULÆ
Tropicus Cancri
ANTILLÆ
INSULÆ
MEXICANUM
ESPAÑOLA
Porto rico
Jamaica
CARIBE
INSULÆ
MAR DEL NORT
INSULÆ SOTTAVENTO
RIO DE LA HACHA
S. Martha
Cartagena
NUEVO REYNO DE GRANADA
VENEZUELA
NOVA ANDALUSIA
CARIBANA
TERRA FIRMA
GUIANA
Miliaria Gallica 20 in uno Gradu.

Plate CVI

'Septemtrionaliora Americae,' Louis Renard, 1703. What had and had not been explored is fairly clear from this Renard chart of the Hudson Bay area. The Bay, the Strait, Labrador and the eastern part of Baffin Is make some pretense of accuracy, but western Baffin Is and everything to the north of Baffin Bay are fantasy.
480 x 560 mm.

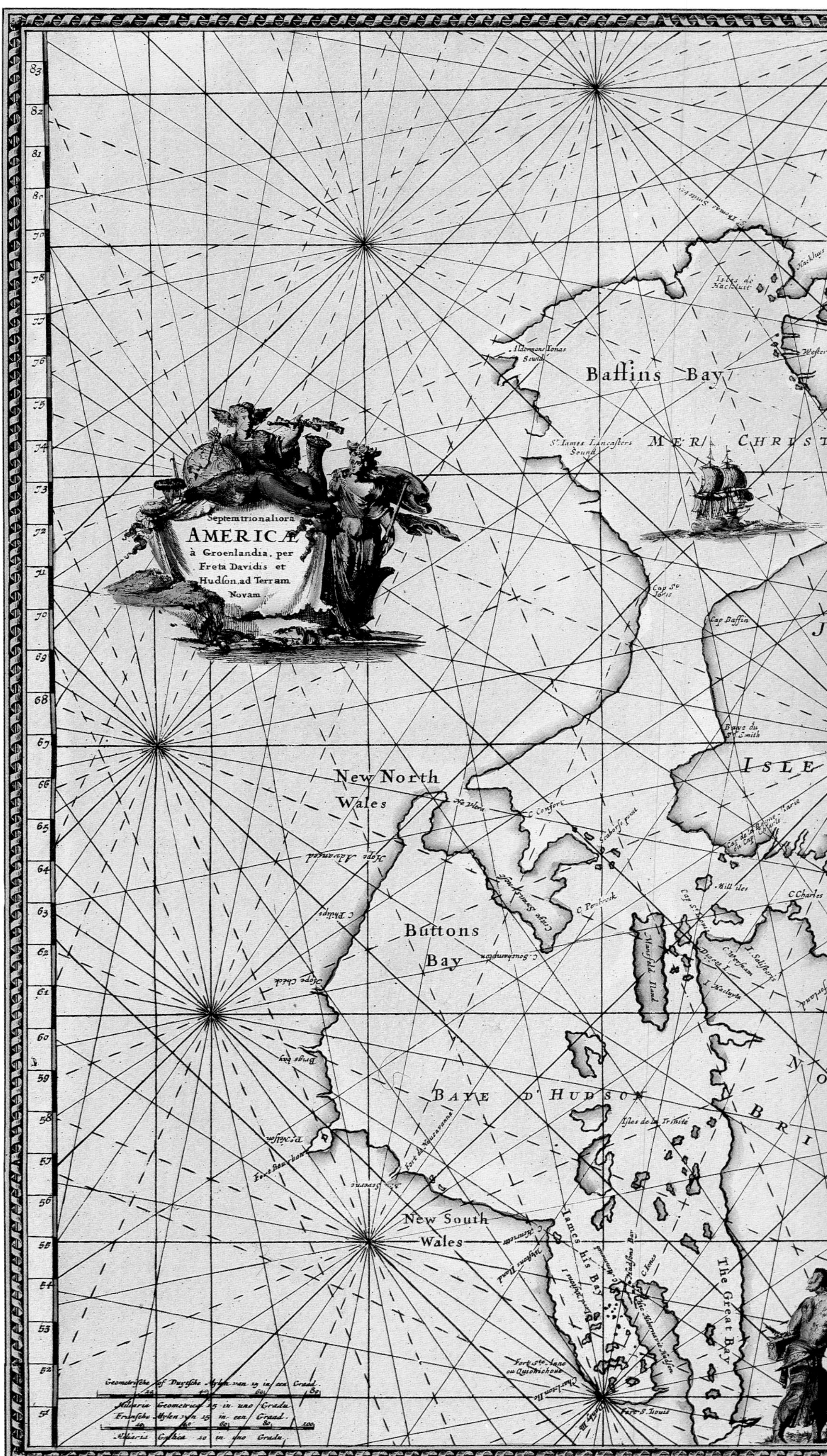

Horne sund
Hope Sanderson
Womens Ile
Vrouwen Eylanden
Londen cast.
G R O E N L A N D
Hier is varsche Visch doode Walvisch Witte Vossen en varsche Salm
Comberlants Bay
S T R E T D A V I S
J A Q U E S
Iland of good fortuyn
Islas Resolution
L A B O R A D O R
Cardinaels hoed
C. Confort
C. Desolation
Staten hoeck
Cap Fareuel
N O V A
F R A N C I A
Grein Blanche
Bolle Ile
C Range
B de Orge
Terra Nova
Golfo St Laurent
MERICA
d door de Straet Davis ende
Hudson tot Terra Neuf

Plate CVII

'Totius Terrarum Orbis,' Louis Renard, 1703. This elaborate Renard planisphere contains nothing new geographically, but the marginal decorations, allegorical renderings of the four elements, are arresting.
580 x 550 mm.

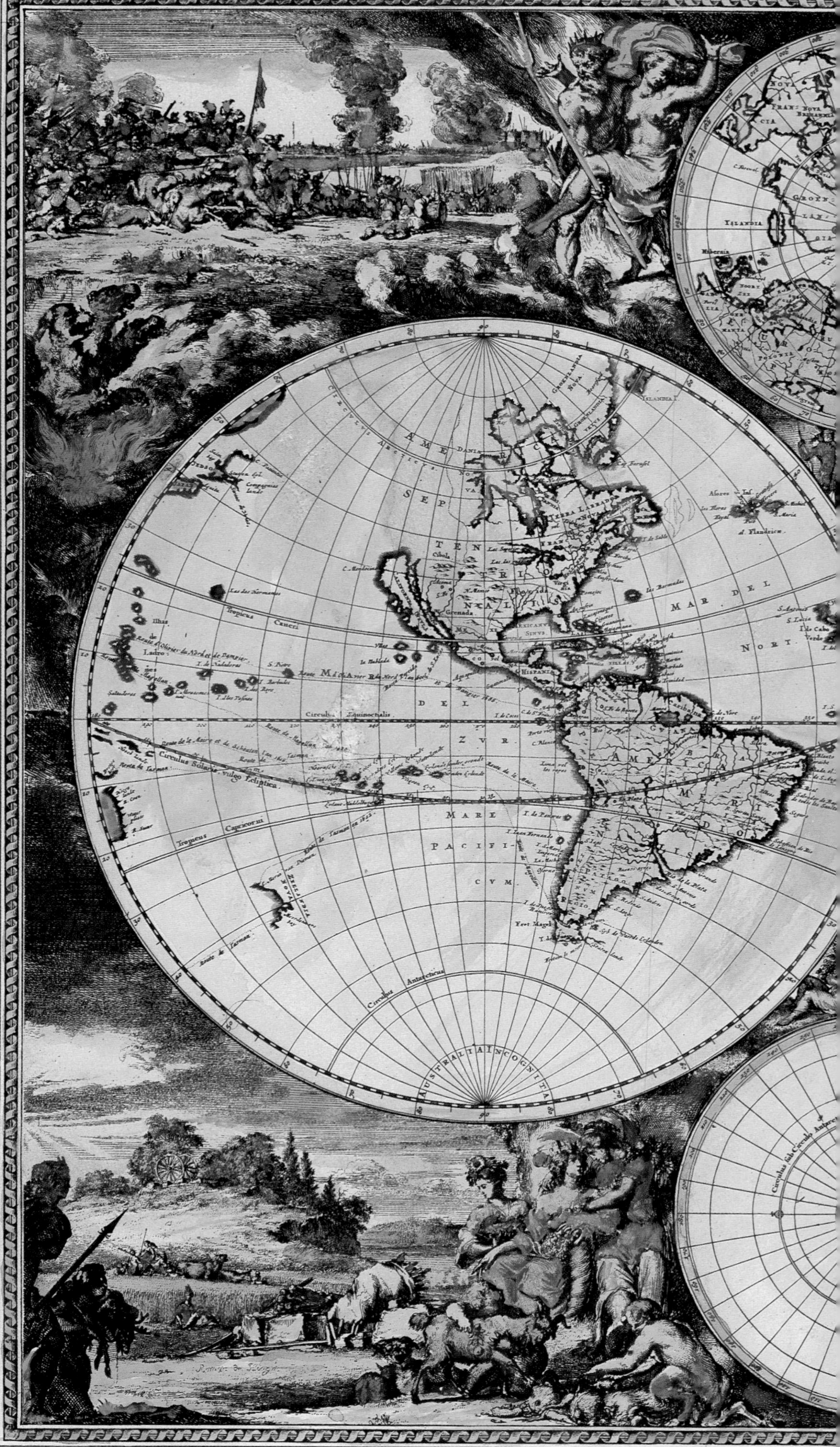

Nova Totius
TERRARUM
ORBIS
TABULA,
ex officina L. Renard
Amstelodami
HOLLANDIA
NOVA
MADAGASCAR
S. LAURENTII
MAR DI INDIA
MARE ARABICUM
ÆTHIOPICUS

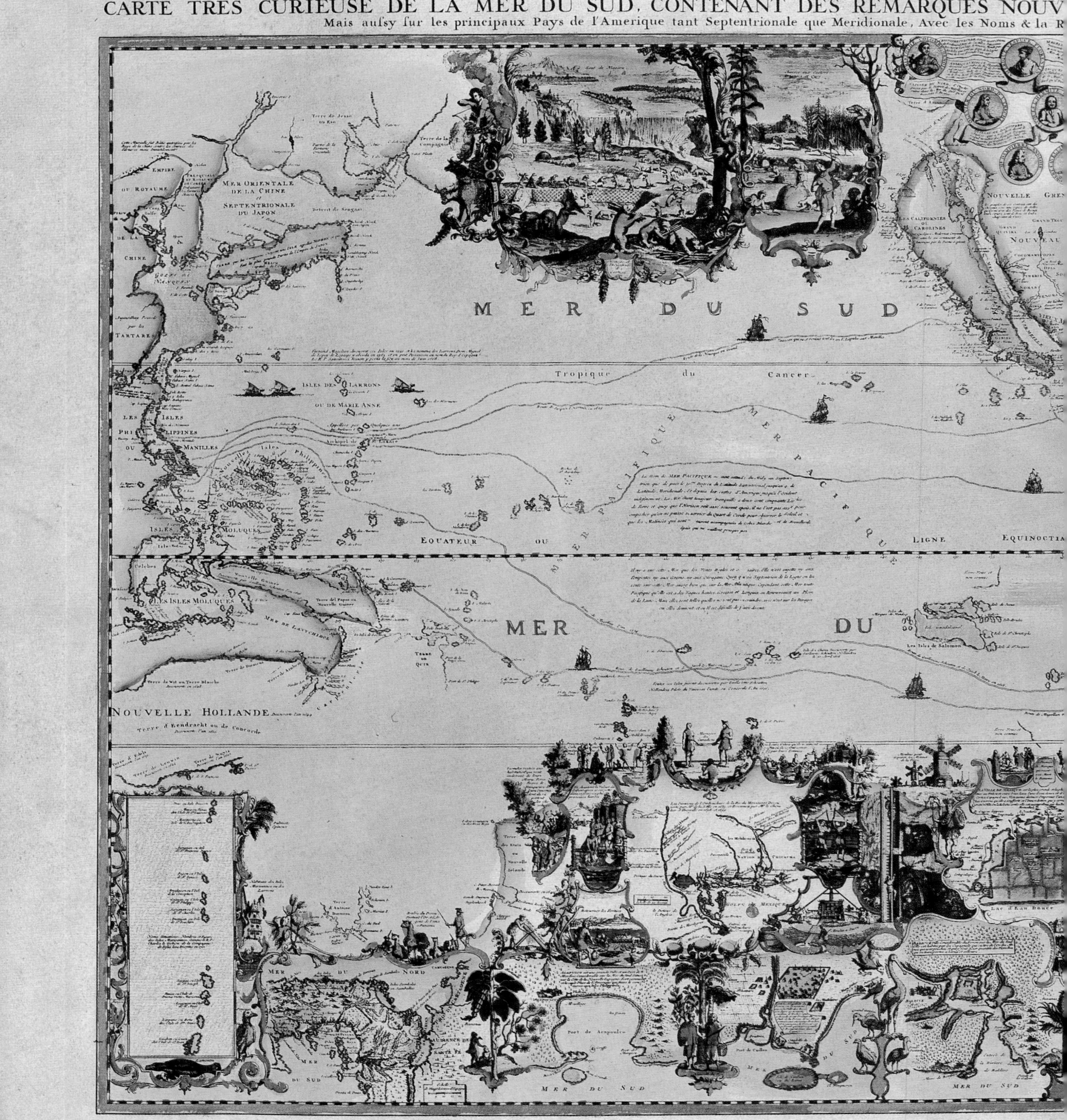

Plate CVIII

'Carte très Curieuse...,' Henri Abraham Chatelain, 1719. Chatelain's large copperplate of the Atlantic and Pacific basins is both lavish in its decoration and full of eccentricity. (Note, for example, how the Solomons appear on the same longitude as the California island.) The scenes and city plans that fill the bottom of the map relate mainly to South and Central America. The vignette in the upper left is of Niagara Falls.
850 x 1450 mm.

ET TRES UTILES NON SEULEMENT SUR LES PORTS ET ILES DE CETTE MER,
yageurs par qui la decouverte en a été faite. Le tout pour l'intelligence Des Dissertations suivantes
MER DU
NORD
SUD
OCEAN
MERIDIONAL
Tropique du Cancer
Tropique du Capricorne
GOLFE DE MEXIQUE
BARBARIE
AMERIQUE
MERIDIONALE
TUCUMAN
PATAGONS
TERRE MAGELLANIQUE
RIO DE LA PLATA
GUIANE ou UAIANE
AMAZONES
BRESIL
COSTE DU BRESIL
FRANCE
ESPAGNE
MEDITERRANEE
ROY. DE FEZ
ROY. DE MAROC
ROY. DE TAFILET
NIGRITIE
GUINEE
ROY. DE BENIN
BASSE GUINEE ou ETATS
ROY. DE CONGO
Royaume de Benguela
ISLES CANARIES
ISLES DU CAP VERD
ISLES ANTILLES
TERRE FERME
NOUVELLE GRENADE
TUNIS
MER DU SUD

The frontispiece of a 1720 edition of Johann Baptiste Homann's Atlas Novus, *first published in 1714.*

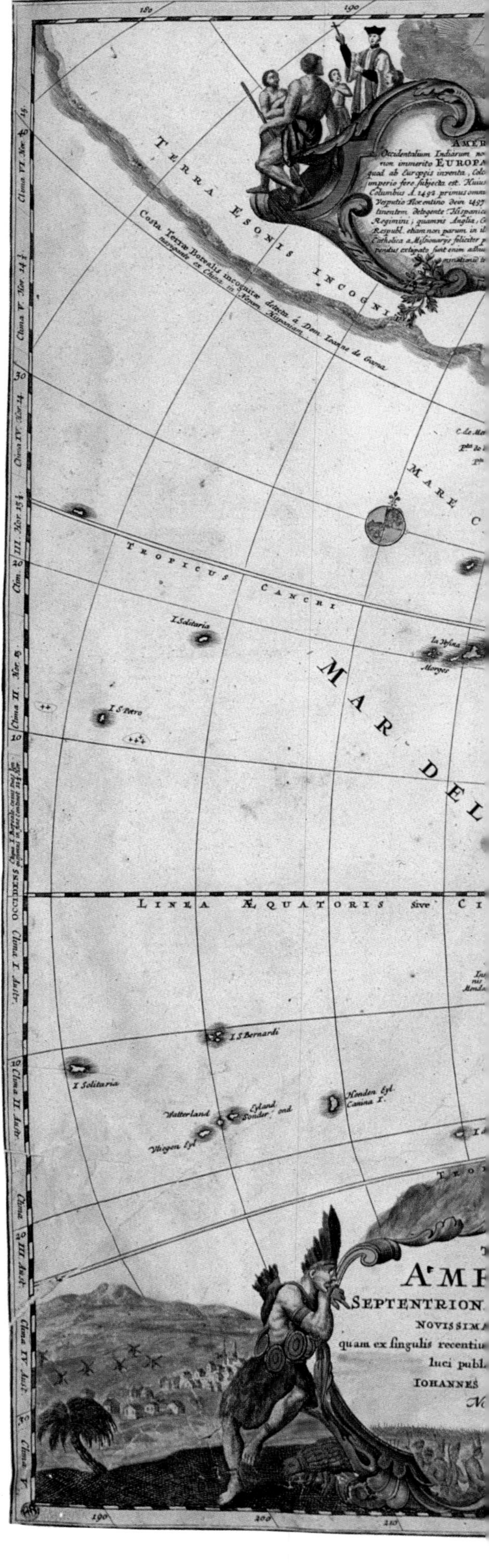

Plate CIX

'Totius Americae,' Johann Baptiste Homann, 1720. The Americas are well represented, according to the lights of the time, on this copperplate map from the 1720 edition of *Atlas Novus.* The scale is too large to permit much detail, but among the North American place names that can be seen is Philadelphia. Again, the Solomon Islands are placed on the same meridian as California.
500 x 684 mm.

AMERICA
SEPTENTRIONALIS
OCEANUS ATLANTICUS
MARE CANADENSE Sive NOVÆ FRANCIÆ
MAR DEL NORT
MAR DEL ZUR
MARE PACIFICUM
MARE HISPANICUM
MARE GALLICUM
EUROPÆ PARS
AFRICÆ PARS
OCEANUS ÆTHIOPICUS
MARE BRASILICUM
MARE PARAGUAIÆ
MARE DE CHILI
MAGELLANICUM
AMAZONUM REGIO
AMERICA MERIDIONALIS
TERRA FIRMA
GUIANA
PARAGUAY
SINUS MEXICANUS
NOVA MEXICO
FLORIDA
CANADA
NOVA FRANCIA
CIRCULUS ARCTICUS
AZORES INS. et FLANDRICÆ
CANARIÆ INS. al. FORTUNATÆ
INS. DE CABO VERDE, al. SALSÆ
Isles Bermudes
ANTILLÆ INS.
MARE VIRGINIÆ
Terra detecta per David Angl. 1680
CAE
MERIDIONALIS
NTATIO
orum Tabulis collectâ
davit
HOMANN

Plate CX

'Novi Belgii,' Matthias Seutter, 1720. This interesting German map is rich in detail of the northeast coast and especially the Hudson Valley, where many of the old Dutch place names are still current. The perspective view of Neu Jorck at the bottom, with its keyed references, is justly famous and was much copied.
490 x 570 mm.

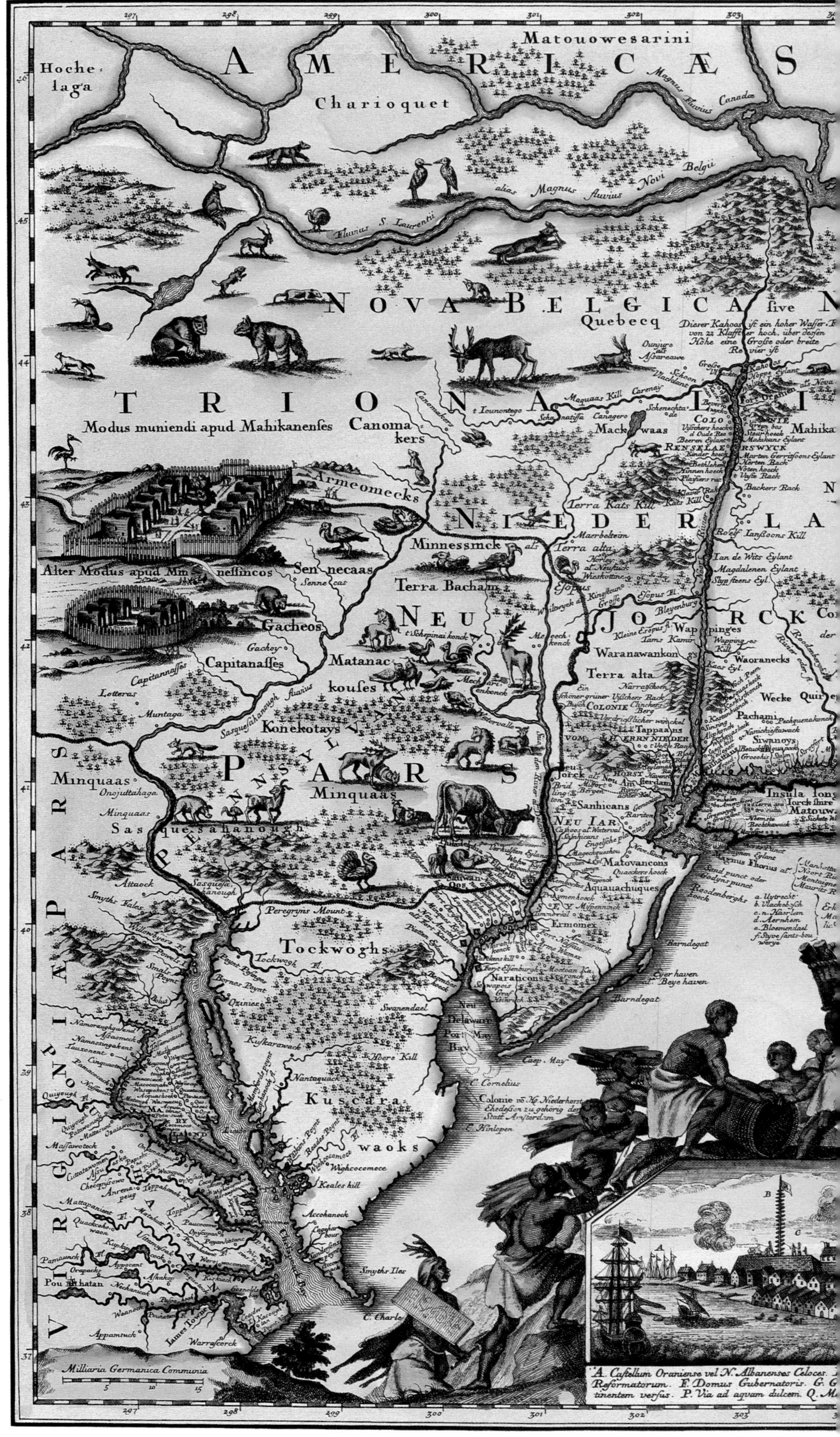

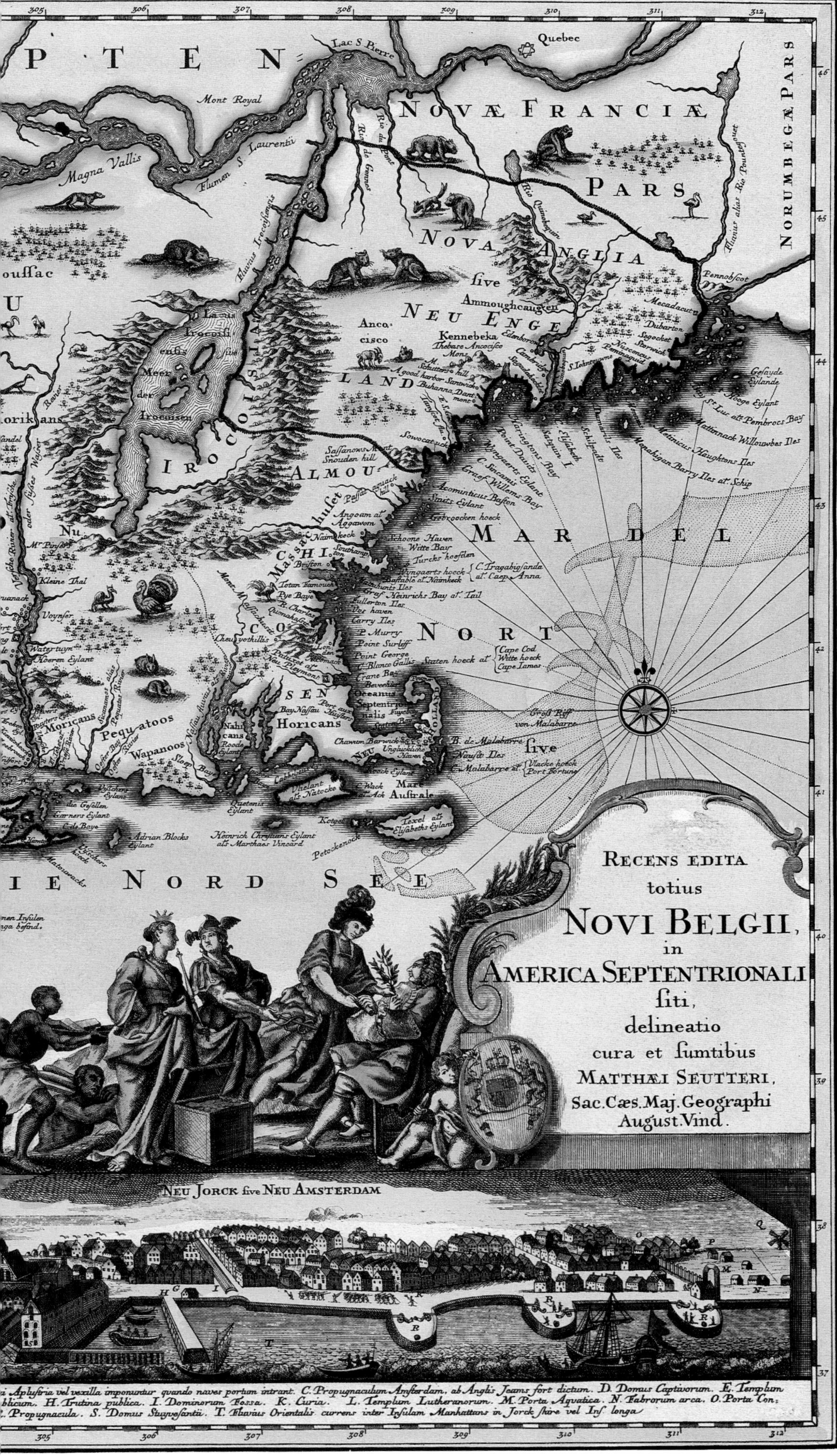

Quebec
Lac S Pierre
Mont Royal
NOVÆ FRANCIÆ
PARS
Magna Vallis
Flumen S Laurentii
NORUMBEGÆ PARS
NOVA ANGLIA
five
NEU ENGELAND
Ammoughcaugen
Kennebeka
IROCOIS
ALMOUCHICOIS
MAR DEL NORT
Cape Cod
Heinrich Christians Eylant als Marthas Vincard
Adrian Blocks Eylant
Texel al. Elyzabeths Eylant
Mare Australe
Pequatoos
Wapanoos
Moricans
SEN Horicans
NIE NORD SEE
RECENS EDITA
totius
NOVI BELGII,
in
AMERICA SEPTENTRIONALI
siti,
delineatio
cura et sumtibus
MATTHÆI SEUTTERI,
Sac. Cæs. Maj. Geographi
August. Vind.
NEU JORCK five NEU AMSTERDAM

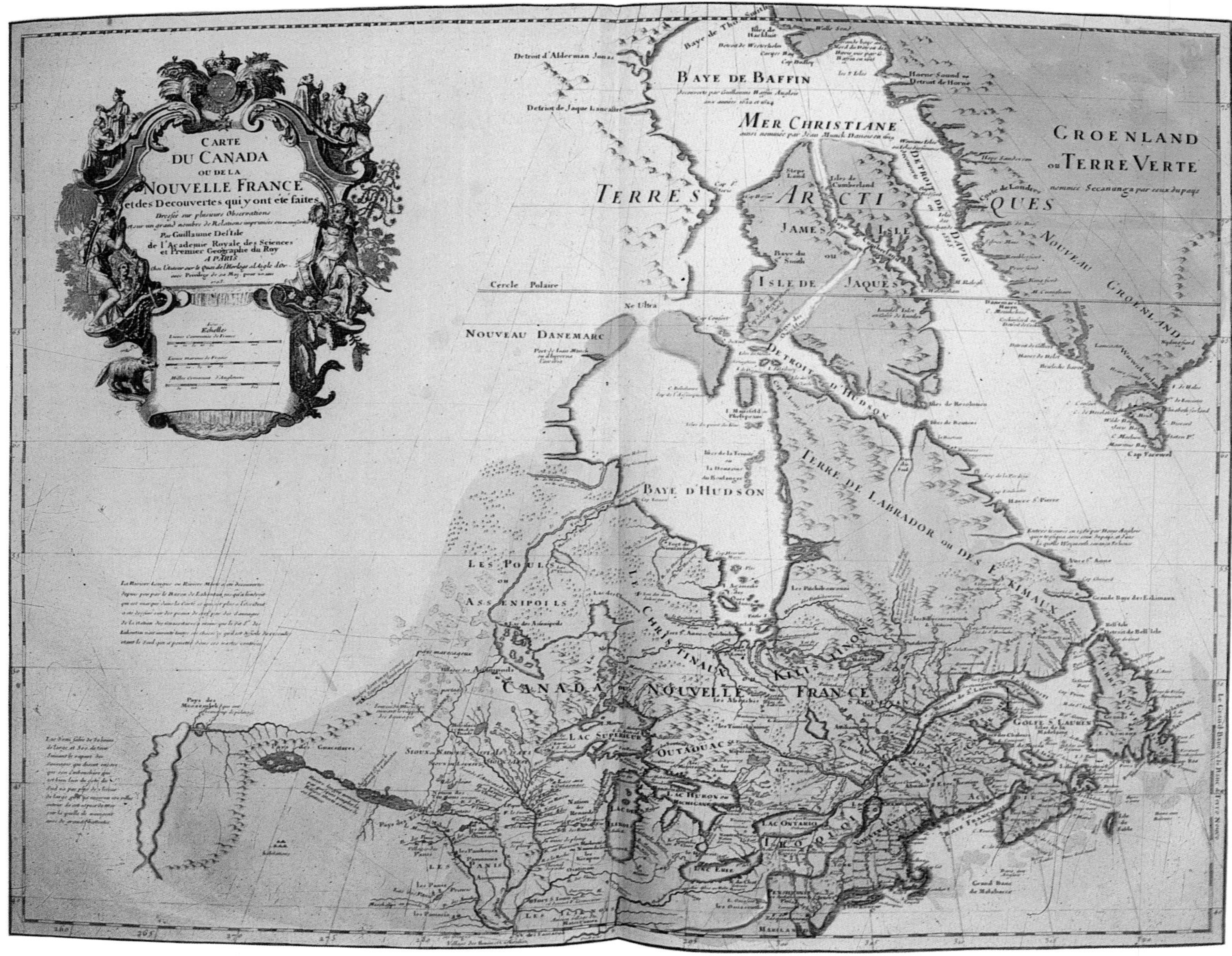

Plate CXI

'Canada,' Guillaume de l'Isle, 1703. This famous de l'Isle map of Canada was almost as, influential as his later 'Louisiane' (Plate CXII). On the plus side, it was the first map to name Detroit, two years after its founding. It correctly sited the Ohio River and connected Lac Assenipoils (Winnepeg) with Hudson Bay. But it also showed the mythical Rivière Longue, a great east-west river that emptied into the upper Mississippi, first hypothesized in 1703 by baron de Lahontan
500 x 650 mm.

Plate CXII

'Louisiane,' Guillaume de l'Isle, 1718. This splendid French map is the first accurately to chart the course of the lower Mississippi and the explorations of de Soto, de Tonty and de St Denis. It is also the first to use the name Texas (Mission de los Teijas). The river's delta and Mobile are shown in the inset, as is New Orleans, founded in 1718.
406 x 510 mm.

Plate CXIII

'Provincae Borealis Americae,' H Scherer, 1720. This crude little map, when compared to the work of such as de l'Isle, is essentially retrograde. Note how the mapmaker attempts to disguise his ignorance of place names by filling the land areas with mountains and trees. 230 x 350 mm.

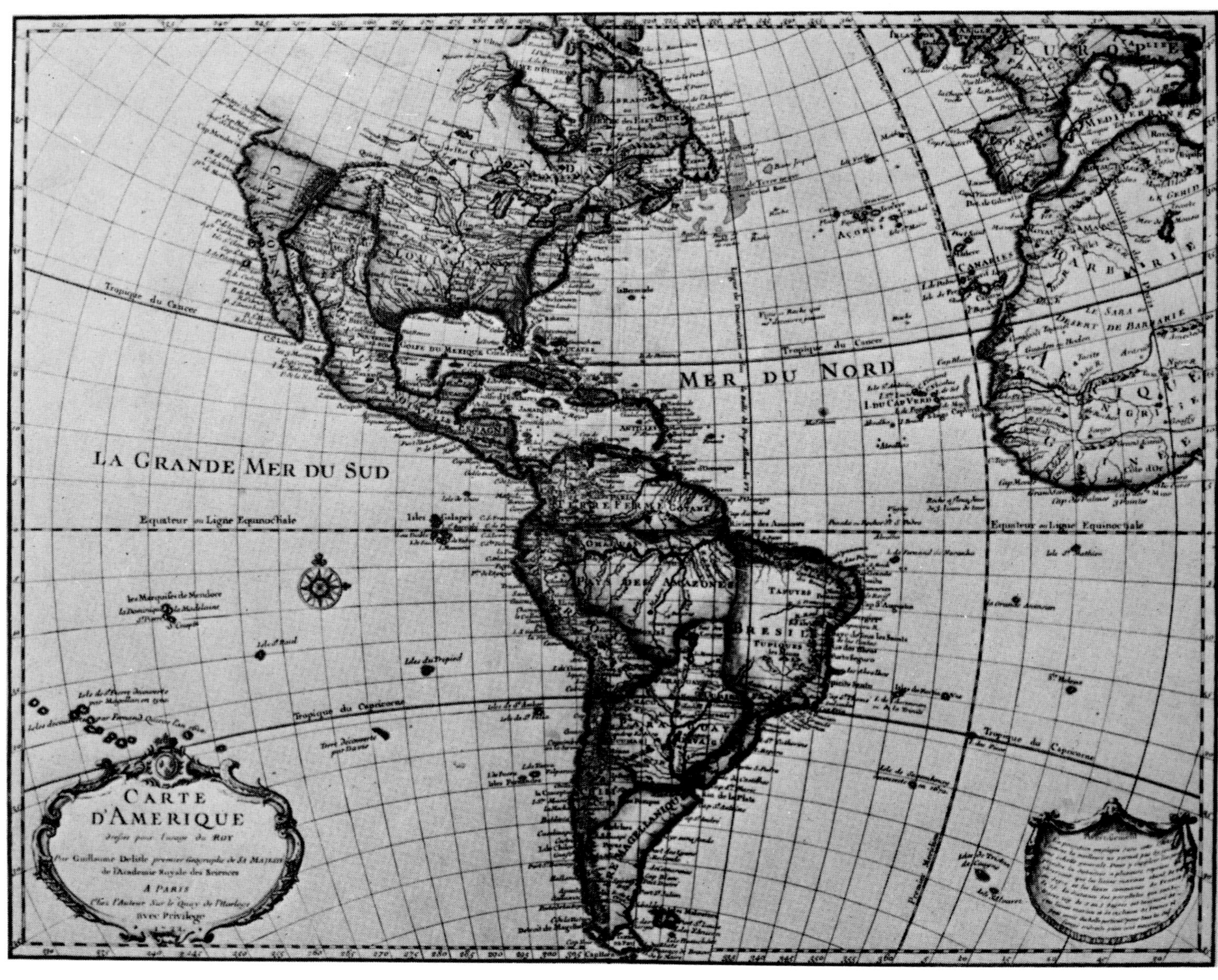

Plate CXIV

'Amérique,' Guillaume de l'Isle, 1722. On this general map of the Americas de l'Isle has incorporated much of the North American detail presented on his smaller-scale maps (see Plates CXI and CXII). With minor variations this map would be copied by other cartographers for almost the next 100 years.
480 x 600 mm.

Plate CXV

'Novae Hispaniae…,' Johann Baptiste Homann, 1725. Dense with place names, Homann's map shows the de facto and de jure political division of North America after the Treaty of Utrecht of 1713 and the French expansion into Louisiana in the following 10 years. The contested southern border of Carolina is drawn to England's advantage, since it pushes deep into Spanish-claimed territory, almost to St Augustine.
420 x 510 mm.

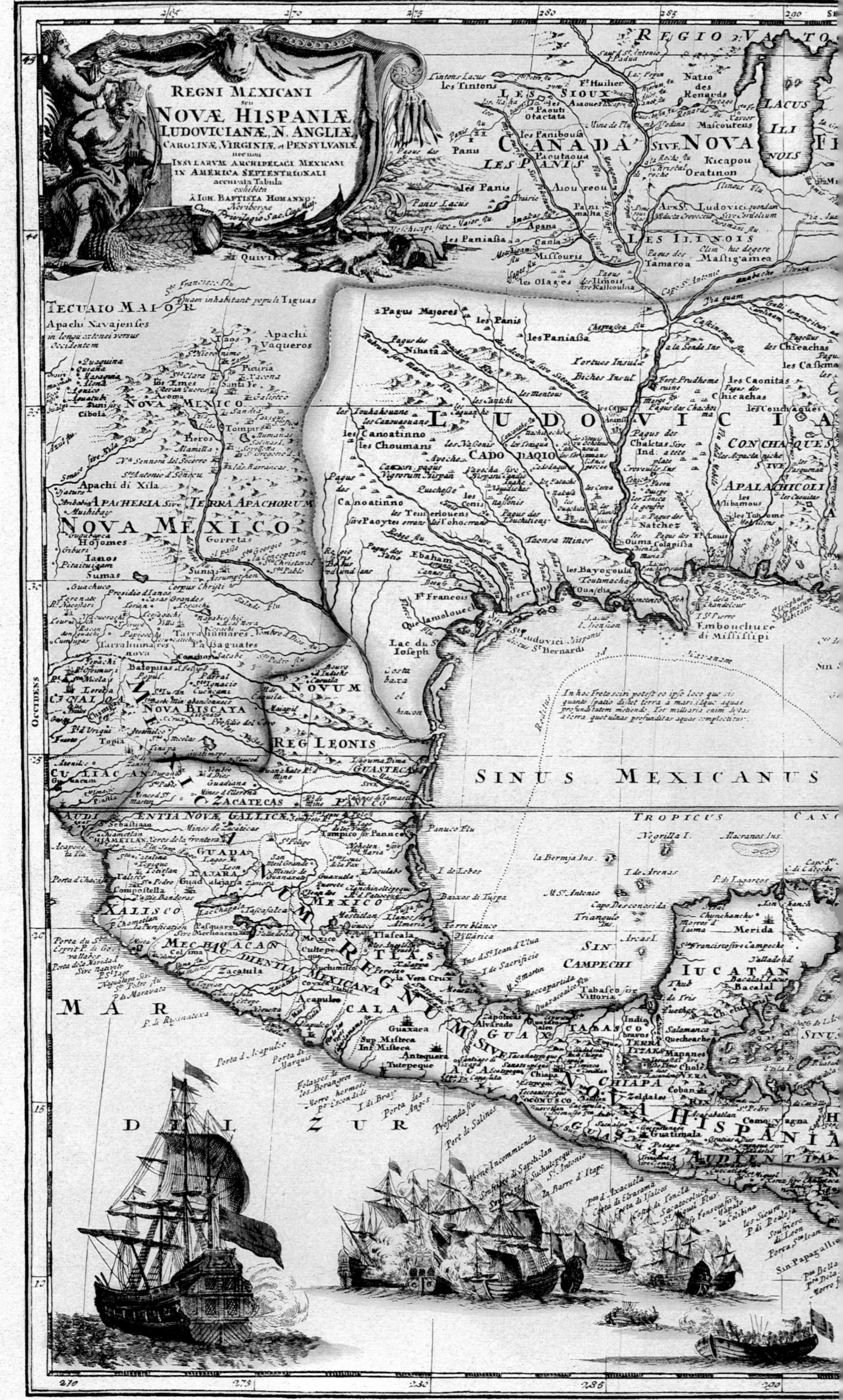

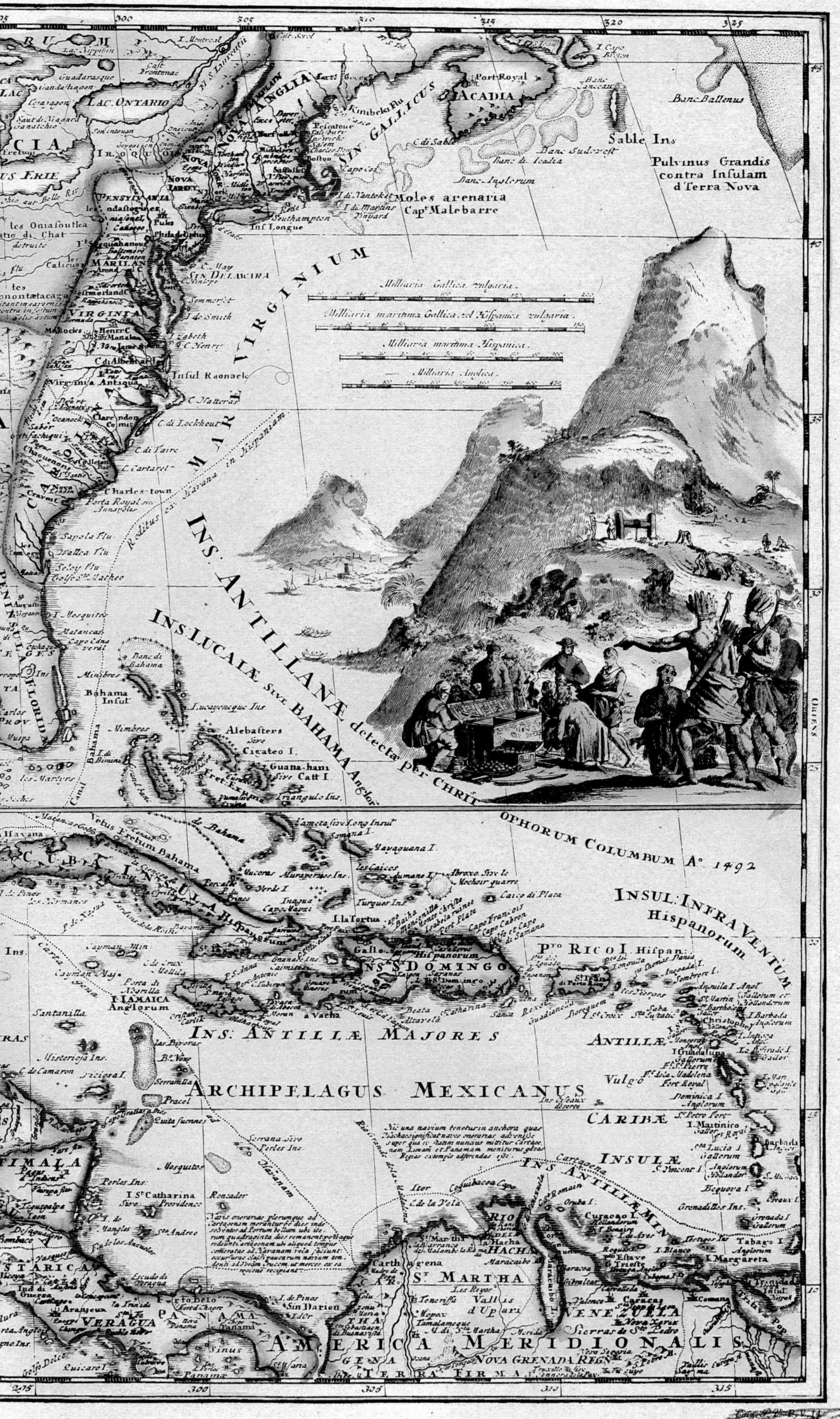
ACADIA
Sable Ins
Banc Ballenus
Pulvinus Grandis contra Insulam d'Terra Nova
Moles arenaria
Capt Malebarre
SIN. GALLICUS
LAC. ONTARIO
NOVA ANGLIA
Mare Virginium
Millaria Gallica vulgaria
Milliaria maritima Gallica, vel Hispanica vulgaria
Milliaria maritima Hispanica
Milliaria Anglica
Charles-town
Reditus ex Havana in Hispaniam
INS. ANTILLANÆ
INS. LUCAIÆ sive BAHAMA detecta per CHRISTOPHORUM COLUMBUM A°. 1492
Bahama Insul
CUBA INSULA Hispanorum
INS. S. DOMINGO Hispanorum
P^{to} RICO I. Hispan:
INSUL: INFRA VENTUM Hispanorum
INS: ANTILLÆ MAJORES
ANTILLÆ
ARCHIPELAGUS MEXICANUS
CARIBÆ INSULÆ
INS. ANTILLÆ MIN.
I. JAMAICA Anglorum
St MARTHA
VENEZUELA
AMERICA MERIDIONALIS
NOVA GRENADA REGN.
TERRA FIRMA
VERAGUA
PANAMA

Plate CXVI

'Nova Anglia,' Johann Baptiste Homann, 1725. Again, place names are much in evidence on Homann's well-drawn rendition of the New England coast, but the interior is not as defined or accurate. Though the New England colonies of Connecticut, Massachusetts, Rhode Island and New Hampshire were well established by this time, their names seldom appear on any but English maps.
420 x 510 mm.

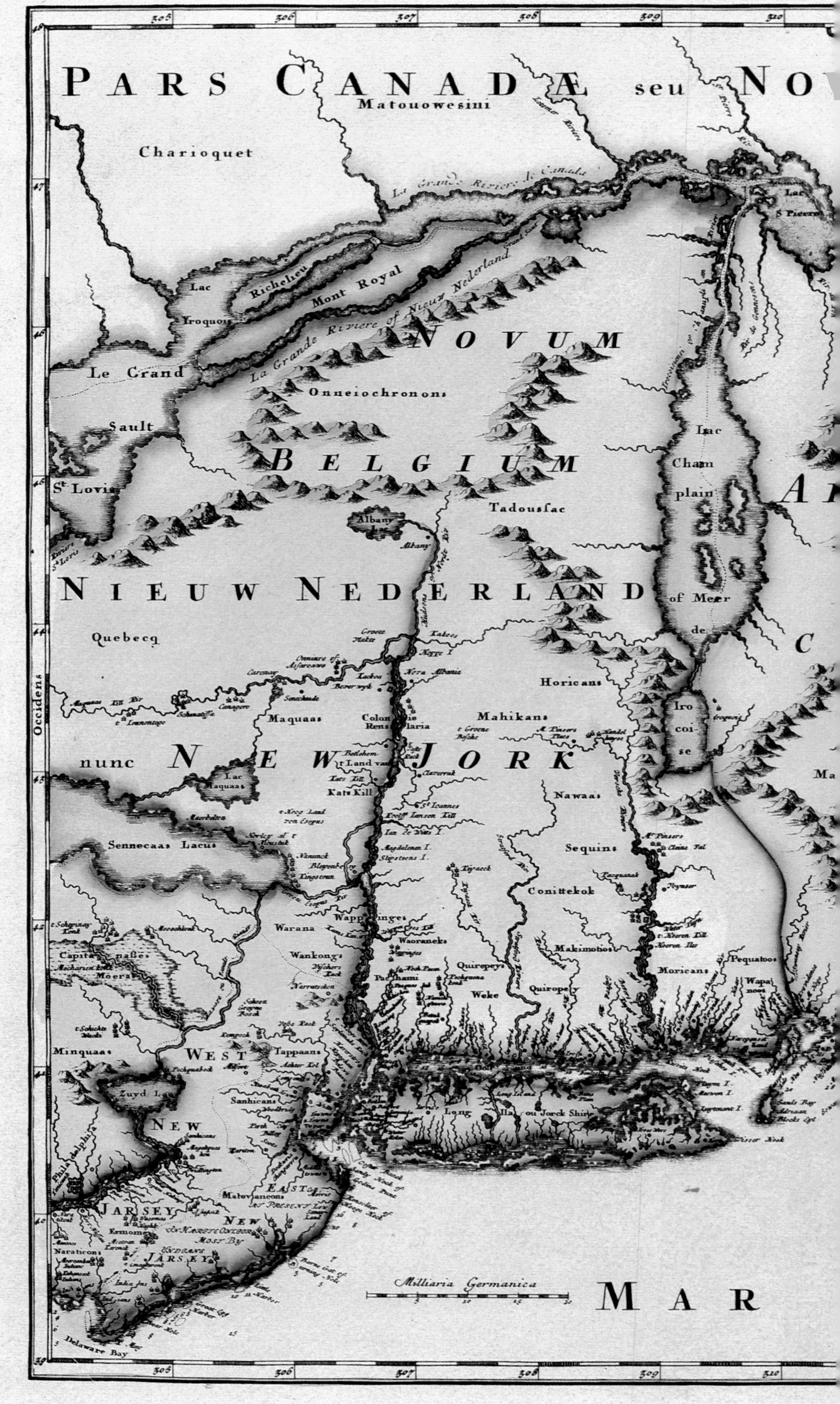

NOVA ANGLIA
Septentrionali Americæ implantata
Anglorumque coloniis
florentissima
Geographice exhibita
a
IOH. BAPTISTA HOMANN
Sac. Cæs. Maj. Geographo
Norimbergæ
Cum Privilegio Sac. Cæs. Maj.
FRANCIÆ
Nouvelle Biscaye
OVA ANGLIA
Incolis dicta
Ammough
caugen
Norum beag
OUCHI
Kennebeka
EN
St GEORGES
CHANNELL
St Georges Banck
EL NORT
Septentrio
Meridies
Oriens

Plate CXVII

'Accurata Delineatio...,' Matthias Seutter, 1730. The Homanns' chief rival in Germany, Seutter published his first major work, *Atlas Novus,* in 1730. This copperplate represents his crisp, precise style well. Its delineation of the American east coast is generally good, though like many other maps of the period it is confused about northern Labrador and Baffin Island. The inset showing the Louisiana-Alabama coast seems to be based on de l'Isle (Plate CXII), but is slightly less accurate.
410 x 480 mm.

Accurata delineatio
celeberrimæ Regionis
LUDOVICIANÆ
vel Gallice
LOUISIANÆ
ol. Canadæ et Floridæ adpellatione
in Septemtrionali America
descripta
quæ hodie nomine fluminis
MISSISSYPPI
vel St. LOUIS
per colonias et navigationes Gallorum
ob immensas opes et adfluentiam
magis magisque inclarescit
ex fide dignissr. Itinerariis consignata
et in lucem edita
cura et manu
MATTHÆI SEUTTERI. S.C.M.G. AUGUSTAN.
Qualis Res Talis Spes
GRANDE MER DU NORD
MER DE VIRGINIE DE LA NOUV. ANGLETERRE
LES ISLES LUCAYES
DETROIT DE DAVID
GROENLANDE
TERRE DE LABRADOR ou LABORADOR Par les Espagnols
NOUV. BRETAGNE Par les Angl.
ESTOTILANDE Par les Dan.
BAYE DE HUDSON
TERRE DES GRANDS ESQUIMAUX
TERRE DES PETITS ESQUIMAUX
L'ISLE DE TERRE NEUVE
Golfe de S. Laurens
NOUV. ANGLETERRE
IROQUOIS
VIRGINIE
Pensilvanie
Les Isles Bermudes
Tropique du Cancer
I. DE S. DOMINGUE

Plate CXVIII

'America,' Matthias Seutter, 1730. On this general map of the Americas, also from *Atlas Novus,* Seutter has much improved his rendering of the outline of Labrador, but otherwise the map abides by conventions in the representation of North America that had been established for at least 50 years (*eg,* California's insularity, an idea that was disproven as early as 1701). Note how much attention is given to the Sargasso Sea and to two related 'seas' that Seutter places in the mid-Atlantic.
486 x 595 mm.

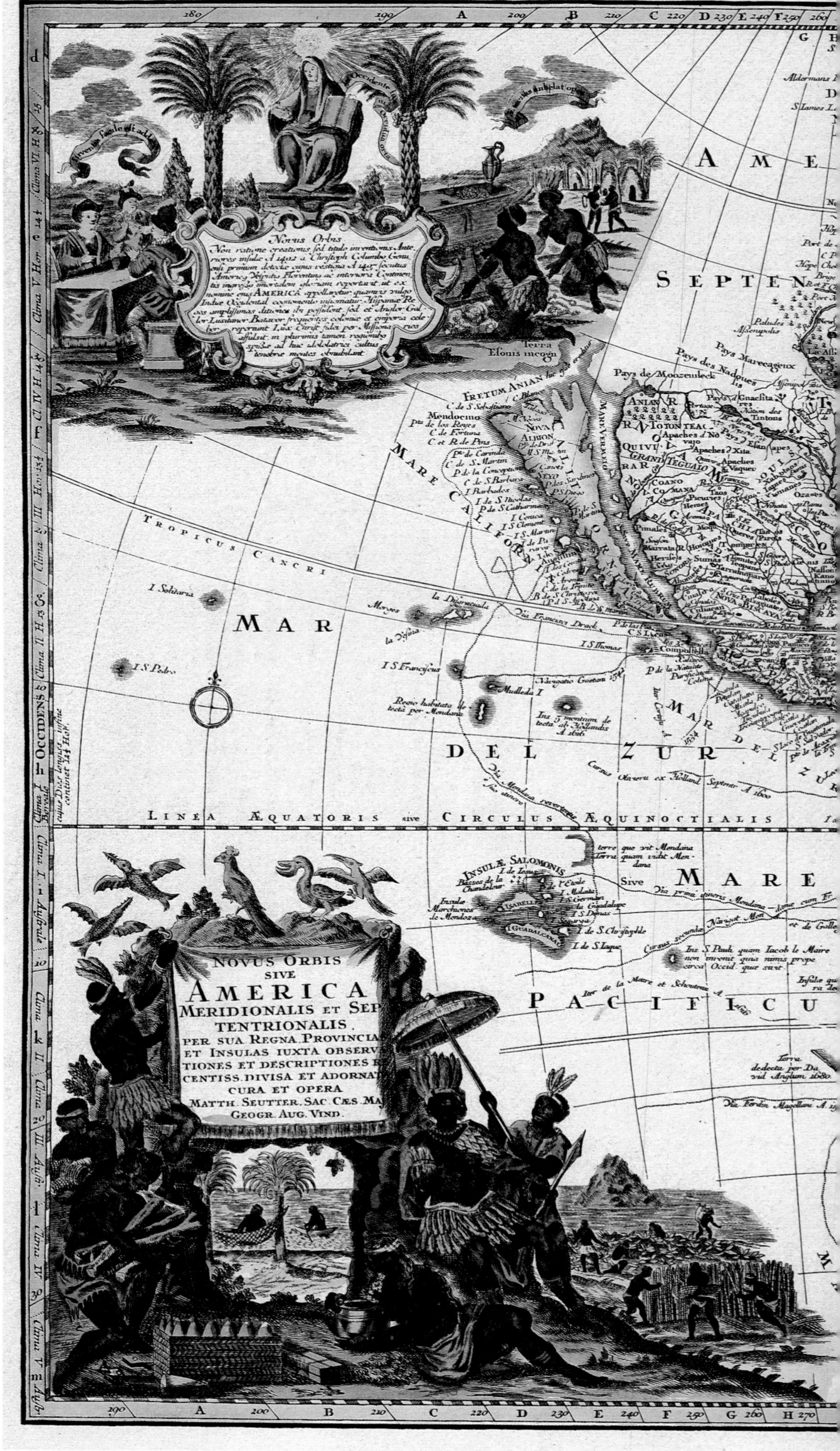

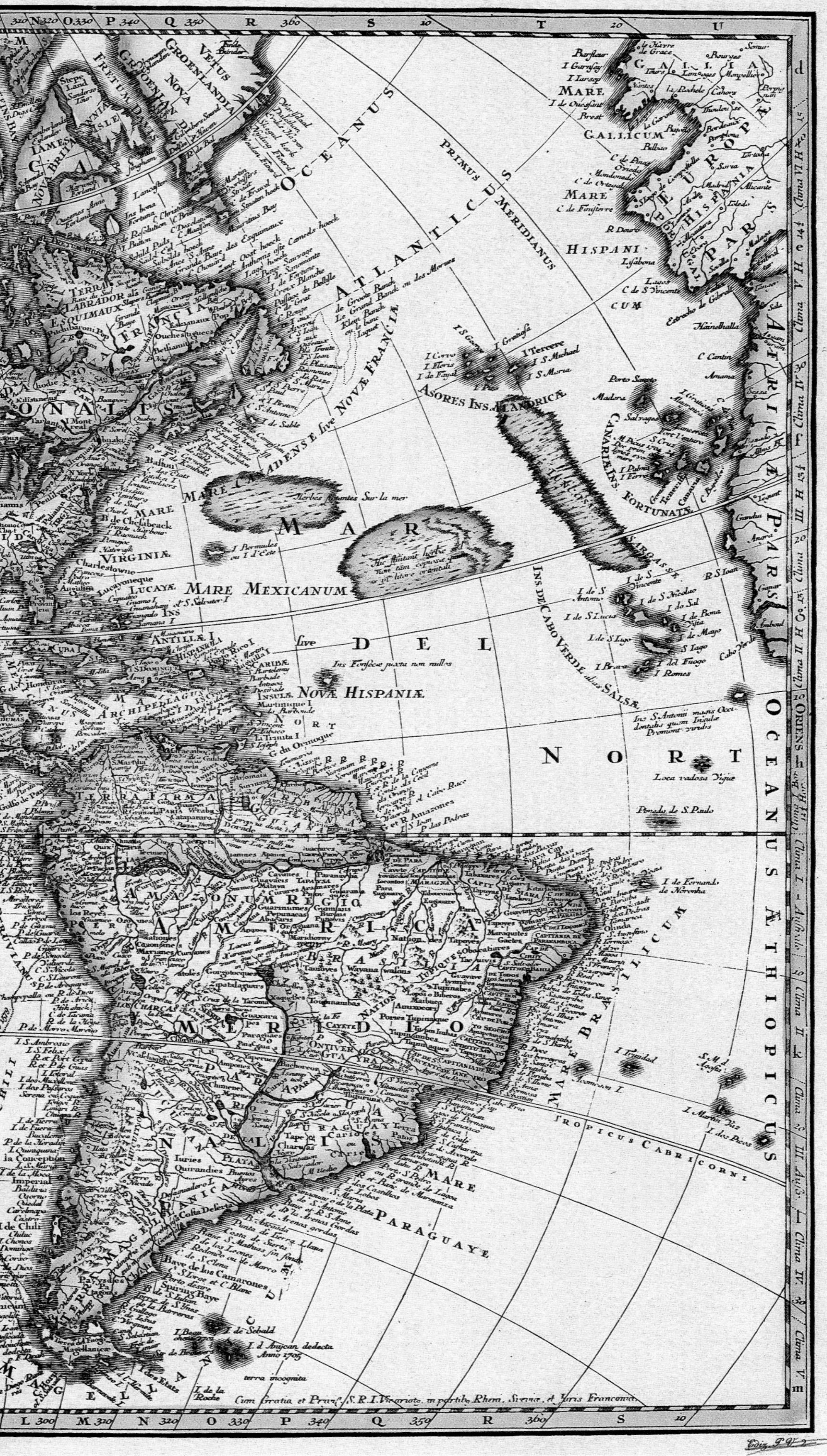
OCEANUS
ATLANTICUS
PRIMUS MERIDIANUS
MARE MEXICANUM
NOVÆ HISPANIÆ
DEL NORT
OCEANUS ÆTHIOPICUS
TROPICUS CABRICORNI
PARAGUAYE
MARE BRASILICUM
AMERICA MERIDIONALIS
MARE GALLICUM
HISPANIA
AFRICÆ PARS
Cum Gratia et Privil. S.R.I. Vicariato, in partib. Rheni, Sueviæ, et Juris Franconici.

Plate CXIX

'Globi Terr-Aquei,' Matthias Seutter, 1740. Essentially based on an old-fashioned model, this planisphere has been only marginally up-graded by the addition of some of the new geographic information that was by the mid-eighteenth century beginning to flood in on cartographers; and the various projections surrounding the main maps are more impressive-looking than useful. Note that on this map the Solomons have edged about 10 degrees closer to South America than they were on Seutter's 'America' (*cf* Plate CXVIII).
440 x 520 mm.

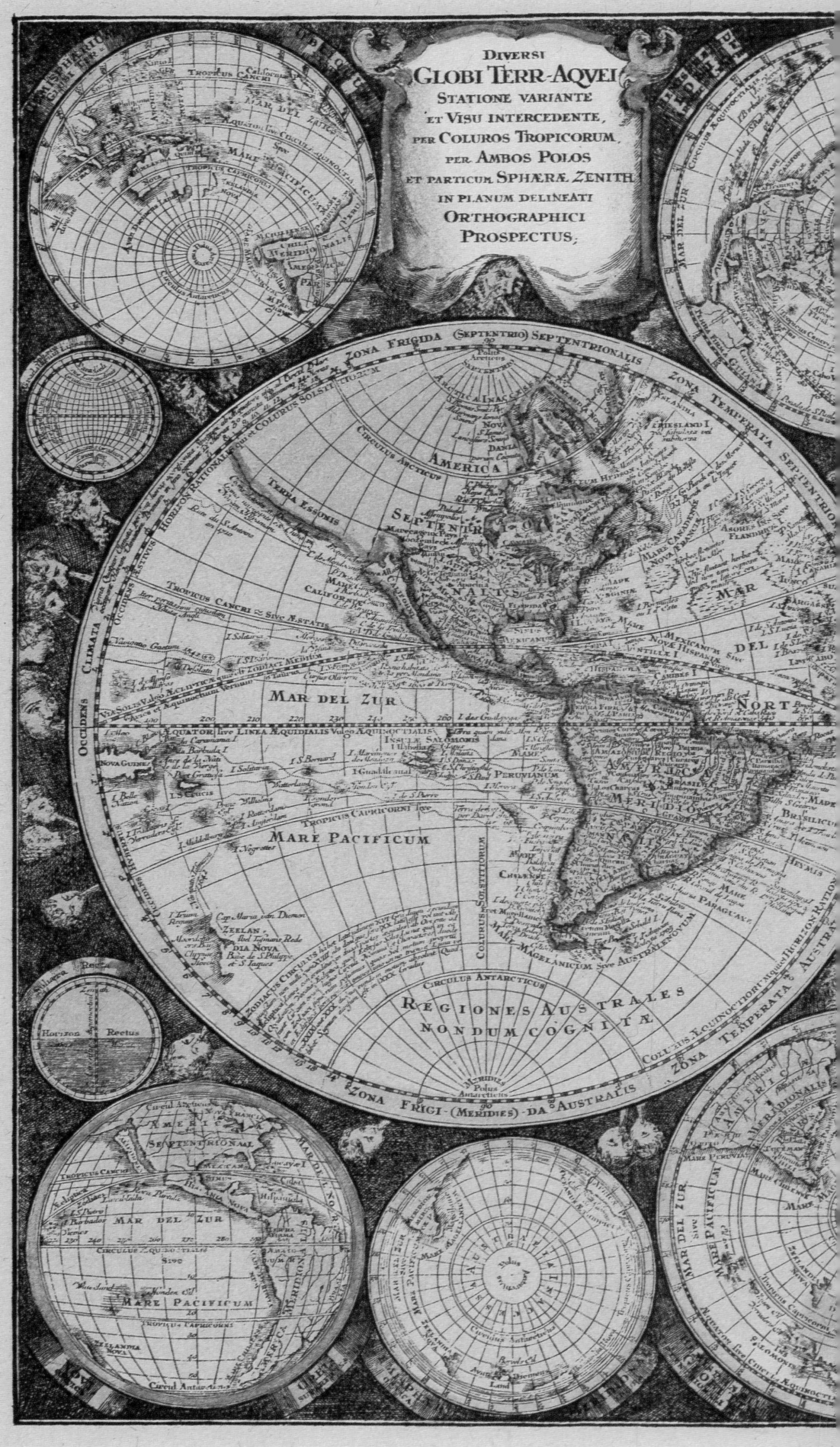

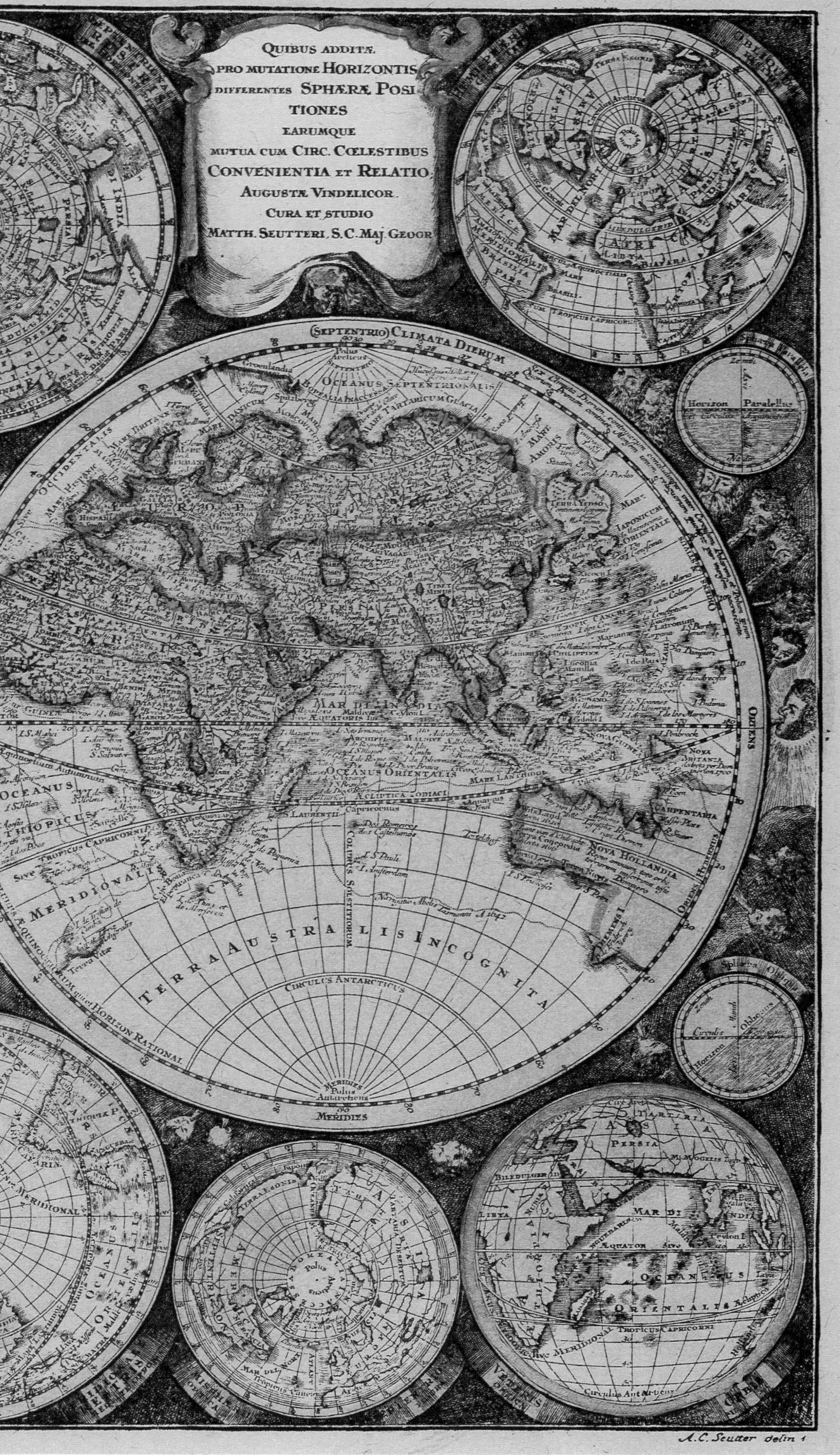
Quibus additæ
pro mutatione Horizontis
differentes Sphæræ Posi
tiones
earumque
mutua cum Circ. Cœlestibus
Convenientia et Relatio.
Augustæ Vindelicor.
Cura et studio
Matth. Seutteri, S.C. Maj. Geogr.
Terra Australis Incognita
Circulus Antarcticus
Oceanus Orientalis
Nova Hollandia
A.C. Seutter delin.

Plate CXX

'America Septentrionalis,' T Lotter, 1757. The rather intrusive coloring on this map by Lotter, a minor German cartographer, cannot disguise the fact that it is a nearly exact copy of Homann's map of 1725 (Plate CXV), even to the naval battle in the left lower corner. Homann's map, in turn, derived from a de l'Isle map of 1703. 450 x 580 mm.

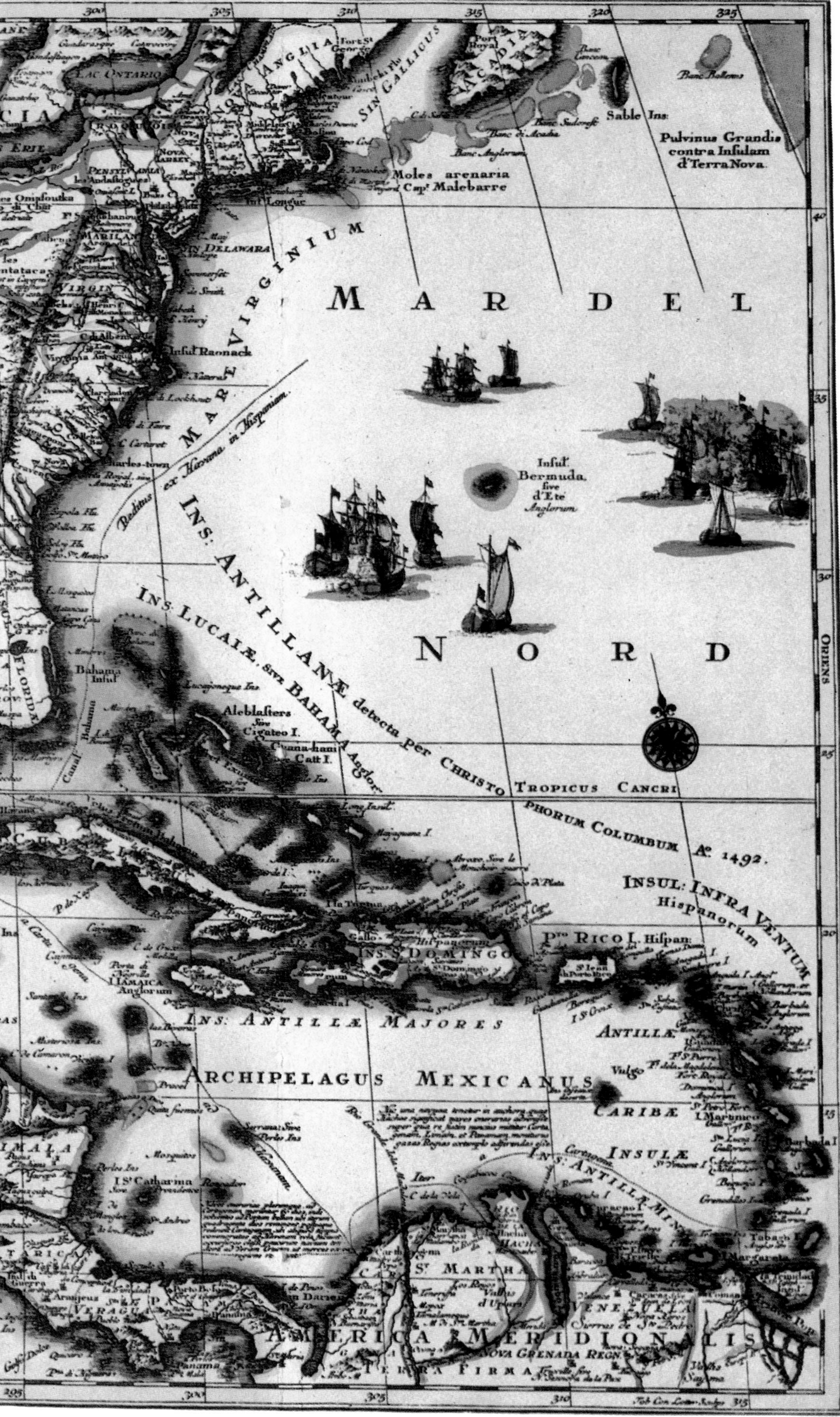
MAR DEL
NORD
MARE VIRGINIUM
Reditus ex Havana in Hispaniam.
INS: ANTILLANÆ detecta per CHRISTOPHORUM COLUMBUM Aº 1492.
INS: LUCAIÆ, sive BAHAMA Anglor.
TROPICUS CANCRI
Insul: Bermuda, sive d'Ete Anglorum
Moles arenaria Capt Malebarre
Pulvinus Grandis contra Insulam d'Terra Nova.
Sable Ins:
Bahama Insul
Aleblasters Sive Cigateo I.
INSUL: INFRA VENTUM Hispanorum
Pto RICO I. Hispan:
INS. S. DOMINGO
INS: ANTILLÆ MAJORES
ANTILLÆ
ARCHIPELAGUS MEXICANUS
CARIBÆ
INSULÆ
AMERICA MERIDIONALIS
NOVA GRENADA REGN
TERRA FIRMA
St MARTHA
ORIENS

Plate CXXI

'The New Continent,' Didier Robert de Vaugondy, 1749. An Italian version of a French map made for the first volume of Buffon's great 44-volume *Histoire Naturelle.* In its effort to work out accurate dimensions for the Americas it succeeds very well. 235 x 135 mm.

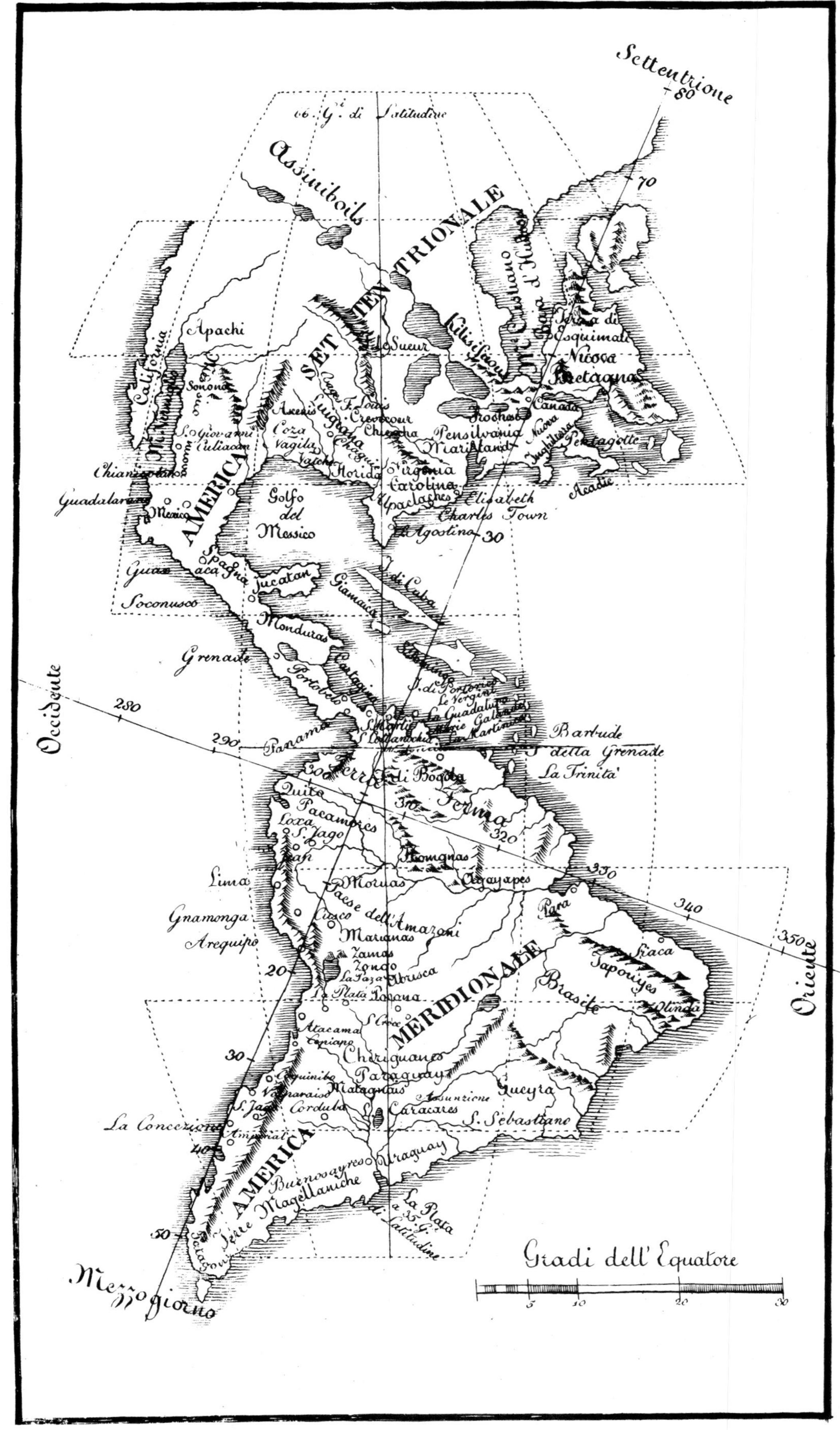

CARTA DEL NUOVO CONTINENTE

nella maggior sua lunghezza diametrale dal Fiume della Plata fin oltre il Lago degli Assiniboil, disegnata sotto gli occhi del Sig. di Buffon dal Sig. Roberto d'Vaugondy Figlio 1749.

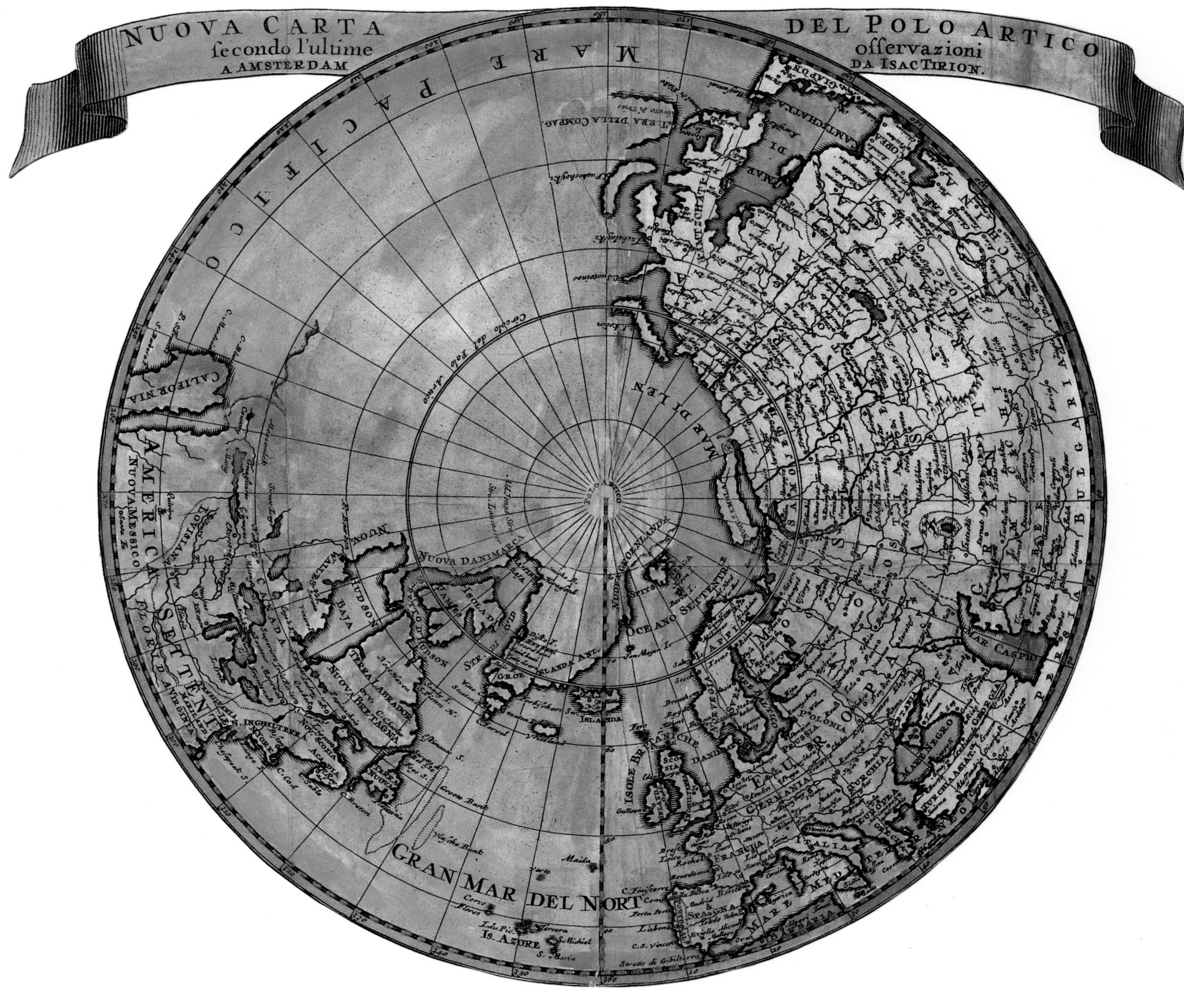

Plate CXXII

'Nuova Carta del Polo Artico,' Isaac Tirion, *c* 1751. A copperplate from Tomasso Salmon's *Lo Stato Presente di Tutti i Paesi e Poppoli del Mondo,* a geography book published in Venice. Conventional in most ways, it nevertheless shows some novel, if garbled, detail of western Alaska, perhaps based on Bering's discoveries. 280 mm (diameter).

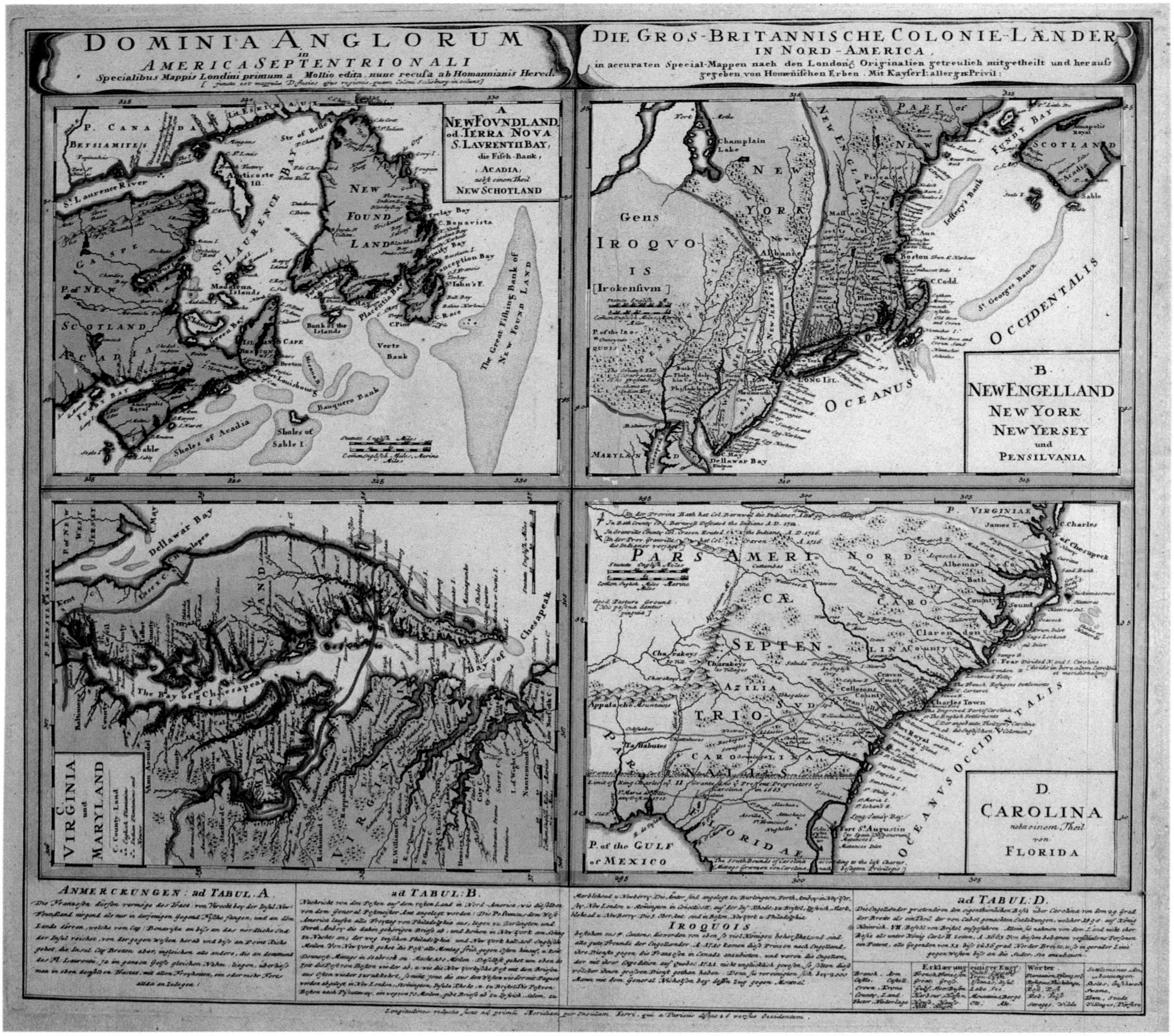

Plate CXXIII

'Domina Anglorum,' the Homanns, 1750. By the mid-eighteenth century almost all the best North American maps were being made by the British and French. They copied freely from one another, and cartographers in other countries copied from them both. These German maps by 'Homann's heirs' are copied from British originals and retain most of the English spellings. Note that on the map of New England both Connecticut and Massachusetts are now named. 500 x 684 mm.

Benjamin Franklin. In addition to his many other accomplishments he was also a cartographer. In about 1770 he and Timothy Folger prepared the first chart of the Gulf Stream.

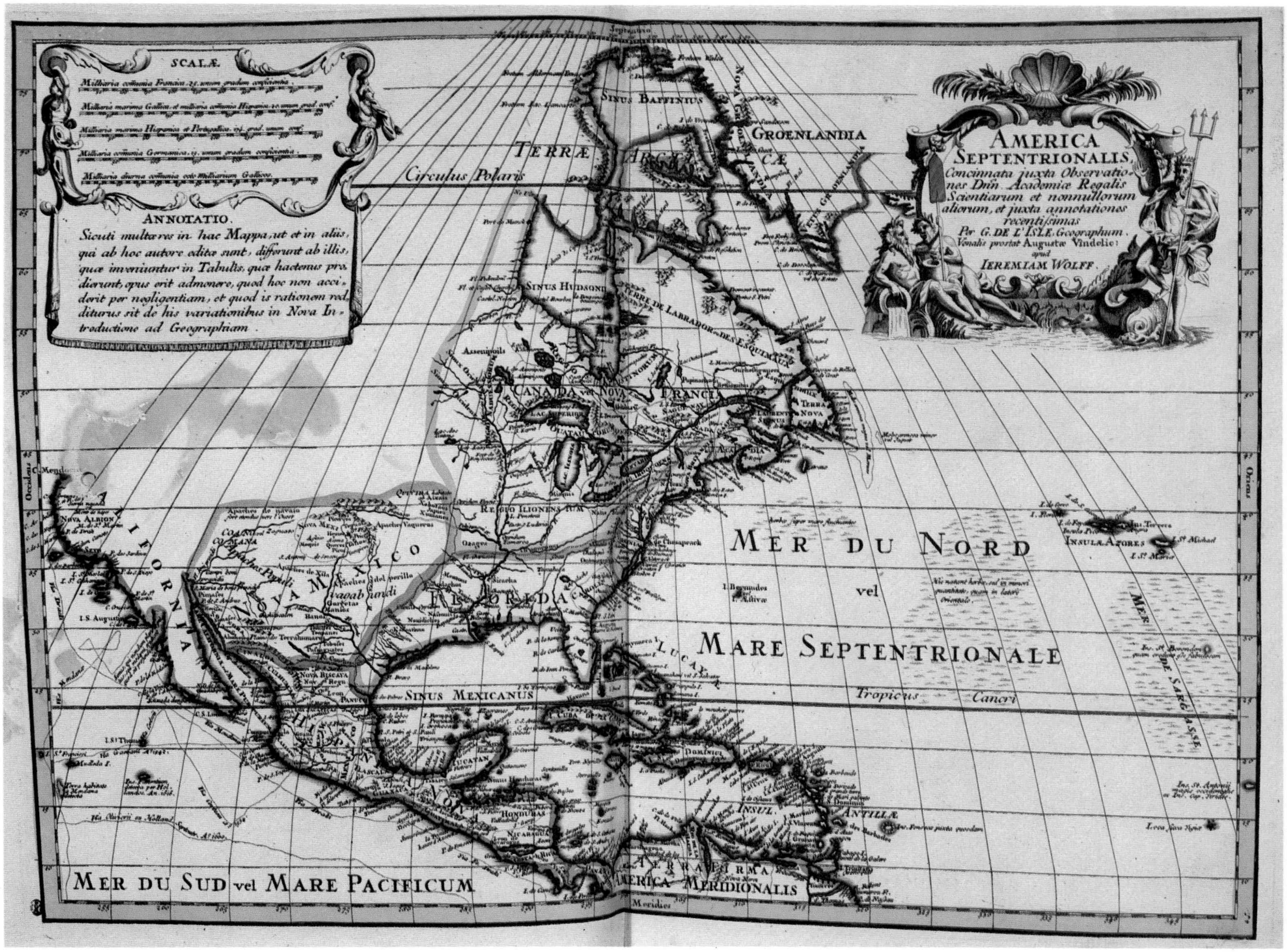

SFERA ARMILLARE

An armillary sphere from an Italian eighteenth-century book.

Plate CXXIV

'America Septentrionalis,' Guillaume de l'Isle, 1750. De l'Isle's *Atlas Nouveau* continued to be published for nearly half a century after his death in 1726, and its maps were widely copied, as in this German map by Jeremiah Wolff.
420 x 560 mm.

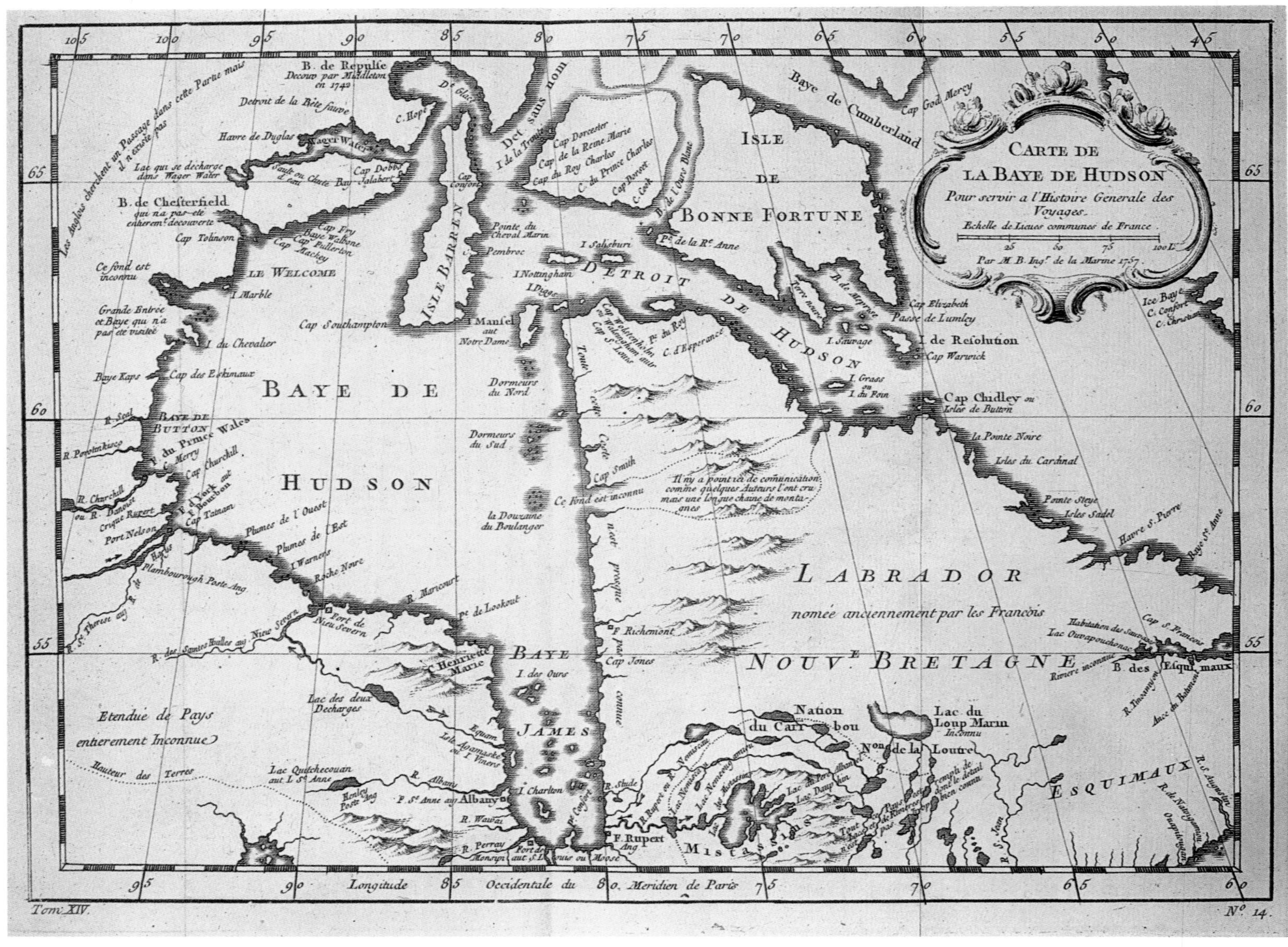

Plate CXXV

'La Baye de Hudson,' Jean Nicolas Bellin, 1757. One of a series of maps that Bellin, Hydrographer to Louis XV, drew for Didot's volume *Histoire Général des Voyages.* Despite its admirable clarity, it perpetuates some of the old confusions about the Hudson Bay-Baffin Island area. Note the legend at the bottom indicating that, as on most French maps of this period, the prime meridian has been drawn through Paris.
210 x 320 mm.

Plate CXXVI (right above)

'Lacs du Canada,' Jean Nicolas Bellin, 1757. Another Bellin map from Didot bearing witness to the excellence of French survey techniques. Except for the distortion of Michigan the map is almost of modern quality. All of the Great Lakes have the names by which we know them, but several islands placed in Lake Superior are based on erroneous reports.
210 x 320 mm.

Plate CXXVII

'La Caroline et Georgie,' Jean Nicolas Bellin, 1757. Bellin's debt to English cartographers, which he acknowledges, does not diminish the superb quality of this elegant map.
210 x 320 mm.

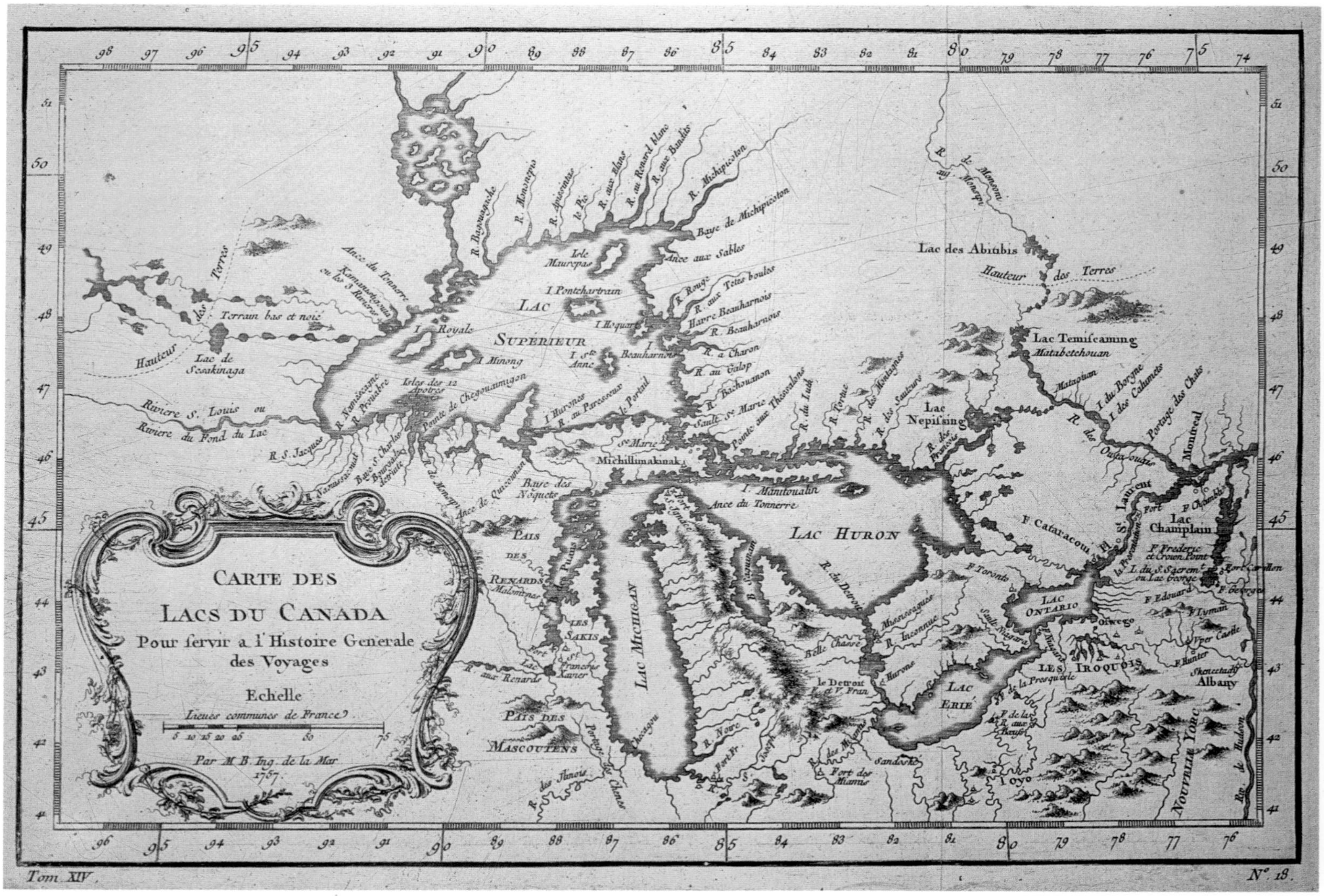

CARTE DES LACS DU CANADA
Pour servir à l'Histoire Generale des Voyages

Echelle
Lieues communes de France
5 10 15 20 25 50 75

Par M B Ing. de la Mar.
1757.

Tom XIV. N°. 18.

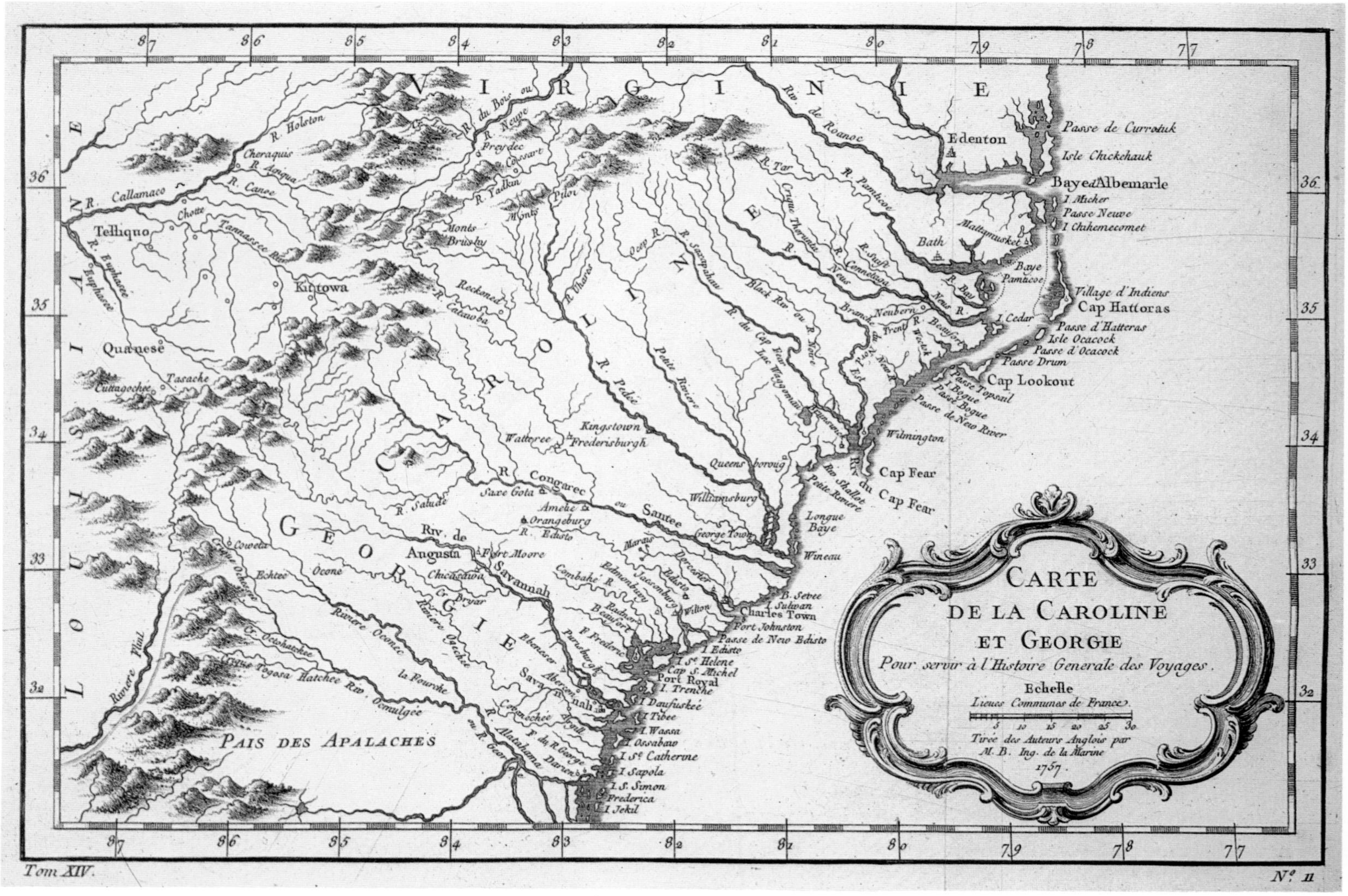

CARTE DE LA CAROLINE ET GEORGIE
Pour servir à l'Histoire Generale des Voyages.

Echelle
Lieues Communes de France.
5 10 15 20 25 30

Tirée des Auteurs Anglois par M. B. Ing. de la Marine
1757.

Tom XIV. N°. 11

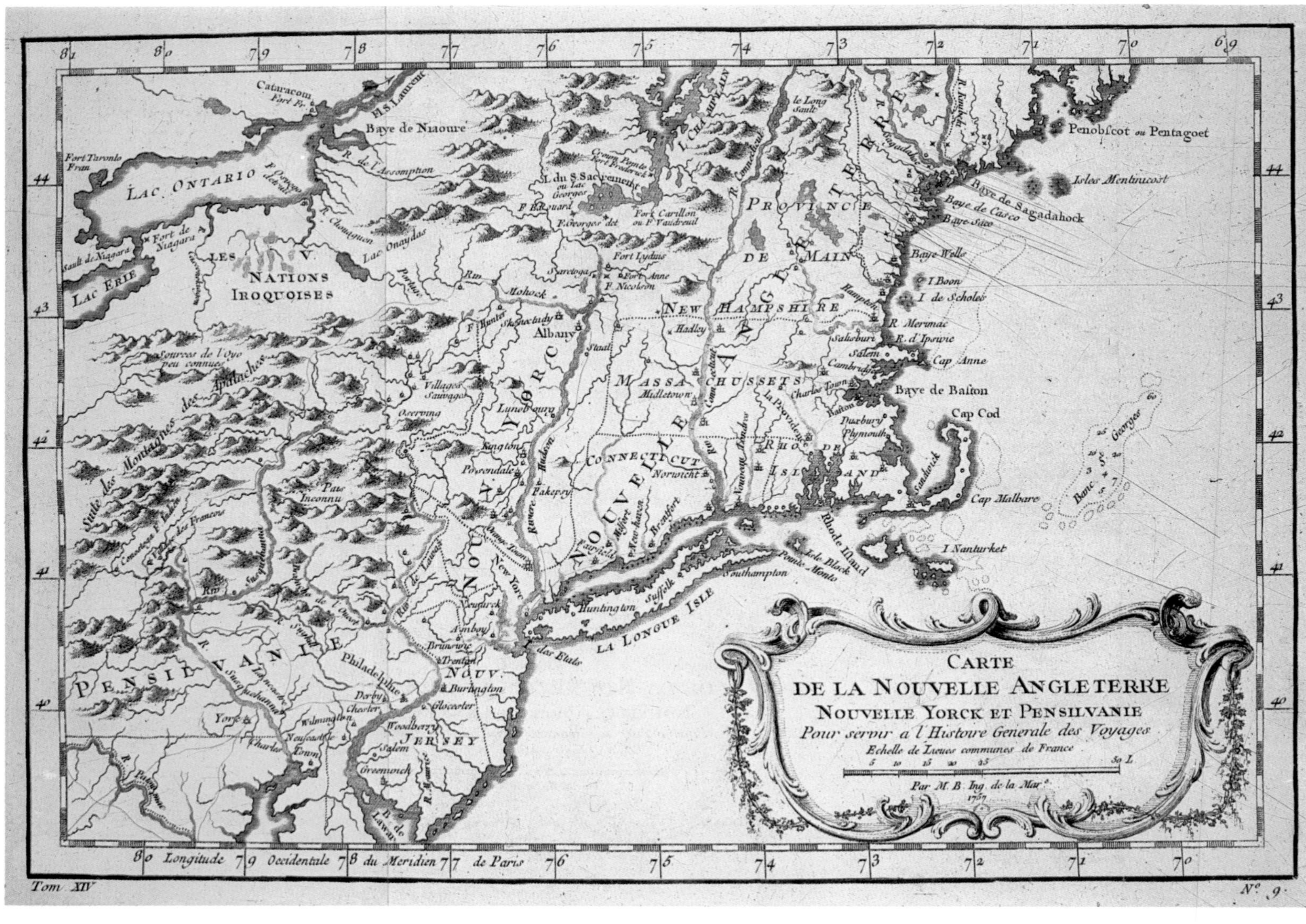

Plate CXXIX (right above)

'The Upper St Lawrence,' Jean Nicolas Bellin, 1757. This and Plate CXXX trace the St Lawrence River from its source in Lake Ontario to the Gulf of St Lawrence. On this map of the upper river Montréal is of course shown, but not Ottowa, which was not founded until 1827. (Its location is the confluence of the Ottowa and the Rideau rivers, both shown.)
210 x 320 mm.

Plate CXXVIII

'La Nouvelle Angleterre,' Jean Nicolas Bellin, 1757. Like his map of the Carolinas and northern Georgia (Plate CXXVII), Bellin's New England is probably based on English models (just as English maps of New France were mostly copied from the French), for by 1757 English mapmakers such as John Mitchell, Lewis Evans, Nicholas Scull and several others had made the then-definitive maps of the American coast between Florida and Nova Scotia. Note that all of the colonies in New England are now named. (Vermont is absent because it was still only a territory disputed between New York and New Hampshire.)
210 x 320 mm.

Plate CXXX

'The Lower St Lawrence,' Jean Nicolas Bellin, 1757. This final map in the series Bellin made for Didot covers the New World area most familiar to the French and is therefore the most accurate of all these remarkably accurate maps.
210 x 320 mm.

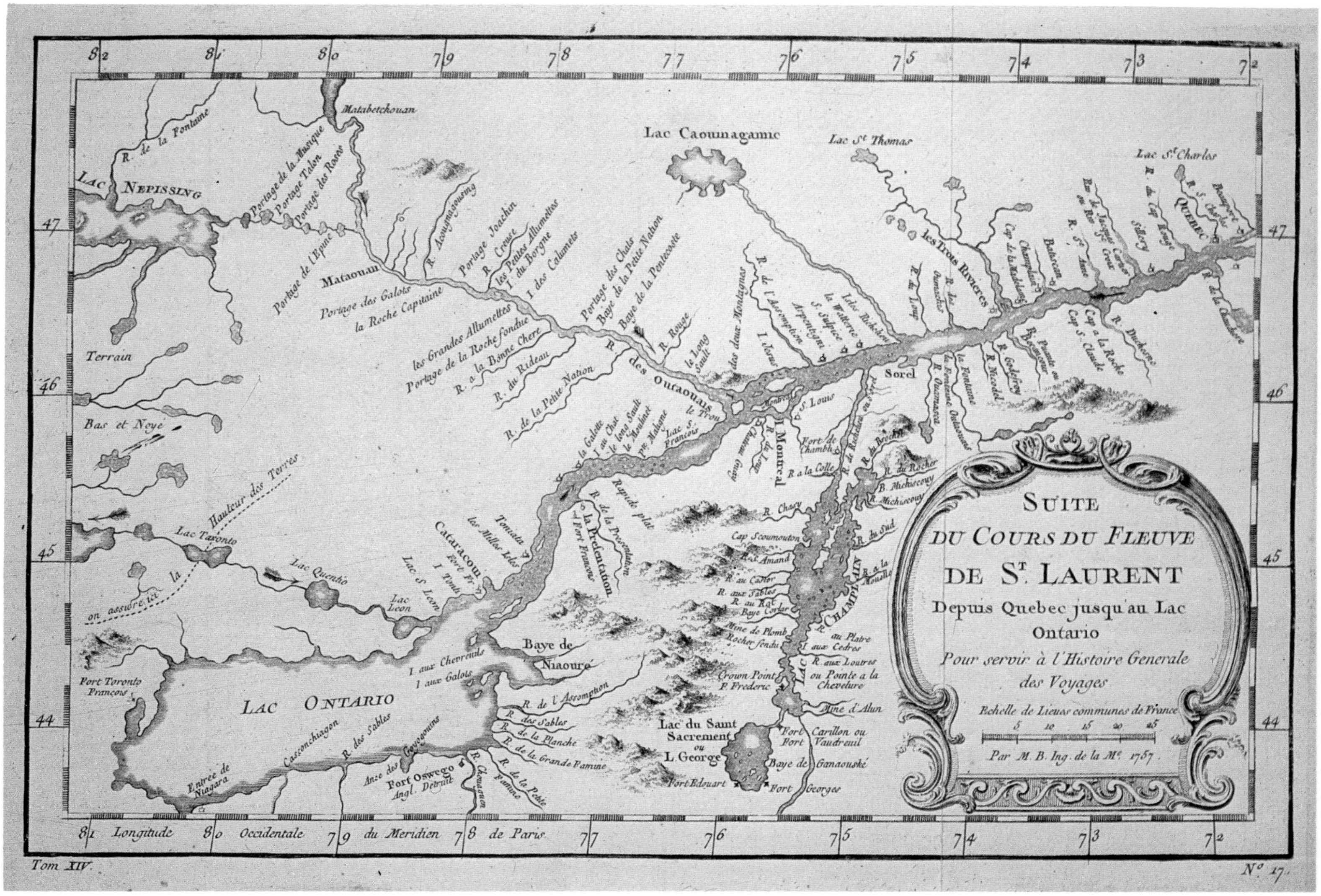

SUITE DU COURS DU FLEUVE DE S.T LAURENT
Depuis Quebec jusqu'au Lac Ontario
Pour servir à l'Histoire Generale des Voyages
Echelle de Lieues communes de France
5 10 15 20 25
Par M. B. Ing. de la M.e 1757.

Longitude 80 Occidentale 79 du Meridien 78 de Paris

Tom. XIV. N.o 17.

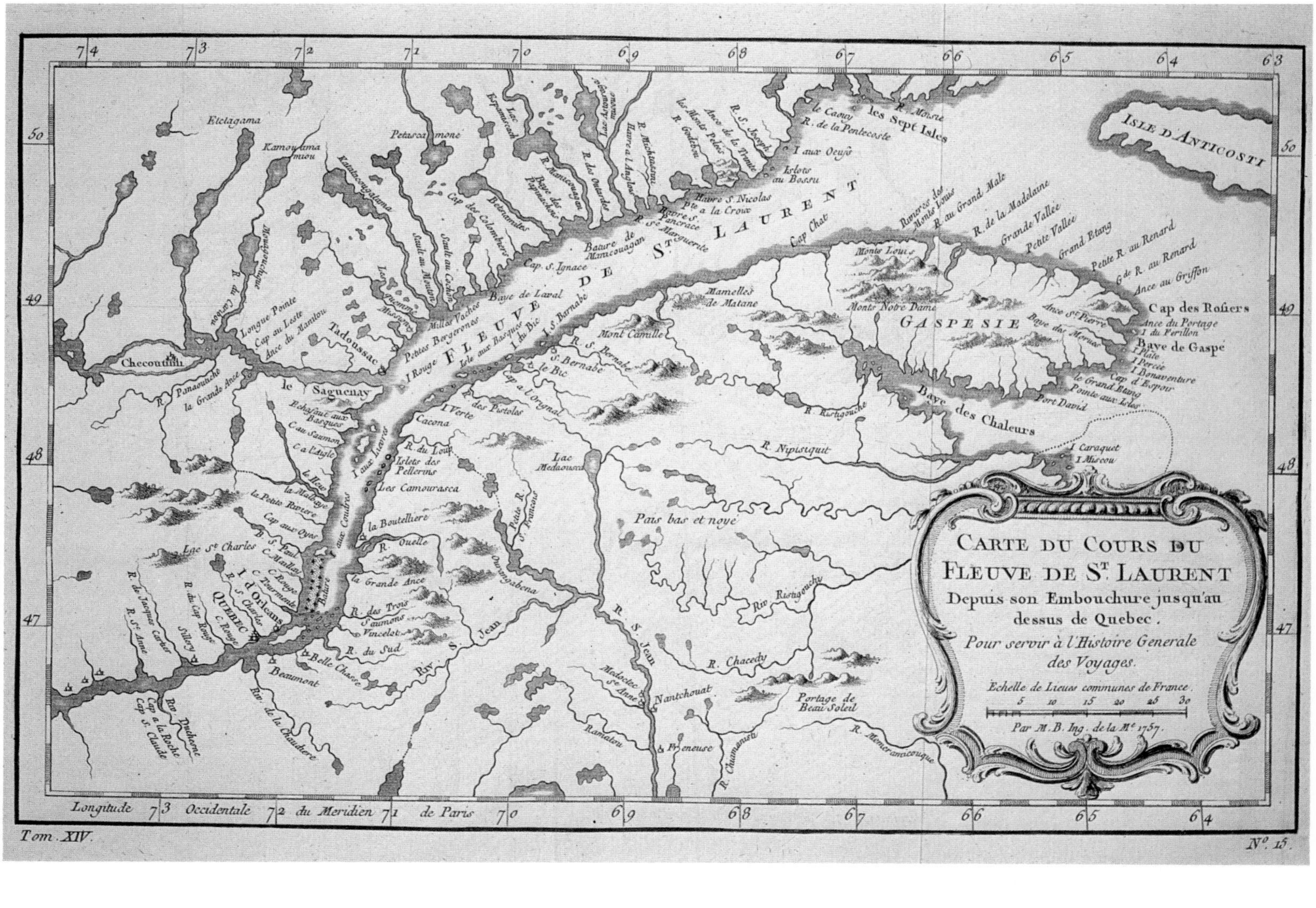

CARTE DU COURS DU FLEUVE DE S.T LAURENT
Depuis son Embouchure jusqu'au dessus de Quebec.
Pour servir à l'Histoire Generale des Voyages.
Echelle de Lieues communes de France.
5 10 15 20 25 30
Par M. B. Ing. de la M.e 1757.

Longitude 73 Occidentale 72 du Meridien 71 de Paris

Tom. XIV. N.o 18.

Plate CXXXI

'L'Amérique Septentrionale,' anon (Thomas Jefferys), 1757. Though not signed, this French map may have been drafted by Bellin. In any case, it is a copy based on the work of English cartographer Thomas Jefferys. As a result, it shows some English claims in the north and west not recognized by France ('pretendues pretentions,' as the cartouche sternly warns). A secondary result is that the prime meridian is here based on London, not Paris, as in other French maps.
210 x 320 mm.

AMERIQUE
SEPTENTRIONALE,
Suivant les Nouvelles Découvertes,
Augmenté des Collonies qui sont
derriere la Virginie et du Cour de l'ohio.
Traduit de l'Anglois d'apres Thos. Gefferys
Geographe du Prince de Galle, et
divisée suivant les pretendues pretentions
des Anglois, sans néantmoins Entendre,
que ce la tire à Consequence
en 1757.
DESCRIPTION HISTORIQUE DE L'AMERIQUE SEPTENTRIONAL
PAYS DES ESKIMOS
DE LA BRADOR
BRETAGNE
selon les Anglais
GOLFE DE S. LAURENT
TERRE NEUVE
ATLANTIQUE
Septentrion
Orient
Midi
CARTE DE L'OCEAN OCCIDENTAL Pour faire voir les Routes des diferents port de l'Europe pour conduire dans l'Amerique Septentrional.
LABRADOR
NOUVELLE FRANCE
LOUISIANE
GOLFE DU MEXIQUE
ISLES ACORES
FRANCE
ESPAGNE
AFRIQUE

Dame Fortune distributes New World treasures to eager traders in this frontispiece of the sixth volume of Guillaume Reynal's 1772 Histoire Philosophique et Politique des Etablissements et du Commerce des Européens dans les deux Indes, *an influential anti-colonialist work.*

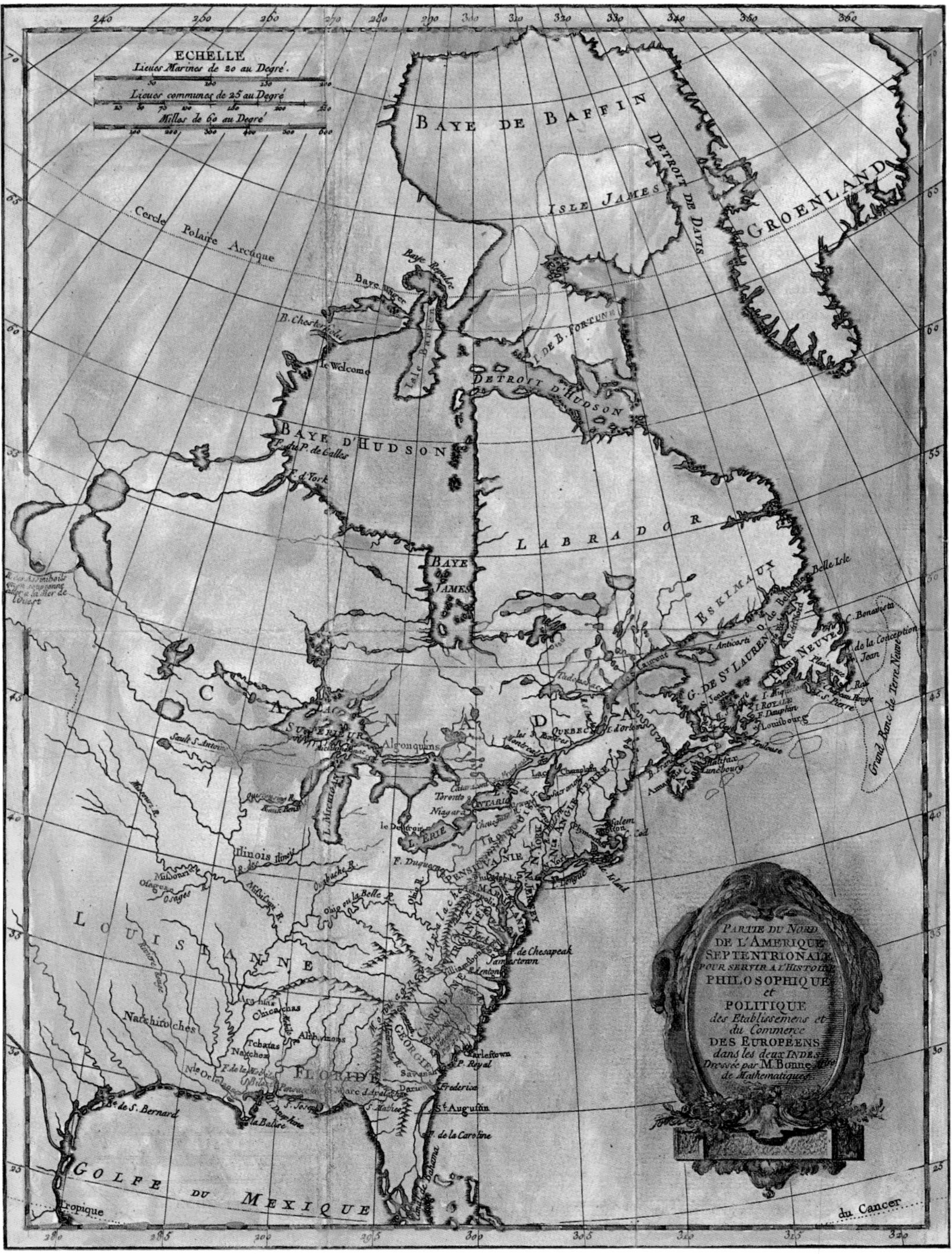

Plate CXXXII

'Partie du Nord de l'Amérique Septentrionale,' M Bonne, 1774. A map that appeared in a Dutch edition of Raynal's *Histoire.* By 1789 some 40 editions of this work had been published, and it has been credited with having more effect on French revolutionary thought even than Rousseau's writings.
320 x 325 mm.

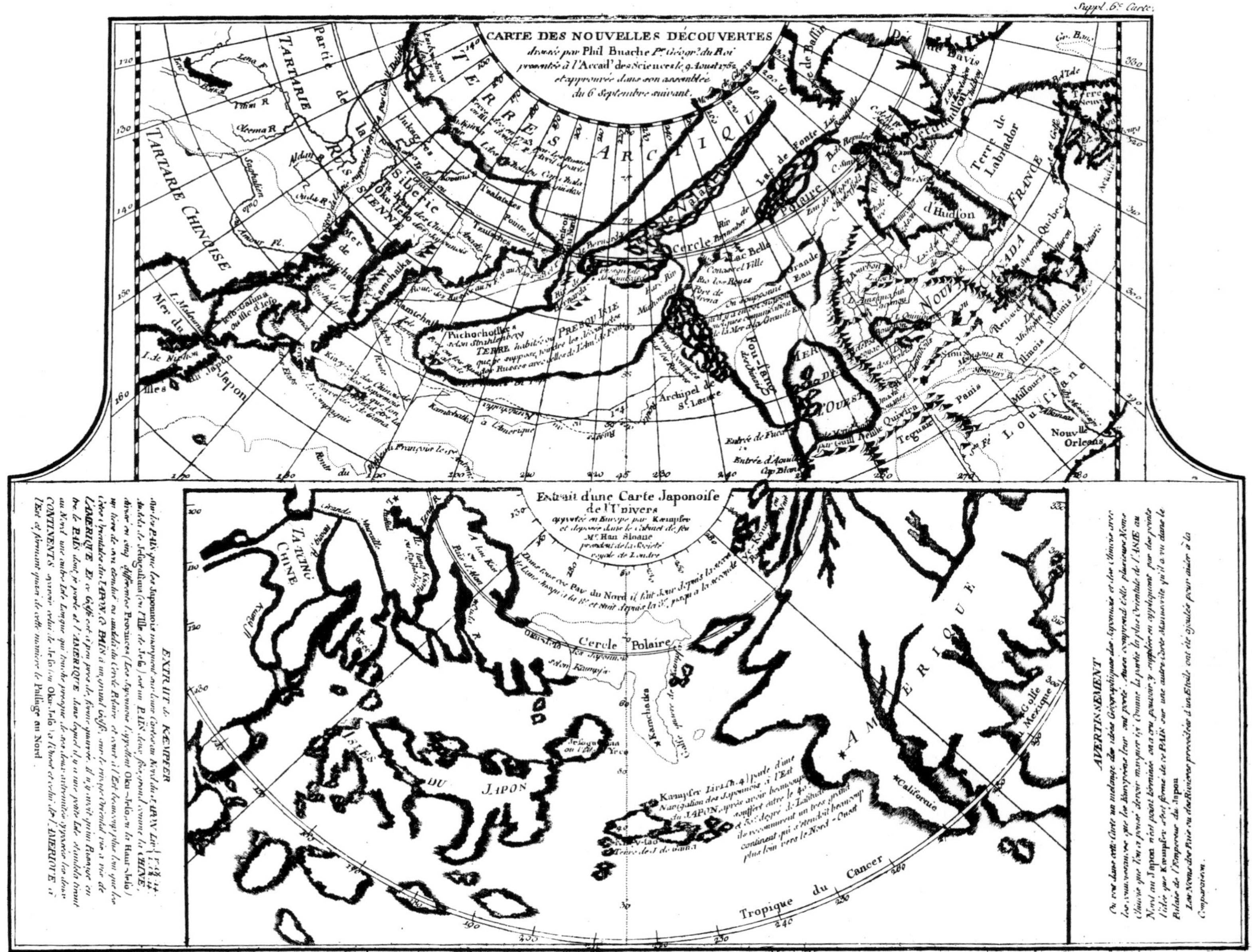

Plate CXXXIII

'Nouvelles Découvertes au Nord de La Mer du Sud,' Phillippe Buache, 1752-76. These maps were included in Diderot's *Encyclopédie* and thus were given wide circulation and much authority. The upper is a simplified version of one made by Buache in 1752, the first to show Bering's two voyages of 1728-30 and 1741-2. It was also the first to show the mythical Mer de l'Ouest in the vicinity of Vancouver, an idea subsequently much copied. Oddly, it gives a Chinese name, Fou-Sang, to British Columbia. The lower map is a detail copied from a Japanese map of the world. 330 x 410 mm.

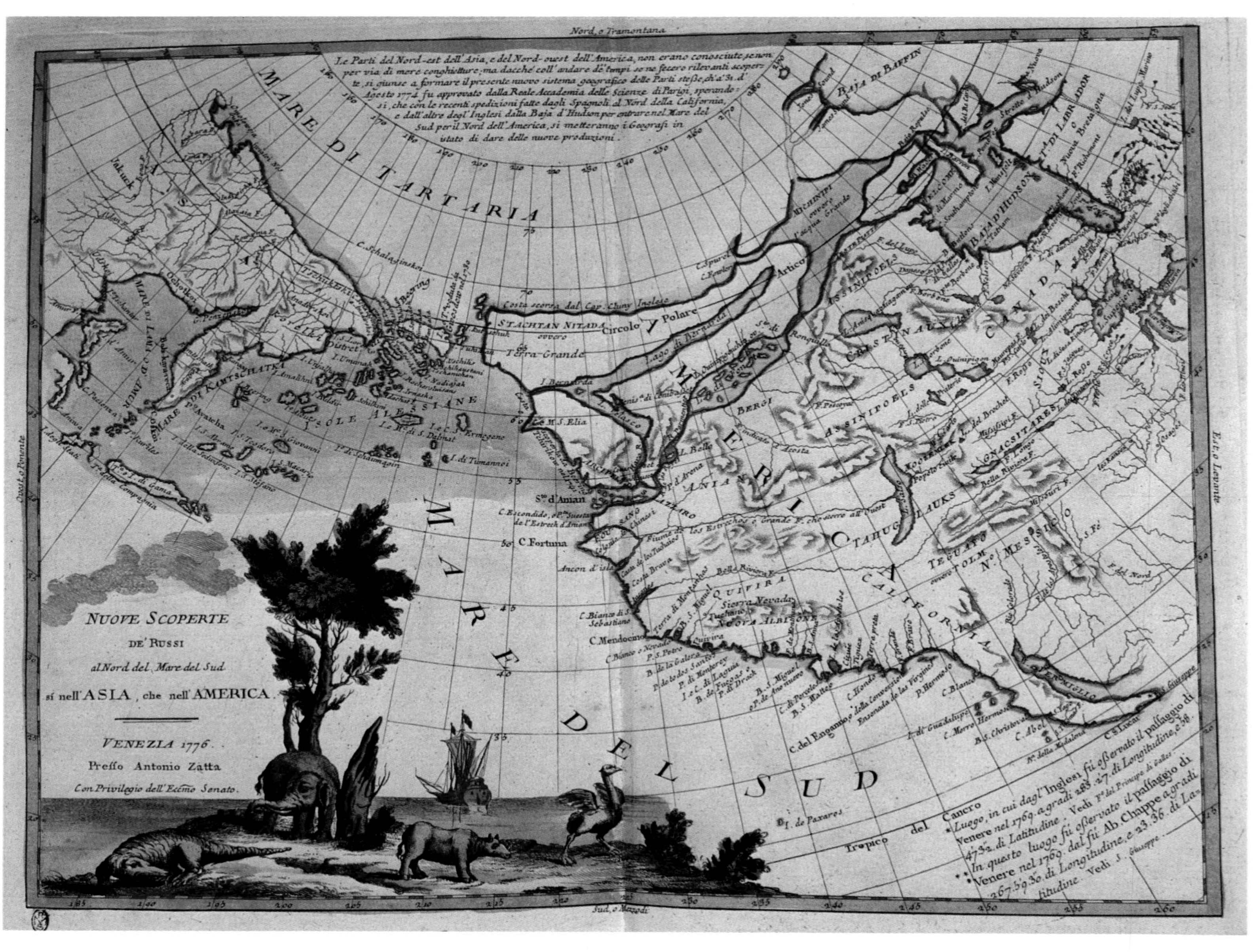

Plate CXXXIV

'Nouve Scoperte de' Russi...,' Antonio Zatta, 1776. This eerily distorted Venetian map purports to show the latest information gathered by the Russians and Bering about the Alaska area, but it is difficult to make out what is being represented. The Northwest Passage, however, is all too clearly visible.
380 x 510 mm.

Plate CXXXV

'Théatre de la Guerre...,' Brion de la Tour, 1777. A French map, copied from British sources, of the theater of conflict between the Americans and the British in the third year of the War of Independence. Note that the only military notation on the map is the one American victory that was instrumental in bringing France into the war on the Americas' side: Burgoyne's defeat at Saratoga.
726 x 540 mm.

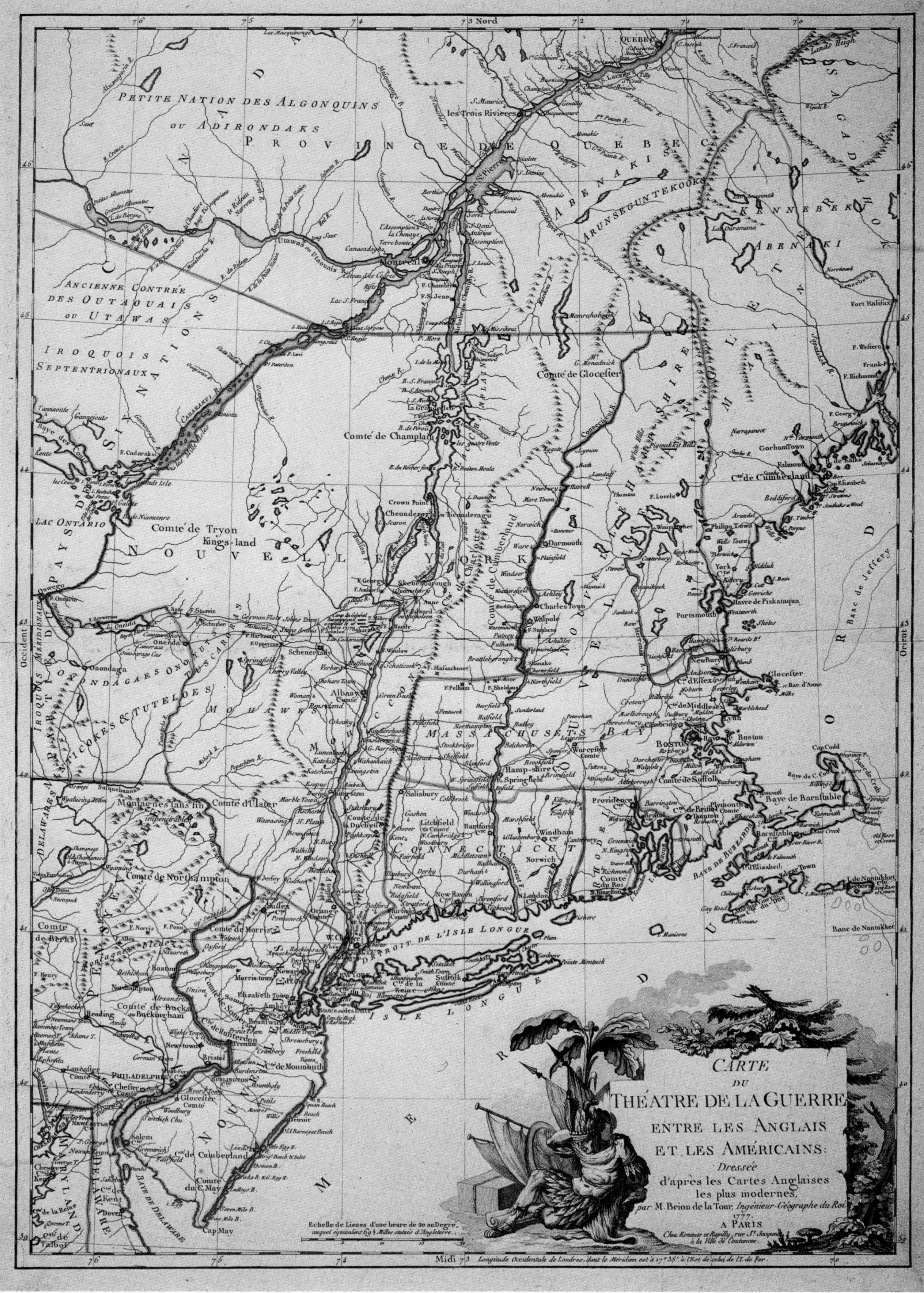
CARTE
DU
THÉATRE DE LA GUERRE
ENTRE LES ANGLAIS
ET LES AMÉRICAINS:
Dressée
d'après les Cartes Anglaises
les plus modernes,
par M. Brion de la Tour, Ingénieur-Géographe du Roi.
1777.
A PARIS

Plate CXXXVI

'Nuova Inghilterra,' Tomasso Masi, 1777. A shamelessly unattributed copy of Bellin's 'Nouvelle Angleterre' (Plate CXXLIII) is this Italian map published 20 years later in Livorno. Even the cartouche is the same. 206 x 304 mm.

Plate CXXXVII

'I Cinque Laghi del Canada,' Tomasso Masi, 1777. Also based on Franco-British sources is Masi's map of the Great Lakes. 240 x 190 mm.

Carta rappresentante i cinque Laghi del Canada
Lago degli Abiubis
Lago de Temifcaming
LAGO SUPERIORE
Algonquini
I Saltatori
LAGO HURONE
LAGO ONTARIO
on Kadarakai
LAGO ERIO
LAGO MICHIGAN
Irocchesi
IROCCHESI
MIAMIS
PENSILVANIA
NUOVA JERSEY
Forte du Quesne
Mataouan

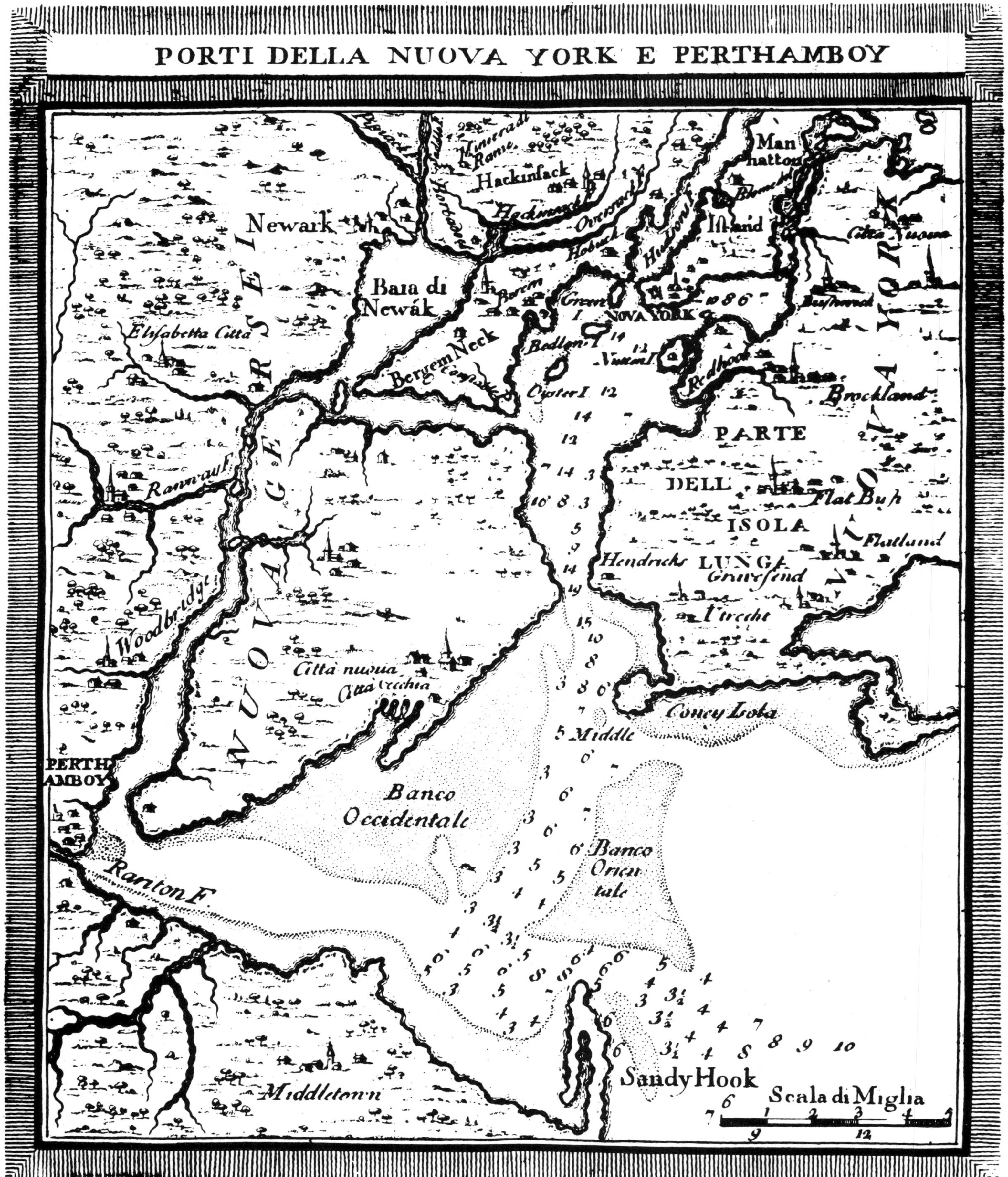

Plate CXXXCIII

'Porti della Nuova York e Perthamboy,' Tomasso Masi, 1777. By the time this map was made far more sophisticated regional maps of New York Harbor and Staten Island were in existence. Presumably Masi would have copied them if he could.
200 x 180 mm.

Plate CXXXIX (right)

'Il Golfo del Fiume S Lorenzo,' Tomasso Masi, 1777. Masi's version of the St Lawrence is essentially that of Bellin (Plate CXXX), with the important political difference that the area is now called Nuova Brettagna.
240 x 190 mm.

CARTA RAPPRESENTANTE IL GOLFO DEL FIUME S.LORENZO

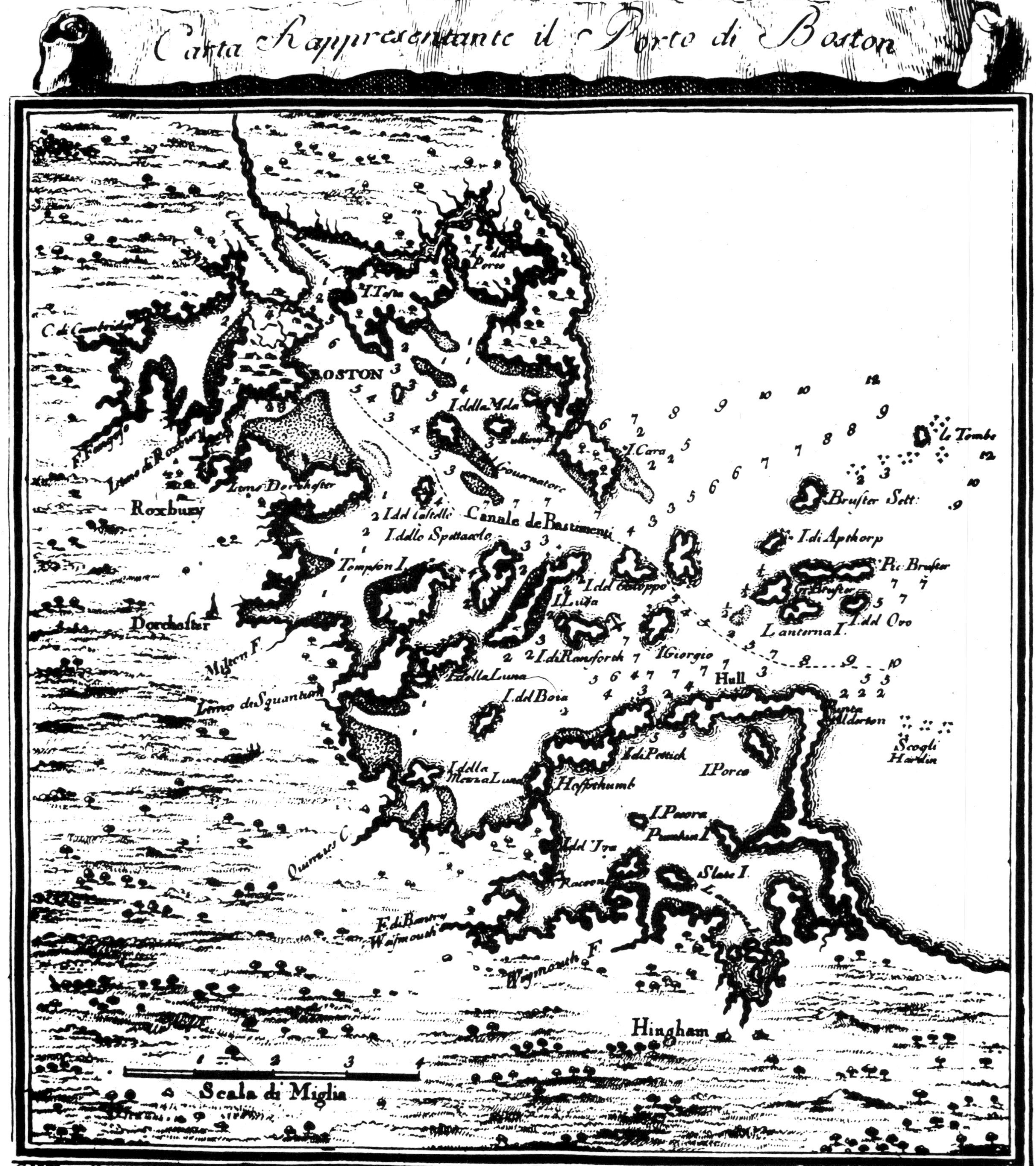

Plate CXL

'Il Porto di Boston,' Tomasso Masi, 1777. Like his New York, Masi's Boston is less inaccurate than old fashioned. But his insistence on using Italian place names (*eg*, Isole di Apthorp) wherever possible lends his pedestrian work a certain charm. 200 x 180 mm.

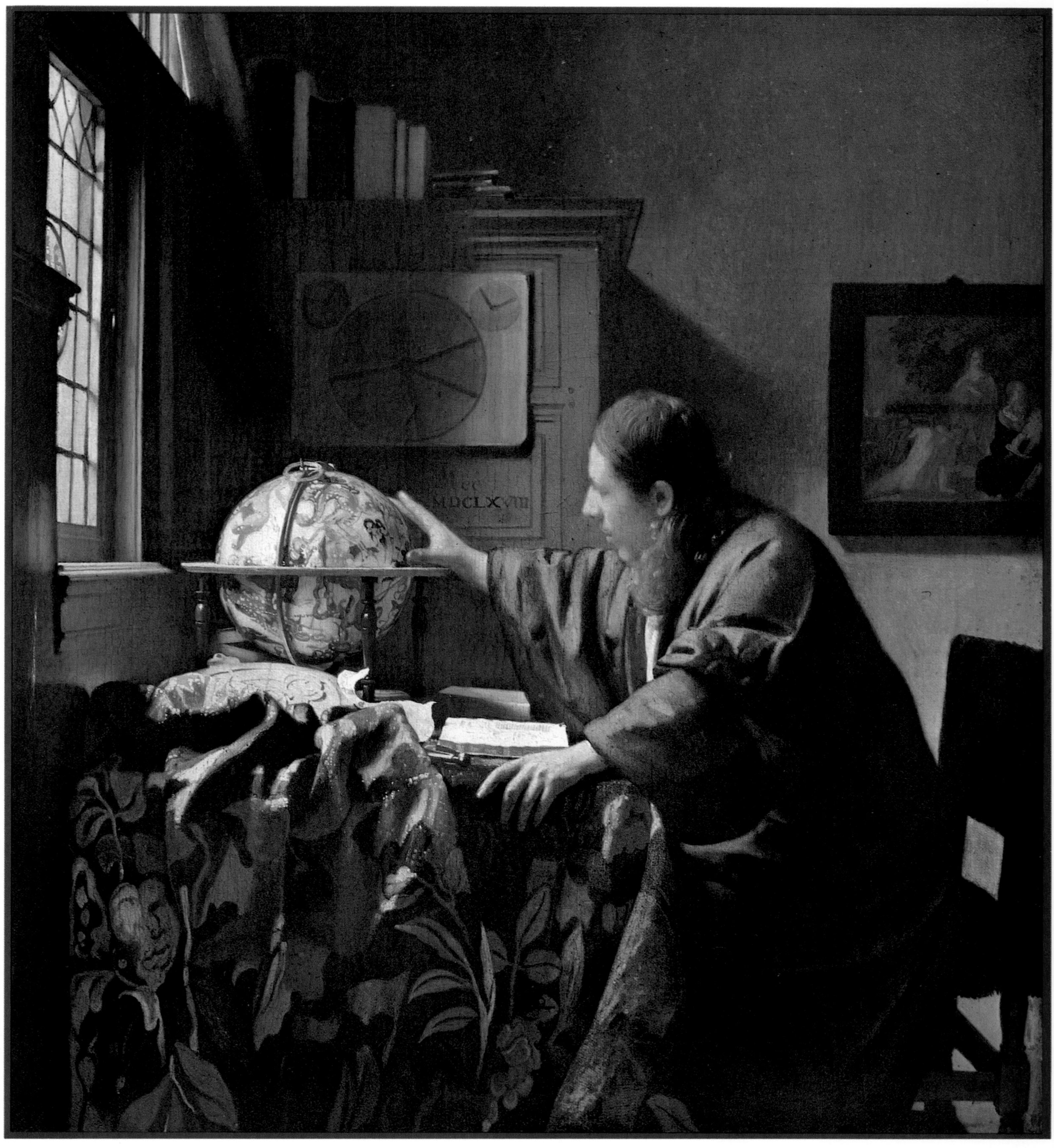

Vermeer's The Cosmographer, *1668.*

Plate CXLI

'Mappamondo,' Antonio Zatta, 1774. By the late eighteenth century if the old tradition of furnishing maps with lavish decoration was being kept alive anywhere, it was in Italy. But even the Italian work was now a pale shadow of sixteenth-century glories, as this no-more-than pleasing Zatta world map suggests. In respect to North America, note the inclusion of Buache's mythical Mer de l'Ouest in the vicinity of Vancouver.
312 x 415 mm.

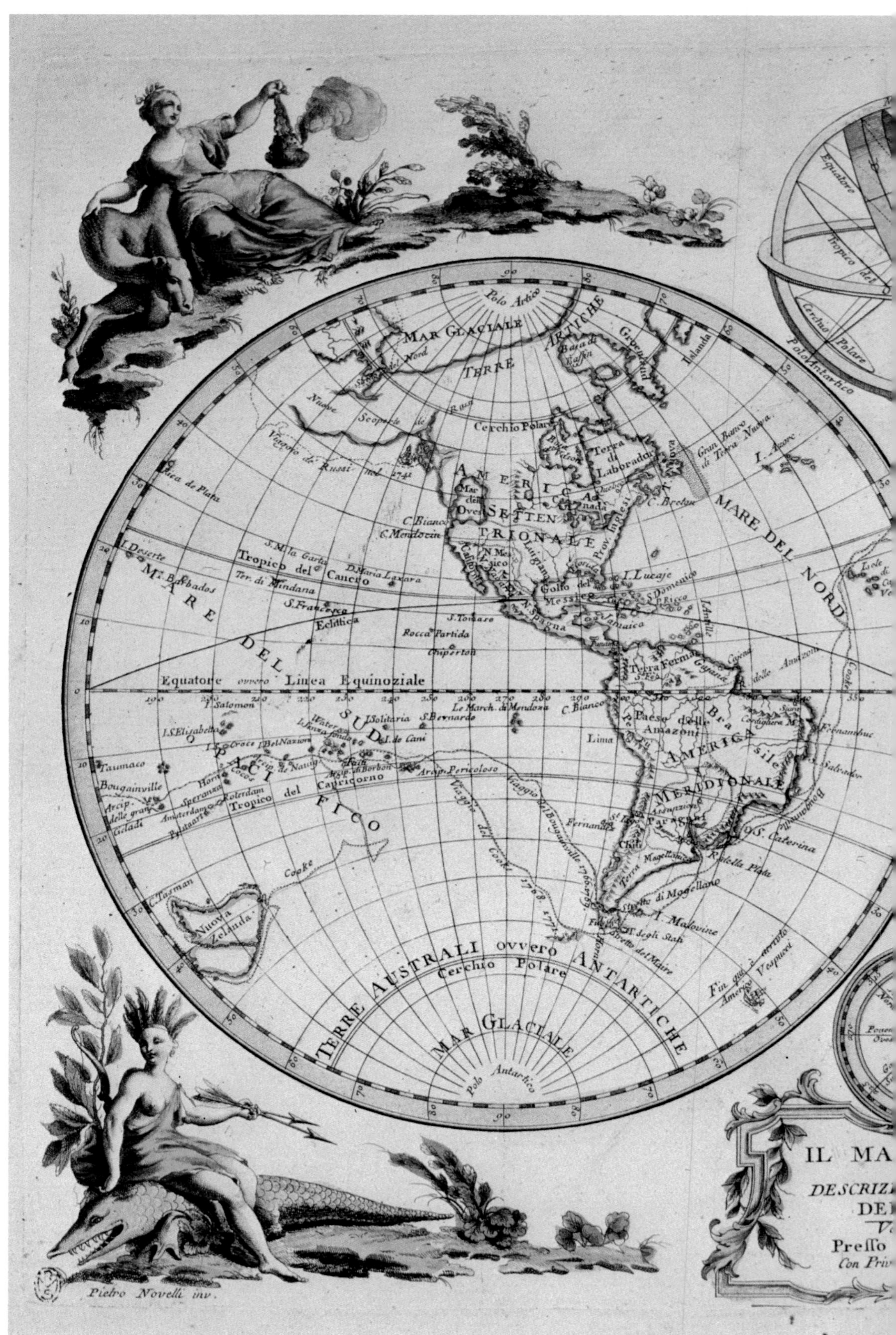

TERRE ARTICHE
MAR GLACIALE
Polo Artico
Cerchio Polare
Tartaria Russa
SIBERIA
ASIA
GRAN TARTARIA
Tartaria Chinese
Tartaria Indipendente
PERSIA
CHINA
L'INDIE
ARABIA
EUROPA
Russia
BARBARIA
NIGRIZIA
AFFRICA
GUINEA
Abissinia
CAFFERIA
Monomotapa
MARE DELL' INDIE
I. Maldive
Ceilan
Filippine
N. Filippine
Is. Mariane
Tropico del Cancro
MARE DEL SUD
Mar del Giapone
Kamtchatka
Nuova Olanda
T. D' Endraet
Terra di Diemen
Viaggio del Cooke
Eclittica
Tropico del Capricorno
Amsterdam
S. Paolo
S. Elena
Congo
Rodriguez
Dromedario
AUSTRALI, o ANTARTICHE
TERRE
Cerchio Polare
Polo Antartico
ONDO
NERALE
BO
Zatta
Valentina Barat scris.
Giulian Zuliani scol.

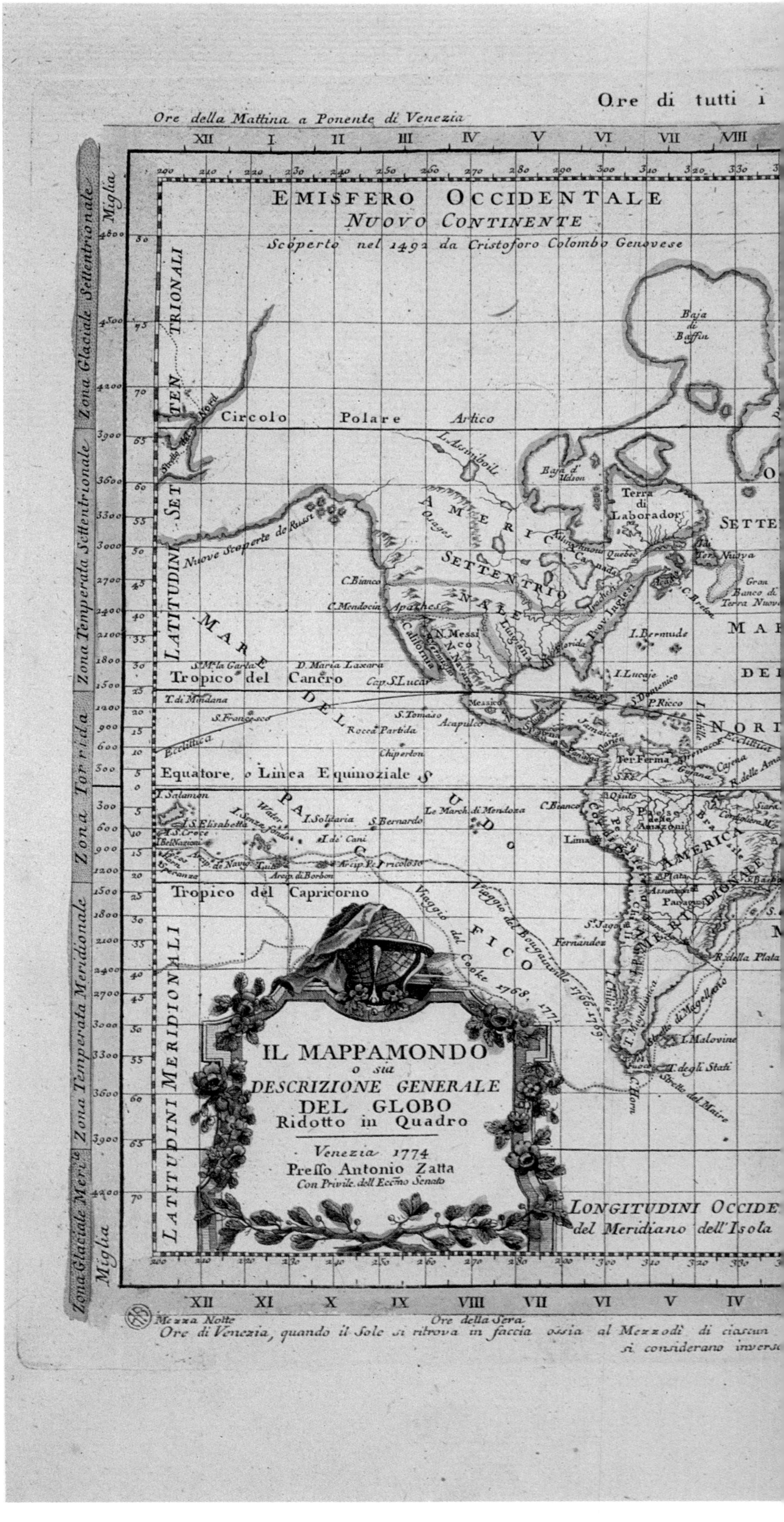

Plate CXLII

'Mappamondo,' Antonio Zatta, 1774.
Though it carries the same date as the Zatta world map shown in Plate CXLI, this one is quite different. The shapes of Labrador and Alaska, for example, are changed, and the Mer de l'Ouest is gone. The scales along the sides explain global time differences, temperature zones, the lengths of days and nights, etc.
312 x 415 mm.

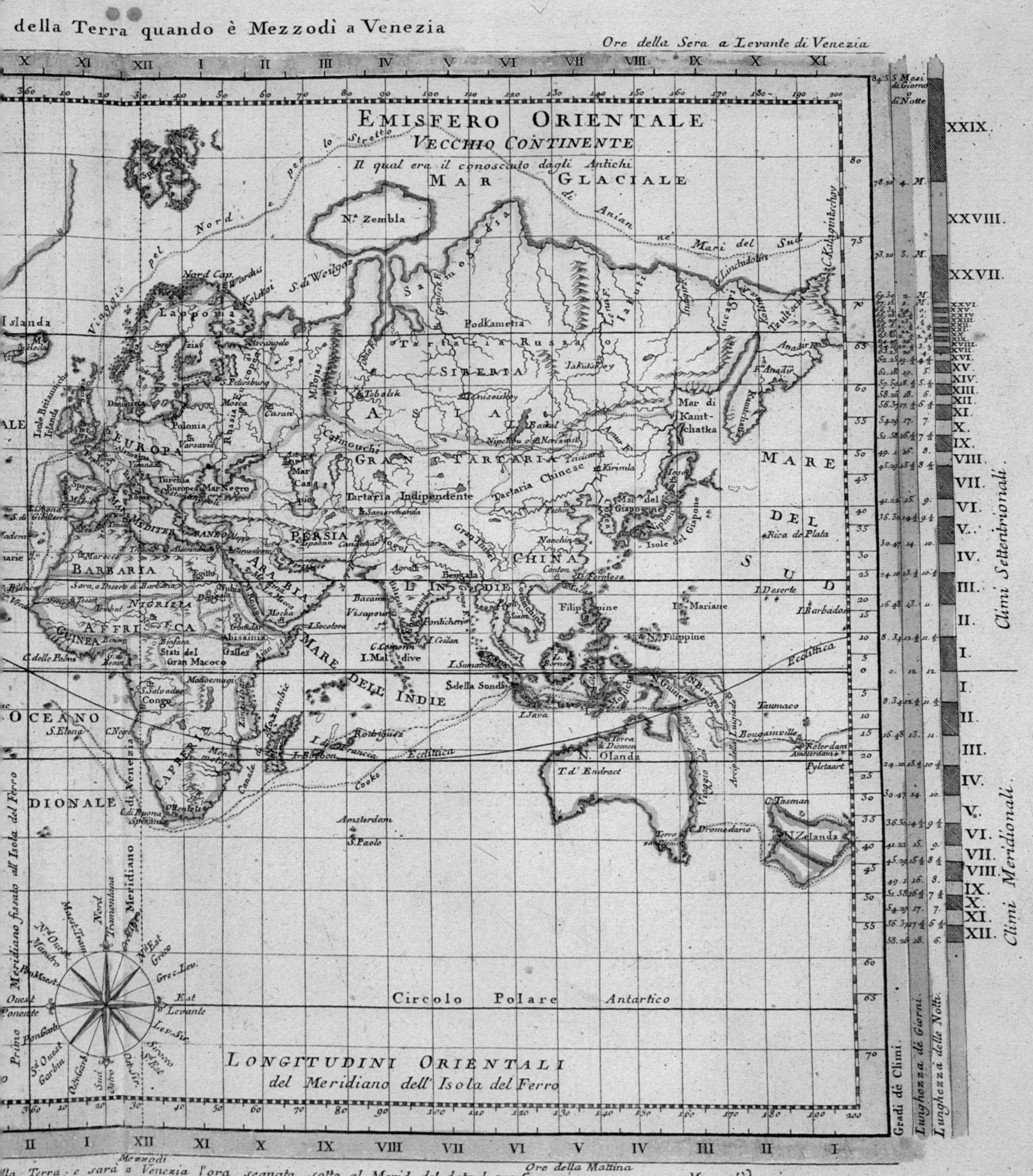
della Terra quando è Mezzodì a Venezia
Ore della Sera a Levante di Venezia
Emisfero Orientale
Vecchio Continente
Il qual era il conosciuto dagli Antichi
Mar Glaciale
Longitudini Orientali
del Meridiano dell' Isola del Ferro
Circolo Polare Antartico
Primo Meridiano fissato all' Isola del Ferro
Climi Settentrionali
Climi Meridionali
Gradi de' Climi
Lunghezza de' Giorni
Lunghezza delle Notti
Ore della Mattina
lla Terra; e sarà a Venezia l'ora segnata sotto al Merid. del dato luogo (ove si suppone essere Mezzodì) ossia sono, e
ore segnate sotto a due Merid. di Venezia e del luogo dato.

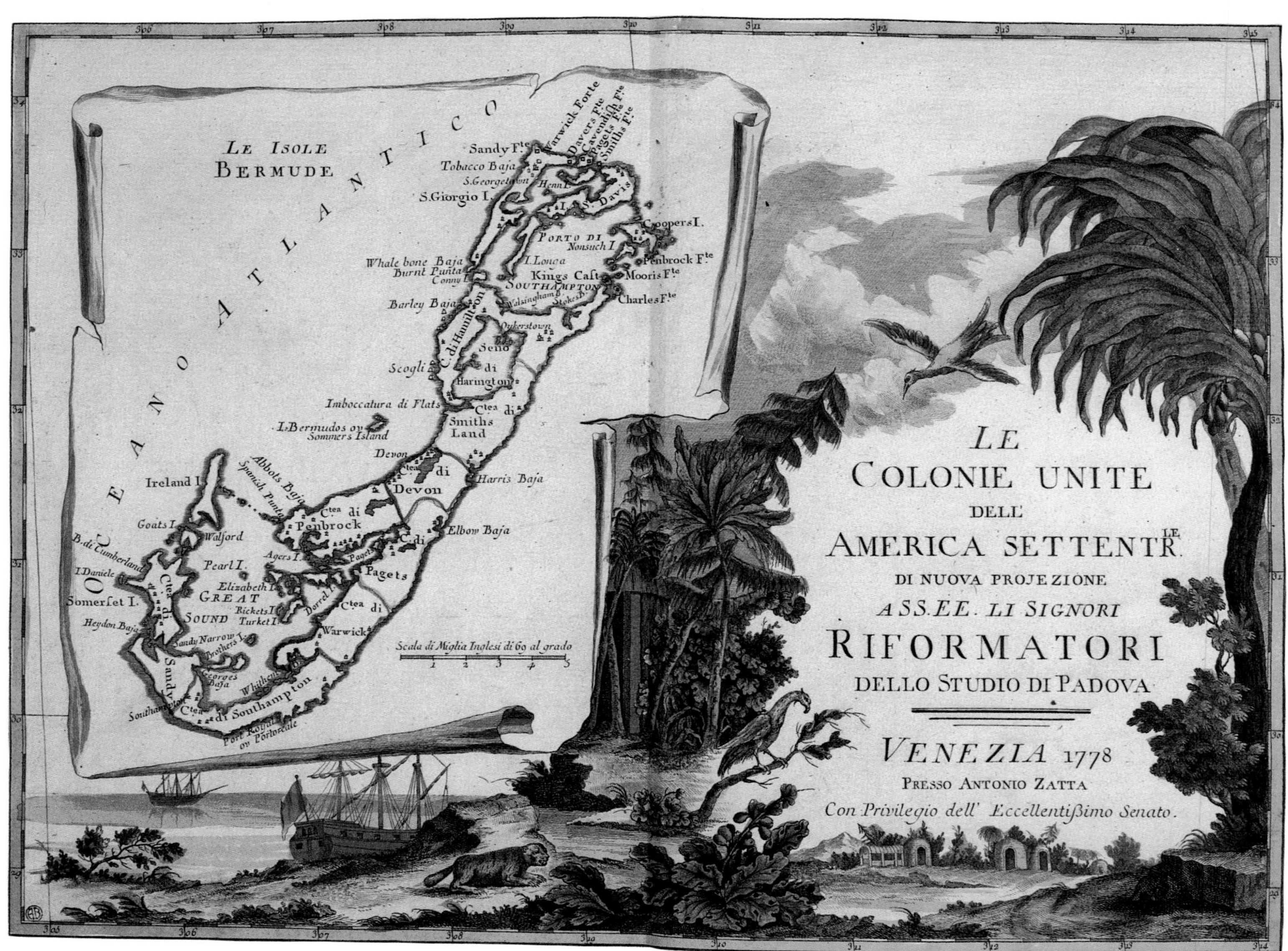

Plate CXLIII

'L'Isole Bermude,' Antonio Zatta, 1778. This frontispiece is from the North American section of Zatta's *Atlante Novissimo,* one of the major Italian atlases of the eighteenth century. The pages that follow (Plates CXLIV-CLIV) reproduce other maps from this famous collection. That they are copies, based primarily on English originals, is less relevant than it might have been 100, or even 50 years earlier, for by now the number of accurate regional maps in circulation was so great that their true proprietorship was becoming more difficult to establish. The Bermuda map above is a case in point. It may derive from a very similar map published in 1763 in *The Gentleman's Magazine,* but the periodical did not even bother to give the name of the man who drew the map.
312 x 514 mm.

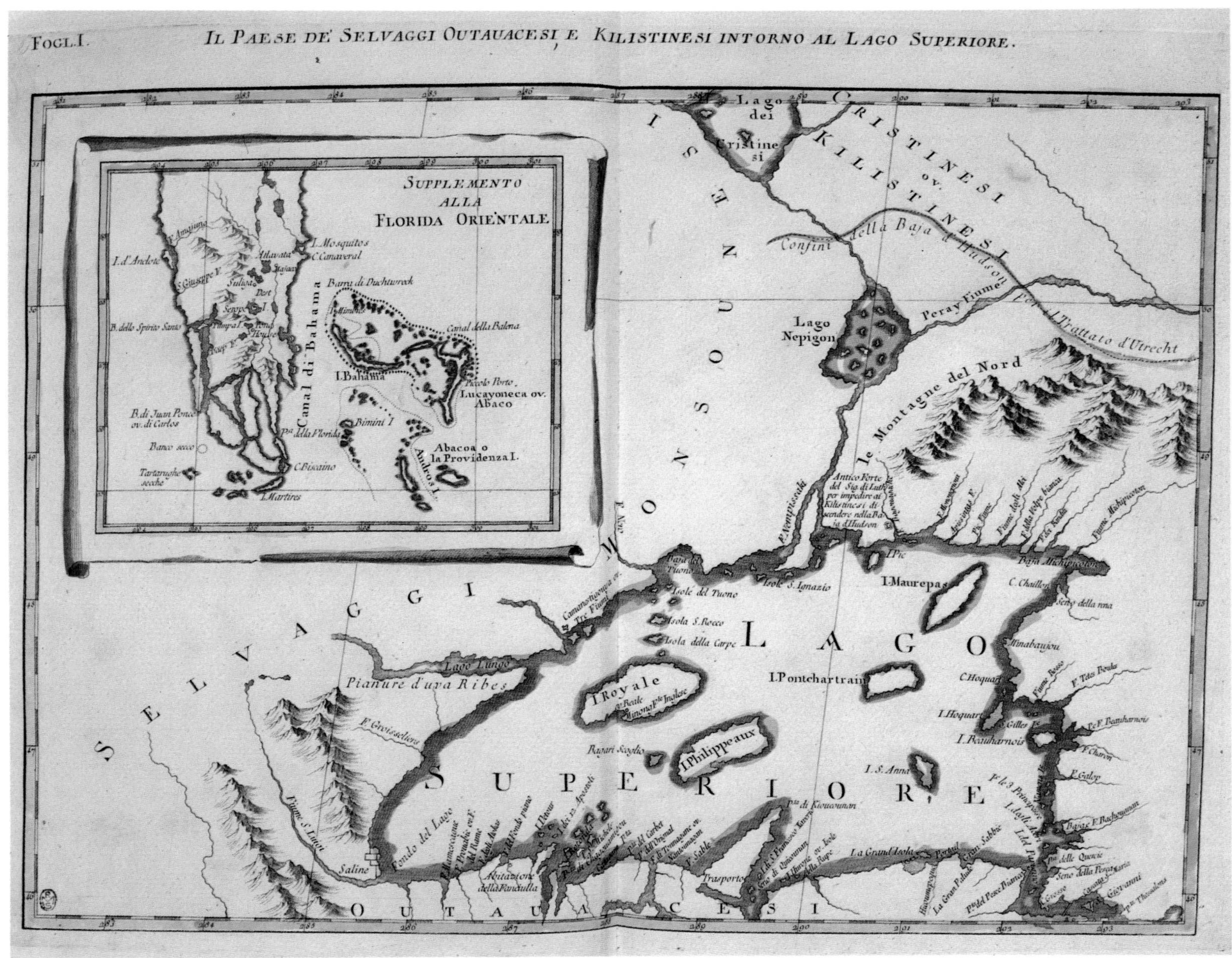

Plate CXLIV

'Il Paese de' Selvaggi...,' Antonio Zatta, 1778. The title, translated, might read, 'The Country of the Savage Ottowas and Christineaux on the shores of Lake Superior.' Except for Ile Royale, the large islands in the lake are fictitious. The somewhat distorted outline of southern Florida in the inset is in keeping with the general lack of British knowledge about this area.
312 x 415 mm.

Plate CXLV

'La Parte Occidentale della Nuova Francia,' Antonio Zatta, 1778. This map covers an area of western Québec and eastern Ontario that is defined by Lake Superior, Hudson Bay and Lake Mistassini, *ie,* part of the area of the Indians' Six Nations. 312 x 415 mm.

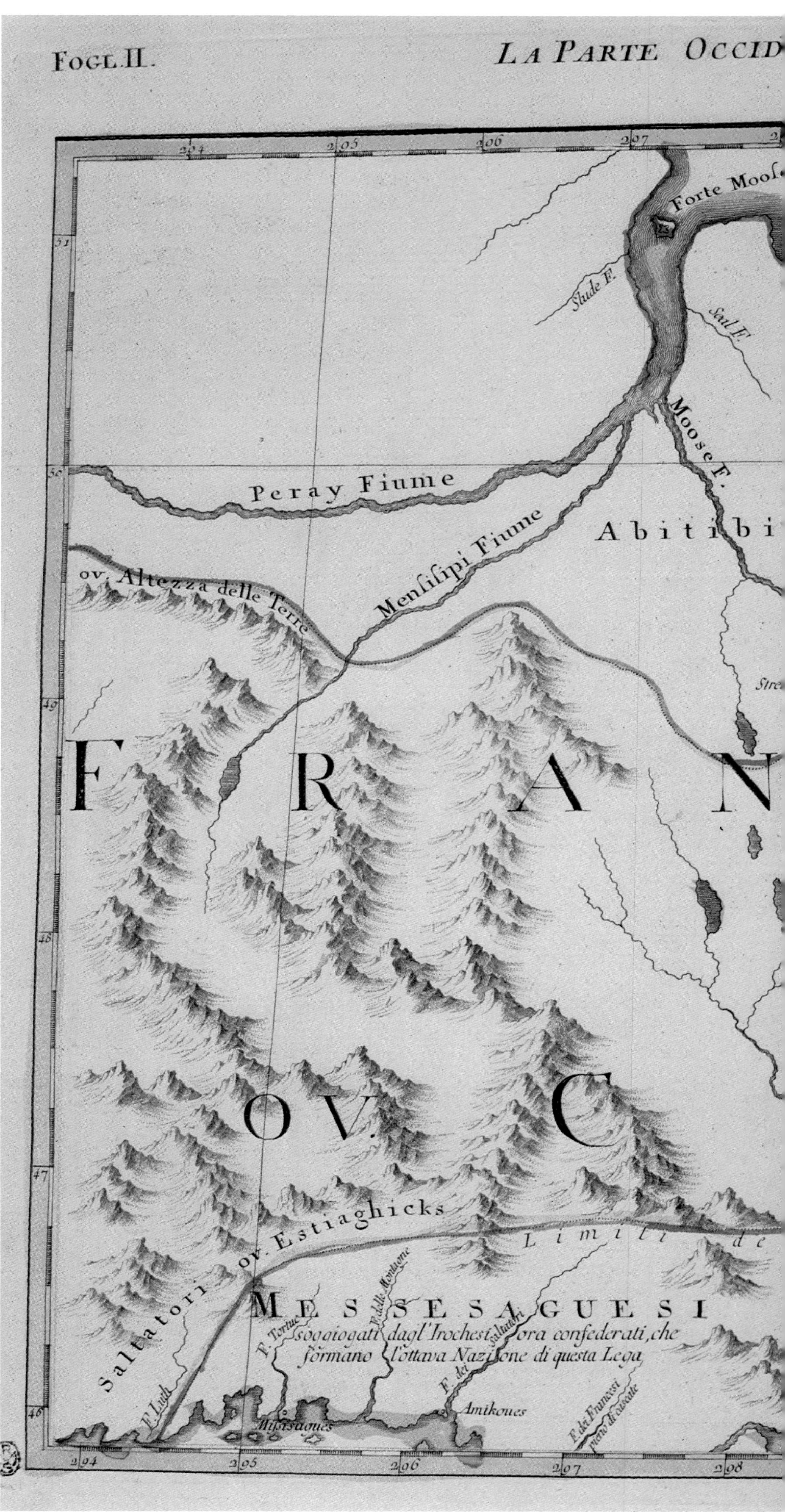

…ALE DELLA NUOVA FRANCIA O CANADA.
Punta Conforto
Fte Rupert abbandonato
Lago Nemiscau
Terre di Gesseirinìouetgz
Lago dei Mistassini
Dureval Missione
Genti di Terre
tutti cacciatori che non coltivano la terra
Oupitchiouen F.
Più alte Montagne
Nekoubàchich L.
L. Nekoubau
Lago Naskatich
go Abitibis
Forte Abitibis
Lago Beauharnois
Nekoubanistesi
Lago S. Pietro
Casa Francese distrutta
Trasporto Ouikouan
Lago Ouichigoubich
Chomomchovanistesi
Lago Miscouaskane
Lago Oumaniouetz
Lago Begon
L. Temiscaming
Miniere di Rame
Seno della miniera
L. Metabetchouan
Cascata lunga
Kaouinnagamich L.
Achoupekahigan F.
Mataouan
Lago Nipissinnis
Trasporto dei Galots
GLI ANTICHI ALGONCHINI
distrutti dagli Irochesi
F. degli Utawasi
F. dell' Assunzione
Monreal

Plate CXLVI

'Parte Orientale del Canada,' Antonio Zatta, 1778. There were by 1778 so many good maps of this region that it is difficult to cite any single source for Zatta's copy. The most probable candidate, a map by John Mitchell, will be discussed at more length in subsequent captions.
312 x 415 mm,

NUOVA SCOZIA SETTENTRIONALE, E PARTE DI LABRADOR.
LABRADOR
L. Ashouanipi
I. ANTICOSTI
Punta d'Anticosti
Capo Rosiers
Gaspesiani
Monti della Madonna
Baya de Calori
B. di Nipisiguit
Banco degli Orfani
NUOVA
SCOZIA
Baya di Miramichi
I. S. GIOVANNI
Shepody Monte
Strada di 120 leghe ascendendo a Quebec
Isola Miscou
Punta delle Isole
Lo Stagno grande
C. Tourmentin
Baya Verde
C. Portepis
Punta del Nord
Niet Isola
Aas Isola
Isola Isser
Duyse Isola
Natiscotec Baja
B. degli Orsi
B. e F. del Buon Soccorso
I. Bonaventura
C. di Speranza
Plate I.
C. e B. di Gaspé
Piccolo Tracadille
Gran Tracadille
Fiume S. Giovanni
L. Freneuse
Villagio dei Cimanisti

Plate CXLVII

'Il Paese de' Selvaggi Outagamiani...,' Antonio Zatta, 1778. This map of the area between the Mississippi and Lake Michigan is, like most of the Zatta maps, heavily indebted to a map made by the English cartographer Dr John Mitchell in 1755, possibly the most influential map of North America made in the eighteenth century. 312 x 415 mm.

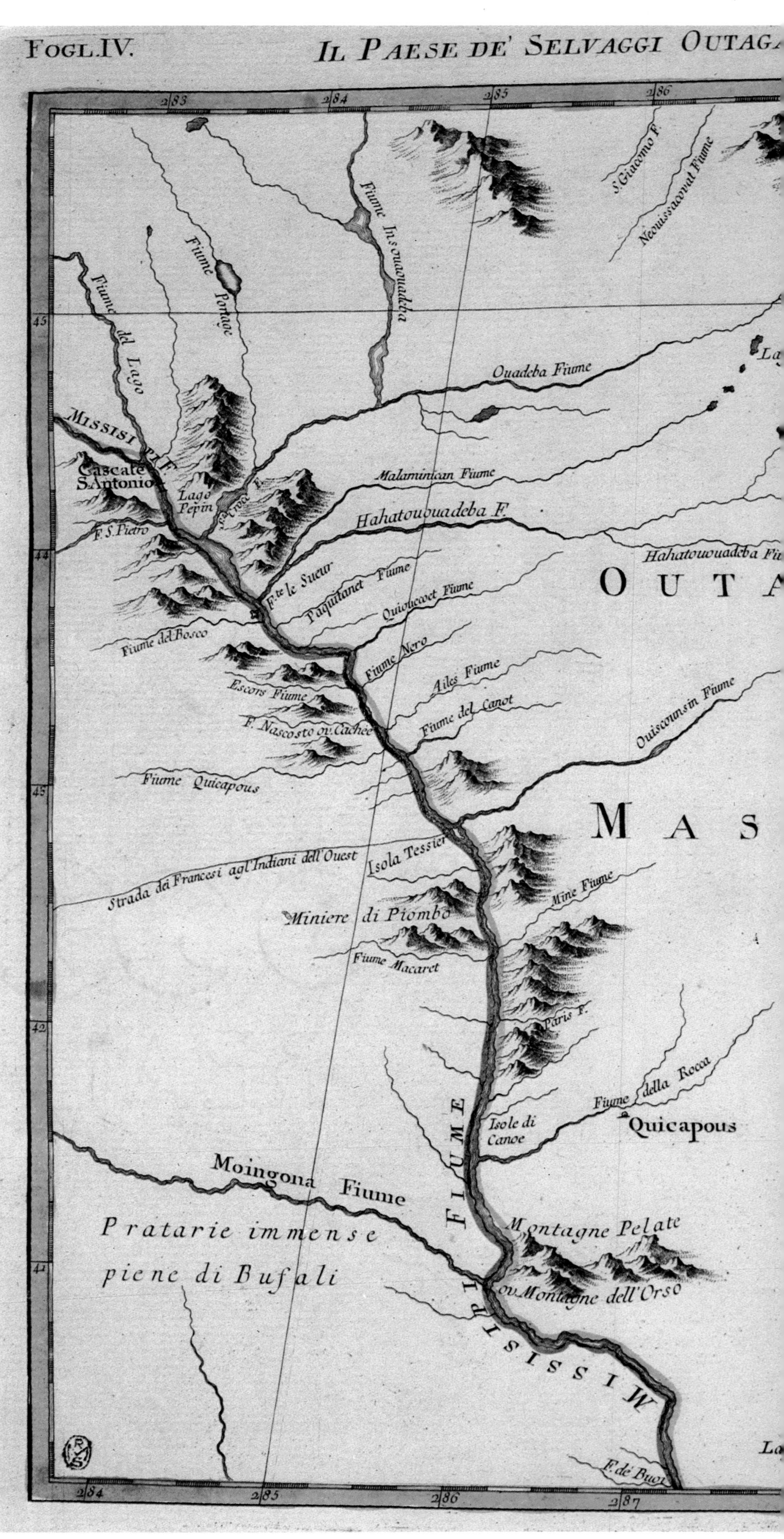

...ANI, MASCOUTENSI, ILLINESI, E PARTE DELLE VI. NAZIONI.
PAESE DELLE VOLPI
...GAMESI
...OUTENSI
LAGO MICHIGAN
LI MIAMESI
INDIANI
Forti e Missioni distrutte
S. Maria
I. S. Elena
Michillimakinak
I. Rotonda
I. del Bosco bianco
Ancoraggio del Tuono
Baja dei Noquets
Isole Poutewatamis
I. del Castoro
Gran Baja
I. Beaver
Fiume Noquets
Gran Pianura molto elevata
Baja di Saguinam
Fiume Buscies
F. d'Oulamanittie
F. Marquet
F. S. Nicolas
Fiume Sable
Fiume Bianco
Maticou
Il Gran Fiume
Fiume Raisin
Fiume Barbue
Fiume Maramег
Fiume Nero
Fiume S. Giuseppe
Malomines ov. Oumalomines
Octagros
li Sakis
Missione di S. Francesco Xaverio
Outagamis ov. F. delle Volpi
Lago
Kitchigamin
Miscouakimina
Mascoutensi ov. Genti del Fuoco
Fiume e Porto Chicagou
Trasporto
Quadoghé cosi nominati dalle Sei Nazioni l'estensione del loro Territorio, ed i limiti secondo il contratto di vendita fatta all'Inghilterra nel 1701. 1726. e 44.
Miamis
Pouteouatamis
Fte S. Giuseppe
Sorgenti del Fiume Teakiki
Fiume degl'Illinesi, strada al Missipi di 250 leghe
Comprati e ceduti
La Forca all'Inghilterra
Fiume della Rupe
Chacaguez Fiume
Miamis F.
Trasporto
Forte di Miamis fabricato dai Francesi nel 1750.
Iroquois ov. Irochese F.
Fiume Teakiki
Antico Villaggio degl'Illinesi distrutto dagl'Irochesi
Fte di Miamis
La Rupe
delle Sei Nazioni
Gli antichi Erii sono stati distrutti dagl'Irochesi già 120 anni sono, e dopo quel tempo questi posseggono il Lago Erio
Croce della metà della strada
Waba che F.
Fte Edward
Pickawillanees ov. Picti
Pickawillany del Ohio Fte Ing. fabricato nel 1748
Miniera di Rame
Pinniteoui
100 Miglia
288
289
290
291
292
293
294

Plate CXLVIII

'La Pensilvania, la Nuova York...,' Antonio Zatta, 1778. This is also a map based on John Mitchell's work, with minor up-datings such as a reference to Burgoyne's defeat at Saratoga. Though Mitchell drew his famous 'Map of the British and French Dominions in North America' in 1755, it was used by negotiators in Paris in 1783 to determine the boundaries of the new United States. 312 x 415 mm.

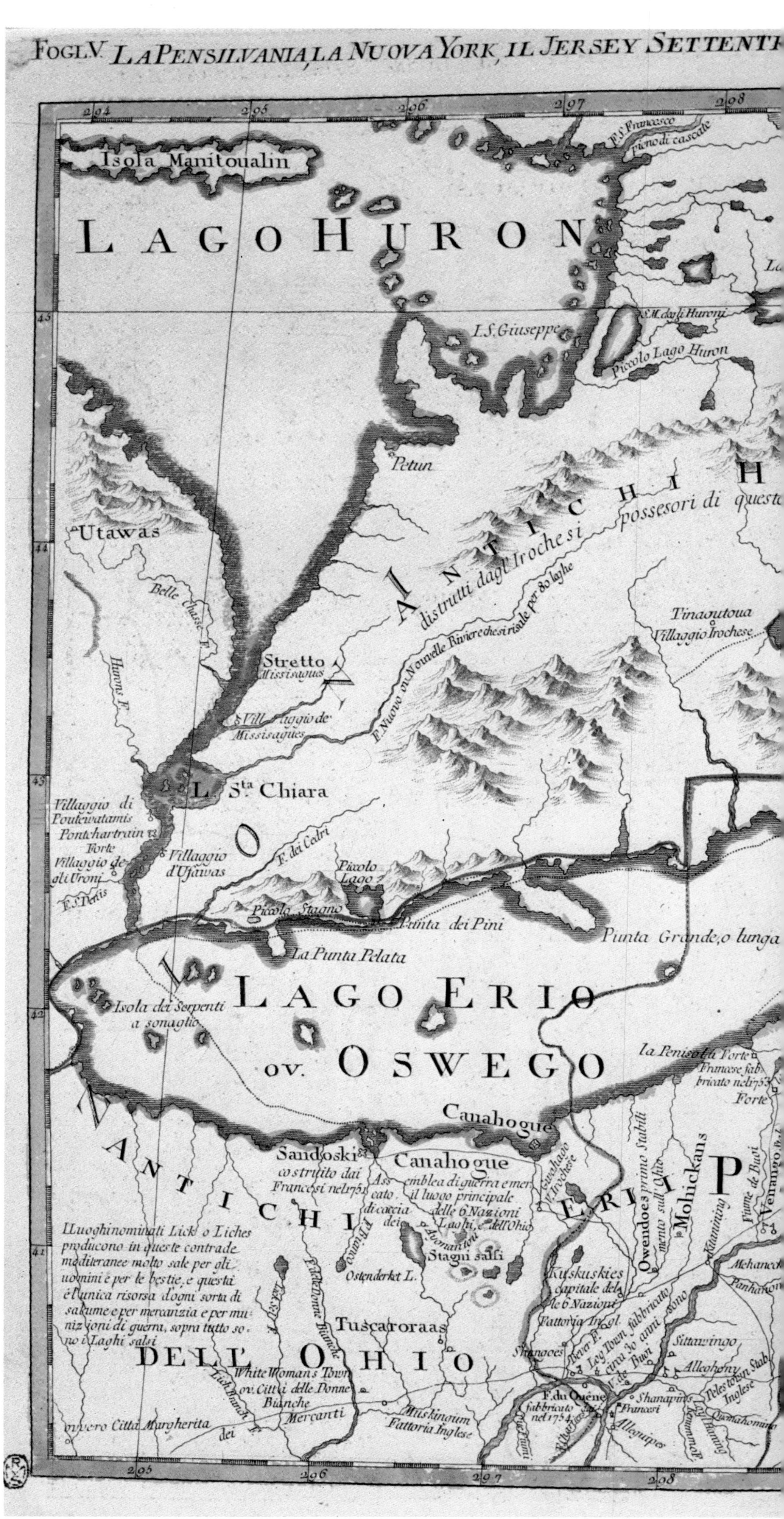

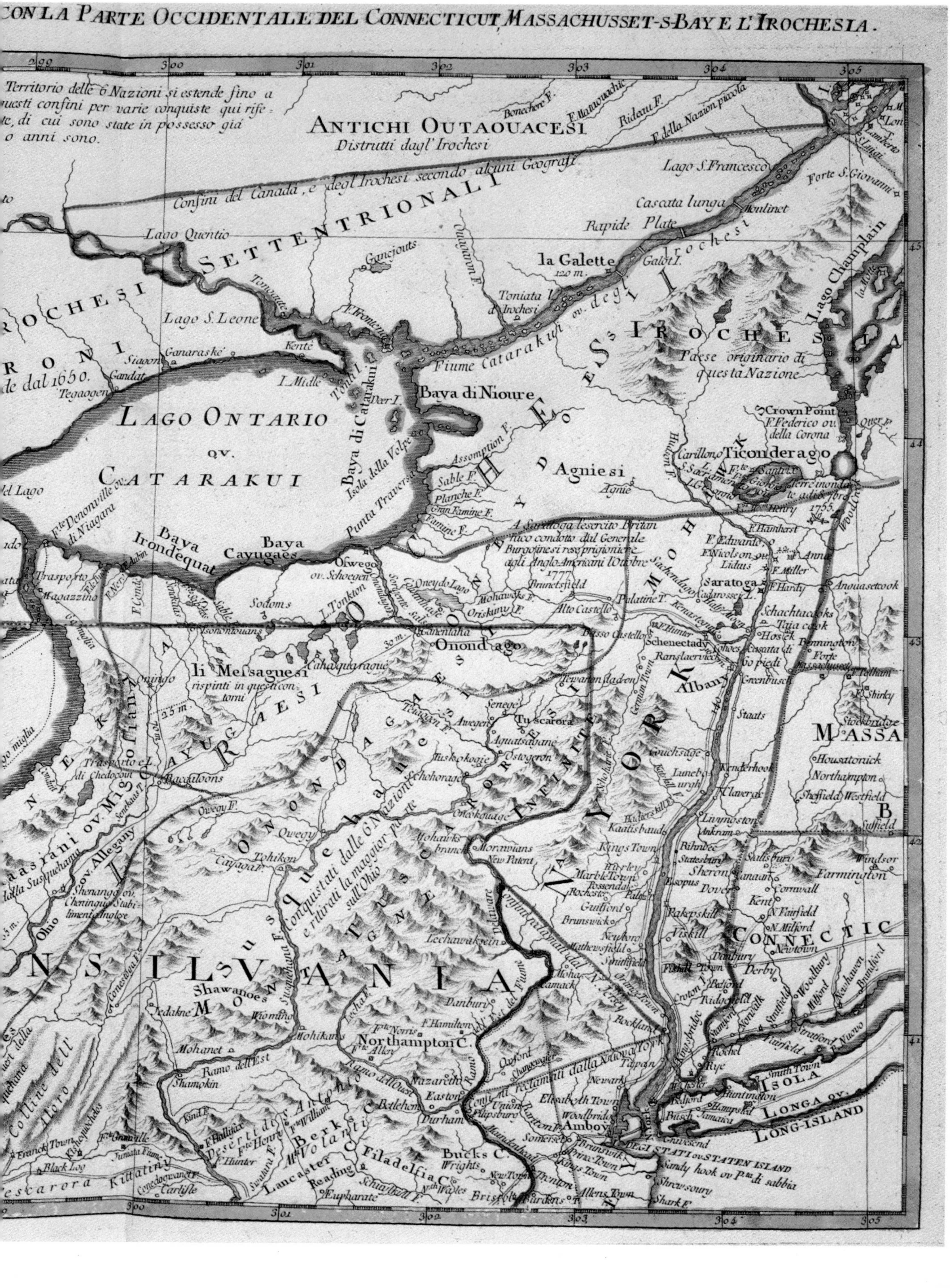

CON LA PARTE OCCIDENTALE DEL CONNECTICUT, MASSACHUSSET-S-BAY E L'IROCHESIA.

Territorio delle 6 Nazioni si estende fino a questi confini per varie conquiste qui rifeite, di cui sono state in possesso già o anni sono.

ANTICHI OUTAOUACESI
Distrutti dagl' Irochesi

Confini del Canadà, e degl' Irochesi secondo alcuni Geografi.

SETTENTRIONALI

Lago S. Francesco
Cascata lunga
Rapide Plate
la Galette
Lago Quentio
Lago S. Leone
Fiume Catarakui ov. degl' Irochesi
IROCHESIA
Paese originario di questa Nazione
Lago Champlain
LAGO ONTARIO ov. CATARAKUI
Baya di Catarakui
Baya di Nioure
Isola della Volpe
Punta Traversa
Crown Point
F. Federico ou della Corona
Ticonderago
Agniesi
A Saratoga l'esercito Britannico condotto dal Generale Burgoine si rese prigioniere agli Anglo-Americani l'Ottobre 1777
Baya Irondequat
Baya Cayugaes
Oswego ov. Schoegen
Saratoga
Schenectady
Albany
Onondago
li Messaguesi rispinti in questi contorni
Tuscarora
NEW YORK
Conquistati dalle 6 Nazioni e ritirati la maggior parte sull' Ohio
PENSILVANIA
Northampton C.
Filadelfia C.
Lancaster C.
Reading
Berks C.
Bucks C.
Easton
Amboy
STATI ov. STATEN ISLAND
Sandy hook ov. P.ta di sabbia
Shrewsboury
ISOLA LONGA ov. LONG-ISLAND
CONNECTICUT
MASSA[CHUSSET-S]-B[AY]
Housatonick
Northampton
Westfield
Farmington
Windsor
Danbury
Stratford
Fairfield
Newhaven
Kingsbridge
Rye
Kinderhook
Livingston
Kingstown
Esopus
Fishkill
Newburgh
Montagne
Colline dell' Oro
Deserti di S. Antonio
Monti Volanti
Tuscarora
Kittatiny
Carlisle
Shamokin
Shawanoes

Plate CXLIX

'L'Acadia... Connecticut,' Antonio Zatta, 1778. This map, along with Plates CXLVII and CXLVIII, form a continuous strip from west to east. (Note, for example, that the missing parts of the words 'Massachusetts,' and 'Connecticut' appear on the preceeding plate.) Again, the basis appears to be one of the editions of Mitchell's great map of 1755. 312 x 415 mm.

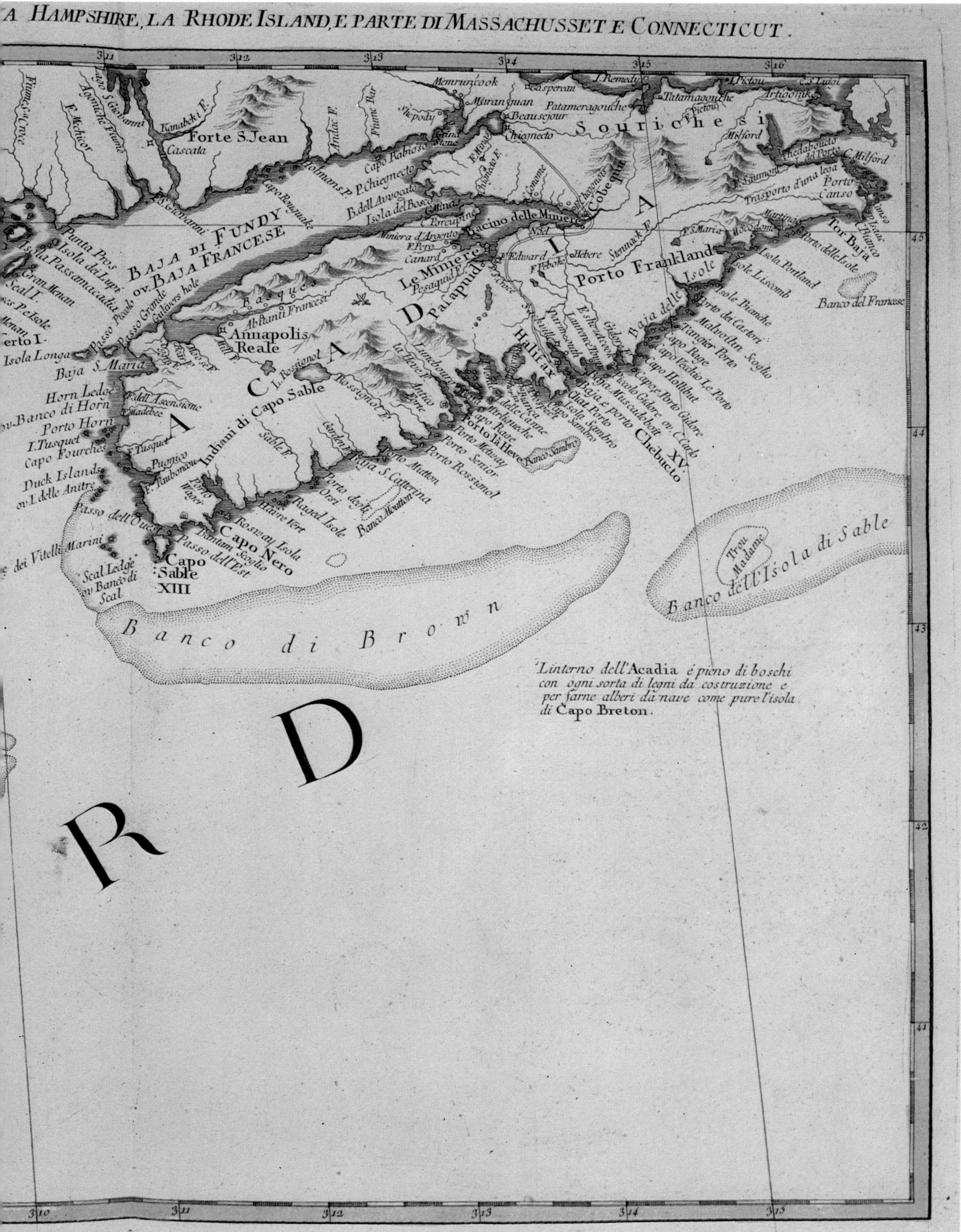
A HAMPSHIRE, LA RHODE ISLAND, E PARTE DI MASSACHUSSET E CONNECTICUT.
Forte S. Jean
Baja di Fundy ov. Baja Francese
Sourichesi
Annapolis Reale
Acadia
Porto Frankland
Halifax
Indiani di Capo Sable
Le Miniere
Bacino delle Miniere
Cobequit
Beausejour
Chebucto
Capo Sable
XIII
XV
Capo Nero
Banco di Brown
Banco dell'Isola di Sable
Trou Madame
Banco del Francese
Tor Baja
Porto Canso
L'interno dell'Acadia è pieno di boschi con ogni sorta di legni da costruzione e per farne alberi da nave come pure l'isola di Capo Breton.
R
D

Plate CL

'Il Paese de' Cherachesi...Virginia,' Antonio Zatta, 1778. This and the following three maps form a unit devoted to the southeastern part of North America. Plate CLI continues this map east, CLII continues it south and CLIII continues CLII east.
312 x 415 mm.

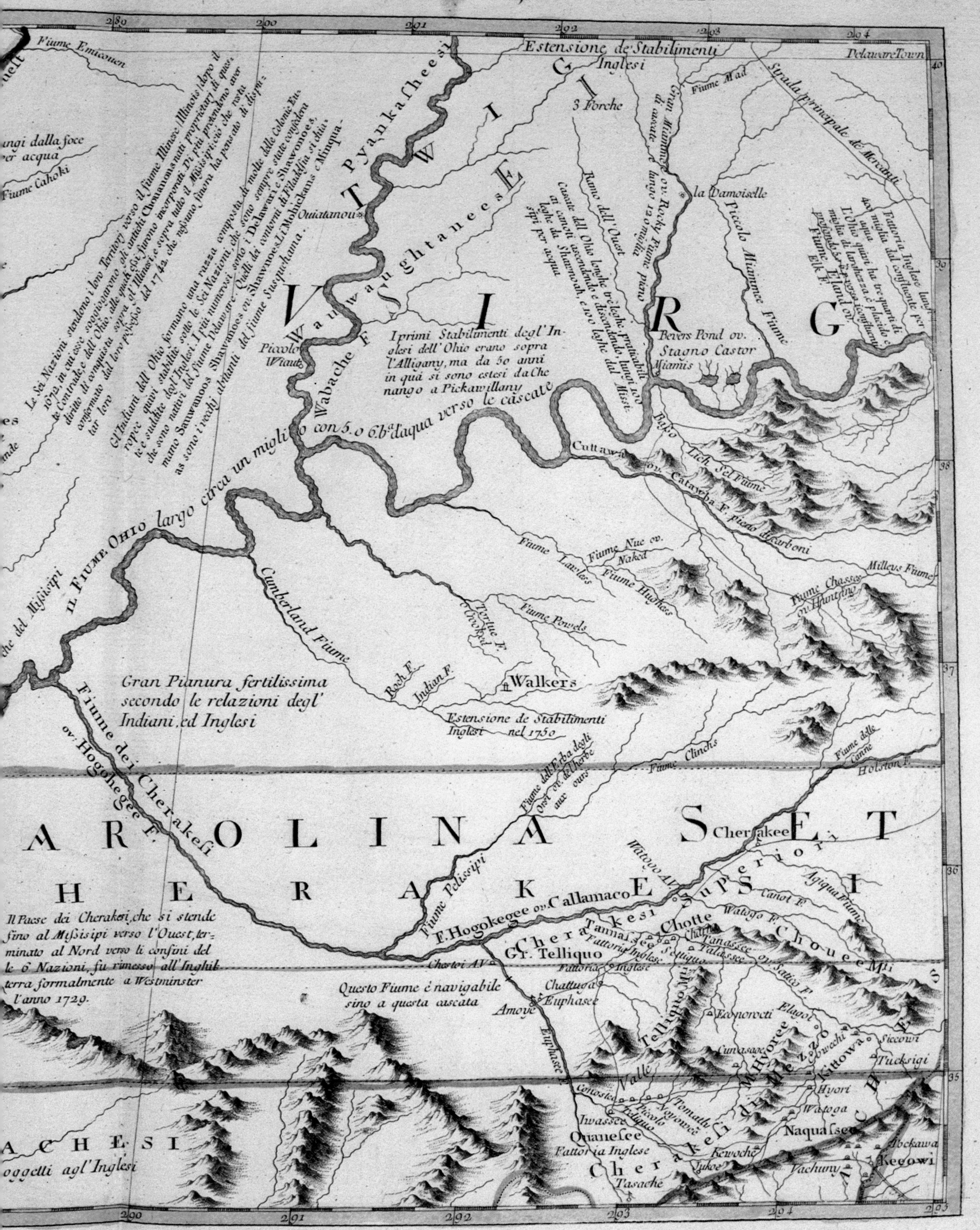

...CCIDENTALE DELLA CAROLINA SETTENTRIONALE, E DELLA VIRGINIA.
Estensione de Stabilimenti Inglesi
Delaware Town
Strada principale de Mercanti
3 Forche
la Damoiselle
Piccolo Miammee Fiume
Bevers Pond ov. Stagno Castor
Miamis
Ouiatanou
Piccolo Wiaut
Wabache F.
Pyankashees
I primi Stabilimenti degl' Inglesi dell' Ohio erano sopra l'Alligany, ma da 50 anni in quà si sono estesi da Chenango a Pickawillany
IL FIUME OHIO largo circa un miglio con 5. o 6.ba d'aqua verso le cascate
Cuttawa ov. Catawba F. pieno di carboni
Cumberland Fiume
Fiume Lawless
Fiume Hughes
Fiume Powels
Walkers
Gran Pianura fertilissima secondo le relazioni degl' Indiani ed Inglesi
Estensione de Stabilimenti Inglesi nel 1750
Fiume dei Cherakesi ov. Hogohegee F.
Fiume Clinchs
Holston F.
CAROLINA SETT
CHERAKESI
Cherakee
Il Paese dei Cherakesi, che si stende fino al Missisipi verso l'Ouest, terminato al Nord verso li confini del le 6 Nazioni, fu rimesso all'Inghilterra formalmente a Westminster l'anno 1729.
F. Hogokegee ov. Callamaco
Fiume Pelisipi
Gr. Telliquo
Chottc
Questo Fiume è navigabile sino a questa cascata
Chattuga
Euphasee
Amoye
Quanesee Fattoria Inglese
Tasache
Naquassee
Keowi
...ACHESI
...oggetti agl' Inglesi

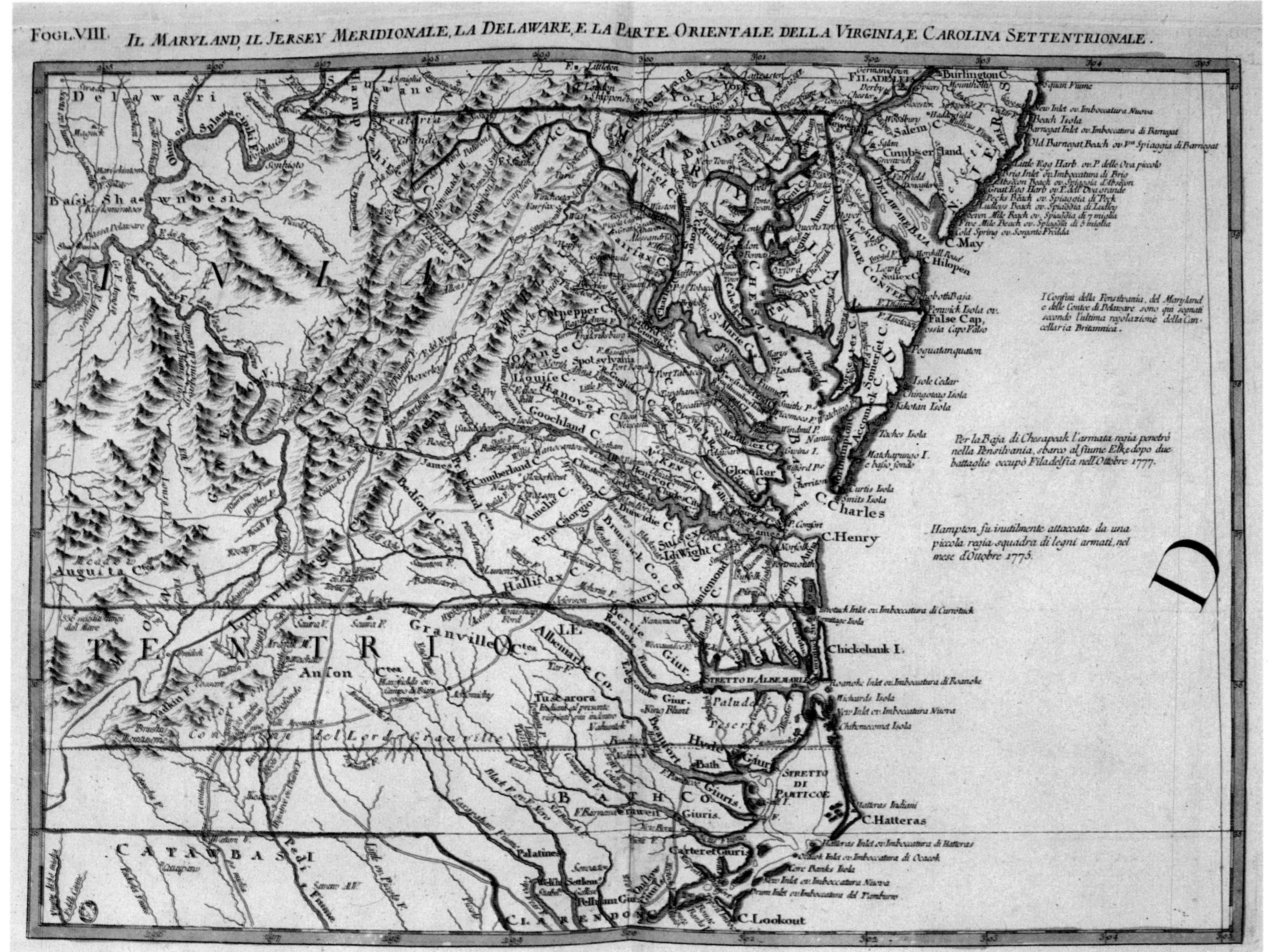

Plate CLI

'Il Maryland...,' Antonio Zatta, 1778. The portion of the Mitchell map shown on this Zatta copy was used as late as 1932 in evidence in a boundary dispute between Delaware and New Jersey. In all, 21 editions of Mitchell's map were published between 1755 and 1781.
312 x 415 mm.

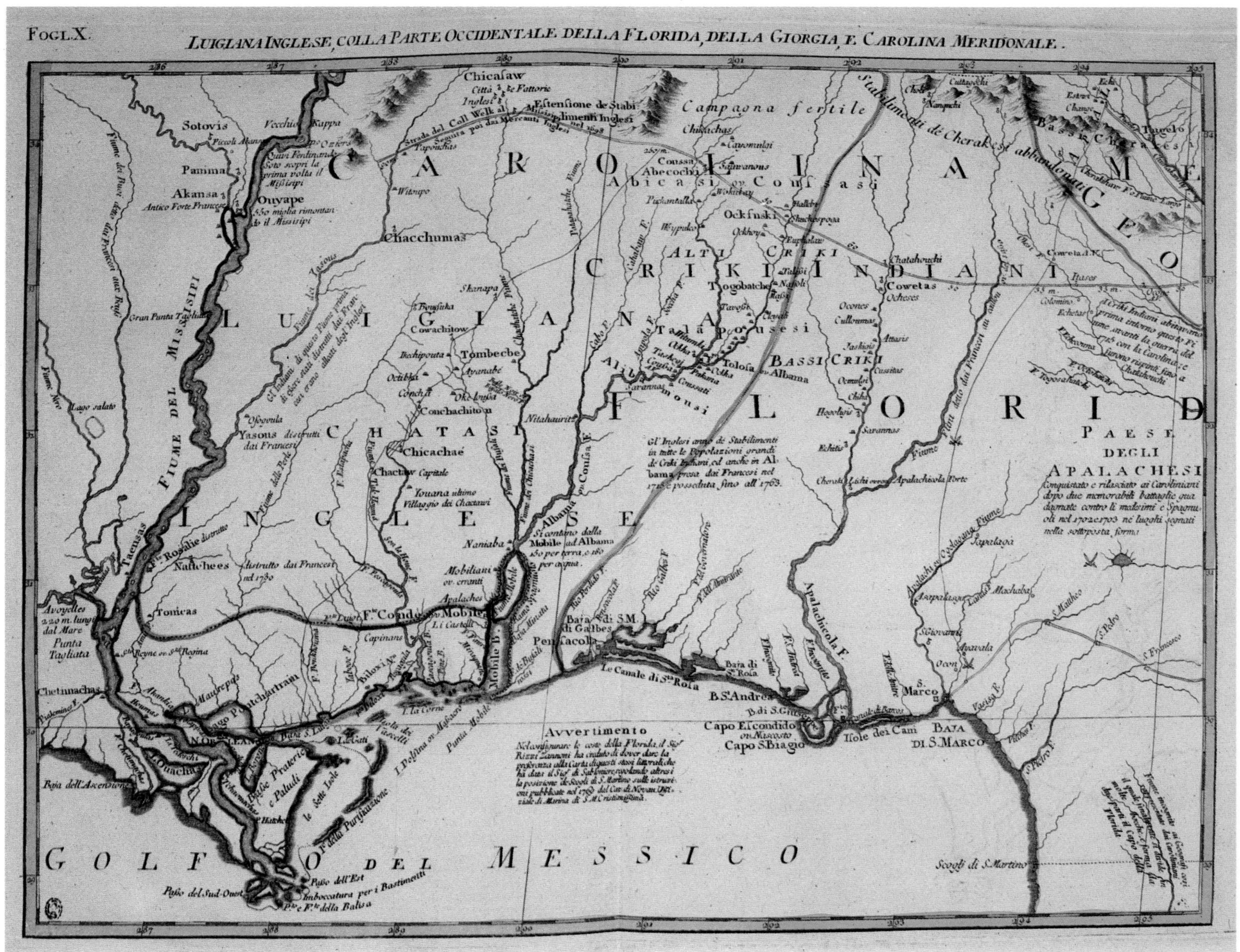

Plate CLII

'Luigiana Inglese...,' Antonio Zatta, 1778. The sole advantage of Zatta's copies over Mitchell's original is legibility. Mitchell's map measures 1016 x 1829 mm, and even to reproduce it on a double-page spread would be to sacrifice much important detail. Also, Zatta's up-dated legends, with their references to the settlement of 1763 and events of the Revolutionary War, are of interest.
312 x 415 mm.

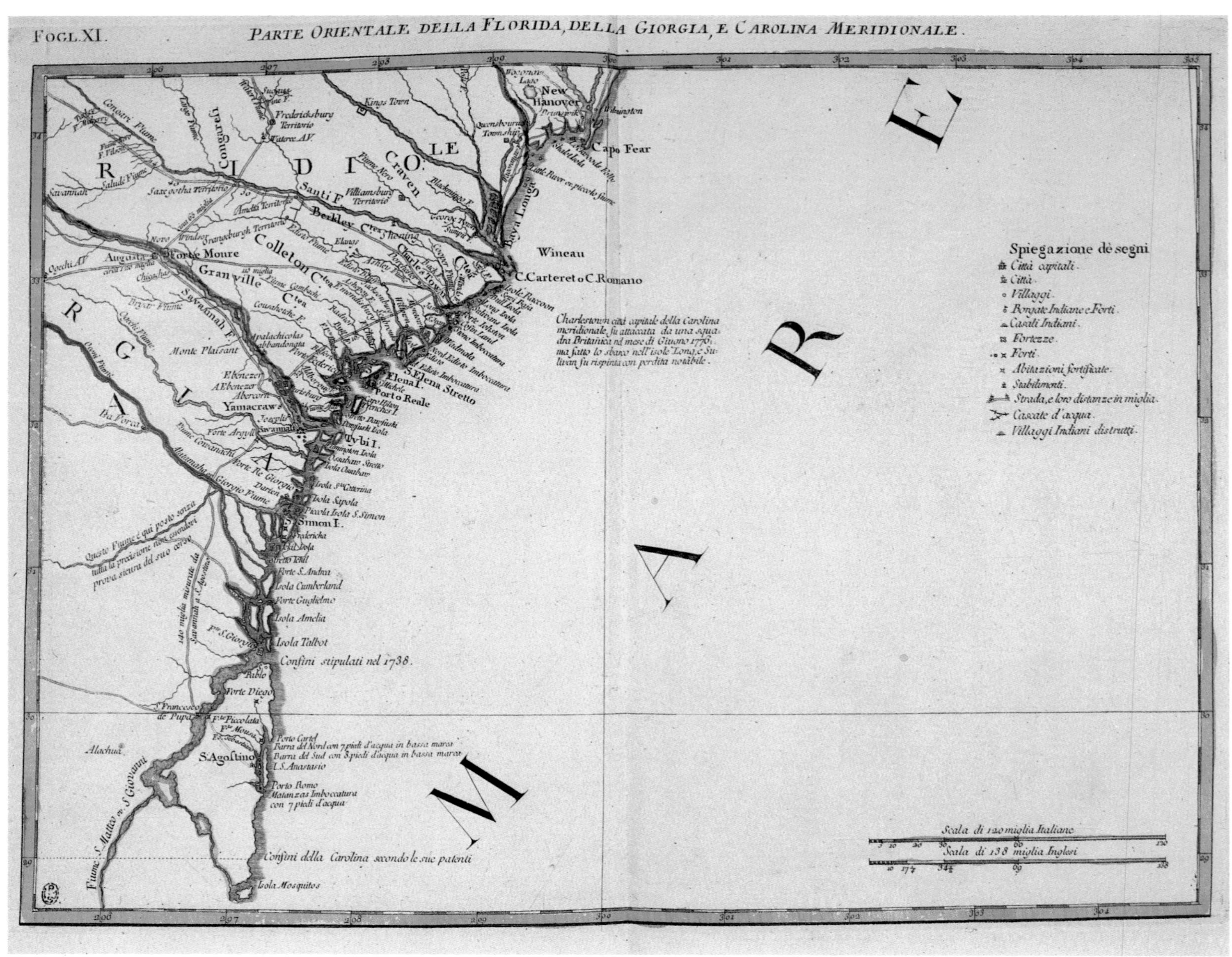

Plate CLIII

'Parte Orientale della Florida...,' Antonio Zatta, 1778. This map, with its note about the British attack on Charleston in 1776, is the last in Zatta's southeastern sequence. At this time Florida was still British, having been acquired from Spain in 1763. It would be returned to Spain in 1783 and finally would be ceded to the United States in 1819. 312 x 415 mm.

Plate CLIV

'La Isole di Terra Nuova...,' Antonio Zatta, 1778. This final map in the series from Zatta's *Atlante Novissimo* was probably derived from Mitchell, but, like the St Lawrence map shown on Plate CXLVI, it refers to an area so often covered by so many others that final attribution is not really very relevant. 415 x 312 mm.

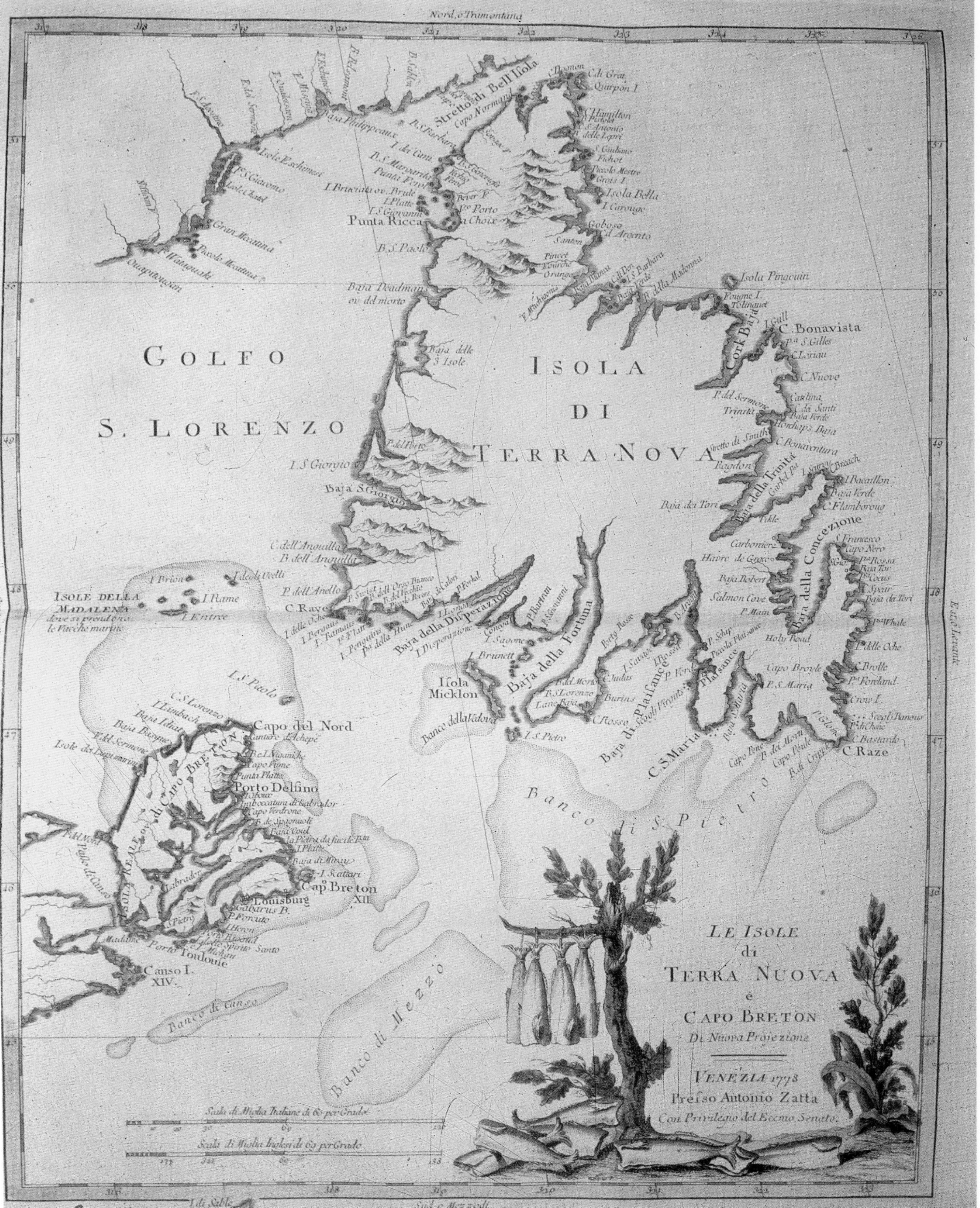
Nord, o Tramontana
Golfo S. Lorenzo
Isola di Terra Nova
Isole della Madalena dove si prend ono le Vacche marine
Capo del Nord
Porto Delfino
Cap.o Breton XII
Louisburg
Porto Toulouse
Canso I. XIV
Banco di Canso
Banco di Mezzo
Banco di S. Pietro
Isola Micklon
Baja della Fortuna
Baja della Disperazione
Baja della Trinità
Baja della Concezione
C. Bonavista
C. Raze
C. S. Maria
Isola Pingouin
Punta Ricca
Stretto di Bell'Isola
LE ISOLE di TERRA NUOVA e CAPO BRETON Di Nuova Projezione
VENEZIA 1778 Presso Antonio Zatta Con Privilegio del Eccmo Senato.
Scala di Miglia Italiane di 60 per Grado
Scala di Miglia Inglesi di 69 per Grado
I. di Sable
Sud, o Mezzodi
Est, o Levante

Plate CLV

'Nouvelle Carte des Découvertes...,' Santini and Remondini, 1784. This curious map is at once a copy and an adaptation of a map first presented to the Imperial Academy of Sciences in St Petersburg in 1758 and later published in the West by Gerhard Friedrich Müller. The unknown author of the original traced the voyages of Vitus Bering and Alexei Tschirikov, including their landings on the west coast of Canada. In the process, he also provided a rough outline of the Alaskan peninsula (*cf* Jefferys's adaptation of the same map shown on Plate CLIX). But for unclear reasons Santini and Ramondini, the Venetian publishers responsible for this 1784 version, have dropped the peninsular theory and have made western Alaska into an island. Otherwise, however, the map exactly copies the original.
540 x 780 mm.

Plate CLVI

'Le Globe...'(detail), Santini and Remondini, 1784. Although published in the same *Atlas Universalis* as the map shown on Plate CLV, this map shows none of the same detail about America's northwest coast. In fact it represents about the same state of cartographic knowledge Guillaume de l'Isle was applying to his maps in the 1720s. Note how far south the Strait of Anian is placed and how it connects with the Northwest Passage.
270 x 390 mm.

The frontispiece of a French edition of Santini and Remondini's Atlas Universalis.

The great English explorer, Captain James Cook. On his third voyage of discovery (1776-9) Cook surveyed the northwest coast of America from 45° north to Icy Cape in the Bering Strait, thus at last providing the world with an accurate idea of how the region was configured.

Plate CLVII

'Mappamondo,' Calcografia Camerale, Rome, 1786. The routes followed by Cook are traced on this Italian map, and the cartographic effect of his discoveries is immediately evident. Northwestern Canada and Alaska are, if not perfect, at least far better represented than ever before. On the other side of the Pacific the same applies, for Cook's surveys now made it possible to show New Zealand and Australia's east coast accurately for the first time.
200 x 280 mm.

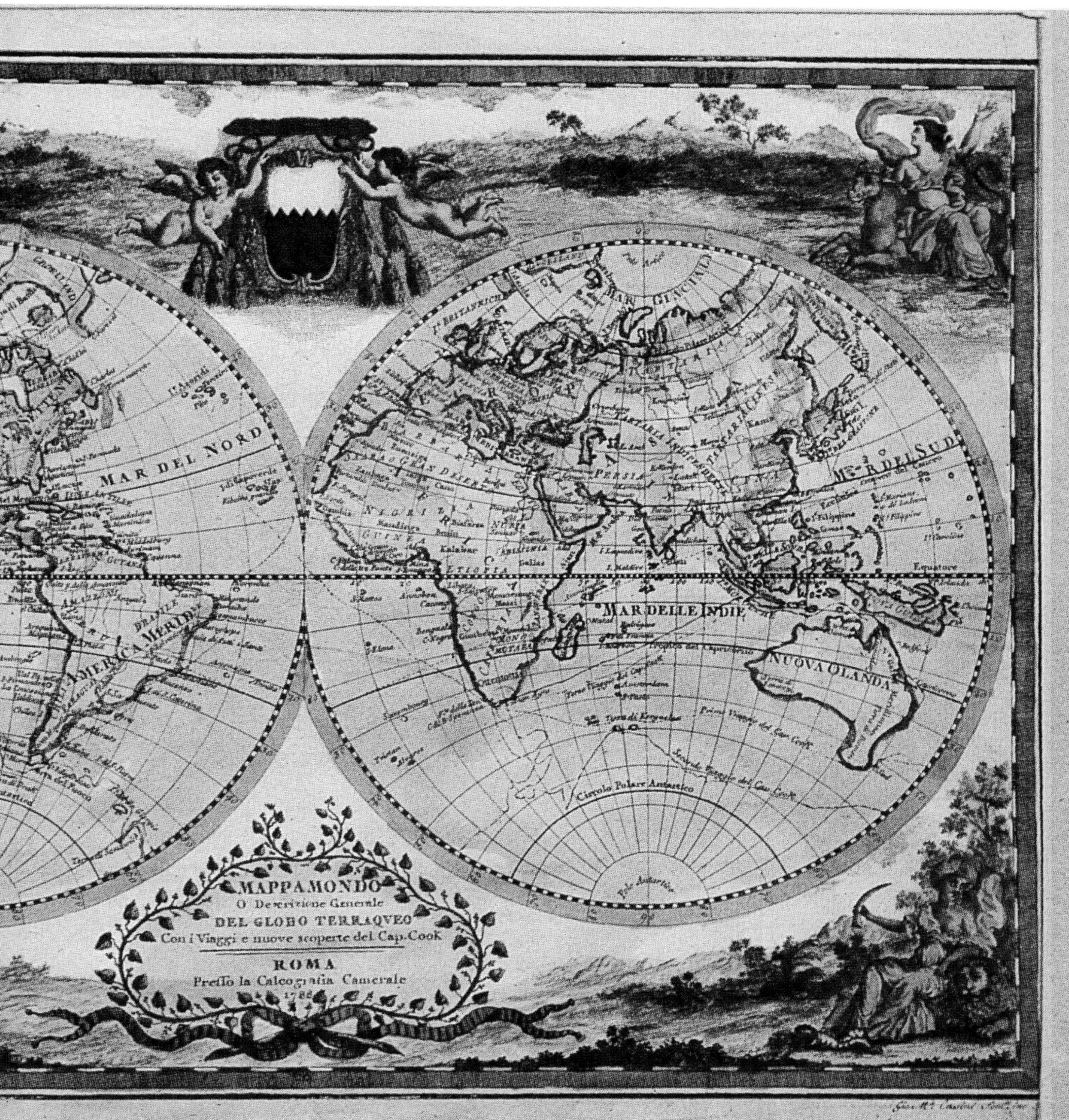

MAPPAMONDO
O Descrizione Generale
DEL GLOBO TERRAQUEO
Con i Viaggi e nuove scoperte del Cap. Cook
ROMA
Presso la Calcografia Camerale
MAR DEL NORD
MAR DELLE INDIE
NUOVA OLANDA
AMERICA MERID.
Circolo Polare Antartico
Equatore

Plate CLVIII

'Parties Nord et Ouest de l'Amérique,' Didier Robert de Vaugondy, 1772-80. Although this Robert de Vaugondy map was published in a 1780 edition of Diderot's *Encyclopédie* (and thereby gained authority and currency), its speculations about the profile of Alaska had already been outdated by Cook's explorations. In fact this is a 1772 revision of a map first drawn in 1764. Note that the Alaska Peninsula (as opposed to the Alaskan peninsula) is broken up into a chain of large islands.
280 x 370 mm.

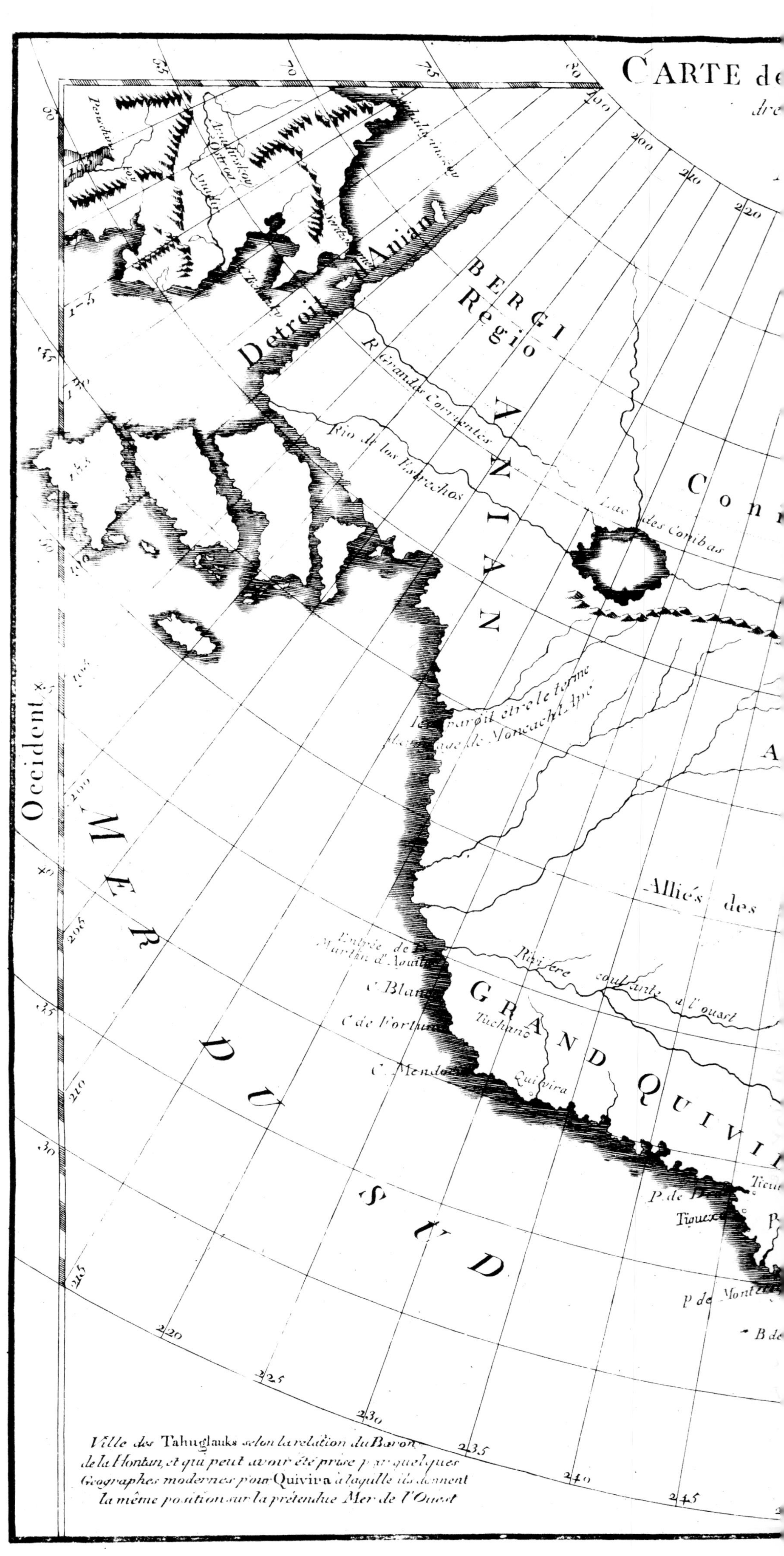

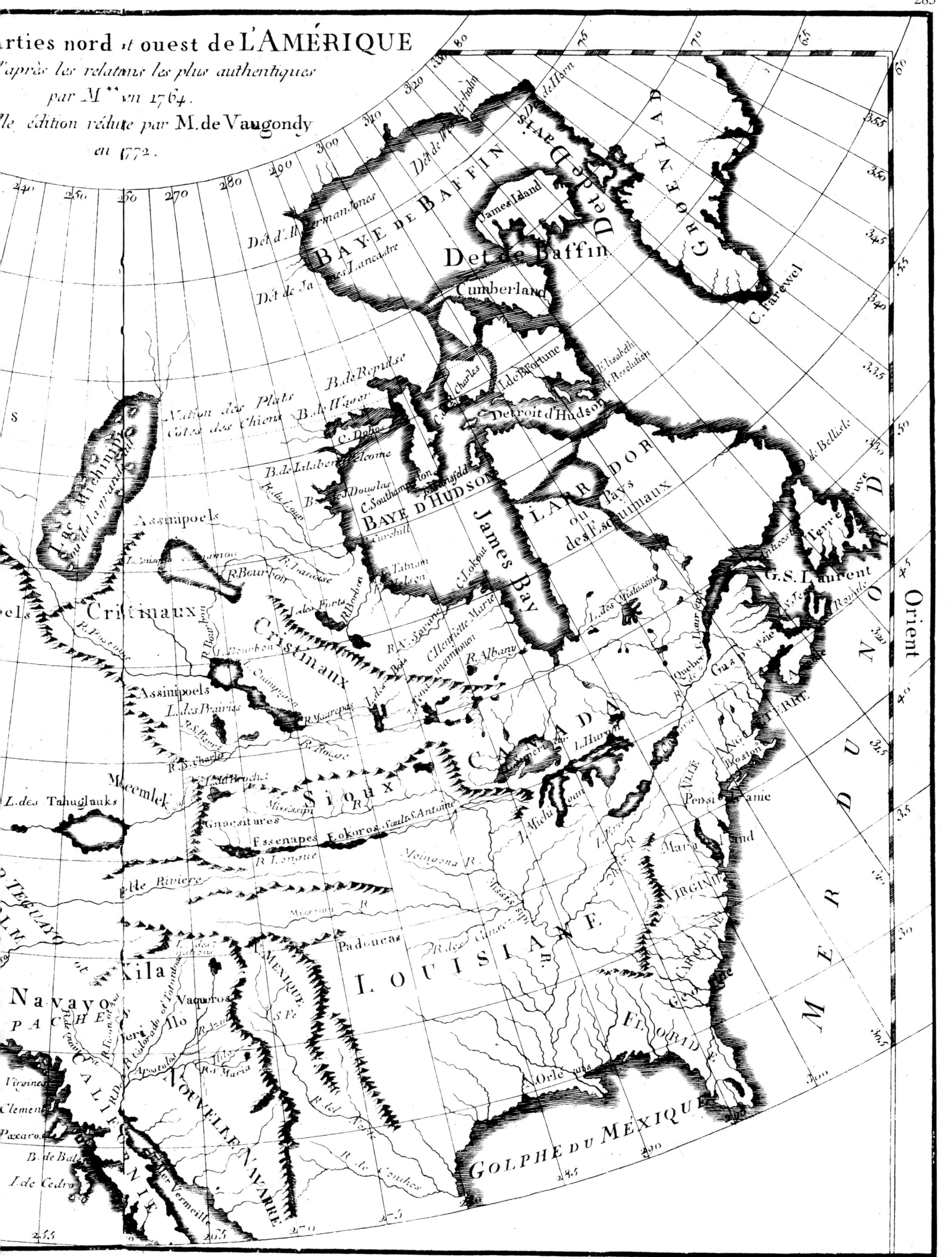
rties nord et ouest de L'AMÉRIQUE
d'après les relations les plus authentiques
par M** en 1764.
lle édition réduite par M. de Vaugondy
en 1772.
BAYE DE BAFFIN
Det de Baffin
Cumberland
GROENLAND
C. Farewel
Detroit d'Hudson
BAYE D'HUDSON
James Bay
LABRADOR
ou
Pays
des Esquimaux
Cristinaux
Assinipoels
CANADA
SIOUX
LOUISIANE
FLORIDE
VIRGINIE
CAROLINE
Orient
MER DU NORD
GOLPHE DU MEXIQUE
NOUVELLE NAVARRE
Navayo
Orleans
Boston
Pensilvanie
Maryland
G. S. Laurent
Quebec
L. Huron
Mississipi
Missouri R.
Padoucas
Vaqueros
Kila
L. des Tahuglauks
Moeemlek
Gnacsitares
Essenapes
Eokoros
Sault S. Antoine
R. Albany
Terre Neuve
NOUVELLE ANGLETERRE

Plate CLIX

'Découvertes de l'Amiral de Fonte,' Thomas Jefferys, 1768-80. Also from a 1780 edition of Diderot is this French version of another pre-Cook map drawn by Thomas Jefferys in 1768. It uses material from both Japanese and Russian maps (*cf* Plates CXXXIII and CLV), but since Jefferys was a Northwest Passage enthusiast, its primary purpose was to show the Passage, and especially its entrance on the west coast, as described by Juan de Fuca in 1592 and in the (apocryphal) story of Bartholome de Fonte's discoveries in 1640. Of all the Northwest Passage maps this is surely the most extravagant.
280 x 370 mm.

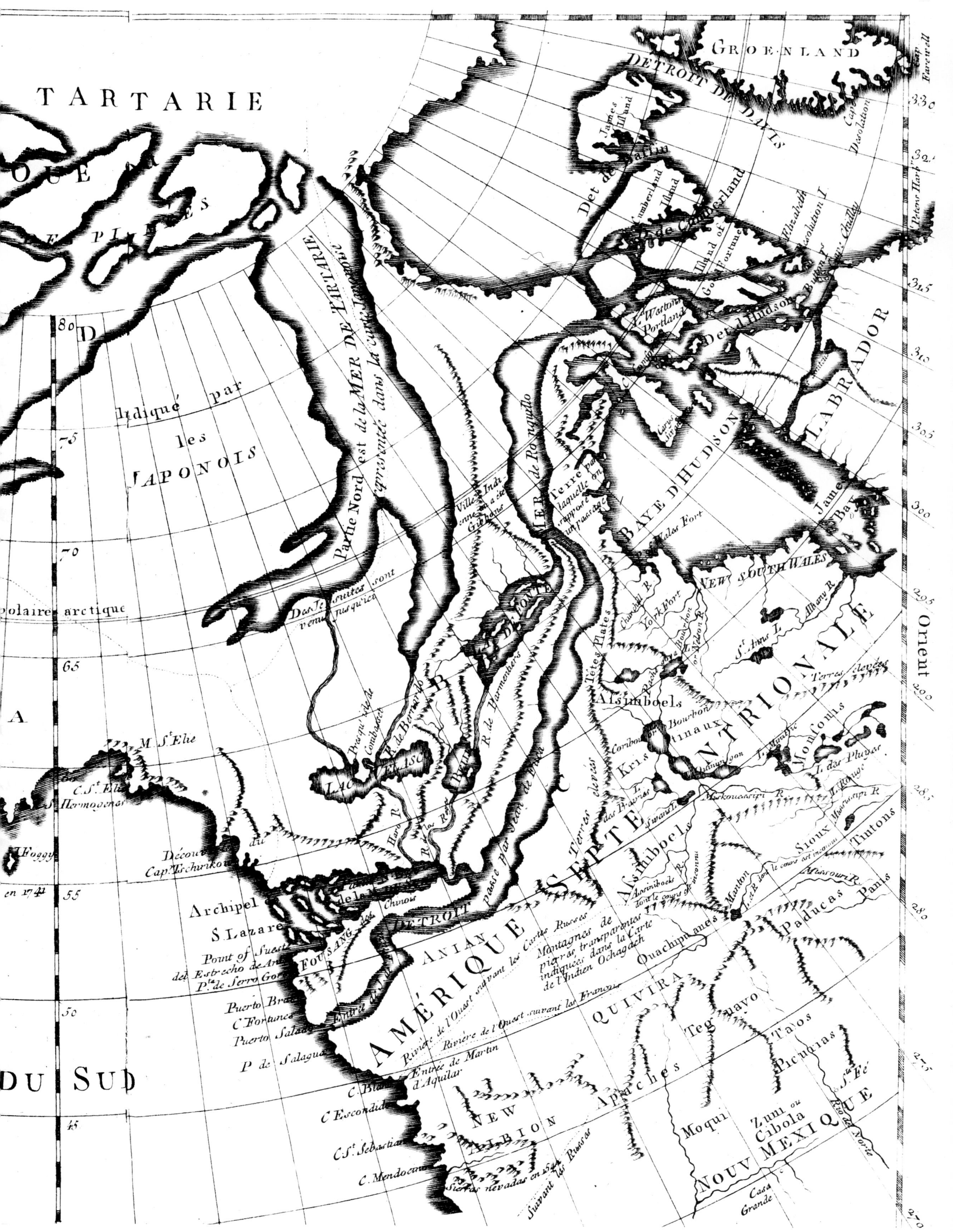
TARTARIE
GROENLAND
DETROIT DE DAVIS
James Island
Det de Baffin
Cumberland Island
D. de Cumberland
Island of Good Fortune
Elizabeth
Resolution I
Det d'Hudson
LABRADOR
BAYE D'HUDSON
James Bay
NEW SOUTH WALES
Parte Nord est de la MER DE TARTARIE
indiqué par les JAPONOIS
polaire arctique
Des Jésuites sont venus jusqu'ici
MER de Ronquillo
Terres plates
Assimboels
Kris
Terres élevées
AMÉRIQUE SEPTENTRIONALE
ANIAN
DETROIT
FOUSANG
Archipel S. Lazare
Point of Suest
Puerto Brava
C. Fortunes
Puerto Salagua
P. de Salagua
DU SUD
QUIVIRA
Teguayo
Apaches
Picurias
Taos
Moqui
Zuni ou Cibola
NOUV MEXIQUE
Rio del Norte
Casa Grande
NEW ALBION
C. Blanc
C. Escondido
C. St. Sebastian
C. Mendocino
Sierras nevadas en 1542
Paducas
Panis
Sioux
Tintons
Missouri R.
Ouachipuanes
Montagnes de pierres transparentes indiquées dans la Carte de l'Indien Ochagach
Rivière de l'Ouest suivant les Cartes Russes
Rivière de l'Ouest suivant les François
Entrée de Martin d'Aquilar
Orient
80
75
70
65
55
50
45
M. St. Elie
C. St. Elie
en 1741
Cap. Tschirikow
Lac
Monsonis
Albany R.
St. Anns L.
York Fort
Wales Fort
Churchill R.
Terres élevées
Cape Farewell
Cape Desolation
Weston Portland

Plate CLX

'L'Amérique,' le Sieur Janvier, 1780. Another pre-Cook map which, though dated 1780, was first drawn in the 1760s. Of interest is the Strait of Juan de Fuca, which leads into the enormous and mythical Mer de l'Ouest. De Fuca's claims about what he had found were ambiguous, but he seemed to imply that his sea and the North Sea (northern Atlantic) were joined, and that was more than enough to excite Northwest Passage partisans.
460 x 640 mm.

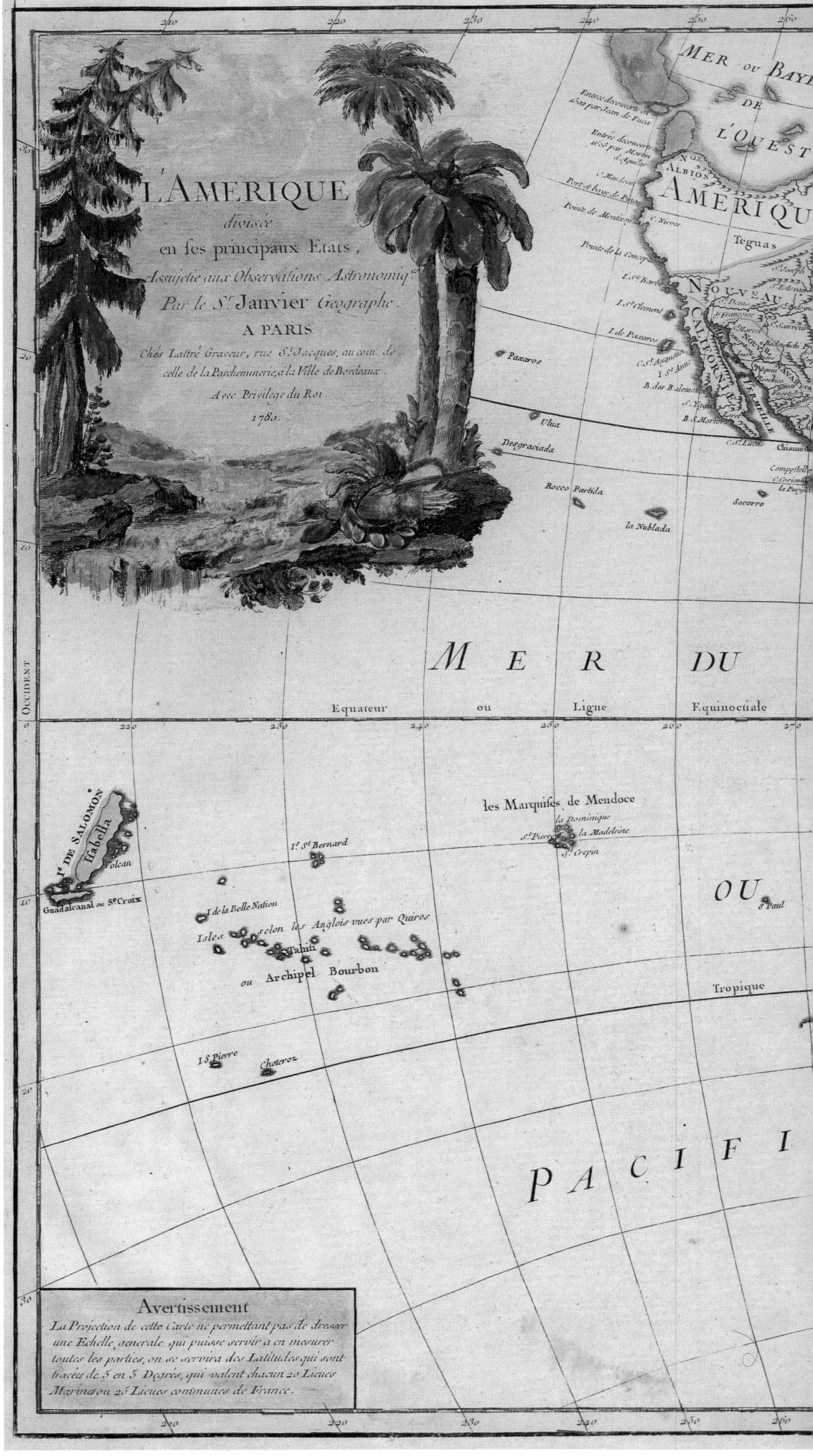

Mer du Nord
Amerique Meridionale
Partie d'Afrique
Isles Açores
Isles Canaries
Isles du Cap Verd
Tropique du Cancer
Capricorne
Golfe du Mexique
Canada
Terre de Labrador
Louisiane
Terre Ferme
Pays des Amazones
Bresil
Paraguay
Terre Magellanique
Pampas
Isles Malouines
Cap de Horn
Petites Antilles ou Isles sur le Vent
Grandes Antilles
Sahra Desert
Zannaga
Zuenziga

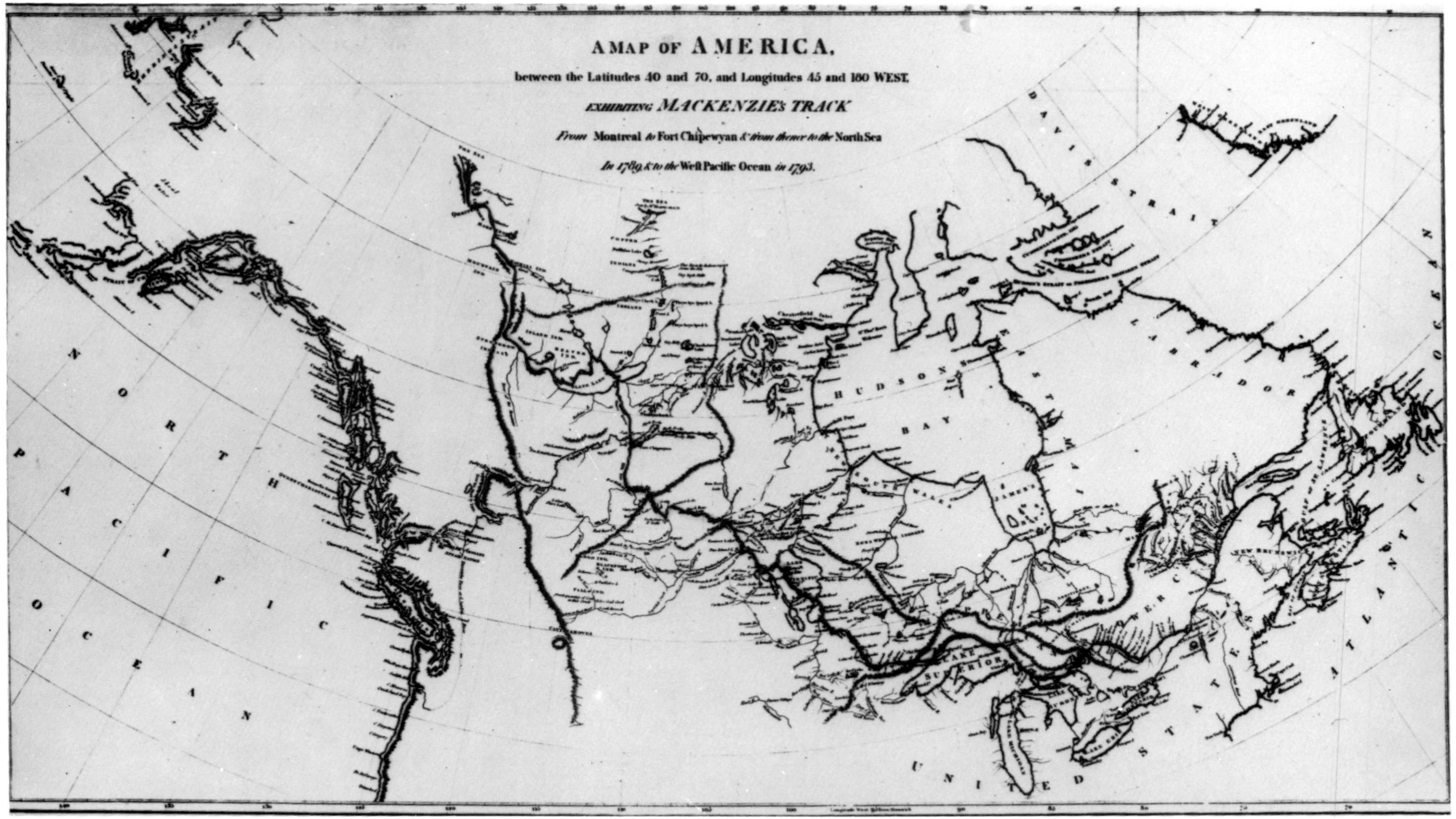

Lawrence's portrait of Alexander Mackenzie hangs in the National Portrait Gallery in Ottowa.

Plate CLXI

'A Map of America...,' anon, early nineteenth century. This historical map traces the route followed by Sir Alexander Mackenzie, who is credited with being the first European to cross the North American continent on foot. After crossing the Rockies, he reached the Pacific in July 1793. 135 x 250 mm.

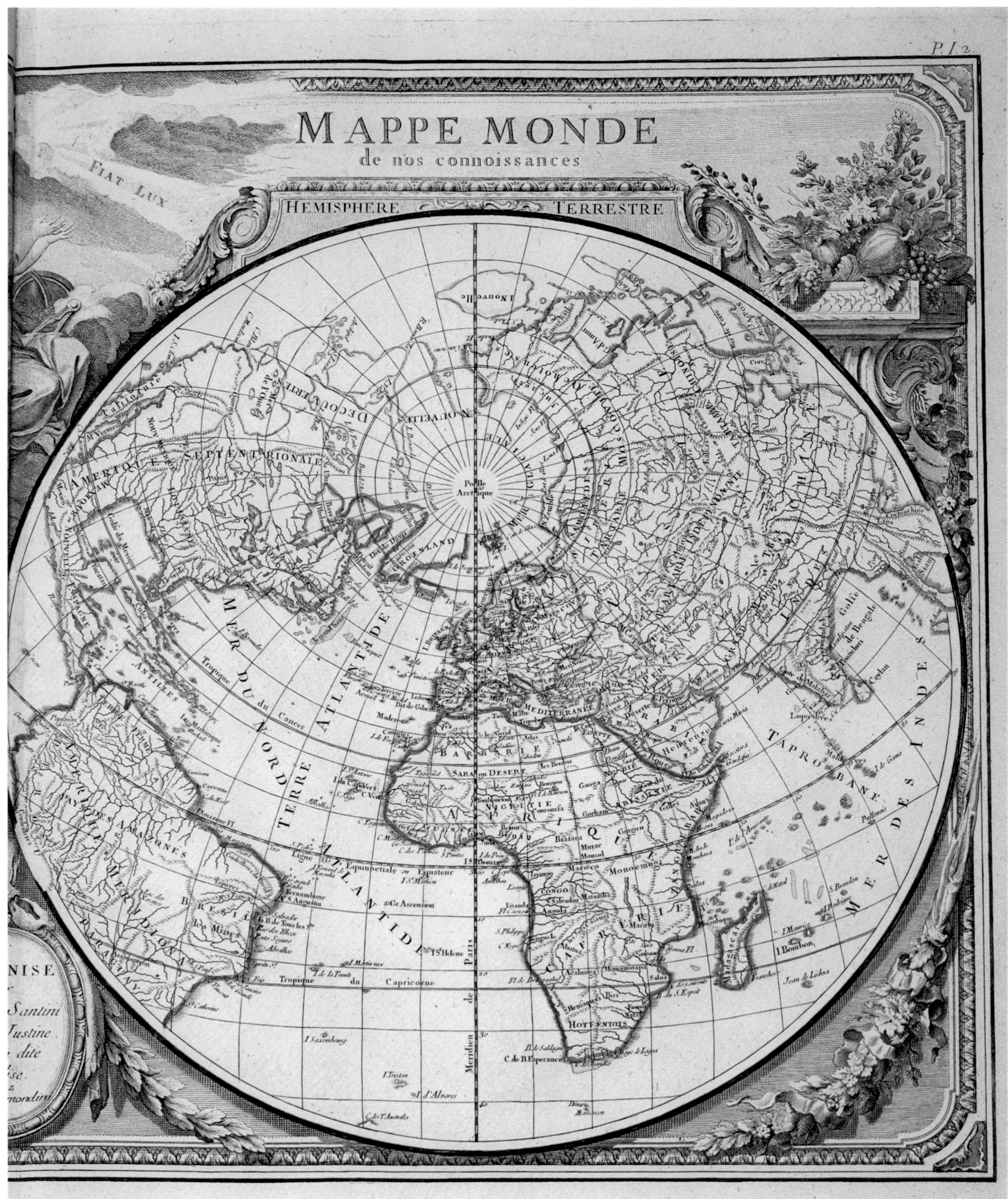

Plate CLXII

'Mappamonde,' Santini and Remondini, 1784. A world map from the *Atlas Universalis* using an unusual type of uncentered azimuthal projection. Geographically it is distinctly old fashioned, showing nothing of Cook's discoveries or even those of Bering or the Russians. The Mer de l'Ouest is evident, and western Alaska is an island (Ile Nouvelle). 540 x 390 mm.

Plate CLXIII

'Gli Stati Uniti...,' Calcografia Camerale, Rome, 1798. This and the following six plates are from the atlas *Atlante Universale,* a work of various anonymous authors and attributed only to the famous Roman print shop that produced it. These maps present a fair summary of what continental Europeans understood of the new-born United States at the end of the eighteenth century. They draw heavily on the old Mitchell map—or more probably upon the Zatta copies (*cf* Plates CXLIV-CLIV)—but they do not show the boundaries of the new states even as well as the Mitchell-Zatta originals. (To be sure, any map attempting to show all the grandiose territorial claims put forth by the various states after 1783 would be nearly unreadable.) For example, here western New York is awarded to Pennsylvania, though in fact it was disputed between New York and Massachusetts and was not even claimed by Pennsylvania.
345 x 475 mm.

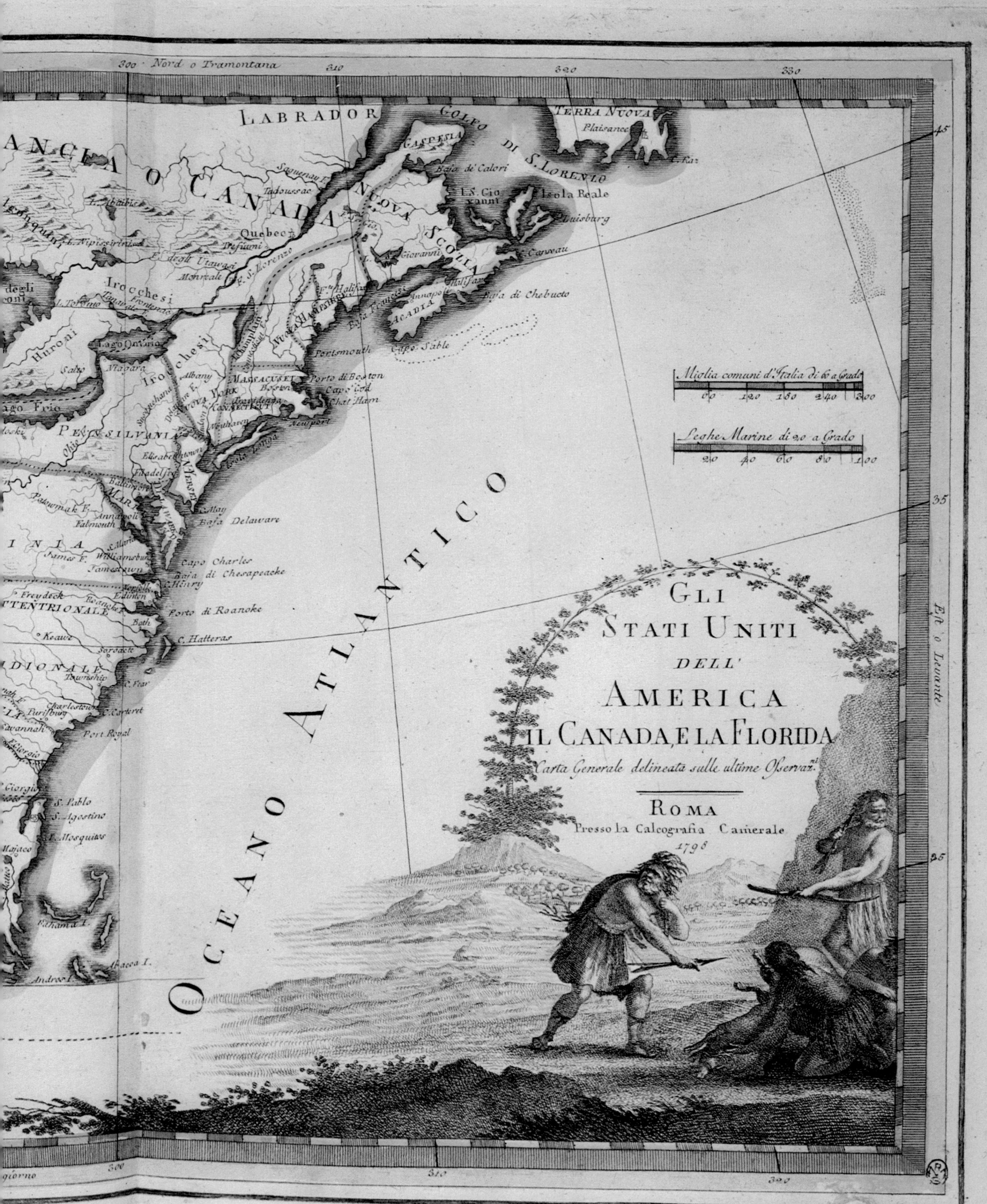
Gli
Stati Uniti
dell'
America
il Canada, e la Florida
Carta Generale delineata sulle ultime Osservaz.ni
Roma
Presso la Calcografia Camerale
1798
Oceano Atlantico
Nord o Tramontana
Est o Levante
Miglia comuni d'Italia di 60 a Grado
Leghe Marine di 20 a Grado
Labrador
Golfo di S. Lorenzo
Terra Nuova
Canada
Nuova Scozia
Acadia
Quebec
Porto di Boston
Capo Cod
Baja Delaware
Capo Charles
Baja di Chesapeacke
Porto di Roanoke
C. Hatteras
Pensilvania
Gio. Cassini Inc.

Plate CLXIV

'Gli Stati...Canada,' Calcografia Camerale, Rome, 1797. This map is a simplified version of an area that was covered in four Zatta copies of Mitchell (Plate CXLIV ff). What is new is the addition of the western and northern boundaries of the United States, the US-Canadian border being essentially as it is today.
345 x 475 mm.

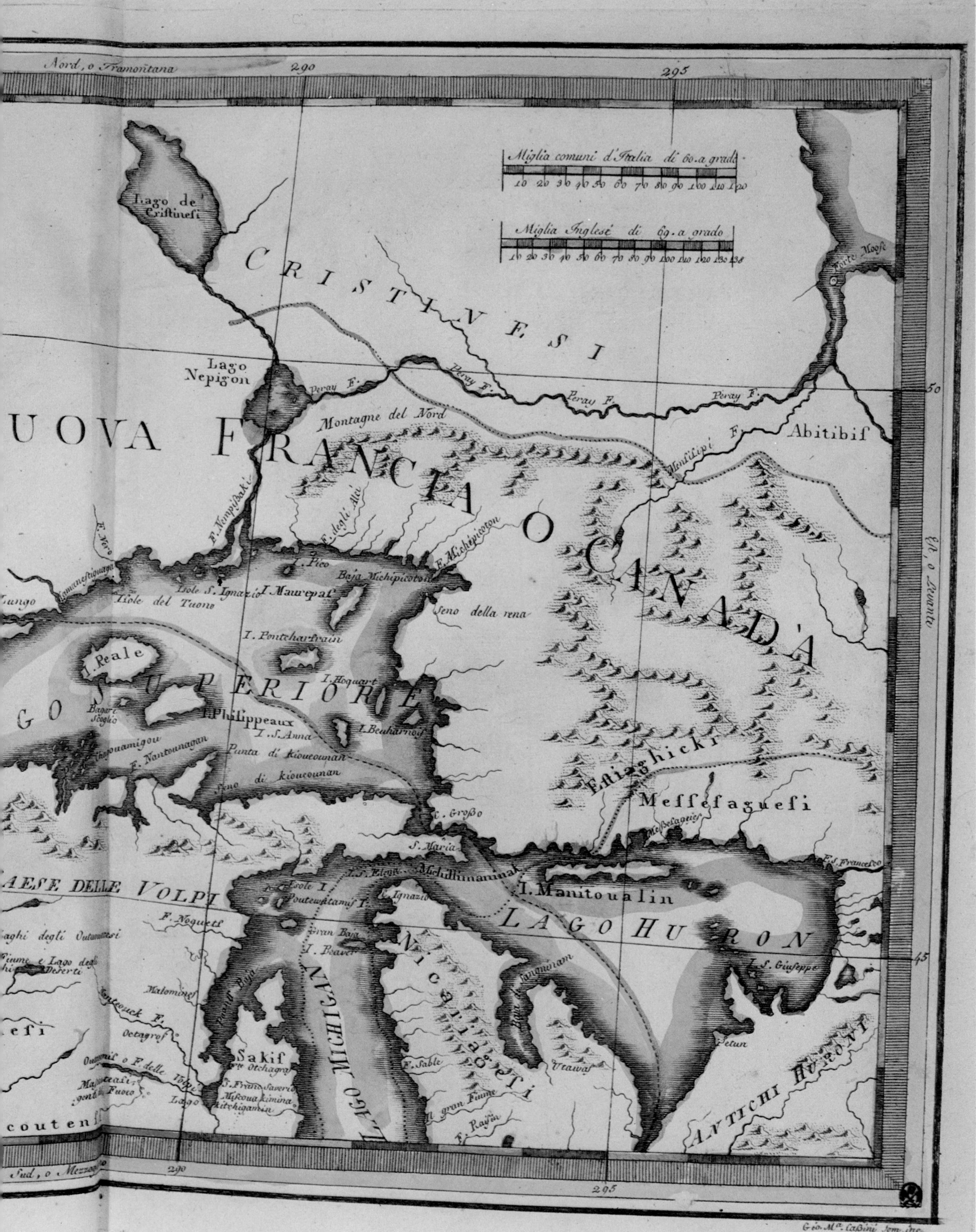
Nord, o Framontana
290
295
Miglia comuni d'Italia di 60. a grado
Miglia Inglese di 69. a grado
Lago de Cristinesi
C R I S T I N E S I
Lago Nepigon
Perray F.
Montagne del Nord
UOVA FRANCIA O CANADÀ
Abitibis
I. Pico
I. Maurepas
Baja Michipicoton
Isole S. Ignazio
Isole del Tuono
Seno della rena
I. Pontchartrain
I. Reale
GO SUPERIORE
I. Philippeaux
I. S. Anna
I. Beauharnois
Punta di Kioueounan
Seno di kioueounan
Essinaghicki
Messesaguesi
C. Grosso
S. Maria
PAESE DELLE VOLPI
I. Manitoualin
LAGO HURON
I. S. Giuseppe
Sakis
Utawas
ANTICHI HURONI
F. Sable
Sud, o Mezzogiorno
290
295
Est, o Levante
50
45
Gio. Mª. Cassini Som. inc.

Plate CLXV

'Gli Stati…Nuova Inghliterra…,' Calcografia Camerale, Rome, 1797. This map is primarily concerned with showing the eastern part of the US-Canadian border. It is reasonably accurate for the time, though of course it does not show the line around Maine as it is today. This was to be a subject of sharp dispute between the two countries until it was finally settled by the Webster-Ashburton Treaty of 1842.
345 x 475 mm.

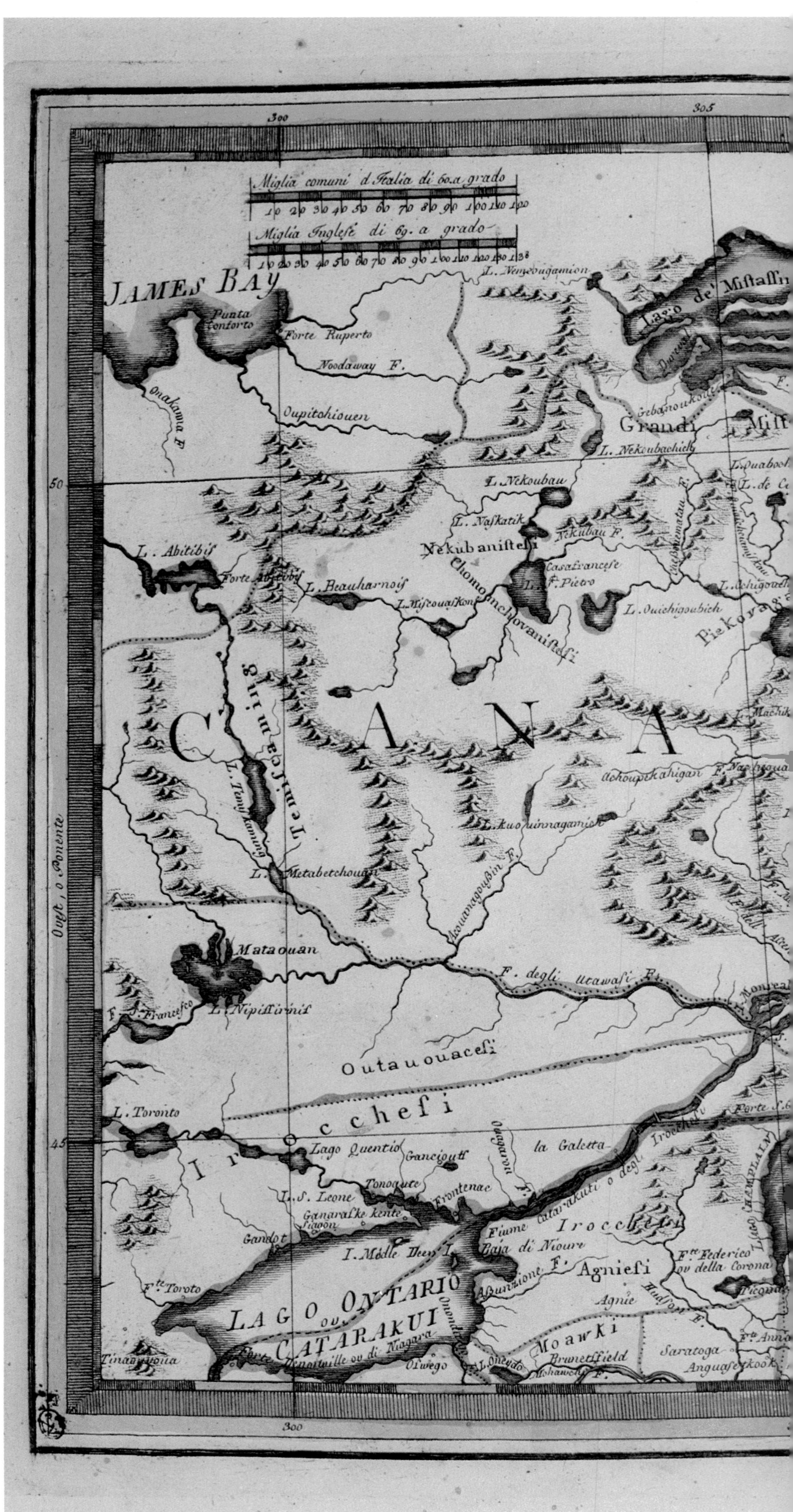

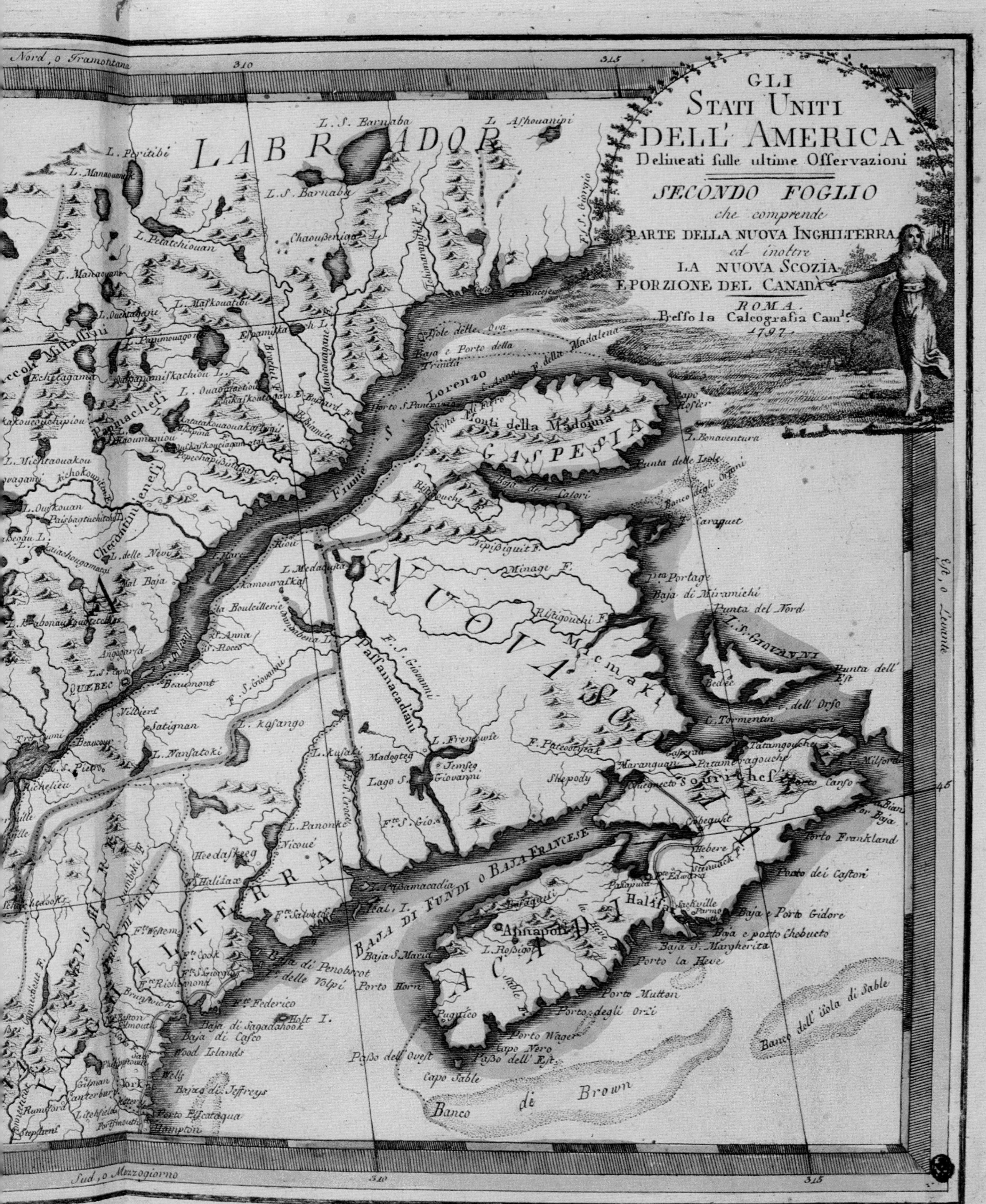
GLI
STATI UNITI
DELL' AMERICA
Delineati sulle ultime Osservazioni
SECONDO FOGLIO
che comprende
PARTE DELLA NUOVA INGHILTERRA
ed inoltre
LA NUOVA SCOZIA
E PORZIONE DEL CANADA
ROMA
Presso la Calcografia Cam.le
1797
Nord, o Tramontana
Sud, o Mezzogiorno
Est, o Levante
310
315
45
LABRADOR
NUOVA SCOZIA
GASPESIA
Monti della Madonna
Fiume S. Lorenzo
Isole delle Ova
Baja e Porto della Trinità
Capo Rosier
I. Bonaventura
Punta delle Isole
Banco degli Orsoni
Caraquet
Baja di Miramichi
Punta del Nord
I. S. Giovanni
Punta dell' Est
C. Tormentin
QUEBEC
L. S. Barnaba
L. Ashouanipi
L. Peritibè
L. Manaouanik
L. Petatchiouan
L. Mistassini
Chicoutimi
L. delle Nevi
Kamouraska
L. Medaouaska
F. S. Giovanni
Passamacadiani
Lago S. Giovanni
Madogteg
Jemseg
Shepody
Chegnecto
Marangouin
Tatamgouche
Porto Canso
Milford
Porto Frankland
Porto dei Castori
Baja e Porto Gidore
Baja e porto Chebucto
Halifax
Annapoli
Baja S. Margherita
Porto la Heve
Porto Mutton
Porto degli Orsi
Porto Wager
Capo Nero
Passo dell' Est
Passo dell' Ovest
Capo Sable
Banco de Brown
Banco dell' isola di Sable
BAJA DI FUNDI O BAJA FRANCESE
Baja S. Maria
Baja di Penobscot
Porto Horn
Holt I.
Baja di Sagadahook
Baja di Casco
Wood Islands
Baja di Jeffreys
Porto Piscataqua
Hampton
York
Wells
Portsmouth
Canterbury
Rumford
Litchfield
INGHILTERRA
Gio. M.a Cassini Som. inc.

Plate CLXVI

'Gli Stati...Virginia e...Carolina,' Calcografia Camerale, Rome, 1797 After 1783 both Virginia and North Carolina claimed broad stretches of territory extending all the way to the Mississippi, and for a time New York also claimed much of the same region.
345 x 475 mm.

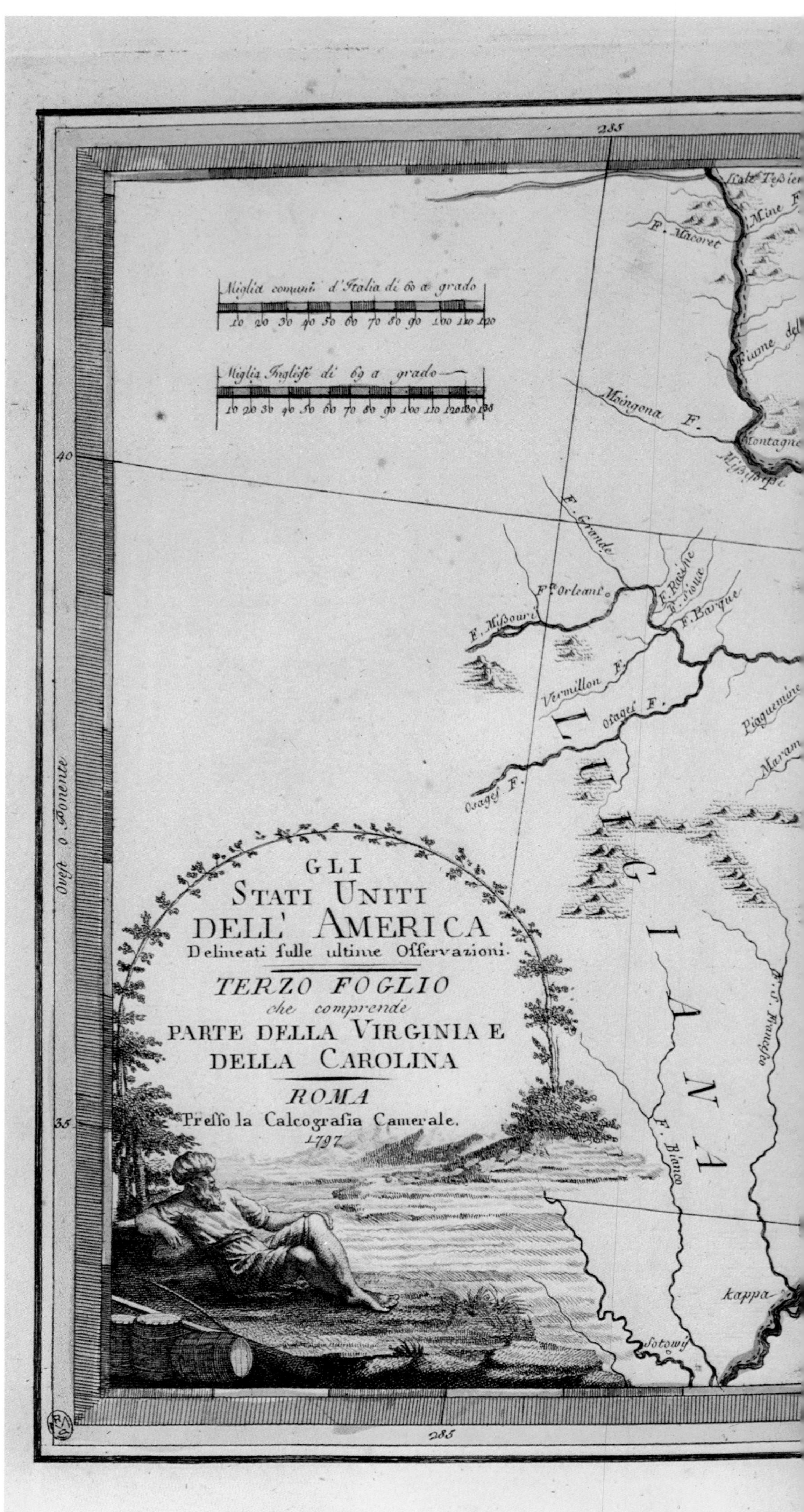

d o Tramontana
290
295
ASCUTENSI
Chiara
LAGO ERIO
Quadoghe
MIAMESI
Pickawillanees
Delawari
Wauwaughtaneesi
VIRGINIA
PYANKASHEESI
Bassi Shawneesi
AUGUSTA CONTEA
CHIRAKESI
CAROLINA SETTENTRIONALE
Chicaesi
LUNEBURG C.
ANSON C.
Sud, o Mezzogiorno
295
Levante
Gio. Mª. Cassini Soma, inc.

Plate CLXVII

'Gli Stati...,' Calcografia Camerale, Rome, 1797. The eastern seaboard from Massachusetts to North Carolina is fairly well shown here, though the error about Pennsylvania's northern border noted previously (see Plate CLXIII) is perpetuated.
345 x 475 mm.

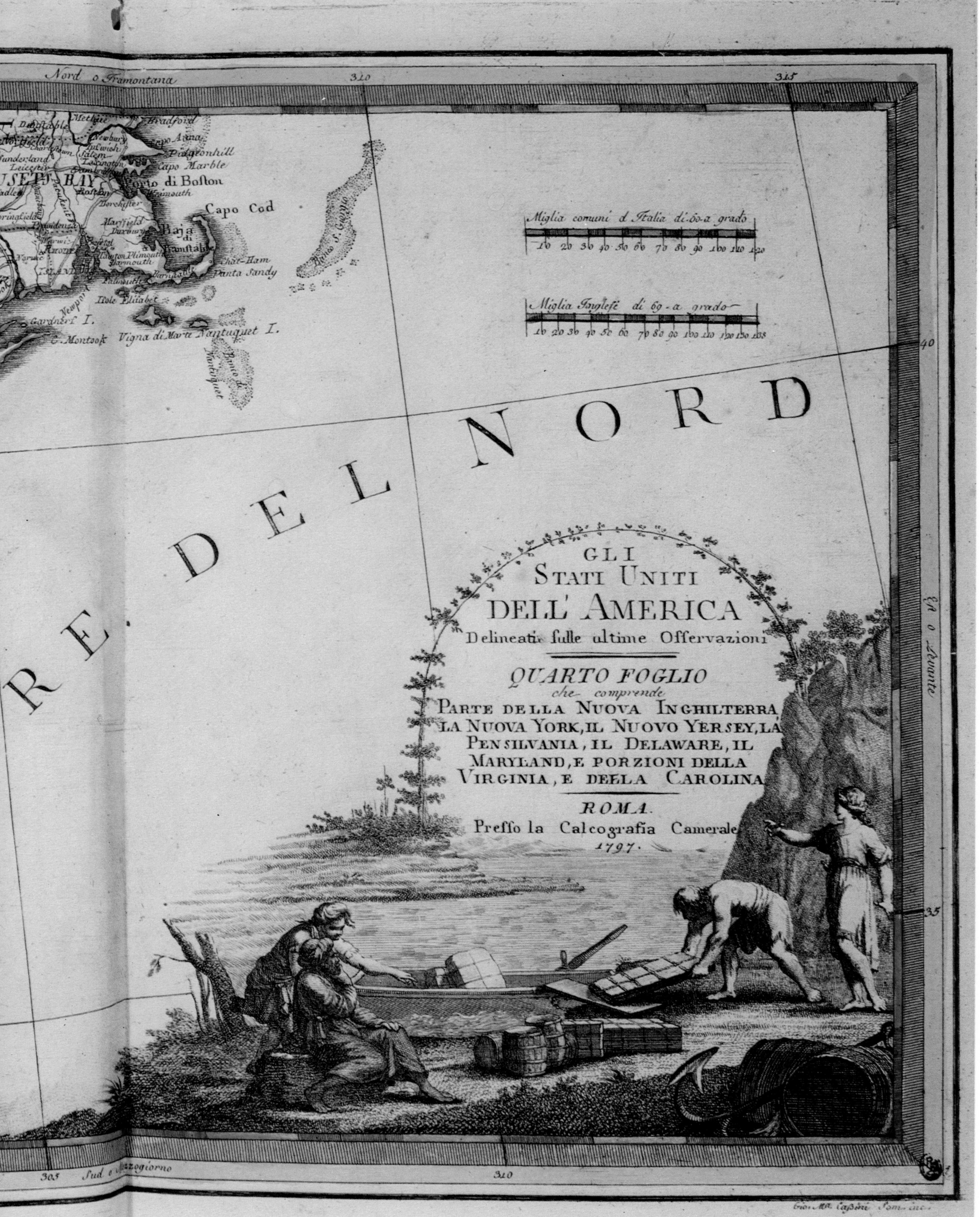
GLI
STATI UNITI
DELL' AMERICA
Delineati sulle ultime Osservazioni
QUARTO FOGLIO
che comprende
PARTE DELLA NUOVA INGHILTERRA,
LA NUOVA YORK, IL NUOVO YERSEY, LA
PENSILVANIA, IL DELAWARE, IL
MARYLAND, E PORZIONI DELLA
VIRGINIA, E DELLA CAROLINA
ROMA.
Presso la Calcografia Camerale
1797.
MARE DEL NORD
Miglia comuni d' Italia di 60 a grado
Miglia Inglesi di 69 a grado
Nord o Tramontana
Sud o Mezzogiorno
Est o Levante
Capo Cod
Porto di Boston
Capo Marble
Pidgeonhill
Capo Anna
Bradford
Baja di Barnstable
Chat-Ham
Punta Sandy
Isole Elisabet
Vigna di Marte
Nantuquet I.
Gardiner I.
C. Montook
Newport
Banco S. Giorgio
Sunderland
Leicester
Providenza
Weimouth
Dorchester
Barnstable
Plimouth
Yarmouth
Newbury
Ipswich
Salem
Lexington
Cambridge
Boston
Marshfield
Duxbury
Taunton
Kingston
Warwick
Norwich
Greenwich
New Bedford
Rhode I.
Dartmouth
Hatfield
Springfield
Gio. Mª. Cassini Som. inc.

Plate CLXVIII

'Gli Stati...Georgia...Carolina...Florida,' Calcografia Camerale, Rome, 1797. The danger of relying on Zatta's 1778 maps for a 1797 map of the United States is well illustrated here. The US-Florida boundary is vaguely drawn; Georgia, whose western border should extend to a line along the Apalachicola and Chatahoochee Rivers, is completely wrong; and the profile of Florida is lamentable.
345 x 475 mm.

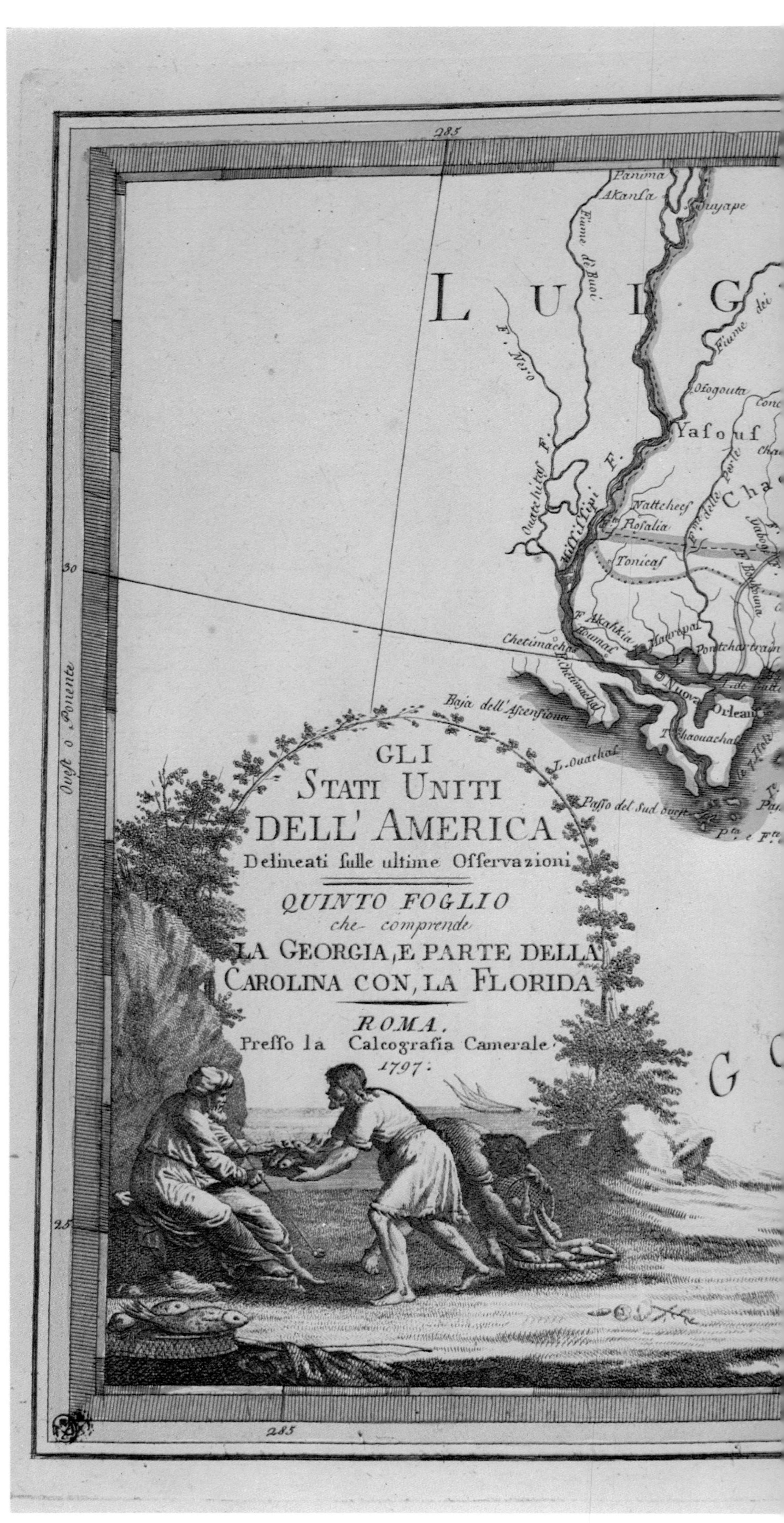

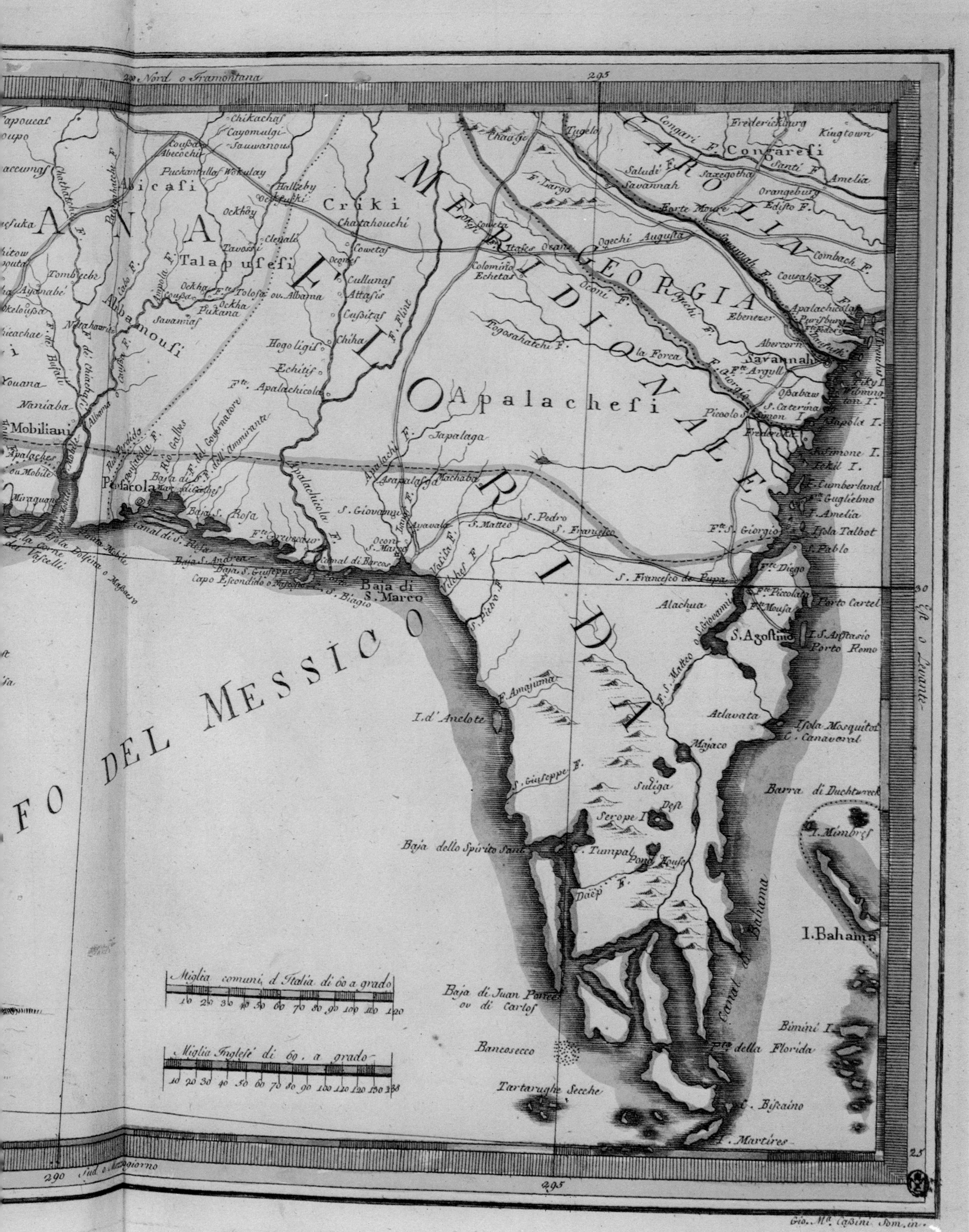
Nord o Tramontana
CAROLINA MERIDIONALE
GEORGIA
FLORIDA
GOLFO DEL MESSICO
Apalachesi
Savannah
S. Agostino
Pensacola
Baja di S. Marco
I. Bahama
Canal di Bahama
Miglia comuni d'Italia di 60 a grado
Miglia Inglesi di 69. a grado
Sud o Mezzogiorno
Est o Levante
Gio. M.a Cassini Som. in.

Plate CLXIX

'Gli Stati…Carolina…Terra Nuova,' Calcografia Camerale, Rome, 1797. Apparently the cartographers for the *Atlante Universale* felt it necessary to include the fragment of the South Carolina coast lost between Plates CLXVII and CLXVIII. The result is a strange map dominated by its oddly-chosen inset of Newfoundland.

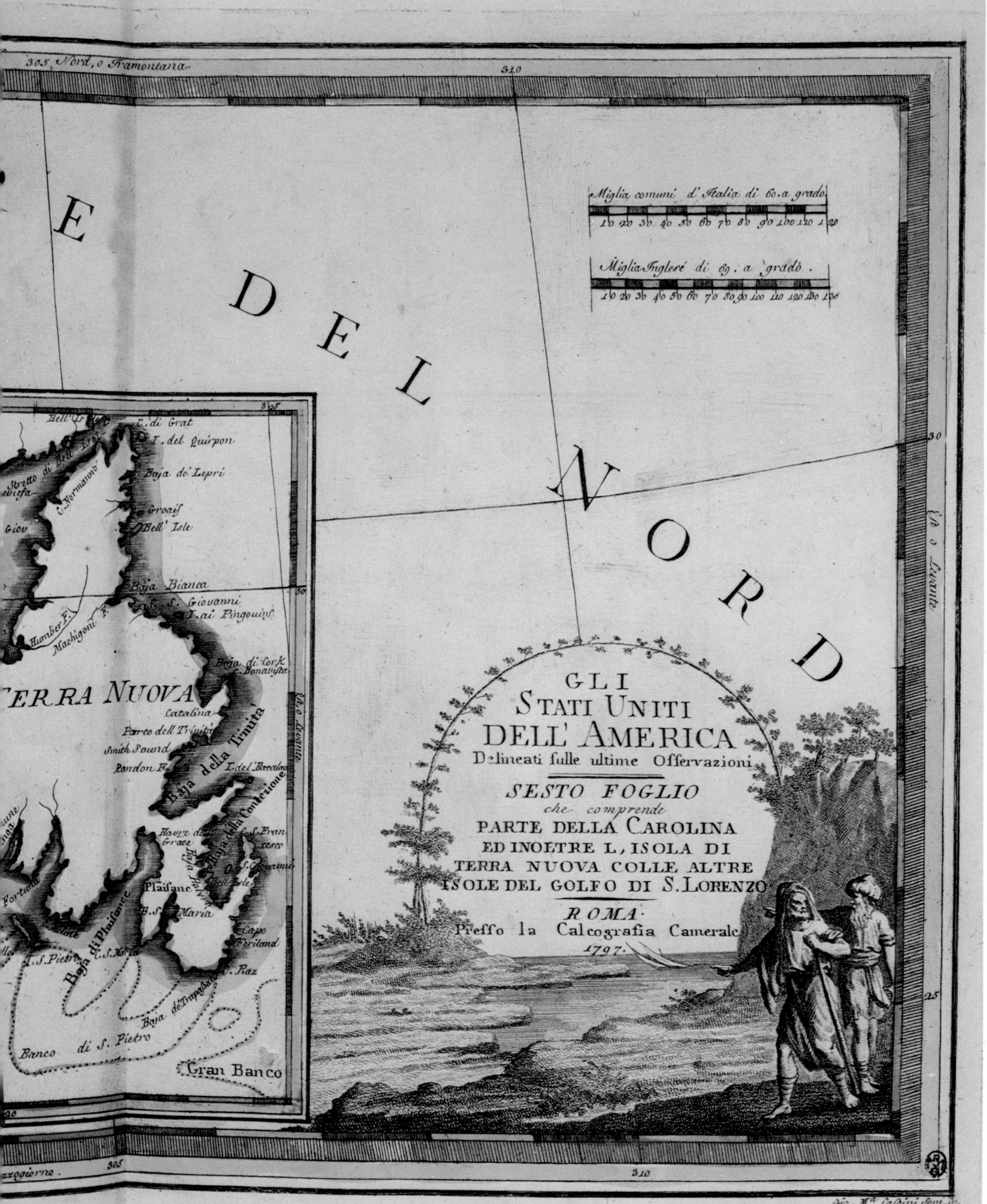

305 Nord, o Tramontana
310
Miglia comuni d' Italia di 60. a grado
Miglia Inglese di 69. a grado
E
DEL
NORD
GLI
STATI UNITI
DELL' AMERICA
Delineati sulle ultime Osservazioni
SESTO FOGLIO
che comprende
PARTE DELLA CAROLINA
ED INOLTRE L, ISOLA DI
TERRA NUOVA COLLE ALTRE
ISOLE DEL GOLFO DI S. LORENZO
ROMA
Presso la Calcografia Camerale
1797.
TERRA NUOVA
C. di Grat
I. del Quirpon
Baja de' Lepri
Groais
Bell' Isle
Baja Bianca
S. Giovanni
I. ai Pingouins
Baja di Cork
C. Bonavista
Catalina
Porto dell Trinità
Smith Sound
Randon F.
Baja della Trinità
Baja della Concezione
Plaisance
Baja di Plaisance
Baja di Trapassa
Banco di S. Pietro
Gran Banco
Ocro, o Levante
310
Gio. Mª. Cassini Som. sc.

A typical illustration from Diderot's Encyclopédie *showing the forging of a ship's anchor in an eighteenth-century foundry. On ships such as Cook's* Endeavour *bow anchors might weigh up to 4000 lbs, and on large warships, up to 9000 lbs.*

Plate CLXX

'America,' anon, late eighteenth century. It was still possible to publish maps as politically obsolete and geographically eccentric as this at the end of the century, but not for much longer. Too many people knew too much about the world. Soon there would be no excuse for all maps not looking the same—a triumph of science and the end of an age in the history of cartography.
502 x 400 mm.

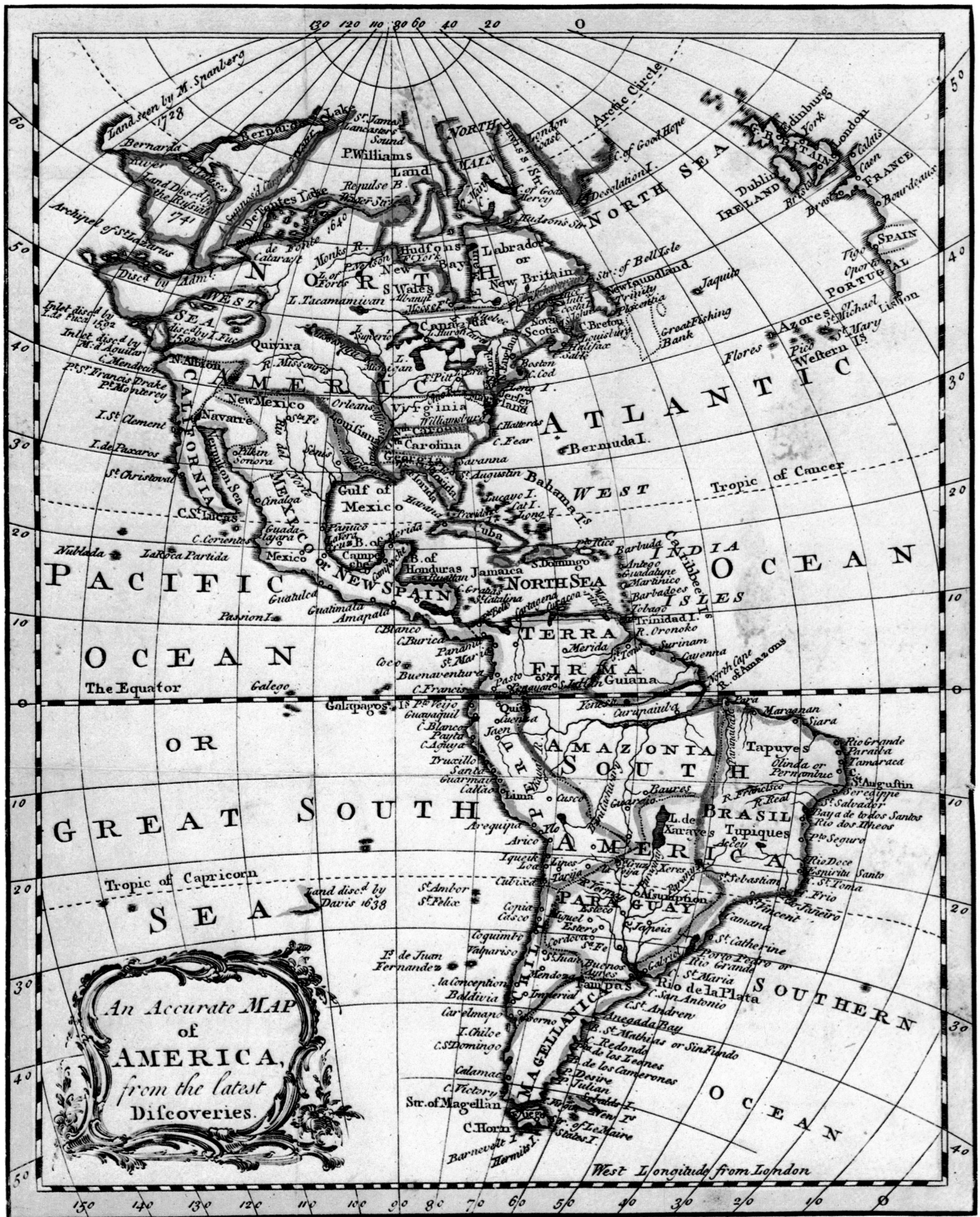
An Accurate MAP of AMERICA, from the latest Discoveries.
NORTH AMERICA
SOUTH AMERICA
ATLANTIC
NORTH SEA
PACIFIC OCEAN
OR GREAT SOUTH SEA
SOUTHERN OCEAN
INDIA OCEAN
Tropic of Cancer
Tropic of Capricorn
The Equator
Arctic Circle
West Longitude from London
Gulf of Mexico
Labrador or New Britain
Hudsons Bay
Newfoundland
Virginia
Carolina
Georgia
Florida
Louisiana
New Mexico
California
Mexico
Terra Firma
Amazonia
Brasil
Paraguay
Peru
Chili
Magellanic
Str. of Magellan
C. Horn
Rio de la Plata
G. Britain
Ireland
France
Spain
Portugal
Azores or Western Is.
Bermuda I.
Bahama Is.
West India Isles
Jamaica
Cuba
Land seen by M. Spanberg 1728

Plate CLXXI

'Mappamondo,' Calcografia Camerale, Rome, 1801. Although this map is based on a seventeenth-century model by Guillaume Sanson, it has been so up-dated that Sanson would hardly recognize it. The proportions of North America, the Great Lakes, the outlines of the northwest coast and Alaska and many other elements, such as the profiles of Australia and New Zealand, mark it as a map of another time—our own. 345 x 475 mm.

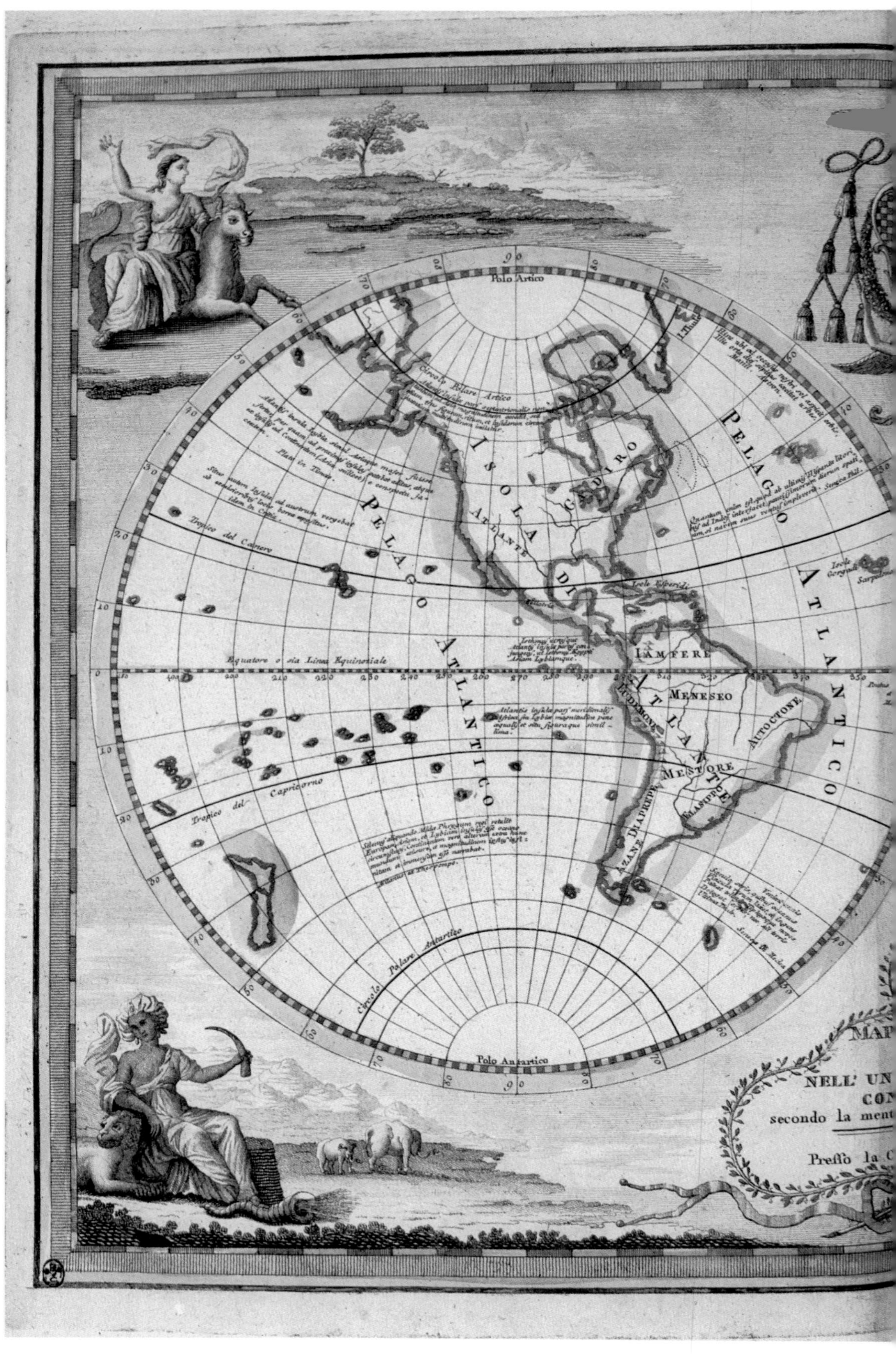

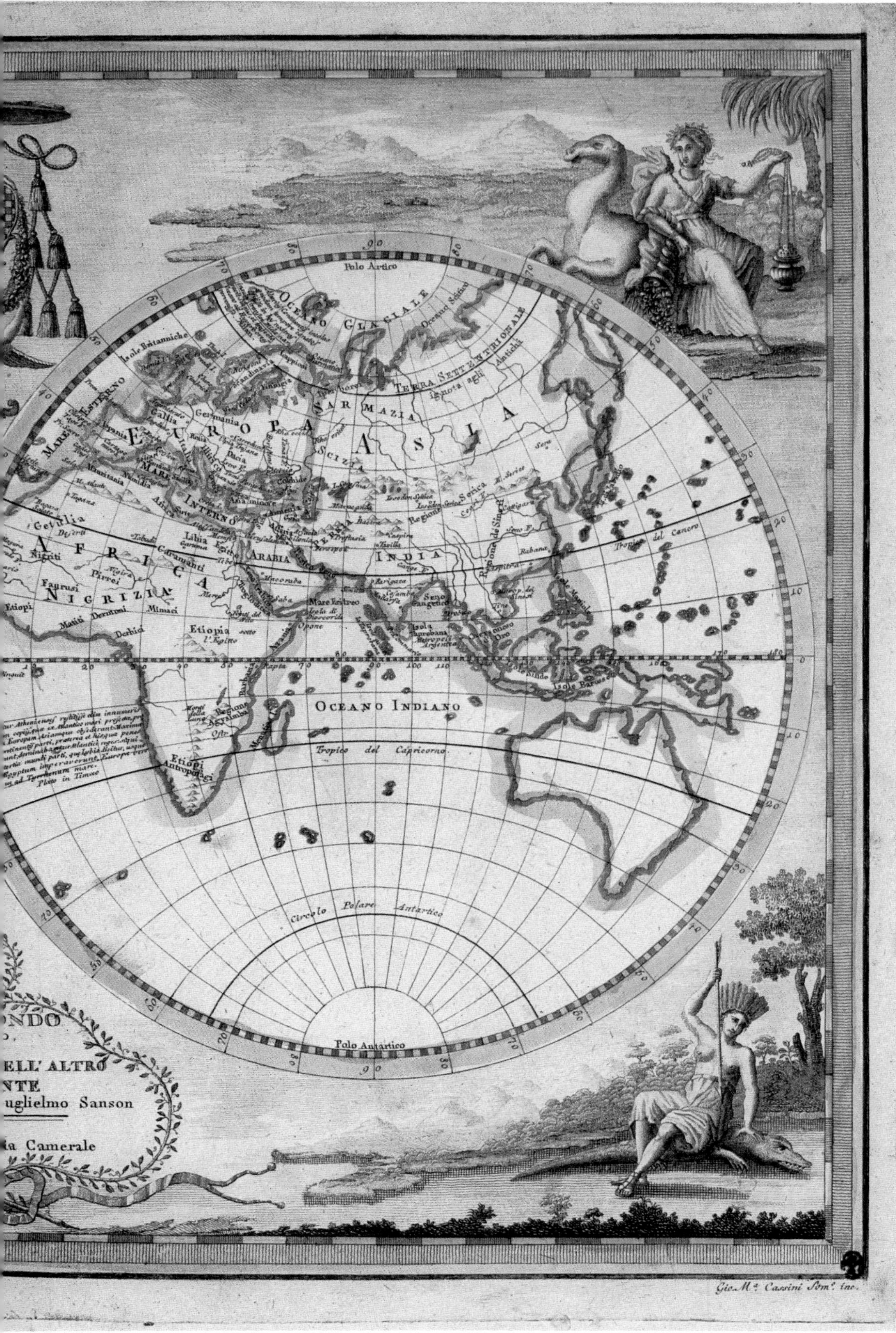
Polo Artico
Oceano Glaciale
Terra Settentrionale
EUROPA
ASIA
SARMAZIA
AFRICA
ARABIA
INDIA
NIGRIZIA
Oceano Indiano
Tropico del Canero
Tropico del Capricorno
Circolo Polare Antartico
Polo Antartico
uglielmo Sanson
Gio. M.a Cassini Som.o inc.

An engraving of a seventeenth-century printing shop of the kind that produced some of the great maps of the 'Golden Age of Cartography.'

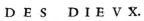

A fifteenth-century carrack.

Selected Biographical Notes

Agnese, Battista
d 1564

Genoese chartmaker who worked mainly in Venice. In technical excellence and aesthetic beauty his charts were much superior to the more utilitarian portolanos of earlier generations. From 1539 his charts were among the earliest to show Lower California as a peninsula.

Apian, Peter
1495-1552

German cartographer, mathematician and astronomer. He published two influential world maps, one in 1520 and one in 1530, as well as several European maps.

Barentzoon, William
c 1560-1597

Dutch explorer-chartmaker active in the search for the Northwest Passage. In addition to many individual charts, he published a highly successful atlas of the Mediterranean. The compass roses on his charts were the first to indicate magnetic variation.

Bellin, Jean Nicolas
1703-1772

A prolific French cartographer mainly concerned with maritime subjects. His many maps and atlases contained much precise information about the Antilles and the North American east coast.

Berlinghieri, Francesco
c 1440-1500

Italian humanist and geographer. He translated (in *terza rima*) and published the first Italian-language edition of Ptolemy's *Geographica* in Florence about 1480. By adding four maps of his own, he made this the first edition of Ptolemy to feature modern geographical knowledge.

Bertelli Family

A large family of Italian cartographic editors and engravers active mainly in Rome and Venice between the mid-sixteenth and mid-seventeenth centuries.

Blaeu, Willem Janszoon
1581-1638

The leading Dutch cartographer of the seventeenth century. He also signed his name Guiliemus Janssonius, Willems Jans Zoon and Guiliemus Blaeu. By 1630 he had produced 17 notable maps, including two world maps and individual maps of the European, Asian, African and American continents. In 1629 he produced the first of a series of atlases based on his own work and that of other cartographers, the most famous of these being *Atlantis Appendix* (1630), *Theatri A Ortelii et Atlantis G Mercatoris* (1631), and *Theatrum Orbis Terrarum sive Novus* (1635). After his death his sons, Cornelis and Joan, continued publication of the *Theatrum,* steadily expanding its size. In 1662 Joan produced the great 12-volume *Atlas Maior.* On aesthetic grounds alone the Blaeus' work would rank among the greatest in cartographic history.

Bordone, Benedetto
c 1460-1539

Italian cartographer whose *Isolario,* a collection of maps dealing with islands, was a sort of precursor of the true atlas. The definitive edition, published in Venice in 1547, contains 107 maps in the text, plus three folding maps.

Bourguignon d'Anville, Jean-Baptiste
1691-1782

A leading French cartographer of the eighteenth century. In addition to several atlases, he published over 200 maps, including several of the world. His maps are notable both for their beauty and their scientific accuracy. His famous personal collection of maps was acquired by Louis XVI in 1779.

Braun, Georg
1541-1622

One of the leaders of a school of cartographers that flourished in Cologne in the sixteenth century. Between 1573 and 1598 he and Franz Hogenberg (*qv*) produced the five-volume *Civitates Orbis Terrarum,* a work devoted to topographical views of cities and towns, some in America.

Buache, Philippe
1700-1773

French cartographer, successor to de l'Isle (*qv*). His atlases include *Cartes et Tables de la Géographie Physique* (1754), *Atlas Géographique et Universelle* (1762) and *Atlas Géographique des Quatres Parties du Monde* (1769-99).

Cabot, Sebastian
1474-1557

English explorer-cartographer. He accompanied his father, John, on his famous 1497 voyage of discovery to Nova Scotia and Cape Breton Island and later made explorations on his own. On his world map, published in 1544, he displaced, perhaps deliberately, the site of his father's landings to the Gulf of St Lawrence.

Contarini, Giovanni Matteo
Early 16th century

Italian cartographer. His 1506 world map contains the first extant printed representation of the New World. Almost nothing is known of Contarini, who may have been a member of a prominent Venetian family. This is the sole example of his work.

Cook, James
1728-1779

English explorer-cartographer. His 1758 survey of the St Lawrence River (later published in 1760 as a 12-sheet 'New Chart of the St Lawrence') contributed to Wolfe's victory at Québec in 1759. He was the first (1778) to chart the northwest coastline of North America accurately, and did more than any previous navigator to explore the Pacific.

Danckerts Family

A dynasty of Dutch cartographer-publishers that flourished in Amsterdam between 1630 and 1727.

de Champlain, Samuel
1567-1635

French explorer and geographer who is known as 'the father of New France.' Between 1607 and 1632 he drew a series of four maps of New England and southeastern Canada that were, in their time, definitive.

de Fer, Nicholas
1646-1720

French cartographer and atlas publisher. More highly regarded for his decoration than his geographic precision, he produced many maps of France and Europe, and, between 1700 and 1705, three major atlases.

de Jode, Gerard
1646-1720

One of the foremost Dutch cartographers of the sixteenth century. His major work, the 65-map atlas *Speculum Orbis Terrarum,* published in 1578, was perhaps somewhat unfairly overshadowed by the *Theatrum* of his rival, Ortelius (*qv*), and the subsequent *Atlas* of Mercator (*qv*).

de la Cosa, Juan
c 1460-1510

Basque explorer-cartographer. He accompanied Columbus on his first and second voyages and was pilot and owner of the *Santa Maria.* His 'Portolan World Chart,' painted on oxhide and dated 1500, contains the first authenticated representation of the New World.

de l'Isle, Guillaume
1675-1726

The leading French cartographer in the early eighteenth century. He was noted for his prolific production (over 100 maps) and exceptional accuracy. His influential *Atlas Nouveau* was published around 1700. He was appointed Premier Géographe du Roi in 1718.

de Wit, Frederick
1616-1698

Dutch map publisher and cartographer. He founded an important three-generation dynasty that continued to produce maps and atlases far into the eighteenth century.

Dudley, Sir Robert
1573-1645

Expatriate English cartographer who settled in Florence. His major work, *Arcano del Mare,* was first published in 1646-7 and is widely considered to be the best Italian atlas of the seventeenth century.

Duval, Pierre
1619-1683

A French cartographer who was the son-in-law and disciple of Sanson (*qv*). His major work, an atlas of 102 maps, was published after his death by his daughter in 1688-9.

Finé, Oronce
1494-1555

The most prominent French cartographer of the sixteenth century. He published an influential large-scale world map, *De Novus Orbis,* constructed on a double heart-shaped projection in 1532. In 1536 he published a second such map using a single heart-shaped projection. A third world map appeared in 1544, but no known copy exists.

Gastaldi, Giacomo
1500-1565

Piedmontese cartographer-publisher who was appointed cosmographer to the Republic of Venice. He published many maps individually and in collections, including an important amended edition of Ptolemy's *Geographia* in 1548. He was the first to posit a strait separating the Asian and North American continents.

Hogenberg, Franz
1535-1590

A Flemish cartographer-engraver. He collaborated with Braun *(qv)* on *Civitates Orbis Terrarum* and with French cartographer André Thevet *(qv)* on a 1581 map of the New World, 'Le Nouveau Monde Déscouverte et Illustré de Nostre Temps.'

Homann, Johann Baptiste
1663-1724

The founder of the dominant dynasty of German eighteenth-century cartographers. He established a calographic workshop in Nuremberg in 1702 and published his first atlas in 1707. A succession of atlases produced by Homann and/or his children followed, culminating in an *Atlas Maior* of over 300 maps published *c* 1780. He was one of the first to color his maps at origin, although, except for special clients, he usually left his cartouches and scrolls plain.

Hondius, Jodocus
1563-1612

Dutch cartographer-publisher, also known as Joost de Hondt. He established himself in Amsterdam *c* 1693 and in 1604 acquired posession of Mercator's *(qv)* stock. In 1606 he published an important edition of Mercator's *Atlas* with 37 additional maps of his own. He also produced large scale world maps in 1608 and 1611. After his death, his sons, Jodocus and Henry, along with their brother-in-law, Jan Jansson *(qv)* continued to produce Mercator *Atlases* throughout most of the remainder of the century, thereby doing much to establish acceptance of the Mercator projection.

Jaillot, Alexis Hubert
1632-1712

French cartographer and founder of the cartographic dynasty that succeeded that of the Sansons *(qv)*. His most important work was his *Atlas Nouveau,* first published as a work of 45 maps in 1681. The fifth edition, published in 1695, was re-titled *Atlas François* and had 115 maps. The final edition, completed by his children around 1750, had 167 maps. Those relatively few copies of his maps that Jaillot fully colored and illuminated with gold are much prized by collectors.

Jansson, Jan
1596-1664

Dutch cartographer and son-in-law of Jodocus Hondius . He took over the Hondius business about 1657 upon the death of Henry Hondius. He had previously constructed globes and had issued an edition of Ptolemy in 1617. In 1633 he and Henry Hondius produced the major two-volume edition of the Mercator *Atlas.*

Jefferys, Thomas
d 1771

A prolific English engraver and map publisher and the geographer to the Prince of Wales (later George III). More than any of his contemporary English mapmakers he concentrated on American subjects. His *American Atlas,* 22 maps on 29 sheets, was published posthumously in 1776, as was his *North American Pilot* (1775). To his industry we owe the existence of many of the historically most important eighteenth century maps of North America and the West Indies.

Lafreri, Antoine
1512-1577

A French engraver and map publisher (also known as Antoine Lafréry) active in Rome after 1544. Although, in collaboration with Antonio Salamanca *(qv)*, he published some maps of his own devising, he is chiefly remembered as a publisher of map 'collections' that were, in effect, proto-atlases of the world. In one of these collections is a 1566 map by one Zaltieri of Bologna that is the first to show a strait separating North America from Asia.

le Moyne de Morgues, Jacques
d 1587

French artist and explorer. He accompanied René de la Laudonnière on the second French gold-hunting expedition to Florida in 1564 and produced the first detailed map of the region—a map that Francis Parkman was later to charcterize as 'curiously inexact.'

le Rouge, Georges-Louis
fl 1741-1779

French cartographer and atlas publisher. His *Atlas Amériquain Septentrional* (1778), was one of the best French collections of North American maps of the period, and his *Neptune Américo-Septentrional* (1778), a collection of North American hydrographic charts, became the official reference of the French Navy.

le Testu, Guillaume
mid-sixteenth century

French pilot and hydrographer. His 1555 manuscript atlas, *Cosmographie Universelle,* contained 56 maps, including seven world maps, all with different projections. His new world maps were used by French Huguenots when they began colonizing North America in 1564.

Mercator, Gerard
1512-1594

Dutch cartographer, considered by many to be the greatest name in geographical science after Ptolemy. He began as a maker of globes and turned to mapmaking *c* 1537. By 1538 he had produced his first world map. Though much admired and copied, it was eventually completely overshadowed by his enormous 18-sheet world map of 1569. The first part of his best known work, the *Atlas,* appeared in 1585, and the third and final part in 1595, a year after his death. His sons, grandsons, Hondius *(qv)* and Jansson continued to publish the *Atlas,* and by 1642 no fewer than 47 editions had been published in Latin, Dutch, French, German and English. Mercator had first used his famous cylindrical projection on a 1569 world map, but not until after his death did mariners begin to realize the extreme importance of this innovation to the science of navigation.

Mitchell, John
c 1690-1768

An American physician, chemist, biologist and botanist of considerable note, Mitchell emigrated to England in 1746. There, at the request of the earl of Halifax, in 1755 he made the only map he is known to have drawn, 'A Map of the British and French Dominions in North America with Roads, Distances, Limits and Extent of the Settlements,' 21 editions of which were published in the next 25 years. It enormously influenced subsequent cartographers, was used by the Treaty of Paris negotiators in 1783 to help determine the boundaries of the United States and continued to be used to settle territorial disputes into the twentieth century. It has been called the most important map in US history.

Moll, Herman
d 1732

Dutch cartographer who lived in London after *c* 1680. He published numerous maps and atlases, and some of his North American maps were used to support British claims in boundary disputes with France after the War of the Spanish Succession (Queen Anne's War),1702-13.

Mortier, Pierre
d 1724

A French map publisher based in Amsterdam. He produced many of the maps of the most important French and Dutch cartographers of the late seventeenth and early eighteenth centuries.

Münster, Sebastian
1489-1552

German humanist, philologist and cartographer. His major geographical works were *Typus Cosmograph Universalis* (1532), *Geographia Universalis* (1540) and *Cosmographia* (1544). The last work, published in Basle, was highly influential and editions of it continued to be published well into the next century. He established the convention of devoting separate maps to each of the four then-known continents (*ie,* Europe, Asia, Africa and America).

Ortelius
1527-1598

Although christened Abraham Ortel, this great Dutch cartographer is universally known by the latinized version of his last name. He began as a colorer and salesman of maps but by the 1560s was making widely acclaimed maps of his own, among them a major eight-sheet world map published in 1564. In 1570 he published his masterpiece, the revolutionary *Theatrum Orbis Terrarum*, history's first 'modern' atlas, in that it was systematically organized, uniformly sized and based solely on contemporary knowledge (*ie*, was non-Ptolemaic). Between 1570 and 1612 42 editions of this hugely influential work were published.

Olaus Magnus
1490-1558

The first of the major sixteenth-century Scandinavian cartographers. His 1539 'Carta Marina,' the first large-scale map of Europe, was embellished with over 100 small engravings.

Plancius, Peter
1552-1622

Dutch cartographer of considerable importance at the end of the sixteenth century. Although he never produced an atlas, his more than 80 individual maps, including two large planispheres, or world maps, were highly regarded by his contemporaries.

Ptolemy
87-150

By far the most influential of ancient—or, for that matter, modern—geographers, Ptolemy, also known as Claudius Ptolemaeus, was an astronomer, mathematician and geographer who flourished in Alexandria between 120 and 150. For 14 centuries after his death his geocentric astronomic system and geographical concepts dominated Western and Middle Eastern thought. The first edition of his major geographical work, the *Geographia*, to be translated into a language fully accessible to Western scholars was published in 1475 without maps, and an edition with maps followed two years later. Although the discoveries of Columbus and others subsequently disproved many of Ptolemy's theories, he continued to exert a powerful influence on European geographical thinking for at least another 100 years.

Robert de Vaugondy Family

A prominent family of French eighteenth-century cartographers and map publishers. Their major product was the *Atlas Universel,* of 1757, a work still highly regarded for its exceptional precision and great beauty.

Rocque, John
fl 1746-1762

An English cartographer of Huguenot extraction. Although he devoted himself mainly to English subjects, one of his most interesting (and now rarest) works was his posthumously-published 1765 *Set of Plans of Forts in America*, which contained, among other things, city plans of New York, Albany, Québec, Montréal and Halifax.

Rosselli, Francesco
1445-1515

Italian cartographer, engraver and map seller. He is popularly accounted the first seller of printed maps, among them the Contarini (*qv*) map of 1506.

Salamanca, Antonio
fl 1540-1560

A Roman map publisher who contributed many of the maps that went into Lafreri's (*qv*) collections.

Sanson, Nicolas
1600-1667

Founder of the first great dynasty of French cartographers. He published some 300 maps and two world atlases, the more important being his *Cartes Générales de Toutes les Parties du Monde* of 1658. He also produced a series of four octavo volumes, each devoted to one of the four known continents. (The American volume was published in 1656.) After his death his work was carried on by his sons, Nicolas, Guillaume and Adrien, and by a grandson, Pierre.

Schöner, Johann
1477-1547

German astronomer, mathematician and geographer. A globe that he constructed in 1515 is said to have shown both a then-undiscovered strait to the south of South America and the Northwest Passage to India.

Seller, John
fl 1665-1705

English cartographer who was Hydrographer to Charles II and James II. He published a world atlas, the *Atlas Terrestris*, between 1680 and 1685, but he is even more famous for his marine atlas, *The English Pilot*, the first edition of which appeared in 1671, and the last in 1803!

Seutter, Matthias
(1678-1757)

German cartographer who was the principal rival of the Homanns (*qv*) in the early eighteenth century. His atlases include his *Tabulae Geographicae* (1720), *Atlas Novus* 1730, *General Atlas* (1735) and *Atlas Minor* (1744). In execution and coloring his maps are similar to those of Homann *(qv)*.

Smith, John
1580-1631

English adventurer and early colonizer of Virginia. His famous 1612 map 'Virginia' (graven by William Hole) was the first cartographic representation of the Chesapeake Bay area.

Speed, John
1544-1641

English cartographer. His 1627 *Prospects of the Most Famous Parts of the World* was the first printed general atlas by an Englishman.

Thevet, André
1502-1590

French Cosmographer to the French court. He was the author of the atlas *Cosmographie Universelle* (1575). He also produced separate maps of the four continents and is said to have made a map of the world (now lost) in the shape of a fleur-de-lis.

Thorne, Robert
d 1527

English merchant, geographer and friend of the Cabots. He was an early advocate of exploring for a Northwest Passage to India. His 1527 woodblock world map, 'Orbis Universalis Descriptio,' shows North America as a large continent separate from Asia and is among the first to show the newly-discovered Strait of Magellan and the Philippine Islands.

Visscher Family

An important dynasty of Dutch cartographers and publishers that flourished in Amsterdam between 1587 and 1702. Notable members were Claes (1587-1637), Nikolaus, Sr (1618-79) and Nikolaus, Jr (1649-1702). Among their many products were an *Atlas Contractus* of *c* 1660 and an *Atlas Minor* of about 1680. The work of Claes was, if not on a level with that of his contemporary Blaeu (*qv*), nevertheless of a very high order.

Waghanaer, Lucas
fl 1583-1596

Dutch cartographer based in Leyden. He was the first to publish a maritime atlas, the *Spieghel der Zeevaerdt*, the two volumes of which (44 charts) appeared in 1584-5. These volumes became models for other sea atlases produced in the following century by such authors as Donckert, Goos and Van Keulen.

Waldseemüller, Martin
1470-1518

German cartographer who lived in St Die, Lorraine, from *c* 1490. He first suggested that the New world be called 'America' in his book *Cosmographiae Introductio*, published in 1507, and in the same year he used the name on an immense (36 sq ft) 12-sheet world map called 'Universalis Cosmographia' which shows the New World as separate from Asia. He was also responsible for inserting some 'modern' maps in a famous edition of Ptolemy published in Strassburg in 1513. In 1516 he produced another great 12-sheet wood-block world map called 'Carta Marina Navigatoria.' Waldseemüller's influence on contemporary mapmakers and on the future evolution of cartography is difficult to overestimate.

Wright, Edward
1558-1615

English cartographer and explorer. His influential 1599 book *The Correction of Certaine Errors in Navigation* did much to popularize the Mercator (*qv*) projection, since Wright, unlike Mercator, took pains to elucidate the mathematical principles on which the projection was based. In the book is 'A Chart of the World on Mercator's Projection,' which many consider to be the most accurate world map produced in the sixteenth century.

Zatta, Antonio
1757-1797

Venetian publisher. He was probably the most important Italian map publisher of the late eighteenth century and is responsible for a large number of atlases and single maps of considerable aesthetic and scientific merit.

INDEX

(Numerals in italics indicate plates. For individual maps see Index of Plates p. 31.)